*Victorian Investments*

# *Victorian Investments*

## New Perspectives on Finance and Culture

*edited by*

NANCY
HENRY
*&*
CANNON
SCHMITT

Indiana University Press

*Bloomington and Indianapolis*

This book is a publication of

Indiana University Press
601 North Morton Street
Bloomington, IN 47404-3797 USA

http://iupress.indiana.edu

*Telephone orders*   800-842-6796
*Fax orders*   812-855-7931
*Orders by e-mail*   iuporder@indiana.edu

Library of Congress Cataloging-in-Publication Data

Victorian investments : new perspectives on finance and culture /
edited by Nancy Henry and Cannon Schmitt.
    p. cm.
 Includes bibliographical references and index.
 ISBN 978-0-253-22027-1 (pbk. : alk. paper) 1. Investments—
Great Britain—History—19th century. 2. Finance—Social
aspects—Great Britain—History—19th century. 3. Finance in
literature. I. Henry, Nancy, date II. Schmitt, Cannon.
 HG5432.V53 2008
 332.60941′09034—dc22
                                                    2008017202

1 2 3 4 5 14 13 12 11 10 09

*To Tom and Dana*

# Contents

*Victorian Investments*

# Introduction

## Finance, Capital, Culture

### *Nancy Henry and Cannon Schmitt*

The temptation is to begin with a contemporary reference—and there are so many to choose from. In *Every Man a Speculator: A History of Wall Street in American Life* (2005), for instance, Steve Fraser quantifies the late twentieth-century surge in investment by noting that "[m]ore was invested in institutional funds between 1991 and 1994 than in all the years since 1939. And the biggest share of that capital was deposited in pension plans" (583). Or, more anecdotally, in a memoir about the bursting of the dot-com bubble titled *American Sucker* (2004), David Denby observes that by the end of the 1990s, "[i]nvestment had become as much a part of popular culture as baseball, fishing, and bar-hopping" and "pension funds and 401(k) plans had turned factory workers and even university intellectuals into investors" (24). Such a beginning would do double duty. It would not only indicate our sense that the rising tide of scholarly interest in investment in other places and times derives at least in part from investment's new visibility in this place and time, North America and Europe at the start of the twenty-first century; it would also convey the consensus among our contributors that a signal moment in the genealogy of the economic world we now inhabit is to be found in nineteenth-century Britain. The developments in investing that transformed Victorian society—including the proliferation of global markets, the passage of laws establishing limited liability, and the creation of new knowledge disseminated through financial journalism—established a reality that now seems familiar to us, one in which participation in equities markets is (relatively) democratized, the stock exchange serves as the economic pulse of many nations, and investing itself takes on the status of a ubiquitous preoccupation encouraging hopes of financial security even as it forces difficult moral and social as well as economic questions.

If such assertions about novelty, origins, and continuity are demonstrably valid, however, they are also dangerous. For they not only give short shrift to the long and vibrant history of scholarship on the Victorian economy, investment included; they also risk eliding the historical, cultural, and textual specificity to which the contributors to *Victorian Investments: New Perspectives on Finance and Culture* are committed. Nonetheless, there has certainly been a recent intensification of attention to all facets of the Victorian culture of investment among academics who are witnessing if not actively participating in our own intensified culture of investment. In the special issue of *Victorian Studies* published in 2002 that stands at this book's own origins, we and our co-editor, Anjali Arondekar, argued that the articles we had gathered together showed a commonality of intent that "begins to define a field" (Schmitt, Henry, and Arondekar 9). Since then, a host of new studies has appeared in that field on topics ranging from the identities of investors in the East India Company and the extent and significance of investing by women to the centrality of speculation in the plots of Victorian novels and plays. This focus on what Victorians chose to do with—and how they chose to write about—their unprecedented excess capital forms part of a broader historical interest in analyzing the role Victorian financial instruments and institutions played in the daily lives of Britons across a remarkably wide spectrum of society.

Expanding on the journal issue with which it shares a title, *Victorian Investments* brings together work by historians and literary and cultural critics that illuminates and interrogates the place of finance capital not only in the Victorian period but also in scholarly approaches to that period. Perhaps the most notable aspect of the latter is the degree to which most of our contributors concentrate less on a critique of Victorian capitalism per se than on overlooked dimensions of the culture of investment such as the rise of financial journalism, the centrality of insurance, changes in the liability laws, the mingling of investing and gambling vocabularies, and the overlap of financial with romantic or sentimental plots in Victorian literature. This marks a change from past scholarship; the difficulty, however, lies in how best to characterize it. Reviewing a set of books on the economic aspects of Victorian literature that proceed in the absence of what he sees as a Marxist-inspired condemnation of capitalism, Jonathan Rose has asserted: "We are now witnessing the emergence of something quite unprecedented—a capitalist criticism" (489). We cannot embrace such a tag, in part because a number of our contributors make the inequities and inhumanity of the system they examine central to their analyses, but like Rose we do recognize the emergence of an approach to the Victorian economy at once more wide-ranging and more fine-grained than those versions of Marxist critique focused on industrialism have fostered. In this regard and others *Victorian Investments* constitutes a break. But, of course, such a departure would have been impossible were the collection not also responding to recent scholarship in the field—and so it is to the ways our contributors both build upon and contest that scholarship that we turn for the remainder of our introduction.

## The History of Finance as the History of Society and Culture

Were it possible to identify a single overarching axiom among historians of the Victorian economy over the last twenty years, it would have to involve the inextricability of business and finance from the rest of Victorian society—from class, race, and gender; religion, law, and politics; and literary as well as other artistic and cultural production. Now-classic works such as Boyd

Hilton's *The Age of Atonement: The Influence of Evangelicalism on Social and Economic Thought, 1785–1865* (1988), assessing the role of evangelical Christianity in how economics was understood and practiced, and Leonore Davidoff and Catherine Hall's *Family Fortunes: Men and Women of the English Middle Class, 1780–1850* (1987), looking at the impact of financial organizations and opportunities on middle-class families, paved the way for later investigations that begin with the assumption that finance intersected forcefully with other aspects of life in nineteenth-century Britain. Historical studies such as George Robb's *White-Collar Crime in Modern England: Financial Fraud and Business Morality, 1845–1929* (1992), Thomas L. Haskell and Richard F. Teichgraber's collection *The Culture of the Market: Historical Essays* (1993), Timothy Alborn's *Conceiving Companies: Joint-Stock Politics in Victorian England* (1998), and Margot Finn's *The Character of Credit: Personal Debt in English Culture, 1740–1914* (2003), to name a few, parlayed that understanding into expansive, inclusive, and innovative accounts of Victorian business and finance. Literary scholars and critics, too, have turned their attention to how Victorian literature was affected by and reflected on dramatic financial change. Studies such as John Vernon's *Money and Fiction: Literary Realism in the Nineteenth and Early Twentieth Centuries* (1984), Barbara Weiss's *The Hell of the English: Bankruptcy and the Victorian Novel* (1986), and Norman Russell's *The Novelist and Mammon: Literary Responses to the World of Commerce in the Nineteenth Century* (1986) have been followed by ever more probing investigations of the imbrications of the financial and the literary, including Paul Delany's *Literature, Money and the Market: From Trollope to Amis* (2002), the essays in Andrew Smith's special issue of *Victorian Review* on "Literature and Money" (2005), and Francis O'Gorman's collection *Victorian Literature and Finance* (2007).

This work is characterized above all by an intense interdisciplinarity, with historians drawing frequently on the literary realm, literary and cultural critics taking care to situate their analyses in specific historical contexts, and both historians and critics attending closely to economic history in particular. The essays collected here also feature this trademark—as it were—disciplinary cross-fertilization. Historians George Robb, Timothy Alborn, David Itzkowitz, and Donna Loftus make literature central to their arguments, while critics Ian Baucom, Mary Poovey, Audrey Jaffe, Nancy Henry, and Cannon Schmitt place their readings of literary and visual texts in direct relation to the state of "the financial system in nineteenth-century Britain" (to borrow a phrase from the title of Poovey's influential collection on financial writing). Another sort of inter- or transdisciplinarity is in evidence as well: many of these essays demonstrate the potential for bringing philosophy and literary and cultural theory to bear on the history of finance, seeking to explain the complexities of investment's place in culture (and culture's place in the system in which investment loomed so large) by way of Immanuel Kant, Jacques Derrida, Fredric Jameson, and Gérard Genette, among others. Furthermore, several contributions enable us to see the transatlantic and indeed global implications of Victorian Britain's culture of investment: the long shadow of the slave trade (Baucom); the comparative progress of women's rights in the United States and Britain (Robb); the influence of Victorian financial plots on American novelists (Henry); and the imperialist contours of British and U.S. investment in Latin America (Schmitt).

On one hand, these essays may be distinguished from other scholarship engaging Victorian writing on political economy and economic theory such as the contributions to Martha Woodmansee and Mark Osteen's collection *The New Economic Criticism: Studies at the Intersection of Literature and Economics* (1999), Regenia Gagnier's *The Insatiability of Human Wants: Economics and Aesthetics in Market Society* (2000), and Catherine Gallagher's *The Body Economic: Life, Death, and Sensation in Political Economy and the Victorian Novel* (2006) by their empirical interest in Victorian finance capital. On the other, they differ from more narrow histories of business, finance, or economics in their insistence that the history of business and finance, and especially of investment practices, is also the history of culture and cultural change. The contributors do not, that is, speak of a "business culture"—how business is done—so much as of the ways in which developments within the realms of business and finance shaped the everyday lives of Victorian Britons: the kinds of knowledge to which they had access, the economic opportunities open or closed to them, and their involvement in the everyday lives of the inhabitants of other parts of the globe. To take only one example: widows, children, single women, and the elderly were becoming increasingly dependent on the Funds (national debt promising a fixed return), annuities, and shares in joint-stock companies. An entire service sector grew up to cater to this growing class of investor—and among the consequences were a new professional class (including financial journalists and what Alborn calls "the first fund managers"), new forms of social protocol (in response to puzzling questions such as how much businesses should disclose about their operations or whether women should vote at shareholder meetings), and new plots for fiction (in the novels of authors ranging from Charlotte Riddell and Arthur Conan Doyle to Anthony Trollope, George Eliot, Joseph Conrad, and Edith Wharton).

## Insurance, Investment, and Empire

Work on the Victorian culture of investment has displayed an interest both in statistical trends in investing over the course of the nineteenth century and in the identities of the ordinary investors behind companies and enterprises. Nowhere, perhaps, have the two sides of that interest resulted in such thoroughgoing rethinking of received wisdom than in the case of work on investors' role in the expansion of the British Empire. In *Mammon and the Pursuit of Empire: The Political Economy of British Imperialism, 1860–1912* (1986), a monumental instance of sustained statistical analysis, Lance E. Davis and Robert A. Huttenback sought to document the "direction and volume of portfolio finance that passed through the London capital market between 1865 and 1914" in the service of, among other things, settling the still-controversial question of whether empire was on the whole profitable for Britons (1). The answer they provide achieves something of a compromise: elites, in their estimation, did profit, while for the middle class empire was generally a losing concern financially. In *British Imperialism: Innovation and Expansion 1688–1914* (1993), P. J. Cain and A. G. Hopkins similarly focus on the economics of imperialism. Whereas Davis and Huttenback largely follow established verities about what the British Empire was, however, Cain and Hopkins prosecute a sweeping revisionist argument: namely, that what they call "gentlemanly capitalism"—"a means of generating income flows in ways that were compatible with the high ideals of honour and duty"—underwrote imperial expansion not only in the nineteenth century but before and after as well (1: 46). Such capitalism is represented in the main by activities falling within the so-called service sector, including insurance, banking, and investment. The somewhat startling claim that follows is that British imperialism was not centrally about the acquisition of territory. Cain and Hopkins see such acquisition as merely the occasional by-product of what they argue was the essence of imperial expansion: the extension of the British service sector over ever-greater areas of the globe.

Animated, like *British Imperialism*, by the conviction that metropolitan and imperial economies were intimately linked in the eighteenth and nineteenth centuries, H. V. Bowen's *The Business of Empire: The East India Company and Imperial Britain, 1756–1833* (2006) poses what at first seems to be a disarmingly modest question about "how the acquisition and expansion of an empire in India affected the development of the East India Company in Britain" (ix). But proposing an answer involves Bowen in the larger project of assessing the complex influences of the East India Company itself on British society in general and shareholders in particular. He seeks to establish "why [shareholders in the East India Company] held stock, how they acted, and how their group compositions altered over time" (84). Less driven than either *Mammon and the Pursuit of Empire* or *British Imperialism* by an argumentative thesis, *The Business of Empire* puts its faith in the empirical, presenting a heretofore unknown wealth of data about one group of investors. If on one hand those data promise future revelations, on the other they foreground a question central to the work of Cain and Hopkins: to what extent are data hostage to the interpretive assumptions brought to bear on them?

In his contribution to this volume, which we consider an indispensable sort of prehistory of Victorian investment, Ian Baucom takes up that question by considering what might be thought of as the elided other half of Bowen's object of inquiry, detailing not who investors were but what "goods" they invested in. We have placed quotation marks around "goods" because in this case that "what" is also a "who": slaves aboard the *Zong* en route from Africa to markets in the Americas. Facing a shortage of drinking water on board, the *Zong's* captain and crew, invoking a clause in the ship's insurance contract that allowed some cargo to be jettisoned if it meant saving the rest, forced 133 slaves into the sea. All but one drowned. Baucom offers a philosophical and historical meditation that insists we view as persons this sacrificed "cargo." Taking the incident and its aftermath as a defining event of modernity, he provides a point of departure for the emergence of the money culture that this volume seeks to define and understand. But, surprisingly, it is not the ethically revolting practice of treating humans as so much insurable property that constitutes the *Zong* massacre as an event for Baucom. It is, rather, what such treatment reveals about insurance per se: that "a money culture cannot exist without insurance," and further that the "genius of insurance, and the secret of its contribution to finance capitalism, is its insistence that the real test of something's value comes not at the moment it is made or exchanged but at the moment it is lost or destroyed" (30). The spectral but quite real effects of the money form that is finance capital are made possible by that capital's detachment from the specific properties of the things in which it speculates—and by the guarantee against loss that insurance, with its prospective-retrospective valuation achieved precisely and only from the vantage of loss, provides.

Timothy Alborn takes up the spectacular rather than the spectral side of insurance in his chapter on Victorian life insurance bonuses. Examining all aspects of those occasions on which life insurance companies' surpluses were either added to the value of policyholders' policies or paid out directly to shareholders, from the actuarial to the theatrical, Alborn argues for the importance of declarations of such bonuses in "attracting attention to investment as a social practice" and "publiciz[ing] money's reproductive powers" (59). Here, too, there is an engagement with the question of what it means to insure a human life—not least in Alborn's documentation of the efforts made in the eighteenth and nineteenth centuries to establish who might be considered to have a legitimate financial interest in the life insured. But the focus is elsewhere, on how the deliberate cultivation of suspense around the dispersion of surpluses affected individuals and how insurance companies learned the value of marketing and structuring their dividend and bonus payouts to appeal to a diverse company of investors.

"Without insurance," Baucom writes, "there is no finance capital" (29). One need not uncritically agree with Cain and Hopkins's redefinition of empire to endorse the corollary dictum that without finance capital there is no modern imperialism as we know it. Joseph Conrad, among others, understood as much. Conrad's *Nostromo* (1904) reveals Britain's tentacular extension of its financial sector into ever more remote parts of the non-European world to be, as Cannon Schmitt writes in his contribution to this volume, "a kind of imperialism that, however different from classic imperialist expansion in its workings, is similar in its results" (188). Schmitt goes on to argue that Conrad's novel is not simply an indictment of informal imperialism but a harrowing examination of some of the consequences of the culture of investment, consequences that follow from a world in which value accrues or dissipates in response to the aleatory force of rumor. But Conrad in this regard cannot do without the system he excoriates, for he enlists rumor to bring pressure on the form of the novel that, beginning with works such as *Nostromo,* broke down realist conventions through the formal experimentation we call modernism.

## The Role of the Working Classes and Women as Investors

Although the expansion of Victorian financial markets into Britain's formal and informal empires and the diversification of investment opportunities at home contributed to what we have described as a relative democratization of the stock market, Conrad insists on the limits encoded in the word "relative." *Nostromo* depicts finance capital as the concern of male European elites, signaling that, like other forms of democratization—particularly the extension of the franchise—the prospect of empowering women, the working classes, or non-Europeans to become investors was controversial. In her contribution, Donna Loftus explores the debates surrounding the Limited Liability Act of 1855 to show that the apparent laissez-faire ideal of turning everyone into an investor was not considered an unqualified good: "Despite its potential for the promotion of market democracy, limited liability confirmed the separate interests of capital and labor" (80). Exactly who would benefit from limited liability was bound up with questions about the value and efficacy of political and educational reform as well as with broader issues of communal identity. Would limited liability help working men by allowing them to increase their capital via investment? Or, as John Stuart Mill believed, would its benefits accrue to them only indirectly by increasing the wealth of capitalists who might in turn lend money to the poor? The likelihood of the former made limited liability a liberal cause epitomizing the potential of the market. At the same time, the debate about liability encompassed "the role of the state in relation to working men" and proved to be "an issue of knowledge of, and authority over, prices and profits in local communities" (83, 93). Hovering somewhere between a right and a privilege, investment, like voting, had to be exercised responsibly (even in the absence of individual liability), and responsibility itself was understood to depend on the possibility or impossibility of education: "Reform," notes Loftus, "was about instructing the working classes in the intricacies of the market and skills associated with capital" (87).

In showing the class implications of this aspect of financial history, Loftus points out that the terms of the debate were also gendered in that they focused exclusively on working men: "The debates around limited liability provided a platform for one of the most wide-ranging public discourses of the relationship between (male) labor and capital" (97). In contrast to controversies over political reform and male suffrage, there was never much public debate about the right of women to invest their money in the stock market. Perhaps as a consequence, there was never any barrier to single women doing as they pleased with their money, and never any blanket prohibition on women participating in the government of joint stock companies in which they held shares. The right of married women to invest was of course inseparable from larger po-litical debates about their property rights that raged throughout the nineteenth century, but in terms of pure gender discrimination, the stock market seems to have offered a uniquely egalitarian opportunity for women who had the means to participate.

Pioneering archival work by Janette Rutterford and Josephine Maltby has revealed the unexpected presence of women investors in the nineteenth cen-tury in all forms of public and private companies and so started the critical conversation about the social significance of this presence. In "'She Possessed Her Own Fortune': Women Investors from the Late Nineteenth Century to the Early Twentieth Century" (2006), for example, they consider previously un-asked questions about the extent and nature of women's shareholding. In doing so they show that, in contrast to married women (at least before the Married Women's Property Acts of 1870 and 1882), spinsters and widows held shares with the same rights as men and, whether they exercised their rights or not, were allowed to vote in shareholder meetings long before they were granted the political franchise in stages following World War I (see also Rutterford and Maltby, "The Widow").

In a special issue of *Accounting, Business and Financial History* devoted to "Women and Investment" (2006), Rutterford and Maltby gather both broad surveys of women's roles as investors and case studies from British and colonial (Australian) contexts. One essay in that volume, "'A Doe in the City': Women Shareholders in Eighteenth- and Early Nineteenth-Century Britain," by Mark Freeman, Robin Pearson, and James Taylor, offers the broadest published survey of company records and quantitative data on women shareholders in joint-stock companies, showing fluctuations in the number of female shareholders and the percentages of shares held. These numbers demonstrate that there were more women in the capital market than previously thought: "Women's investment in the corporate economy though not deep was extensive" (287). Further, Free-man, Pearson, and Taylor's analysis reveals that women were involved in corpo-rate governance and identifies an increasingly positive attitude toward women shareholders beginning in the mid-nineteenth century, tracing this acceptance to historical practices by which "stock companies placed female proprietors, if often only by default, on largely the same constitutional footing as men" (288).

In his essay in *Victorian Investments*, George Robb adds to the growing body of knowledge about women investors by examining both British and American women's financial activities. While acknowledging important differences be-tween the two national investment cultures, he argues that the similarities are important as well, and that the research need not remain segregated. Robb in-terrogates the stereotype implied in such phrases as "a doe in the city," empha-sizing that "while the corporate economy welcomed capital investments from women, it offered them little protection from unscrupulous promoters" (120). Weighing the benefits and dangers of investing to women and examining the rhetoric of victimization and empowerment connected with female investors, he finds that women were often prey to frauds and scams and "dependent on the riskiest and most vulnerable kind of economic activity: 'gambling' on the stock market" (126). But public discourse about these dangers, Robb contends, was exaggerated, and that exaggeration served a purpose: the female victim was frequently invoked in literature and in the press "to marginalize women's role in the economy" (137). By the same token, however, and following the trend of the contemporary women's movement generally, by the Edwardian period women's vulnerability to financial victimization became a central tenet of British and American feminism. Despite cultural prejudices that encouraged passive investment through male mediators and threatened active women investors by associating them with transgressive, unfeminine behavior or exposing them to the designs of swindlers, as "the century progressed and as some middle-class women longed to escape the Doll's House," Robb concludes, "they came to see economic empowerment and financial regulation as key to their liberation" (139–40).

Robb joins Rutterford and Maltby, Freeman, Pearson, Taylor, and other historians in the project of giving us a much clearer picture of just how involved women were in managing their money, adding to the chorus of voices now revisiting and complicating both the separate spheres ideology and assumptions of female disempowerment in the nineteenth century. Significantly, he makes fiction central to his discussion of cultural stereotypes of women investors, invoking a range of nineteenth-century authors from Trollope to Catherine Gore, Mrs. Henry Wood, and Charlotte Riddell. While historians have looked to literature in support of their contentions about cultural attitudes to certain kinds of investors and investment activities, literary critics have in turn suggested that the investment activities of authors deserve heightened scrutiny. In *George Eliot and the British Empire* (2002), for instance, Nancy Henry documents George Eliot's extensive colonial holdings and speculates on the degree to which knowledge of those holdings forces us to regard aspects of her fiction in a new light. Similarly, Gail Turley Houston, in *From Dickens to Dracula: Gothic, Economics, and Victorian Fiction* (2005), examines Charlotte Brontë's investments in connection with her novels to illustrate how familiarity with the financial system manifests itself in the deployment of Gothic tropes. Among other things, what Henry and Houston reveal is a curious bifurcation: while writers such as Elizabeth Gaskell and George Eliot produced fiction in which bank failures that cost women money and status figure centrally (see Miss Matty in *Cranford*, Gwendolen and her family in *Daniel Deronda*), the authors themselves were responsible, educated investors who took advantage of the stock market to supplement their incomes. Perhaps, as Robb might contend, the notion of women as victims of the market proved more powerful—more literarily useful or compelling—than these authors' own experience of market success.

## Form and Finance

To note that Victorian novelists found failed investment an alluring plot device is of necessity to make a point about form. And although such a point might appear to be of narrowly literary interest, a number of the contributors to this volume suggest that attention to form—in connection with institutions and subjectivity no less than the novel—is required of any meaningful analysis of the new culture of investment in nineteenth-century Britain. This should come as no surprise. It was, after all, Marxism that kept attention to form alive during those not-too-distant dark ages when formalism was a methodology that dared not speak its name, and did so precisely by insisting on the economic "base" or mode of production itself as a form or structure. Fredric Jameson's *Marxism and Form* (1972) details the twentieth-century history of this tradition, which may be said to reach its apogee in Jameson's own *The Political Unconscious* (1981). Thus, as Baucom observes, when he refers to the "ever more exhaustive, ever more total, ever more complex, ever more ubiquitous and (*because* ever more ubiquitous) ever more unremarkable penetration of the Heideggerian life-world by the cultural logic of finance capital," his mode of thinking is recognizably "Jamesonian" (32). This is in large part because his reflections on insurance and money culture—as may also be said of Schmitt's contentions about rumor, investment, and modernism—are enabled by the proposition that *finance* capital entails a specifically *cultural* logic.

In her contribution, Mary Poovey takes a different approach to explaining the relationship between finance and form. Tracking the emergence of a new kind of "financial writing," she shows how it functioned to "normalize or naturalize the workings of financial institutions" (45). At the center of that writing, and of the culture of investment out of which it grew, she locates a kind of double bind—at once contradictory and constitutive—between the imperative to disclose as much information as possible and the necessity of keeping some information secret. Having demonstrated the presence of this relationship between disclosure and secrecy in financial writing and institutions, Poovey turns to George Eliot's *The Mill on the Floss*. What in financial writing itself works to naturalize the financial system, in a novel provides the opportunity for its defamiliarization: *The Mill on the Floss* and other realist novels "enabled readers to experience imaginatively the dynamic by which Britain's financial institutions generated monetary value and to reflect upon the affect this dynamic created" (55). In this sense, formal features of the novel including the shape of its plot recreate the pervasive structure of disclosure and secrecy, but with the effect of rendering it visible and, therefore, subject to critique. "Having experienced this [structure] in an arena in which they might reflect upon it," Poovey writes, "readers might even have been encouraged to wonder if the dynamic of disclosure and secrecy that financial journalism sought to normalize was quite as natural as journalists wanted it to seem" (55).

One of Poovey's key contentions is that *The Mill on the Floss* features two distinct plotlines, financial and sentimental, and that by novel's end the latter overwrites and displaces the former. For Audrey Jaffe, however, reading Anthony Trollope's *The Prime Minister,* no such distinction exists: "The marriage plot *is*, in fact, the financial plot: the lesson Emily Wharton learns about

Lopez is taught by way of her increasing knowledge of his financial dealings" (148). Further, in contrast to Poovey's reading of Victorian realist novels as potentially affording critical distance on the culture of investment, Jaffe emphasizes the degree to which their disruptive or defamiliarizing effects are recontained. "After the narrative of Lopez's exuberance, of Emily's mistake, and of the degradation that results from their entanglement," she writes, "comes the embrace of what might now have to be called rational exuberance: the ordinary emotions of the married, middle-class subject, whose choice, shaped by life's hard lessons, is articulated by that narrative as a choice of investment over speculation" (157). The disagreement here, although routed through works by George Eliot and Trollope, is not about differences in individual Victorians' view of the system in which they found themselves enmeshed but inheres in divergent estimations as to the function of realist fiction—and, by extension, aesthetic production as such—vis-à-vis the economic realm.

## Investment, Speculation, or Gambling?

The distinction Jaffe perceives in *The Prime Minister* between investment and speculation, as well as the novel's representation of speculation as a game and a form of irresponsible gambling, underwrote moral concerns about the nature and state of the stock exchange and the City throughout the nineteenth century. Most of the contributors address or at least mention this fundamental problem of definition, which emerged repeatedly in financial writing: was there really any difference between investing and speculating and, furthermore, were speculators nothing more than glorified gamblers?

Writing about the appearance of "bucket-shop keepers" who served a growing number of working-class investors and advertised themselves in ways similar to sporting bookmakers, David Itzkowitz shows that many feared that they were "turning the world of financial speculation into a new form of popular entertainment whose morality was ambiguous at best" (99). His essay explores that anxiety as it was reawakened in the 1870s, when the bucket-shop brokers challenged the uneasy legal acceptance of the distinction between speculating and gambling that had allowed speculation to flourish in an increasingly free market even while gambling was outlawed. Such anxiety, which Itzkowitz argues never totally disappeared, was "at least partially responsible for the continued existence of the discourse that equated speculation and gambling" (118). Scrutinizing the lines between investing, speculating, and gambling, lines that fluctuated continually in legal, financial, and popular writing throughout the Victorian period, Itzkowitz reveals one constant: the function of the specter of "gambling" in maintaining speculation's legitimacy.

To return to the pages of realist fiction after this foray into the world of bucket shops and bookmakers is to perceive the legal, political, and terminological disputes around gambling and speculation carried on via characterology. Several contributors consider the way cultural fears about the market are displaced onto that mid- to late Victorian novelistic mainstay, the disreputable and dangerous stockbroker or financier. Both the thrill and the danger of speculating attached to this ubiquitous figure, who is often explicitly depicted as or implicitly understood to be Jewish. As Jaffe suggests, in the treatment of such a character may be found the roots of our own contemporary vilification of financial transgressors: "In offering up as villains stock-market characters whose particular forms of exuberance are routinely characterized as reverberating beyond the market, contemporary culture demonstrates the persistence and the usefulness of a Victorian master narrative within which matters not otherwise easily regulated may be placed" (145). In her essay examining the recurring trope of the financier's suicide in fiction by Dickens, Trollope, Gissing, and Wharton, Henry shows that the financier-speculator became a point of intersection for a variety of discourses (sensational, melodramatic, gothic) employed by realist novelists as part of their "attempt to find the right language and images with which to represent a financial sector that had long been considered unsuited and inappropriate for fiction because of genteel and literary society's distaste for trade, business, and finance" (163). Alternately viewed as Corsair and vampire, New Man and straw man, the financier is frequently most powerful in the aftermath of his (often self-inflicted) death. The perpetuation of the image of the financier-suicide epitomized the ambivalence of many Victorian authors toward a money culture they might be critical of but in which they were inevitably implicated.

## Conclusion

The watchword of this volume in its entirety is *transformation*. Rapid changes in Victorian financial markets and investment practices reflected and influenced broader social changes: political and moral reform, the struggle for women's rights, the growth of empire. The Victorians developed new kinds of financial writing in a flourishing press as well as in manuals, advice books, advertising, and novels; new knowledge was produced and consumed by a growing number of readers—shareholders and non-shareholders alike. Impossible any longer to consider as a thing apart, investment cut across all aspects of life: the financial sphere overlapped with the domestic sphere, overseas expansion promised to fund comfortable retirement, speculation rewrote the plots and themes of Victorian fiction and reshaped its form. In his afterword, Martin Daunton extends this list still further, signaling that more work remains to be done on moral attitudes toward saving and investing, the politics of joint-stock companies, monopolies, and taxation—all of which were in flux throughout the period. *Victorian Investments* bears witness to such transformations even as it manifests a corresponding transformation in critical approaches to studying and understanding the multiple and complex intersections between culture and high finance.

# PART 1

*A Prehistory of Victorian Investment*

# 1 "*Signum Rememorativum, Demonstrativum, Prognostikon*"

## Finance Capital, the Atlantic, and Slavery

## *Ian Baucom*

On November 29, 1781, Luke Collingwood, captain of the slave ship *Zong,* ordered his crew to bring onto the deck of his vessel and begin throwing overboard scores of the slaves imprisoned in the holding pens of his ship, citing as his rationale and justification for this action a shortage of drinkable water in the *Zong*'s provisioning supplies and a clause in his ship's marine insurance contract that permitted him to jettison any portion of his "cargo" he deemed it "necessary" to destroy in order to preserve the rest. Over the days that followed 122 of the captives on the ship were forcibly drowned. Ten more, on being hauled onto deck by the crew, elected to jump into the fatal sea before they could be forced overboard. They also perished. One more inmate of the holds, having been brought on deck and thrown into the sea, managed to catch hold of a trailing rope and crawl back on board. On Collingwood's return to England, he convinced the owners of the *Zong* (three of whom were, at one time or another, mayors of Liverpool) to demand compensation from the ship's insurers for the drowned slaves. The owners pursued that claim. The insurers refused to pay, and the matter went to court, where to win their case the owners had to convince the bench that the slaves had actually existed and that their captain had actually drowned them. A jury at the Guildhall Court heard the case, decided in favor of the owners, and ordered the insurance agents to pay £30 for every drowned slave. The insurers appealed and the case went back to court, this time to the King's Bench, where it was argued before Lord Mansfield. In the meantime, Ouladah Equiano and Granville Sharp gained news of the case, brought it to the attention of the abolitionist community in England and abroad, and Sharp also sent a letter with various accompanying documents to the Lords Commissioners of the Admiralty requesting them to open a murder investigation.

The essay that follows is taken from a larger book project in which I have tried to trace a history of this atrocity and the discourses that have surrounded it; to identify the *Zong* massacre as a horrifically defining event in a long twentieth-century history of Atlantic capital; and to discover in it an exhortation to a knowledge of history more than rhetorically haunted by the specter of the *Zong* (see Baucom, *Specters*). To encounter this event at the closing end of the long twentieth century and the beginning of the twenty-first, it is my purpose to argue, is not to encounter a "past" incident within the violent archive of the trans-atlantic slave trade but to encounter a moment of human and speculative (capital) violence within which we are still living; to find ourselves, however unexpectedly, encountering an event that falls somewhere between what Walter Benjamin called an image of "now-being" ("wherein what has been comes together in a flash with the now to form a constellation") and what Immanuel Kant identified as a "*signum rememorativum, demonstrativum, prognostikon*": a historical sign within whose recollective, demonstrative, and predictive code it is possible to trace a trajectory of modern history. And though it is the event of the *Zong* massacre and the capital history that it brings to light that are my primary concerns, it is, thus, with Benjamin and Kant and their theories of the "event" that I wish to begin.

* * *

"We desire a fragment of human history and one, indeed, that is drawn not from past but future time, therefore a predictive history." Thus said Kant, in the first sentence of his essay "An Old Question Raised Again: Is the Human Race Constantly Progressing?" (137). The "fragment of human history" he has in mind, the revelatory object he wishes to snatch from future time "as a possible representation *a priori* of events that are supposed to happen then" is among the more extraordinary and complex figures of his philosophy of history, one that offers to make him less the precursor antagonist whose modern "time consciousness" Walter Benjamin will drastically reverse 150 years later (as many standard accounts of Benjamin's work suggest) than an anterior interlocutor whose work functions, quite precisely, as "a representation *a priori*" of the Benjaminian work to come.

If Benjamin's *Arcades Project* is the "fragment of human history" Kant can be said, perhaps to his great surprise, both to anticipate and to desire (not as an event, to be sure, but as a meditation on the reiterative temporality of events), that is, however, not yet clear from these first sentences of Kant's essay. For despite the striking similarity of his concept of the "representation *a priori*" to the Benjaminian notion of the redemptive, messianic future-present that retroactively redeems the contemporary present as its "what has been," Kant's account has not yet established as its point of view that "future time" that will code the present as its past, thus discover the future fully "imminent" in the past/present, and so sever this philosophy of history from that "horizons of expectation" discourse that Reinhart Koselleck identifies as the Enlightenment's prime contribution to a modern consciousness of time. Koselleck's argument is well known, and it certainly accommodates these sentences by Kant within its general discussion of a future-oriented Enlightenment time-consciousness licensed by the growing gap "societal modernization" opens between the anterior and the lived "space[s] of experience" and an anticipated, transformed-and-transforming future that functions, in Habermas's gloss on Koselleck, as the present's ever more rapidly approaching "horizon ... constantly subject to being overlaid with utopian conceptions" (*Philosophical* 12). Benjamin's prime contribution to the philosophy of history, Habermas argues, is, in fact, to overturn precisely this conception, to reverse flow by identifying as the present's key "horizon" not the future but the past.

The Kant/Benjamin opposition thus seems, at least so far, to hold. The "future," however, does not wait the 150 years that pass between Kant and Benjamin to find itself replaced by the "past" as the present's governing horizon of expectation. That reversal comes a scant few pages later in Kant's text when he comes to identify his desired "fragment of human history" not with an event to come but with one that has already, if still quite recently, passed:

> There must be some experience in the human race which, as an event, points to the disposition and capacity of the human race to be the cause of its own advance toward the better. . . . Therefore, an event must be sought which points to the existence of such a cause and to its effectiveness in the human race, undetermined with regard to time, and which would allow progress toward the better to be concluded as an inevitable consequence. This conclusion could then be extended to the history of the past (that it has always been in progress) in such a way that that event would have to be considered not itself as the cause of history, but only as an intimation, an historical sign (*signum rememorativum, demonstrativum, prognostikon*) demonstrating the tendency of the human race viewed in its entirety.

The event Kant has in mind, he then goes on to clarify in the succeeding paragraph, is the sublime spectacle of the French Revolution, the occasion for "disinterested sympathy it affords," the power it possesses to make of itself "a phenomenon in human history [that] is not to be forgotten" (143, 147). The crucial turn in this sequence from Kant's opening desire for "a fragment of human history . . . drawn not from past but from future time," to his discovery of that future in a past event that is "not to be forgotten," is the phrase "This conclusion then could also be extended to the history of the past" in the middle of the paragraph I have cited. Up to that point, Kant's horizon remains future oriented. In troping his turn to the "history of the past" as an "extension" rather than a reversal of this forward-looking gaze, he seems, indeed, to wish to counter the suggestion that he has reversed field at all, to cover, or disavow, the dramatic shift of perspective that is about to ensue. And it is crucial to note that it is Kant's *perspective* that has shifted, not his method or his desire. He continues to search for "fragments," "intimations," or "signs." But now those intimations come to the present not from the future but from the past, they "demonstrate the tendency of the human race viewed in its entirety" by discovering that tendency not in a "fragment of future history," but in a "*signum rememorativum, demonstrativum, prognostikon.*"

Kant is not Benjamin. And I have no interest in arguing that he is. What I do want to suggest is that his philosophy of history is far less inimical to Benjamin's than we might think, that, most specifically, this complex Kantian "*signum*" grounds a reiterative philosophy of history markedly like that Benjaminian philosophy of history grounded in the "memory as it flashes up" (as Benjamin has it in the "Theses") or the dialectical image "that wherein what has been comes together in a flash with the now to form a constellation" (as he puts it in the *Arcades Project*), and that one way to apprehend the form of this "likeness" is through the terms these "like" philosophies define. The form of the relation of Kant and Benjamin is apprehensible, in other words, as something like "that wherein what has been [Kant] comes together in a flash with the now [Benjamin] to form a constellation"; and the names for that "constellation" are the "*signum rememorativum, demonstrativum, prognostikon,*" the "dialectical image," and the "representation *a priori.*"

Kant is not Benjamin. But they do seem to agree that the modern is, in one way or another, apprehensible and condensed within a field of resonant and reiterative images or signs, and that, condensed within such signs, modernity articulates itself not as the universalization of a homogeneous empty order of time but as a labor of repetition and recollection. I agree. Subsequent to that moment of agreement, however, it becomes important to decide which type of event serves as the sign in which modernity might find itself demonstrated, recollected, and anticipated. For much continental philosophy, the French Revolution (and the Enlightenment discourses subtending and attending that revolution) has functioned as that sign—whether happily or unhappily so. What I want to suggest is that it seems equally possible to identify the *Zong* massacre as an alternate *signum rememorativum, demonstrativum, prognostikon* in which our long contemporaneity finds itself demonstrated, anticipated, and recollected.

* * *

To grasp what might be at stake in making such a claim, however, we need to get a slightly fuller sense of what Kant and Benjamin intend by such terms (sign, image, event) and of how these terms, in turn, relate to some of those other key figures of historical thinking by means of which we might make sense of this "event." In the sentences immediately prior to his recoding of the "event" as the *signum rememorativum, demonstrativum, prognostikon* and his immediately ensuing discovery of this sign in the sublime spectacle of the French Revolution, Kant establishes this circular methodological rule: "From a given cause an event as an effect can be predicted [only] if the circumstances prevail which contribute to it" (143). This is tricky, in part because the sentence seems to shift, midway, from a general account of the nature of predictive causality to an analysis of the relation of circumstance to event. The event is thus doubly predicated *from* a cause and *by* a set of circumstances. The implicit syllogism would thus align circumstances with (and as) causes and so produce a general—if bare bones—historicist conception of events as the determinate "effects" of prevailing circumstances. The sentences that follow, however, complicate this. For here it seems apparent that Kant's interest is not in predicting or predicating events from prevailing circumstances (which function as these events' "cause") but in predicting or predicating circumstances from determinate events. The sentences in question read so: "That these conditions [circumstances] must come to pass some time or other can, of course, be predicted in general, as in the calculation of probability in games of chance; but that prediction cannot enable us to know whether what is predicted is to happen in my life and I am to have the experience of it. Therefore an event must be sought" (143). Part of the confusion here (as events seem now to precede circumstances, now to be caused by them) follows from Kant's use of the word "prediction"—by which he seems to intend something like "predication," though in such a way as to reintroduce a processual, temporal quality to the act of predication such that predication anticipates but does not yet encounter the predicated. If we assume that what Kant has in mind is some such concept of predication then things become a little more familiar (if no less tautological). For here again he defines as the "event" that which is predicated by a set of circumstances whose (future) existence (as recognizability) it at once predicates and predicts; or, alternately put, he envisions a set of circumstances that can be understood to precede the event they are said to predicate only "after" that event has brought them to light as its set of prevailing conditions. That reformulation offers, indeed, to dissolve the tautology, as least in part. For what it suggests is that there are two competing (rather than two circular) modes of precedence in question: the precedence of the "actual" and the precedence of the "categorizable." Circumstances, thus understood, "actually" precede the events they predicate, but it is the "event" that precedes the operations of the categorizing intelligence and that enables that intelligence to retrospectively formulate (or, as Kant might have it, "demonstrate") prevailing circumstances from some singular event.

I have paused over such questions not in order to suggest that in consequence of these several paradoxes and tautologies we should demand some alternate less vexed event-theory, but, rather, because it is precisely in such terms that the *Zong* establishes itself as an event actually determined by its prevailing circumstances and as an event that makes it possible for us to recognize those circumstances in the first place. The *Zong,* in other words, can serve as our long twentieth century's *signum rememorativum, demonstrativum, prognostikon,* can "demonstrate" those "prevailing historical tendencies" that preceded it, that it enables us retrospectively to apprehend and to categorize, and that, re-collecting, it also "predicts," precisely to the extent that it is, in Kant's full sense, also an "event," or, in the words of Alain Badiou, one of Kant's more recent interlocutors, not just an event but a "Truth-Event."

* * *

Badiou, whose work is of importance to Slavoj Žižek, defines the Truth-Event in contradistinction to what he calls the "Knowledge" of the "multiplicity of Being."[1] And his importance for Žižek, and also for the argument I am making here, lies at least in part in his capacity to reconcile Kant both to a tradition of French Marxist thought and, most crucially, to Benjamin.[2] The Kantian register of Badiou's thought, Žižek argues, is strong and persistent, subtends his frequent and explicit disagreements with Kant, and assumes form in his fundamental categories of analysis: "at a deeper level his distinction between the order of the positive Knowledge of Being and the wholly different Truth-Event remains Kantian: when he emphasizes how, from the [neutral] standpoint of Knowledge, there simply is no Event—how, that is, the traces of the Event can be discerned as signs only by those who are already involved in support of the Event—does he not thereby repeat Kant's notion of signs that announce the noumenal act of freedom without positively proving it (like enthusiasm for the French Revolution)?" (Žižek, *Ticklish* 166). The Kantian "notion of signs" Žižek has in mind is, obviously enough, that indexed to the *signum rememorativum, demonstrativum, prognostikon*.

For Badiou, as Žižek further indicates, the Truth-Event belongs to an epistemological domain fundamentally distinct from that encompassed by Knowledge. Knowledge, he maintains, pertains to the realm of facticity and is thus properly the province of science. Its only true discipline, he argues, is mathematics. Truth, on the other hand, implies a fidelity to (and a "decision for") a motivated delimitation of the totality of Being into concrete sets, conditions, states, or "situations." Truth is thus, always, not the truth of Being but the truth of a situation, the truth of a singular state of history. It includes not just the "situation" it names but the determination to name a situation as such (i.e., it acknowledges that the act of defining a situation, the act of deciding to "count a situation as One," is fundamental to, and constitutive of, the Truth it seeks to describe). And its condition of possibility is the generally sudden, generally surprising emergence of a Truth-Event, the dramatic appearance of a disturbance (sign, image) within the field of Knowledge that, precisely because it cannot be accounted for by the prevailing regimes of knowledge, precisely because it appears as an anomaly, demonstrates the repressed or previously unrecognizable truth of a historical situation. Among Badiou's premier test cases for such an event is, unsurprisingly, the French Revolution, whose appearance as a Badiouvian Truth-Event Žižek glosses so:

> Take French society in the late eighteenth century: the state of society, its strata, economic, political, ideological conflicts, and so on, are accessible to Knowledge. However, no amount of Knowledge will enable us to predict or account for the properly unaccountable event called the "French Revolution." In this precise sense, the Event emerges *ex nihilo*. . . . The Event is the Truth of the situation that makes visible/legible what the "official" situation had to "repress." The French Revolution, for example, is the Event which makes visible/legible the excesses and inconsistencies, the "lie," of the *ancien regime*. . . . An event thus involves its own series of determinations: the Event itself; its naming . . . its ultimate Goal . . . ; and, last but not least, its *subject*, the agent who, on behalf of the Truth-Event, intervenes in the historical multiple of the situation and discerns/identifies in it signs-effects of the Event. (*Ticklish* 130)

As Žižek's comments suggest, the full scope of Badiou's conception of the Truth-Event is entirely complex. And it is not my object here to provide a full account of his theory but, rather, as a first step to returning to the *Zong* as such a

Truth-Event, to emphasize a few of its elements: centrally what Žižek identifies as the Truth-Event's "determinations," but also its status as what we might think of as a representative anomaly and its mode of appearance as at once Kantian "sign," Benjaminian "image," and Derridean "specter."

The spectral quality of the Truth-Event pertains to its uncanny and reiterative temporality. For the event, like the specter, is an untimely apparition: untimely in the sense that it first appears as the re-apparition of itself, emerges into visibility (as an Event) not at the moment of its happening but only within the retrospective purview of what Žižek calls its subjects—those who, having made a decision for the Truth of the Event, belatedly call the Event into being (as "One") by naming it as such and naming themselves as those who are faithful to the Truth they have discerned in it. Derrida, in *Specters of Marx,* proves himself, in this precise sense, a faithful "subject" of Marx and of a Marxian project for the emancipation of the society, much as Kant, in his essay, identifies himself as a "subject" of the French Revolution: subjects whose "faithfulness" to the event is indexed not so much to the "events" of the Event but to their determination/decision to be faithful to the "spirit" of the Event (whether, as in Kant's case, that "spirit" is attached to its spectacularly sublime quality or, in Derrida's, to its hauntological refusal ever to assume a final, empirical, "ontologized" form).[3] And the event is spectral in the sense that like Kant's *signum rememorativum, demonstrativum, prognostikon* and Derrida's "revenant . . . to come," it exists, for Badiou, as a promise to come again in some full, final, and absolute form.

Spectral, or at least quasi-spectral, the Truth-Event is also, in the terms I have used, a representative anomaly, in Žižek's terms a "symptom": "What Truth does is to reveal that (what Knowledge misperceives as) marginal malfunctionings and points of failure are a structural necessity. . . . With regard to the *ancien regime,* what the Truth-Event reveals is how injustices are not marginal malfunctionings but pertain to the very structure of the system which is, in its essence, as such 'corrupt.' Such an entity—which, misperceived by the system as a local 'abnormality,' effectively condenses the global 'abnormality' of the system as such, in its entirety—is what, in the Freudo-Marxian tradition, is called the *symptom*" (Žižek, *Ticklish* 131).

Spectral or quasi-spectral, symptomatically anomalous, the Truth-Event is also, as Žižek stresses, visible as the effect of a decision, as the belated determination not merely to regard it as such but as the typical sign that brings to light the "prevailing tendencies" of a surrounding set of historical circumstances. And it is with regard to this belated partisan decision for the existence and the truth of an event that Badiou's conception of the Truth-Event reveals, Žižek suggests, not only its Kantian but its Benjaminian character:

> Within the Marxist tradition, this notion of partiality as not only an obstacle to but a positive condition of Truth was most clearly articulated by Georg Lukács in his early work *History and Class Consciousness,* and in a more directly messianic, proto-religious mode by Walter Benjamin in "Theses in the Philosophy of History":

"truth" emerges when a victim, from his present catastrophic position, gains a sudden insight into the entire past as a series of catastrophes that led to his current predicament. (*Ticklish* 137)

How, we might then ask, does that truth emerge for Benjamin? The "Theses" outlines the perception, the *Arcades* "demonstrates" the method. Benjamin makes his decision for the truth as (and *as*) he writes the *Arcades*: by developing "to the highest degree" the art of citational montage; by accumulating fragments of human history drawn not from future time but from the archives of the "what has been"; by arraying and juxtaposing these fragments alongside one another in the interest of producing the resultant "dialectical image": "that wherein what has been comes together in a flash with the now to form a constellation." Benjamin's "dialectical images" *are* his decision, his determination to discern from the multitude of "what presents itself" a series of Truth-Events, his motivated, partial resolution to seize hold of one or other of the fragments or shards of wreckage piling up at the feet of the backward-glancing angel of history and to discover in this a Truth-Event, a demonstration of the coincidence of "now-being" with "what has been," an intimation of the future agreement between "past generations and the present one," a *signum rememorativum, demonstrativum, prognostikon.*

Kant-Benjamin-Badiou: between these three my understanding of the form of the event as apparition and re-apparition; symptomatic anomaly; sign, image, and decision is balanced. What remains is to turn from the form of *the* event, *the* image, decision, sign, to what is also under discussion here: *an* image, *an* event, *a* symptomatic anomaly, a *signum rememorativum, demonstrativum, prognostikon.* What remains is what is long past overdue: a return to the *Zong*, the sign it writes into the history of the modern, the state of history it reveals. And one way to begin to read that sign is to return, at last, to the decision that Kant's contemporary Granville Sharp made in identifying not the French Revolution but the *Zong* massacre as the age's decisive truth-event, the decision he made in putting pen to paper and dispatching to the Lords Commissioners of the Admiralty his account of this event and the awful truth it demonstrated.

\* \* \*

The 138-page handwritten packet of material Granville Sharp sent to the Lords Commissioners of the Admiralty on July 2, 1783, consisted of five documents: the first comprised a transcript of the appeals hearing on the case of the *Zong* held before Lord Mansfield at the court of King's Bench; the second was a letter Sharp addressed to the Lords Commissioners asking that they open a murder investigation; the third was his brief account of the massacre together with his arguments against the legal case for compensation advanced by the attorneys for the ship's owners; the fourth was a copy of another letter he had written, this to the Duke of Portland; the fifth was a copy of a petition the

*Zong*'s insurance underwriters had sent to William Pitt in his capacity as chancellor of the Court of Exchequer requesting that the initial verdict reached in favor of the owners be set aside and a new trial ordered.[4]

Read in its entirety, Sharp's dispatch presents itself as a formal imitation of both the events it seeks to describe and the mode of appearance of the "Truth-Event." It constructs itself, that is, via a logic of reiteration and a logic of surrogation. The reiterative quality of Sharp's submission is its most obvious but perhaps also its most perplexing quality. Read from beginning to end, it presents the story of the *Zong* massacre, then re-presents that story, then re-presents it not one but seven more times: the story is heard four times in the trial transcripts; once in Sharp's "cover letter" to the Lords Commissioners; once more in his succeeding "Account" of the massacre; again in the copy of his letter to the Duke of Portland; and then twice more in the petition of the underwriters with which he concludes the submission. The narrative of the massacre is thus presented nine times in 138 pages, or perhaps more than that if one also counts the testimony of the two chief witnesses that was read into evidence at the trial and the summarizing comments of Lord Mansfield.

Five documents, at least nine and as many as fourteen accounts: why this manner of representing "one" event (or, at least, one "Event" that in Badiou's full sense Sharp had decided "to count as One")? Why this insistence that his readers encounter the detailed horror of the massacre over and over and over again?

* * *

But what are those details? We, at least, have not yet encountered them in full. Whatever their inevitable differences, the nine or fourteen successive versions of the massacre agree on this basic history:

> **On September 6, 1781,** the *Zong* weighed anchor and sailed for Jamaica from the island of St. Thomas, off the west coast of Africa. There were 440 slaves on board and a crew of 17 men.
>
> **On November 27,** the ship came in sight of Jamaica, but the vessel's commander, Captain Luke Collingwood, ordered the *Zong* back out to sea. At the time over sixty of the slaves and seven of the crew had died of disease, and many of the remaining slaves were in ill health (and thus unlikely to fetch a good price on the Jamaican market).
>
> **On November 29,** Collingwood called a meeting of his ship's officers, informed them that the vessel's water supply was running dangerously low and that he intended to throw overboard that portion of his cargo necessary to preserve the life of the rest. The massacre began that day. Fifty-four of the sickest slaves were singled out and thrown into the ocean.
>
> **On November 30,** forty-three more slaves were thrown overboard. One of these, while in the water, managed to catch hold of the ship's

ropes and to drag himself up to a porthole, through which he climbed back into the ship.

**On December 1,** rain began to fall, and the crew collected six casks of water. Collingwood ordered the murders to proceed regardless. Thirty-six more slaves were brought on deck. Twenty-six were cast overboard. The last ten, as crew members were about to seize hold of them, jumped overboard rather than being thrown. They also drowned.

\* \* \*

133 human beings thrown or driven overboard over a period of three days. One survivor. 132 individual human beings methodically slaughtered, one by one by one. One killing after another. One murder after another imitating the one that had preceded it. One slave after another brought on deck and then thrown into the fatal sea. Below deck, in his cabin, unwilling either to participate or to protest: the retiring governor of the West African slave fort at Annamabo, Robert Stubbs, who, by the testimony entered into evidence at the trial, passed these three days by watching the bodies of the slaves falling past his window. 133 window-framed moments. 133 appearances and re-appearances of the same image. 133 repetitions of what even the attorney for the Liverpool owners could not avoid calling "this melancholy event" (NNM, REC/19). 132 deaths. One event.

One?

The logic of his decision to testify to the catastrophic truth of what had taken place aboard the *Zong* over the three days from November 29 to December 1, 1781, obliged Sharp to "count" this event as one. He was not alone in this. Everyone who spoke at the appeal evinced the same determination, a determination, perhaps, to limit the manifold horror of what they were discussing by unifying it. The psychology underlying such a decision may readily be parsed. Its ethics is, however, far from simple or simply suspect. There is ample and good reason to resist an easy nominalism that would refuse to recognize this as a coherent event, that would refuse to count this event as one, either as each of its moments of horror relate to one another or as this event, as an event, relates to all the other eventualities of history, capital, and knowledge that bear upon it and that it brings to light. But there are also good reasons to make another decision, reasons to recognize that this is also a singular and a melancholy event, or, perhaps more accurately, a melancholy conjunction of singular atrocities, reasons to recognize that the number we need to find some way to comprehend is neither 133 nor 132 but one, one, one.

\* \* \*

133. One. Whatever we decide, Sharp, for his part, made his decision for neither and both. One event. 133 singular acts of atrocity, iterated and re-iterated. 132 murders. One event. One by one by one. Why does Sharp demand that his readers encounter the details of what transpired over and over and over again?

What if we were to regard history, Cathy Caruth asks, as the history of a trauma? What would such a decision betoken? Among other things, she argues, it would demand that we learn to submit ourselves to a re-iterative practice of listening, a serial willingness to encounter the voice speaking from the "wound" of another: "Trauma is always the story of a wound that cries out, that addresses us in the attempt to tell us of a reality or truth that is not otherwise available. This truth, in its delayed appearance and in its belated address, cannot be linked only to what is known, but also to what remains unknown in our very actions and our language" (4). Trauma, thus understood, speaks its "truth" not only in much the same fashion as Badiou's "Truth-Event" articulates its message, it speaks also with the voice of melancholy. Caruth tends not to use the term, but trauma-theory, as she develops it, is undoubtedly also a theory of melancholy, a theory devoted to the un-exchangeable singularity of loss and what has been lost, a theory that in Nicolas Abraham and Maria Torok's terms "incorporates" its objects of loss rather than "introjecting" them, resolves itself to encrypt within its expressive text the "exquisite corpse" or corpses of its lamented dead and to guard them there.[5]

Melancholy, Abraham and Torok further argue, abhors metaphor, wages war on it. It does so because it regards metaphor as the representational mode of that principle of exchange, that principle of substitution, that is its opposite and the precondition of that "healthy" introjective work of mourning that works by finally surrendering the object of loss and replacing it with some other affective attachment. The dilemma for melancholy, as it seeks to express itself in language, is thus its profound mistrust of representation per se. How then does melancholy refer its text to the object whose loss that text laments, but that it cannot permit itself to represent? It does so, Abraham and Torok's work suggests, through an anti-metaphoric hyper-realism, through a cryptonymic mode of reference that aims to pass itself off not as a representation of the lost thing but as that lost thing itself. Hence the frequent impossibility of parsing the melancholic text. Hence its paradoxical, and anxious, re-iterativity. Hence its attempt to reduce representation to the exclusive domain of the nominative, to the speaking, over and over again, of the secret name of the dead. Hence its attempt to strip language down to the barest, most utterly literal, and most cryptic realism.

Is Sharp's submission such a cryptic, melancholically realist text? I mentioned earlier that it runs to 138 numbered pages. That is both the case and not quite the case. Between the second and third, third and fourth, and fourth and fifth sections of the manuscript there is a blank page. One would expect the same between the first and second sections, for a total of four unwritten pages. Inexplicably, however, between the first and second sections there are three blank pages. So, instead of four blank pages between five sections, as might be expected, there are six. Why? 138 pages in all. Six blank pages. In total, then: 132 handwritten pages secreted within the larger total; 132 inked pages, that is, unless one also counts that floating, un-numbered, extra page—the index, which, if added, makes 133. 132 marked pages by one count. 133 by another. We know these numbers. They might, of course, represent no more than the greatest of coincidences. Perhaps they do. But we also know a few more things. Sharp was an obsessive copier and re-copier of his correspondence. He wrote and re-wrote drafts of all his letters, often leaving behind as many as five or six different versions until he was fully satisfied with the text he finally dispatched. There is something else also. The 132 or 133 marked pages of his submission are not equally filled with print. Thumbing through the entire manuscript the discrepancies from page to page are obvious. Some pages are entirely filled, some only half so, some pages are less than a quarter full. Beneath the final line of writing on each page there is a neatly ruled border. If Sharp had not set himself these borders, if he had written from the top to the bottom of each page, the manuscript would never have filled anything near its total 132 or 133 pages. Is this number deliberately arrived at? Regardless, it is there. One event. 133 slaves thrown overboard. 132 human beings drowned. Nine or fourteen re-iterated accounts of this singular, melancholy event. 132 or 133 handwritten pages. The text guards its secrets even as it demands that we listen to them over and over and over again.

*  *  *

The *Zong*, Sharp's submission indicates, may well name a trauma and an injunction, a wound and a serial obligation to listen "to the voice and the speech delivered by the other's wound" (Caruth 8). That does not yet make it *either* the "event" in which the "moment" finds itself condensed and realized *or* an event in which our long twentieth century finds itself demonstrated, recollected, and predicted. For that to become clear we need to return to Sharp's manuscript and to the "event" it demonstrates. And we need to recognize that what Sharp quite clearly understood was that the "event" in question entailed more than those three days aboard the *Zong*, more than the massacre: it entailed also, at the very least, what followed—most crucially the original trial in which a jury found for the owners and the hearing in which Lord Mansfield revisited that decision. As the name for an "event," in other words, the *Zong* names both a massacre *and* the set of legal decisions made upon it; both an act of atrocity and the value-form on which that atrocity made its claims.

If the slaughter itself evoked the horror of all the parties discussing it at court, then Sharp's outrage, while clearly inspired by the massacre, was re-doubled by the initial jury verdict and by Mansfield's decision to treat the matter not as a murder case but as a property dispute, and his appeal to the commissioners was devoted not only to demanding that they find some way to see the guilty parties punished but that they see the drowned slaves as something other than the bearers of an abstract, insured quantum of value: "The manuscript book," he informed the Commissioners, "contains a copy of minutes taken in short hand the last term, on the 22d and 23d May, 1783, of the proceedings in the Court of King's Bench, on a motion for a new trial of the cause of the same parties mentioned above, concerning the *value* of those murdered Negroes! Thus the contest between the owners and insurers of the ship, though a mere mercenary business amongst themselves about the *pecuniary* value, and not for the blood, of so many human persons wickedly and unjustly put to death, has, nevertheless, occasioned the disclosure of that horrible transaction, which otherwise, perhaps, might . . . have never been brought to light" (emphasis original) (NMM, REC/19). Sharp's syntax suggests that the "horrible transaction" he has in mind is, primarily, the massacre itself. His diction, however, is precise in *its* ambiguity. For it suggests that what inspires horror and outrage is not only the massacre but a massacre that was, itself, solely interpretable to the court as a financial dispute. If his horror is for murder as a form of fiduciary transaction then it also attends the financialization of a system of justice, the transformation of the courtroom into a scene of exchange, its reinvention as a mechanism designed not to dispense justice but money, not to insure the existence of human beings as the holders of rights but to investigate their properties as the bearers of a quantum of value underwritten by the slave ship's insurance contract.

* * *

A brief note: if mourning is the opposite of melancholy then, in the realm of capital transactions, so is insurance. Which is to say that insurance is the form that mourning takes when it equips itself for the market. For what else is mourning—upon the completion of its "work"—but the determination to exchange some lost thing for a viable substitute; and what else is insurance but that determination monetarized? Putting on trial a form of value that finds its perfect realization in the practice of insurance, the case of the *Zong* thus also puts mourning on trial. No wonder then that Sharp's outrage should have taken the form it did. No wonder that he understood that, no matter what Mansfield ruled, the terms to which he had bound his ruling had already confirmed that the law could treat the slaves as no more than the bearers of an abstract measure of value. No wonder, also, that in embarrassment of this fact, virtually all the parties before the court found themselves obliged, at one moment or another, to at least pay lip service to the language of melancholy. But while the attorneys for both the owners and the underwriters may have mouthed that language, they knew that the bench was by no means inclined to enshrine it as a principle of law. Instead, as all the parties seemed to agree, the case would be decided on the technical question of "necessity." It is the most frequently spoken word in the transcript, and as Mansfield indicated in his final judgment, the sole matter at issue as a point of law. Even Sharp, in his letter to the Duke of Portland, sought to strategically redeploy the term, opening and closing his appeal by insisting that the facts of the case demonstrated the "absolute necessity to abolish the Slave Trade" (NMM, REC/19).

Sharp's use of the term is, however, at odds with the meaning it held in Mansfield's courtroom. For there "necessity" referred not to an abstract ethical obligation but to a particular stipulation within the *Zong*'s insurance contract and to the general insurance principle underlying that stipulation. As far as the court was concerned the question of necessity was circumscribed not by a code of ethics but by the terms of a contract. In raising the question of "necessity" the court did not ask whether or not it had been ethically necessary for Collingwood to sacrifice some lives to save some others. It asked instead whether his actions met the standard of necessity (for the throwing overboard of "goods") of his contract's jettison clause and whether, accordingly, the ship's owners were or were not entitled to compensation for those lost "goods" in accord with the rules laid down by the bedrock insurance principle of the "general average."

This then was the question before the court: whether or not the loss to the overall value of the *Zong's* cargo was or was not a general average loss "according to the Stipulation and Agreement" of its insurance policy. And there were two main ways in which the underwriters' attorneys could have pursued that question: either by suggesting that that policy did not include slaves among the list of "goods" that could be treated as a general average loss; or by suggesting that the policy did include slaves among that full list of "commodities that had become the subject of insurance," but that, in this case, it had not been necessary for Collingwood to destroy these "goods" and thus no compensation was owed. The first option would have entailed a fundamental engagement with the extant law and theory of property. The second, which is the option that the attorneys chose to pursue, depended more simply on a matter of fact. Like any "standard" marine insurance policy of the period, the ship's insurance contract stipulated that

> Whatever the master of a ship in distress, with the advice of his officers and sailors, deliberately resolves to do, for the preservation of the whole, in cutting away masts or cables, or in throwing goods overboard to lighten his vessel, which is what is meant by *jettison* or jetson, is, in all places, permitted to be brought into a general, or gross average: in which all concerned in ship, freight, and cargo, are to bear an equal or proportionable part of what was so sacrificed for the common good, and it must be made good by the insurers in such proportions as they have underwrote: *however, to make this action legal, the three following points are essentially necessary; viz—1st. That what was so condemned to destruction, was in consequence of a deliberate and voluntary consultation, held between the master and men:—2dly. That the ship was in distress, and the sacrificing the things they did was a necessary procedure to save the rest:—and 3dly. That the saving of the ship and the cargo was actually owing to the means used with that sole view.*[6]

"A necessary procedure to save the rest": this is the crucial condition, and the issue on which both the original trial and the subsequent appeal rested. In disputing the "absolute," "inviolable," "indispensable," or "extreme" necessity of Collingwood's actions, the attorneys for the underwriters were trying to establish, as a simple matter of fact, that the *Zong* was not in such a condition of distress that Collingwood's actions had proved necessary to save it. They granted the first condition and concentrated all their energies on the second, arguing that there was ample water to permit everyone aboard ship to survive, on half allowance, for upward of two weeks.

In electing to argue their case so the attorneys for the underwriters had, however, already conceded a fundamental point, indeed *the* fundamental point. They had admitted, by refusing to contest, the conviction that slaves were, as a matter of law, commodities just like any other, interchangeable before the law with alabaster, beads, china, deal, glass. . . . The attorneys for the underwriters assumed this as a given. Lord Mansfield assumed it. The ship-owner's attorney was, in fact, the only person to raise the issue, and then only to assert its unquestionability: "[They] are made the subject of property. . . . Your Lordship knows they are real Property . . . not only Property but of the species Value of 30 a head. . . . This is the case of Chattels, of Goods, it is really so, it is the case of throwing over Goods—for to this purpose and the purpose of Insurance they are real goods and property" (NMM, REC/19). This is shocking, must be shocking, even if, two centuries later, we are no longer shocked by it, no longer surprised to discover that slaves were regarded as commodities. There is nothing new in *this* discovery. But there is, nevertheless, something new here, something that does in fact mark this case as an "event" in the history of the slave trade and the modern history of capital.[7] The entire proceeding in Lord Mansfield's courtroom proceeds on the basis of an assumption, assumes—and by assuming makes appear for the first time in the legal record—an a priori truth: that slaves are not only the "subjects of property," not only commodities, but commodities "which have become at some or other time the subjects of insurance." This is the news the *Zong* trials announce, this is the truth they belatedly testify to by assuming that slaves are, like quills, rice, rosin, sedans, and silks, subject to the "general average."

But what is this "general average"? The passage I cited above detailing the stipulations of the jettison clause of the *Zong's* marine insurance policy is more than a clause specific to that contract. It is, in fact, the definition of the "general average" provided in John Weskett's 1781 manual *A Complete Digest of the Theory, Laws, and Practice of Insurance,* and as such, as Weskett makes clear, the definition of *the* bedrock principle of insurance law, the definition of that practice by which finance capital insures not only its objects but, more importantly, insures its capacity to value (and to *guarantee* the value) of objects regardless either of their thingly existence or their actual marketplace exchange. Without insurance there is no finance capital. And without the concept of the average, as Weskett makes clear, there is no modern practice of insurance. Indeed, as his text demonstrates, to speak of the average is to speak not only of insurance's most complex work of valuation, it is also to speak of a general damage—or loss—theory of value, of that full range of circumstances that might degrade a good's thingly existence, without—if it was insured—effecting its ultimate "value."[8] The average begins with damage or loss, computes the extent of loss, and then substitutes as a sort of prosthesis for what has been lost, the "what would have been." "Average" is then the word insurance gives to that paradigmatic finance-culture procedure by which lost singulars find themselves re-expressed as speculative but exchangeable typicals. And *its* paradigm, *the* "typical" situation from which its protocols are deduced, is the *Zong* massacre—

not to be sure as a unique event but, precisely, as a type of event, a paradigm of that typical event that the theory of the average establishes as its general precedent and test case. Such, certainly, was Collingwood's determination when in November of the year that Weskett's *Complete Digest* was published, he called together his officers and crew, informed them that their ship was in distress, its water and food supplies running out, and, having sought their advice, as he was obliged to do, "deliberately resolved . . . for the preservation of the whole . . . [to throw] goods overboard" with the intention of justifying his acts under the law of jettison and claiming "average" compensation for "what was so sacrificed" on the basis, to quote Weskett again, of "what would have been the value of the goods if they had arrived safe and undamaged." The *Zong* I am thus suggesting was not an aberration, not some wildly exceptional event that could nevertheless, somehow, just barely, be encompassed or made sense of by the dominant cultural logic of its age. It was, instead, the very "type" of the type of case that that moment's value theory had identified as its test case, *the* typical sort of loss-event from which this age deduced its speculative procedures, average theories, theoretical realism, and money-form of value.

Let me put this another way.

The genius of insurance, and the secret of its contribution to finance capitalism, is its insistence that the real test of something's value comes not at the moment it is made or exchanged but at the moment it is lost or destroyed. In a pure commodity culture (if there ever was such a thing) that value would cease to exist the moment the commodity ceased to exist, the moment there was no longer something to exchange, the moment Marx's paradigmatic yards of cloth, burnt up, no longer existed to express the value of the shirts for which they could have been exchanged. In a money culture or an insurance culture (the distinction, I am suggesting, is irrelevant—a money culture cannot exist without insurance), value, however, survives its objects, and in doing so does not just reward the individual self-interest of the insured object's owner, but retrospectively confirms the system-wide conviction that that value was always autonomous from its object, always only a matter of agreement. Insurance-value, a more durable precisely because a less material, contingent, or mutable form than either use-value or exchange-value, does not await the moment of loss to become real. It exists the moment an object is insured, and effectively abridges Marx's full formula for capital at that moment, conferring upon that object a value that depends neither on its being put to use nor entered into exchange as a commodity but results purely from the ability of two contracting parties to imagine what it would have been worth at that imaginary future moment in which it will have ceased to exist. The insurance that covers an object has not ensured that it will survive destruction. Anticipating that future moment of destruction, insurance proleptically visits its consequences upon the object. It annuls the object, abolishes it as a bearer of value, and so frees value from the degradation of thingly existence.

Insurance thus does not confer a monetary value upon lost things; it sets the money-form of value free from the life of things, insures its existence, instantly speeds whatever it touches to the money-form of value. It does not ensure things, it ensures a form of value, serves as that form's word of guarantee. Absent the security insurance provides, finance capitalism could not exist. The world of things would stage its revenge on value each time some object or another was destroyed, would re-fasten value to embodied things and make one as mortal as the other. Licensed by insurance to utterly detach value from the material existence of objects, however, finance capital is free to speculate in and profit from its imaginary markets, imaginary transactions, imaginary valuations, to exchange both use-values and exchange-values for the indestructible money-form.

We have not yet, I believe, grasped the consequences of this, not yet appreciated what it means for slavery to name an extension not only of commodity capitalism into the domain of the human, but the colonization of human subjectivity by finance capital. The *Zong* trials constitute an event in the history of capital *not* because they treat slaves as commodities but because they treat slaves as commodities that have become the subject of insurance, treat them, in Žižek's terms, not as objects to be exchanged but as the "empty bearers" of an abstract, theoretical, but entirely real quantum of value, treat them as little more than promissory notes, bills of exchange, or some other markers of a "specie value," treat them as suppositional entities whose value is tied not to their continued, embodied, material existence but to their speculative loss-value. The *Zong* trials constitute an event not because they further subject the life-world to the principle of exchange but because they subject it to the hegemony of that which super-ordinates exchange: the general equivalents of finance capital.

Luke Collingwood's catastrophic decision signals the completion and the bringing-to-light of *this* financial (and financializing) revolution. His step-by-step determination to treat the slaves aboard his ship as bearers not simply of a commodified exchange-value but of an utterly dematerialized, utterly speculative, and utterly transactable "pecuniary value" represents the symptomatic manifestation of this revolution. Precisely because his act was regarded as an anomaly, precisely because his decision was treated as an exception that "a general normative schema" could nevertheless incorporate within its system of rule, it functions as the test case and truth-event of the "situation" it brings to light (as, in Žižek's terms, that "which, misperceived by the system as a local 'abnormality,' effectively condenses the global 'abnormality' of the system as such").

The *Zong*, thus, was not only a name for a late eighteenth-century *legal* case, it was, as James Chandler has taught us to re-understand the word, an eighteenth-century "case" par excellence; a "situation" that a casuistic jurisprudence ("casuistry," Chandler reminds us, is, most simply put, "a discipline for dealing with the application of principles to cases") could submit to the test of "a general normative scheme," precisely, if tautologically, because it defined the type of situation *from which* that general normative scheme had deduced itself (Chandler 195, 209). If the case, like the historicist situation, thus generates a bidirectional interpretive practice, "a two way-movement in which now the general normative scheme, now the particular event or situation, is being tested," a process of simultaneously reading the meaning and value of the particular off the grammar of the general *and* construing the general from the representative particular, then it is, I am suggesting, as such a situation, as such a two-way "case," that the *Zong* at once falls within, and can be made sense of by, the general normative schemes of its moment *and* defines the very type of situation on which the normative schemes of that (long, repeating) moment depend.

Precisely because the casuistic system of jurisprudence operative in Lord Mansfield's courtroom could apply its general principles to this aberrant case in which those principles find themselves most absolutely demonstrated, this case can serve as one of those "events" in which the age sees itself revealed, as a counter-*signum rememorativum, demonstrativum, prognostikon* by which this age of speculative revolutions is predicated. Sharp recognized this. And it is because he recognized it that *his* act of decision, his determination to bring this event to life, demanded that he bear outraged witness not only to the slaughter aboard the *Zong* but to the "horrible transaction" that slaughter betokened, to the culmination of this event in a hearing not on the murder but on the "value" of the *Zong*'s drowned slaves.

\* \* \*

*Signum demonstrativum?* So much may be granted. *Signum rememorativum?* This perhaps also. But *signum prognostikon?* That, certainly, is not yet established. Nor will I establish it with anything like the detail I have attempted thus far. The late twentieth century that bookends the long twentieth century whose emergence the *Zong* massacre and trials bring to light represents not only a repetition but an intensification of its moments of "beginning." In this case, however, intensification assumes the form less of concentrating the operations of finance capital in one or other signature event than of distributing its modes of speculation, speculative epistemologies, and abstract value forms more fully across the global spectrum, by finding for itself ever more points of application along the exchange networks of the globe. Intensification, here, manifests itself as the ever more exhaustive, ever more total, ever more complex, ever more ubiquitous, and (*because* ever more ubiquitous) ever more unremarkable penetration of the Heideggerian life-world by the cultural logic of finance capital. This is, obviously enough, a Jamesonian argument, as it is Jamesonian shorthand for what we have taken to calling the postmodern. And if part of the implied argument of this essay is that the postmodern is less original to the period with which we tend to associate it than we might think, that the postmodern is, indeed, a period concept that requires its own adjustment, then the version of the contemporary I have in mind is, nevertheless, largely Jamesonian in its understanding of this contemporaneity's dominant cultural logics (with both the caveat drawn from Giovanni Arrighi that like any regime of capital this regime moves "forward" by "moving backward at the same time," cyclically "resurrecting" the capital and cultural logics of a mode of accumulation that seems to have preceded it, and the Benjaminian qualification that this contemporaneity is, like any other, non-contemporary with itself). I do not intend then to offer anything like a comprehensive map of this contemporaneity that the "what has been" I have been charting predicates, and for which that recollected past functions as a demonstrative *signum prognostikon*. Jameson has already undertaken that labor more thoroughly than I could hope to. And indeed, the corrective that Arrighi's argument offers to Jameson's description of our contemporaneity is itself redundant. Jameson has recently taken note of it and has incorporated Arrighi's design within his own system of analysis.

Jameson makes this adjustment to the argument of *postmodernism* in his relatively brief but immensely suggestive essay "Culture and Finance Capital." The essay opens with a consideration of Arrighi's *The Long Twentieth Century* and attributes to it both the framing of "a problem we didn't know we had" and "a solution to it: the problem of finance capital" (246). The "problem" of finance capital that Jameson suggests Arrighi has discovered is its anachronism, its appearance not only as the dominant form of capital within capital's most recent stage of development (and thus also, by the arguments of prior models, its most "advanced" or its "final" stage), but its untimely prior appearances in both the eighteenth and the late sixteenth centuries. Arrighi's solution, Jameson approvingly notes, is to index these serial appearances of finance capital to a set of "cycles of accumulation," each of which begins and ends with a moment of finance capital, and each of which plays out, over the course of its "long durée," the tripartite sequence of Marx's full formula for capital. With this in mind, Jameson indicates that what he had previously referred to as the "late capitalism" of the postmodern is better understood both as its finance capitalism *and* as a mode of accumulation that marks the postmodern not as a break with what has preceded it but as the culminating moment of a long durée that repeats, by intensifying, the moment with which it began:

> Capital itself becomes free-floating. It separates from the concrete context of its productive geography. Money becomes in a second sense and to a second degree abstract. . . . Now, like the butterfly stirring within the chrysalis, it separates itself from the concrete breeding ground and prepares to take flight. We know today only too well (but Arrighi shows us that this contemporary knowledge of ours only replicates the bitter experience of the dead . . . ) that the term is literal. This free-floating capital, in its frantic search for more profitable investments . . . will begin to live its life in a new context: no longer in the factories and the spaces of extraction and production, but on the floor of the stock market, jostling for more intense profitability. But it won't be as one industry competing against another branch, nor even one productive technology against another more advanced one in the same line of manufacturing, but rather in the form of speculation itself: specters of value, as

Derrida might put it, vying against each other in a vast, world-wide, disembodied phantasmagoria. This is of course, the moment of finance capital as such. (251)

Jameson is here describing the "today." As he indicates, however, he might equally, and indeed *is* equally, describing a yesterday this today replicates. At the heart of that yesterday-constellating-today, as he indicates, is the separation of value from the concrete, the emergence of speculation as a hegemonic enterprise and of speculative forms as the bases for and objects of a new form of knowledge/power, and the global circulation of what, paraphrasing Derrida, he calls "specters of value." The phrase is as striking as it is apt, more resonant, even, than Jameson's usage indicates. For the "specters of value" he envisions vying with one another in a "world-wide, disembodied phantasmagoria" (which itself reads like a precise analog of "Lady Credit's" fantastical realm of speculation alternately extolled and lamented by eighteenth-century public-sphere discourse) are at least doubly "spectral": they are both the imaginary, disembodied, value forms trading on the floor (or across the digital circuitry) of the globe's money markets and stock exchanges, and the ghostly reappearances of such exchangeable abstractions, haunting reminders and revenants of this present's "what has been."

Jameson's primary concern, however, is not with the hauntological doubleness of finance-capital but, characteristically, with a dialectical reading of Arrighi's "comprehensive new theory of finance capital" that will enrich that account by "reaching out into the expanded realm of cultural production to map its effects" (252). In his essay, Jameson restricts himself to one of these: the "effect" of finance capital on the "category of abstraction itself," particularly as abstraction assumes aesthetic life within the postmodern "fragment," which he suggests differs from both the realist and the modernist fragment precisely to the degree that it, like the spectral value forms of finance capital, has now fully escaped the domain of reference, utterly detached itself from some material context, and so set itself free to wander as some narratological specter of historicity (258).[9] Jameson finds his chief instance of this process in the "image fragments" that saturate the films of Derek Jarman, but reminds us that he does so by way of offering what is primarily a "symptomatic" reading of the effects of finance capital in the image-fragment-dominated culture of "late-capitalist everyday life" (252). In concluding, I want to suggest that we follow that lead; which implies, in part, also returning to the statement of method and intentions with which Kant begins ("We desire a fragment of human history") and recognizing that, on this matter at least, Kant and Jameson are not that far apart: that in either case the image-fragments symptomatic of their speculative moments demonstrate the broad historical tendencies of those moments precisely to the degree that they disclose the sovereignty of abstraction over the phenomenal world of persons, events, and things; recognizing, indeed, that it is to the degree that the "fragments" central to both a postmodern culture of speculation and Kant's Enlightenment philosophy of history disclose their common allegiance to the category of abstraction, and to the extent that such abstraction generates, "now" as "then," an oppositional and pervasive counter-discourse of cultural melancholy, that these two "moments" can indeed be said to demonstrate, anticipate, and recollect one another.

## Notes

1. For Žižek's lengthiest discussion of Badiou, see *The Ticklish Subject*, 127–71. The central text to which Žižek refers throughout his reading, Badiou's *L'être et l'événement* (Paris: Editions du Seuil, 1988), has recently been translated as *Being and Event;* here I rely on Žižek's translations throughout.

2. I discuss the Derridean and Benjaminian cast of Badiou's event theory in the pages that follow. Badiou partially reconciles Althusser to Kant, Žižek suggests, largely by conferring on the sympathy-inducing character of the sublime Kantian "event" a strong Althusserian "interpellative" capacity.

3. On Derrida's refusal of the ontologization of the spectral, see *Specters,* throughout but especially 95–124.

4. The complete handwritten set of documents is in the National Maritime Museum, Greenwich, catalogued as REC/19. Subsequent citations will be abbreviated NMM, REC/19.

5. For Abraham and Torok, the cryptic discourse of the melancholic is a discourse that founds itself on the inability to introject the lost object of desire and a consequent incorporation of that object. As Nicholas T. Rand indicates in his "Editor's Note" to Abraham and Torok's *The Shell and the Kernel,* where introjection implies an acknowledgement of loss that allows the mourner to transform the self "in the face of interior and exterior changes in the psychological, emotional, relational, political, [and] professional landscape," incorporation "is the refusal to acknowledge the full import of the loss, a loss that, if recognized as such, would effectively transform us" (127). A form of disavowal, incorporation also implies a secret labor of compensation: "The words that cannot be uttered, the scenes that cannot be recalled, the tears that cannot be shed—everything will be swallowed along with the trauma that led to the loss. Swallowed and preserved. Inexpressible mourning erects a secret tomb inside the subject" (130). Within that tomb, Abraham and Torok continue, within that cryptic vault of memory, the mourner hides the terrible, fascinating, strangely "exquisite" corpse of the lost, violated, beloved, and suffers its serial hauntings.

6. This text is from Weskett's *Complete Digest of the Theory, Laws, and Practice of Insurance;* I cite it as evidentiary of what the *Zong*'s insurance contract would have stipulated because while the contract itself has not survived, testimony entered at Mansfield's hearing indicated that the contract was a thoroughly standard policy in all respects. Weskett's 1781 framing of the principle of the "general average" and of the legal restrictions applying to it may thus be taken as describing the terms under which the *Zong*'s policy, drawn up that same year, would have been written. Testimony and argumentation throughout the hearing further indicate that it was exactly the set of stipulations Weskett defines that were at issue before the court.

7. If, that is, we continue to regard the event not as that which marks a moment of absolute rupture but as that which offers its retrospective testimony to a pre-existing "situation"; as the mode of appearance of the "what has been"; as the re-apparitional appearance of what has been brought to light.

8. The initial work of establishing the value of a cargo was a simple matter of

agreement, and, so long as the intention of fraud was not suspected, could easily be set higher than market value if the "owner" was willing to pay the correspondingly higher premium; in the case of the total loss of a cargo no valuation was necessary, the amount having already been set by the terms of the contract; the computation of "average" value in the case of total or partial loss was thus the fundamental work on which the fortunes of an insurance underwriter depended.

9. Jameson summarizes his argument so: "What does all this have to do with finance capital? Modernist abstraction, I believe, is less a function of capital accumulation as such than of money itself in a situation of capital accumulation. Money is here both abstract (making everything equivalent) and empty and uninteresting, since its interest lies outside itself. It is thus incomplete like the modernist images I have been evoking; it directs attention elsewhere, beyond itself, towards what is supposed to complete (and abolish) it. It knows a semiautonomy, certainly, but not a full autonomy in which it would constitute a language or a dimension in its own right. But that is precisely what finance capital brings into being: a play of monetary entities that need neither production (as capital does) nor consumption (as money does), which supremely, like cyberspace, can live on their own internal metabolisms and circulate without any reference to an older type of content. But so do the narrativized image fragments of a stereotypical postmodern language; they suggest a new cultural realm or dimension that is independent of the former real world, not because as in the modern (or even the romantic) period culture withdrew from that real world into an autonomous space of art, but rather because the real world has already been suffused with culture and colonized by it, so that is has no outside in terms of which it could be found lacking" (264–65).

# PART 2

*Cultures of Investment*

# 2    Writing about Finance in Victorian England

## Disclosure and Secrecy in the Culture of Investment

*Mary Poovey*

The circulation of regular, reliable information about financial matters has always played a critical role in the modern market economy. Since at least the sixteenth century, when the first lists of prices were published in Antwerp and Venice, such writing has been instrumental in publicizing the availability of specific commodities, prices current in the market, and international exchange rates (Parsons 12). Without this information, early modern merchants would not have been able to conduct the elaborate and geographically extensive business that fueled economies in sixteenth- and seventeenth-century Western Europe, nor would they have been likely to develop the kind of informal associations that flourished in eighteenth-century London coffee houses. By the same token, writing about finance was also essential in creating the public confidence crucial to the refinement of credit instruments (like bills of exchange) and the spread of financial institutions (like banks). In the "remarks on trade" that began to appear in eighteenth-century British newspapers and the editorial statements about business published as early as 1713, interested Britons were able to read about trade negotiations, bankruptcies, shipping news, and debates about tariffs (Parsons 17). Doing so, they could begin to imagine their society as penetrated—if not yet defined—by a system of financial relationships whose most visible signs were the various credit transactions in which nearly every Briton was already involved (Brewer 203–30).

If the development of a modern market economy has always depended in part on the circulation of financial information, then nineteenth-century England witnessed an intensification of the already close relationship between the growth of financial institutions and writing about finance. There are many ways to explain why this relationship became more intimate after the end of the war with France, but the single most important factor was the increase, in number and kind, of shares available for Britons to buy. While only five stocks were available on the still rudimentary London Exchange in 1770, by 1811 government securities and the shares of chartered corporations like the East India Company had been joined by some industrial shares. After Napoleon's defeat, as the peacetime economy of Great Britain expanded and the London

Stock Exchange became more organized, the number of quoted stocks multiplied so that, by 1824, it was possible for an investor to trade in as many as 624 joint-stock companies—a number that signaled a four-fold increase over the previous year (Michie 56; Robb, *White-Collar* 14). This increase in available shares marked the beginning of what eventually became a culture of investment in Britain. Previous investment opportunities had been few in number, and the two leading venues for eighteenth-century capital both posed serious impediments to the would-be investor: lending money for mortgages required expensive lawyers and a long-term commitment of funds, and shipping was a high-risk venture. Most company shares, by contrast, paid a regular dividend and could easily be bought and sold, with only the market to dictate risk and only a broker to pay up front. While individuals did not begin to invest in shares in large numbers until at least the 1870s, the institutions to which individuals entrusted their money did. With banks and insurance companies regularly putting their money at call into the stock market, many individuals were intermittently involved in stocks even before they purchased shares on their own. By the 1890s, when the price of many shares fell to £1, more individuals were prepared to invest, for nearly a century of indirect participation in an increasingly well-publicized activity had made the rapid returns the stock market promised seem within the reach of even the average middle-class Briton.

In this essay, I explore the role that financial writing played in making the allure of investment vivid for Britons. For reasons that are both historical and theoretical, I do not describe this writing as a single discourse. Instead, I identify the features that characterized each mode of financial writing that developed before the mid-1840s, then show how these features were combined and reworked in a genre that was new in that decade. From the mid-1840s forward, the new genre of financial journalism brought the world of investment ever closer to middle-class Britons in articles and books that not only drew their information from other kinds of financial writing but also used many of the narrative conventions popularized by contemporary fiction. Just as financial journalists began to borrow literary conventions in the middle of the decade, so novelists soon began to introduce financial themes into their fictions. The result was a set of (admittedly uneven) exchanges and crossovers at the level of themes and formal features that drew financial journalism and realist novels into a relationship of generic proximity. Thinking about this generic affiliation between financial writing and much of the fiction of the period enables us to specify the formal dimension of a relationship that some literary critics have treated as metaphorical, and others have used simply to launch historical investigations of the nineteenth century's prevailing economic conditions.[1] Identifying the affiliation between financial journalism and many of the canonical novels of the period as formal and generic also enables us to identify a structural dynamic that was central to both the growth of Victorian companies and the appeal of Victorian fiction: the constitutive relationship between disclosure and secrecy.

## From Shipping News to Financial Journalism

As I have already suggested, the first kind of financial writing to appear in Europe was limited to commercial information and typically took the form of lists of numbers. Intended primarily for merchants, this information began to appear in London and European commercial centers in the sixteenth century as lists of prices, tables of exchange rates, and the arrival and departure dates of ships. Such commercial information continued to be published for English merchants throughout the eighteenth century; in 1713 it was joined by another kind of writing, which tended to replace the numerical information and lists that dominated the remarks on trade with the kind of polemical writing typical of the emergent political press. This new political writing was often published as penny sheets; stylistically, it relied on declarative summaries of assumptions presented as common sense; and it was intended for a somewhat different audience than were the lists of prices current in the market, although the readers of these cheap publications could certainly have included merchants who saw their interests affected by political decisions. By the beginning of the nineteenth century, the tendency to replace lists of commercial, often numerical information with discursive prose reached something like a logical conclusion in the long essays published in the *Edinburgh Review*. These essays, which were often reviews of other, fairly technical economic writings (such as Francis Horner's review of Henry Thornton's *Inquiry into . . . Paper Credit*, published in the first issue of the *Edinburgh* in 1802 [Horner 28–56]), drew their stylistic features from moral philosophy and their subdued polemics from the unfolding campaign for free trade. The contributors to the *Edinburgh Review* sought a more intellectually sophisticated audience than did the compilers of the prices current or the authors of polemical pamphlets. Their articles tried to cultivate in these readers an understanding of the new commercial economy that placed specific trade opportunities within a larger social and political context, whose contours were mapped by the new science of political economy (Fontana 112–46).

In the 1820s, another form of financial information began to appear in newspapers like the *Morning Chronicle* and the *London Times*. This financial information was the first direct response (and incentive) to the increased opportunities for investment represented by the expanded number of companies quoted on the London Stock Exchange. Appearing in the form of "money columns" or "City articles" published daily or weekly, this feature built on the closely printed columns listing prices of shares and international rates of exchange that the *Times* had published since 1785 (Parsons 22). Unlike these lists, however, the new articles supplemented columns of prices with brief expository, often chatty, comments on the culture of the City, which began to cultivate the image of London's financial district as a distinct and charmingly idiosyncratic culture. Beginning late in 1825, some City editors also took it upon themselves to issue judgments about the climate of investment as a whole, so that these

City articles became a source of rudimentary, nonspecific investment advice. Following upon this tradition, the *Times'* City editor, Thomas Massa Alsanger, began to warn investors in the early 1840s that the railway bubble was about to burst. That the editors allowed him to so do even though the *Times* accepted extensive advertising from railway companies suggests that his columns had acquired a value of their own, over and above promoting the companies whose advertisements the paper solicited (Parsons 23).

Three additional nineteenth-century innovations in financial writing deserve comment. The first was the development of what we might call business writing, by which I mean regular publications that were both produced by and devoted to various financial institutions or to the financial sector as a whole; this writing subordinated the author's political agenda to what was represented as an impartial presentation of facts. Such writing is epitomized by the *Banker's Magazine,* founded in 1844, but historians have also linked it to the *Economist,* which was launched in 1843 by James Wilson (Edwards 6–84; Parsons 25).[2] In its early years, the *Economist* did not conform to the definition of business writing I have just provided, for the paper was initially an organ of the Anti-Corn Law League. It only assumed the function that became its trademark—explaining the relationship between economic issues and the financial sector in dispassionate, apparently apolitical language—after the free trade campaign had succeeded. The paper had clearly embraced this role by 1853, when the banker Walter Bagehot began to contribute to the *Economist* (Edwards 97; Parsons 25–29), for Bagehot not only increased the attention the paper paid to banking, currency, and investment but did so with an eye to explaining how the financial system worked, why some institutions failed or faltered, and even, in very general terms, what kinds of securities investors should buy (Bagehot, "What to Buy—I" 1449–51 and "What to Buy—II" 31–32).

Another nineteenth-century genre critical to this history was not, strictly speaking, new in the nineteenth century, but the availability and volume of this writing after 1820 make it seem different in kind from its earlier counterparts. This was the publication of official government information about economic and financial matters, typically the reports of parliamentary select committees, which were often issued in the nineteenth century as the so-called Blue Books. Such reports, which originated in the fourteenth century, began to be used to influence public opinion as early as 1825, when the *First Report of the Select Committee on Laws Respecting Friendly Societies* was published (Clokie and Robinson 49, 63–64). By the 1830s, the reports of the select committees established to monitor reform measures like the 1833 Factory Act and the 1834 Poor Law Amendment Act regularly supplied both numerical information and eyewitness accounts describing various social conditions in Britain. With the publication of the *Report on the Sanitary Condition of the Labouring Population of Great Britain* in 1842, the economic theme implicit in many of these reports was brought to the fore, as Edwin Chadwick tirelessly pointed out the national cost of the ailing poor. Beginning in the mid-1840s, with the appearance of the 1844 *Report of the Select Committee on Joint-Stock Companies,* government publications began addressing financial institutions more explicitly, and, in the wake of the crash of the railway boom, at least one parliamentary select committee took up a topic with direct bearing on the emergent culture of investment. At its peak in 1846–1847, expenditure on railways absorbed almost 7 percent of the national income, and, for the first time, a significant proportion of the shares offered on the London Stock Exchange represented companies instead of government bonds (Robb, *White-Collar* 31). When the bubble burst and investors' savings vanished, Parliament had no choice but to investigate company fraud. In 1849, the proprietors of the York, Newcastle, and Berwick railway convened a shareholders' committee to investigate the indiscretions of George Hudson, the so-called Railway King. The publication of their findings, along with those of other committees appointed by the Eastern Counties and the York and North Midland railways, prompted appointment of the Parliamentary Select Committee on the Audit of Railway Accounts, which published its report in 1849 (Robb, *White-Collar* 46–50, 227).

As even this brief survey suggests, the various modes of financial writing developed before the mid-1840s formed a subset of the British press, by which I mean the entire ensemble of newspapers, periodicals, and cheap pamphlets that played so critical a role in constituting a public sphere in England. In some of its guises, moreover, financial writing also belonged to the British press, which some contemporaries called the "Fourth Estate"—more or less explicitly political writing that could mobilize public opinion so as to influence legislation (Koss 2–3). Beginning in the mid-1840s, however, a new mode of financial writing began to appear that performed a function only obliquely related to the financial writing that preceded it and to the activism other journalists embraced in calling themselves "the Fourth Estate." This new mode of writing—which I call financial journalism—often drew information from the numerical accounts that dominated merchants' lists, eyewitness accounts and statistics from government Blue Books, and the stance of impartiality from the kind of business writing that was to be perfected by the *Economist*. This writing differed from its sources in organizing these materials in narrative forms borrowed from contemporary fiction and in framing the presentation of financial information with features like first-person point of view and personification. Sometimes, financial journalists even resorted to thinly disguised fictions, as they sought simultaneously to expose a financial miscreant and to shield their articles from charges of libel. What unites all of these texts, however, is neither the venue in which they were published nor the specific assortment of formal features they deployed. Instead, what unites them was the function they performed: all of the articles and books I call financial journalism sought to depict the financial sector, which they represented as a culture unto itself, as a law-governed, natural, and—pre-eminently—safe sector of modern society. Even when a specific article exposed financial misdeeds, by doing so it implicitly dramatized the financial system's ability to police itself and thus helped normalize the operations of a financial world still subject to catastrophic irregularities and still largely unfamiliar to British readers.

We can identify several reasons why financial journalism began to assume its characteristic form in the mid-1840s. By the middle of that decade, the institutions that composed the British financial system were sufficiently defined to support the in-depth reporting that had already begun to appear in government Blue Books; with the invention of the electric telegraph in the late 1830s, journalists could transmit price information more rapidly; and, by that time, the available modes of financial writing were sufficiently developed to support the kind of second-order commentary that financial journalism provided. Perhaps most important, however, are two additional reasons. The first is the repetition, for the third time in the century, of the boom phase of an economic cycle whose crashes had led ninety-three English and Welsh banks to fail in 1825–1826 and thousands of individuals to lose their life savings between 1836 and 1839. As the railway boom first exploded, then began to implode in the 1840s, journalists rushed first to arouse, then to assuage the public's fears by presenting such swings as normal parts of a mature economy. Finally, financial journalism developed when it did because the radical press of the early 1840s had also begun to publish essays about finance, some of which were trenchant and compelling. These articles demanded a response because they linked their harsh criticisms of financial institutions explicitly to Chartist politics. Thus the four-part series on banks written by R. J. Richardson, a self-described "poor man," charged the Bank of England with impoverishing the nation, robbing working men, and practicing the "GREAT SWINDLE" of taxing the people for managing the national debt (Richardson 91).

With Chartists drawing to a point evidence that everyone could see, middle-class journalists like David Morier Evans, Ronald Laing Meason, Sidney Laman Blanchard, and Laurence Oliphant began to produce a counter-narrative, which stressed the regular, sometimes even comical, characteristics of these institutions. To do so, they borrowed material from existing modes of financial writing and formal conventions from literature; in so doing, they drew the available modes of financial writing into a distinctive relationship with each other that set the terms in which emergent modes, like the business writing of the *Economist*, developed. Thus, in articles like "The State of the Money Market from a Fresh Point of View" (*Speculative Notes*, 1857), Evans constructed a chatty, first-person narrative to conduct readers through the hitherto opaque operations of the City, drawing, along the way, upon his own first-hand knowledge, and published government, business, and newspaper reports as well. In "A Biography of a Bad Shilling," published in Charles Dickens's *Household Words* in 1851, Blanchard used personification to create a voice for the "bad shilling," the bastard spawn of a union between a zinc door plate and a pewter flagon. In 1876, Oliphant also deployed personification to expose Albert Grant's mismanagement of the Credit Foncier and Mobilier of England in the fictionalized form of an "Autobiography of a Joint-Stock Company (Limited)." With the mixed style of financial journalism well established by 1853 and the threat of Chartism long gone, Bagehot adopted the conventions of this writing to give his *Economist* essays a personal, authoritative voice that purported also to be politically impartial. If Bagehot should be called "the greatest interpreter of commercial sentiment and economic ideas of his day," as one modern historian argues, then he became so because he was able to make his middle-class, pro-business ideas seem simply like common sense (Parsons 28). He was able to do this, in turn, because other financial journalists had already popularized a set of stylistic features that presented business as both accessible and a matter about which one might feel "sentiment."

The journalists I have named were not the only contributors to this genre, of course. Indeed, the most famous financial journalist was probably Dickens, although the anonymity and co-authorship of many of the articles in *Household Words* and *All the Year Round* make it difficult for modern readers to see the interest Dickens took in exploring financial topics (Wills and Dickens). Nor were all of the contributions to the genre as playful as some of the examples I have cited here. Arguably, in fact, the combination of a politically corrective agenda and a personable, quasi-literary style that characterized such writing in the late 1840s had metamorphosed into an explicitly didactic, even moralistic mission by the 1860s. The change in tone (although not always in style) that accompanied this shift in agenda was a response to a number of developments during the 1850s and 1860s, but two deserve particular notice. First, by the late 1850s, with Chartism no longer a threat and arguments about the spiritual perils of business no longer so obviously necessary to counter political radicalism, the Christian version of political economy, which had cautioned against capitalists' worst excesses during the first half of the century, began to lose its influence (Hilton 255–97). Second, changes in company law had begun to make it easier for promoters to launch companies, and the passage of limited liability laws had eased the fiscal responsibility of company owners. With no voice from the pulpit rising to chastise unscrupulous businessmen and government officials no longer resisting the expansion of trade, some financial journalists began to serve as moral watchdogs as well as chroniclers of the City. Thus by 1864, the jaunty tone of much of Evans's earlier writing had given way to a more cautious note, as he turned to the fallout of the 1862 Company Law that established limited liability (Evans 228–36), and journalists like Bonamy Price, H. R. Grenfell, and Henry Sidgwick used titles that appeared lighthearted to engage readers in what were actually substantive discussions of the currency debate. In 1886, Meason made this didactic function absolutely clear when he noted that *Sir William's Speculations or, the Seamier Side of Finance* was designed "as a warning to any one intending to dabble in Amateur Finance, or take shares in 'bogus' companies" (vi).

It is important to recognize that this moral mission, which sometimes seems like a rebuke to investment or even to business in general, was always subordinated to the other function that financial journalism continued to perform. This other function—to normalize or naturalize the workings of financial institutions—was actually served by some of the ethical distinctions journalists drew. This was true, for example, of the distinction between investment, which journalists represented as sound, and speculation, which they represented as unwise or greedy. By normalizing the operations of individual institutions through such distinctions, financial articles like W. E. Aytoun's "The National Debt and the Stock Exchange" (1849) and the anonymous "Stockbroking and the Stock Exchange" (1876) also helped make the financial system imaginable *as a system* to Britons whose primary experience of finance was probably limited to transactions with local bankers. Because making the financial system seem regular and systematic was the primary goal of financial journalists, these writers transformed the features adapted from existing modes of writing—especially numerical data—into rhetorical devices. The numbers journalists cited, in other words, helped create an overall image of financial institutions operating efficiently, or at least amenable to the kind of assessment numbers promised; these numbers were never part of specific trading or investment advice (periodicals devoted to investor advice appeared only in the 1880s [Parsons 36; Porter 1–17]). This is one way we know that financial journalism constituted a genre that was new in the 1840s: the features its authors borrowed from other modes of financial writing were rearranged, with the help of literary strategies, to serve a function distinct from that of the other modes in which these devices also appeared.

## The Logic of the Supplement and the Fantasy of Perfect Writing

If financial journalism both took features from existing modes of writing and harnessed them to a new function, it did so in a manner that always implied, and sometimes contained, its own critique. That is, even though the moral agenda visible in journalism after 1860 was always subordinated to the function of naturalizing the financial system, this agenda sometimes called attention to what financial journalism aspired to be but patently was not: an instrument that could actually make business and investment as safe and ethical as journalists proclaimed them to be.

Such morally efficacious writing—writing that could make company promoters and directors moral through its own performative force—is what I refer to in the title of this section as perfect writing. We see how powerful the fantasy of such writing could be in an essay reprinted repeatedly after 1849. In this essay, entitled "The Moral and Religious Duties of Banking Companies," James William Gilbart, the respected director of the London and Westminster Bank, tries to make his writing do what he assumed scripture did: command morality through its own utterance. When Gilbart opens the essay with a note that it was originally composed for a group of company directors, he obviously wants readers to witness his writing at work—to imagine its performative power by imagining company directors reading it. The essay consists of a series of Gilbart's own commandments, interspersed with quotations from the Bible, whose form Gilbart imitates: "Insert no erroneous statements in your prospectus. Make no incorrect calculations in order to deceive a parliamentary committee; circulate no unfounded rumors for the purpose of affecting the market value of your shares; and let your annual reports contain nothing but the truth" (*Practical Treatise* 395). Even if Gilbart wanted such commandments to perform with the efficaciousness of the Word, of course, what such admonitions really did was simply inform readers of the ruses by which company directors repeatedly duped them, not prevent directors from perpetrating fraud.

Other financial journalists expressed their desire to produce such perfect—because morally efficacious—writing less blatantly than Gilbart, but it is obvious that much financial journalism was animated by a similar aspiration. Not only did journalists like Meason explicitly offer their essays as warnings to readers, but others trumpeted the merits of what they, as writers, claimed uniquely to be able to offer: the glare of publicity. It was common knowledge, such writers insisted, that Parliament could not legislate virtue; company directors had to be made to police themselves through fear of being publicly exposed. "Publicity is the great thing wanted, and were it secured, the manner of doing business might be allowed to take care of itself," declared one optimistic writer ("Stockbroking" 103). The fantasy that writing could perform this morally efficacious function—ideally, without the aid of literary devices—was also sustained in the period by a kind of writing that seemed to do exactly this. This kind of writing, which haunts the pages of financial journalists as both the ambition that ennobles their efforts and a reminder of what they could not achieve, is accounting.

We can see that accounting was sometimes imagined to be perfect in the way that financial journalists wished their writing could be in George Rae's journalistic survey of banking practices, *The Country Banker* (1885). Rae, the manager of the North and South Scotland Bank, viewed the certified accountant's balance sheet as an absolutely unimpeachable document, which not only perfectly reflected the transactions in which a tradesman had engaged but, in so doing, also dictated future honesty: "A man's duly certified balance-sheet is the one reliable voucher of his actual position: all other information that we can gain respecting him must be more or less at second hand and imperfect, and it may be delusive. But there is no mistaking the figures of an honest balance-sheet" (15). It was possible for Rae to imagine that a "duly certified balance-sheet" would both accurately reflect current business and entail future honesty because he assumed that accountancy, the practice that certified the tradesman's books, was rule governed, impartial, accurate, and sure. Because it relied on the rules of arithmetic and double-entry bookkeeping, accounting could be imagined to be free from the individual whims of the bookkeeper. Because it was regularly performed by someone chosen by a company's directors, accounting might even enforce the honesty it theoretically measured, for departures from the rules of writing could be punished as deviations from the rule of law (Poovey, *History* 29–65). Finally, because accounting was stylistically so plain, it seemed not even to require the help of literary features, which were always suspected of introducing error-prone creativity or even the moral taint of fiction.

Of course, accounting was no more guaranteed to perform this moral function than was financial journalism, which could only gesture toward accounting as the form of writing that journalists aspired to approach. Accounting did not necessarily ensure morality for at least two reasons in nineteenth-century Britain. First, the various company laws passed after 1844, including the 1856 and 1862 Limited Liability Acts, considerably lightened the already-lax rules governing the publication of company information. These laws did require year-end audits, but company directors could employ friends to look over the books or even participate in the audits themselves (Robb, *White-Collar* 127–29). Second, for the first three-quarters of the century, instruction in accounting was not regularly available, and the manuals that were in print were outdated, obscure, or both. Until the publication of B. F. Foster's *Double-Entry Elucidated* in 1843, the most accessible books of accounting instruction were the 1588 *Briefe Instruction and Maner How to Keepe Bookes of Accompts* and P. Kelly's *Elements of Book-Keeping,* which was in its eleventh edition by 1839. Even with the publication of Foster's guide, reviewers complained that the subject remained opaque and the manuals confusing ("Book-Keeping"). Amateurish bookkeeping was not replaced by a more rigorous system of accounting until amateur bookkeepers were replaced by professional accountants, and this did not even begin to occur until 1870, when the London Institute of Accountants was established. This was followed in 1880 by the Institute of Chartered Accountants in England and Wales, the organization that established the system of training and credentialing that finally made it possible for Rae to speak, in 1885, of a "duly *certified* balance-sheet" (Robb, *White-Collar* 136–37; emphasis added).

Accounting could not always approach its ideal, then, but the periodic references to it in the pages of financial journalism remind us that the fantasy of some more morally efficacious writing always shadowed—and implicitly critiqued—the normalizing function journalism actually performed. Indeed, references to accounting suggest that financial journalists both imagined that their writing supplemented existing financial writing with an ethical agenda and longed for something that could make their own articles morally efficacious in the way accounting promised to be. In both these senses, we can say that financial journalists' vision of the relationship between the various modes of financial writing—including journalism and accounting—corresponds to the definition of the supplement formulated by Jacques Derrida. In "That Dangerous Supplement," Derrida explains that the supplement is simultaneously a surplus, "a plenitude enriching another plenitude," and a substitute that "produces no relief" because its addition only confirms the inadequacy of that to which it adds (144, 145). The relevance of this description for nineteenth-century financial writing should be clear. With the emergence of financial journalism, existing genres were drawn into a relationship with each other that seemed to make financial writing a whole, in the sense of being simultaneously descriptive and morally efficacious; this is a plenitude, to use Derrida's term. But the addition of financial journalism to existing modes of financial writing "produces no relief" because journalism could no more perform a perfectly efficacious role than could the other kinds of writing that it supplemented. Indeed, the fantasies that swirled around publicity and accounting reveal that the system of financial writing as a whole continued to be haunted by the image of another kind of plenitude—one that would have accurately described the world of finance and made company owners honest. Ideally, this would have been possible without the aid of literary devices, which were suspect in exactly the ways that accounting was not. In nineteenth-century Britain, of course, it was not possible to realize the ideal of perfect writing because an accurate description of existing institutions was bound to expose their ethical shortcomings as well as display their virtues. When journalists revealed that ethical transgressions existed in the financial world, they also betrayed their own inability to make companies moral—their failure to make the real and the ideal coincide *except* in a fictional form.

My invocation of Derrida to explain the internal dynamics of financial writing implies that accounting's failure, like the failure of every other link in the supplemental chain, derives from representation's inevitable inability to achieve presence—that is, simply to make whatever language represents exist. While I do believe that all representation fails in this sense, I also want to insist that some of the impediments that simultaneously retarded the development of accounting and kept the fantasy of perfect writing alive emanated from a tension inherent in the operations of financial institutions themselves. This tension—between the imperative to disclose facts about finance and the need to keep aspects of business secret—both made the kind of writing accounting epitomized necessary and rendered the perfection to which financial journalism aspired impossible to achieve. No matter what conventions a writer used, in other words, it was impossible to describe the operations of financial institutions accurately and comprehensively (much less to make them moral) because these financial institutions could not work if they did not keep aspects of their business secret. Thus the tension between the imperative to disclose facts about finance and the incentive to keep aspects of the financial institutions hidden was essential to the financial system's success. By the same token, this tension shaped every contribution to financial writing as well as the fantasy of perfect writing that simultaneously animated and berated everyone who wrote about finance.

The imperative to disclose facts about finance derives from the principle I invoked at the beginning of this essay: the growth of the modern commercial system depended (and continues to depend) on publicizing prices, commodities, and the reliability of credit instruments. If the public did not know what prices were current, what bargains were available, and what shares were on offer, it would not buy; and if the public did not believe that representations of value (like paper money and bills of exchange) functioned as if they were gold, then credit could not exist. By the same token, the need to keep secrets is also as old as commerce, credit, and competitive economies. If merchants revealed everything about their business, they lost their competitive edge; if sectors of the financial industry whose operations depended upon establishing autonomy (like the London Stock Exchange) did not control the terms for membership and participation, they could not create the closed market that guaranteed that transactions would be honored (Michie 31–36).

If the twin imperatives to disclose information and keep secrets are inherent in the modern market economy, then these agendas assumed a particularly intimate—and fraught—relationship in nineteenth-century Britain. On the one hand, the imperative to disclose information was facilitated by the introduction of new communication technologies into the operations of financial institutions; these technologies included the electric telegraph (introduced 1837), the undersea cables between London and Paris (1851) and London and New York (1866), the ticker-tape machine (1867), and the telephone (1878) (Michie 70–74, 82). The imperative to disclose information was further intensified by the combined pressures of increased investor demand and the professionalization of financial reporting. On the other hand, meanwhile, the incentive to keep business secrets was heightened by increased competition in nearly every sector of the business community, and it was supported by the long-standing assumption that every man has a right to keep his financial dealings to himself. The constitutive tension between these two imperatives was further complicated by the way that information could be both circulated by and confused with rumor, which, in the hands of skilled publicists, could mislead investors as it pretended to instruct. Indeed, one sign of the novelty of the emergent culture of investment was the way that modern technologies combined with the professionalization of journalism to so completely confuse the distinction between rumor and information that even a seasoned financial journalist could not always tell whether what he reported was true or simply a cleverly planted tip intended to incite speculation (Shand 313).

Even when rumor did not muddy information, nineteenth-century businesses were committed to keeping aspects of their operations secret. This convention was simply accepted by everyone who practiced or wrote about business and investment. Thus, members of the London Stock Exchange were forbidden to disclose information to non-members lest the exchange's business be usurped by rival brokers, and brokers and jobbers developed a special language to keep their activities secret (Michie 35–37); the directors and investors of joint-stock companies were required to sign an oath of confidentiality in order to protect their competitive advantage (Gilbart 207–208); and individuals could keep their financial transactions hidden even from their bankers by drawing their checks "in blank"—that is, by signifying the payee only by initials or numerals (Rae 11). The English government made sporadic efforts to require businesses to publish more information, but the belatedness of effective legislation makes the government's tolerance for secrecy clear: joint-stock companies were not required to publish balance sheets until 1908, and not until 1948 did a companies act require trust companies to publish consolidated balance sheets (Parsons 39; Robb, *White-Collar* 138).

This tension between disclosure and secrecy within the financial system's institutions both fueled journalists' desire to write about finance and imposed limits on that writing that were more specific than those erected simply by representation's inherent limitations. This tension also dictated the much more encompassing, but more amorphous, cultural atmosphere that increasingly permeated Victorian society. Indeed, what Raymond Williams would have called the period's structure of feeling, which underwrote the emergent culture of investment, can be said to have derived from this tension between disclosure and secrecy. While this tension may be a feature of all modern business cultures—and even of every form of writing that elicits interest through suspense—it had particular salience in Victorian England, as the combination of closely guarded business secrets and the gradual expansion of the investor base helped make Britain the most powerful nation in a world economy increasingly organized by finance and credit.

## Disclosure and Secrecy in *The Mill on the Floss*

Derrida's discussion of the supplement enables us to describe the dynamics internal to the system of financial writing as it was engaged and altered by financial journalism in the mid-1840s, and it helps us understand the kind of fantasies associated with publicity and accounting. Derrida's essay also begins to suggest that addition and displacement—the two characteristic gestures that link and separate the various genres of financial writing (including financial journalism and accounting)—are not the only dynamics of this system. According to Derrida, the substitution of representation for presence does more than inaugurate an endless process of additions that also displace. This substitution actually generates something new, which Derrida calls "value": "The operation that substitutes writing for speech also replaces presence by value: to the *I am* or to the *I am present* then sacrificed, a *what I am* or a *what I am worth* is preferred" (142). In the final section of this essay, I want to pursue the implications of this comment. While they do not generate "value" in a form that financiers would have understood, I suggest that nineteenth-century literary texts did more than simply contribute formal features to financial journalists eager to engage their readers. Literary texts generated an imaginative form of value for contemporaries by exploring the "what I am" and "what I am worth" available to the individuals who inhabited the emergent culture of investment. In so doing, literary texts constituted another supplement in the chain of financial writings I have described. Because they were not primarily devoted to the normalizing agenda that dominated financial journalism, however, literary texts were able to generate an imaginative alternative to both accurate description and the perfectly efficacious writing epitomized by accounting. Because they offered readers something different from information or promises to incite honesty, literary texts could produce a form of value generated by the imaginative engagement that novels encouraged readers to develop with the culture of investment's ethical complexities.

As late as the 1840s, novelists were still struggling to overcome the old charges that fiction was immoral or irrelevant, even though literature in the form of poetry was generally considered a reliable arbiter of values. A powerful weapon in novelists' rebukes to these charges was the development of a set of formal features we now call realism: the combination of a single-point perspective that positions the reader outside and in the future of the fiction's action and the control of narrative attention and focalization by an implicit and sometimes explicit omniscient narrator. Realism, or the "grammar of single-point perspective," produces a formal kind of neutrality by creating within a unified narrative system numerous points (in time, space, and character perspective) that do not contradict each other; the consistent use of past tense verbs makes these events seem simultaneously always to have already happened (in the sense that their outcome is known to the narrator) and to be unfolding before the reader (Ermarth, "Realism" 1074). Financial themes could easily be incorporated into this kind of narrative system because financial plots lent themselves to this mode of presentation and to the complicated model of causation realism excelled at resolving. From the late 1840s on, British novelists increasingly turned to these themes because, unlike the inheritance plots that dominated eighteenth-century novels, financial plots allowed writers to explore matters involving personal agency and individual will, like financial temptation and fiscal responsibility. Thus, although mid-century novelists did not use the most characteristic feature of financial writing (numerical lists), many of them did refine a formal (not political) version of the impartial stance cultivated by the *Economist,* and many used financial plots to enhance their genre's reputation for relevance and seriousness. For my purposes, the most important component of novelists' adaptations of financial themes to the formal conventions of realism is the way that novelists' control of narrative attention, which leads the reader to focus on some details and ignore others, reproduces for the reader the very dynamic of disclosure and secrecy that was also essential to the emergent culture of investment.

To demonstrate how realism's reliance on the control of narrative attention reproduces this dynamic imaginatively, I could use any of a number of canonical Victorian novels, including, to name just two, Dickens's *Our Mutual Friend* (1864–1865) and Anthony Trollope's *The Way We Live Now* (1874–1875). For this brief discussion, I have chosen instead George Eliot's *The Mill on the Floss* (1860) because this novel provides a succinct and particularly clear example of the way that a realist narrator manages financial themes by controlling the reader's attention through alterations in the figure and ground of narration. Anyone who has read Eliot's novel will recall the novel's most obvious financial theme: Mr. Tulliver's bankruptcy, which has such far-reaching effects on Maggie and Tom. But bankruptcy is only the most dramatic of the financial events in this novel, and it is actually simply the climax of a series of financial entanglements that may go unnoticed by many readers. These entanglements are easy to miss because the emphasis of the narrative directs the reader's attention elsewhere—not to the financial plot, but to what I want to call the sentimental plots, which focus on Maggie, Tom, Philip, and Stephen.[3] Indeed, in each of the novel's first six books, we can identify a constitutive relationship between the financial plot and the sentimental plot, in which the financial plot—

which is presented largely in narrative summaries—actually determines the events in the sentimental plot, which is lavishly narrated and punctuated with those magisterial asides for which Eliot is justifiably famous. Thus in book one, the sentimental plot consists of the developing relationship between Maggie and Tom, and the financial plot, which is relegated to the narrative's summary commentary, consists of two loans—one made by Mrs. Glegg to her brother-in-law Tulliver, and the other by Tulliver to his sister, Mrs. Moss (73, 76). In book two, the sentimental plot focuses on Tom's exploits at school, his rancorous relationship with Philip Wakem, and Maggie's desperate efforts to win some kind of recognition from the boys; and the financial plot (again presented largely in narrative summaries) arises from the lawsuit that Mr. Tulliver brings against Mr. Privart (186, 188). In book three, the financial plot and the sentimental plot seem to converge, for when Tulliver loses the lawsuit, he falls ill and his family must be recalled. But book three also contains another financial plot, which is revealed to the reader in such scant detail that it is quite difficult to reconstruct. This plot turns on securities that Tulliver has guaranteed to back other people's debts and bills of sale he has offered as security on loans he has taken (196, 198). It is the failure of the people for whom he holds these securities—"poor Riley," then Mr. Furley (196, 198)—that causes Mr. Tulliver to lose all of his household furnishings, which, for his wife at least, is worse than his loss of the mill.

This structural pattern continues in books four, five, and six, where Maggie's involvements, first with Thomas à Kempis, then with Philip Wakem, then with Stephen Guest, provide material for the sentimental plots that constitute the figure of the narrative, while Tom's efforts to acquire business skills and sufficient money to repay his father's debts constitute the subject of the financial plots, which provide the narrative's ground. As early as book five, however, something about the relationship between the figure and ground begins to shift. For the first four books of the novel, the dynamic between secrecy and disclosure might be said to characterize the relationship between the sentimental plot and the financial plot. That is, details of the financial plots are largely occluded by the attention the narrative pays to the sentimental plot, so that what Eliot presents as the action's determining agents—the details contained in the financial plots—are constituted as the sentimental plots' secrets and are disclosed only intermittently, in the narrative summaries to which I have alluded. But in book five, which is entitled "Wheat and Tares," Eliot introduces disclosure and secrecy as *themes* that are also *psychological problems* in the sentimental plot. When Maggie agrees to meet Philip in the Red Deeps, she begins to harbor a secret from her brother, who has forbidden such meetings. In so doing, she is afflicted with what the narrator calls "doubleness" (304), a psychological state that extends the self-renunciation she initially embraced through reading Thomas à Kempis and that prepares the reader for the dangerous mixture of passion and passivity that leads Maggie nearly to succumb to Stephen Guest's allure. At this point, then, the dynamic between secrecy and disclosure, which still characterizes the relationship between the sentimental and the financial plots, not only appears as a theme within the sentimental plot but also begins to receive the kind of narrative attention that other themes in this plot receive—not, let me emphasize, as a relation between financial determinants and subjectivity, but as a constitutive feature of a subjectivity divided against itself.

By the beginning of book seven, the shift that began in book five is complete: disclosure and secrecy have been completely redefined as themes, and they are located exclusively in the sentimental plot. Indeed, by the opening of that final book, all of the problems of what had previously constituted the novel's structural secret or ground—the financial plot—have been resolved, and the narrative result is that the financial plot ceases to have any importance at all. At the beginning of book seven, Tom is master of the mill and he has paid off his father's debts, but none of this matters because Maggie has run off with Stephen Guest. Eliot's focus in book seven is exclusively on the sentimental plot, where personal and social disclosures gradually and painfully triumph over secrecy, but these issues appear, once more, solely as themes that are psychological and ethical, not as characteristics of the relationship between plots, where they had provided Eliot the opportunity to explore a model of causation that transcends individual psychology.

This brief analysis of the novel's engagement with, then redefinition of, the dynamic that also informed both financial institutions and nineteenth-century writing about finance illuminates one contribution that Eliot's novel made to readers' experiences of the culture of investment. By using the dynamic between disclosure and secrecy as an organizing principle for the first six books of *The Mill on the Floss,* Eliot enables her reader to experience imaginatively the tensions and moral discomfort that this dynamic produces. By introducing the various facets of a plot of economic entanglements as determining factors in the novel's action but withholding the details of those entanglements, Eliot incites the reader both to want to know more and, gradually, to relinquish this desire as the sentimental plot becomes more engaging. In so doing, she explores the emotional response that many contemporaries must have had to that half-visible, half-hidden financial system that was simultaneously inescapable and elusive. *The Mill on the Floss* thus shifts the emphasis away from informing readers about the facts of finance, which was one agenda of so much financial writing, and she never gives financial institutions enough attention to help naturalize them (unless one reads their relative neglect—their relegation to the fiction's ground—as a mode of naturalization). Instead, her novel invites the reader to explore the subjective meanings—the implications for subjectivity itself—created by the central dynamic of the culture of finance. This kind of exploration may be said to have constituted value, in Derrida's terms, because it spoke directly to issues of "what I am" and "what I am worth" raised in a society permeated by forces that threatened to convert subjectivity into sheer enactments (or failures) of economic rationality.

Relegating the financial plots to the level of the narrative's ground introduced its own problems, of course, as well as generating an alternative form of value in the imaginative engagement the novel solicited. When Eliot converts the financial plot into the sentimentalized themes of disclosure and secrecy, she effaces, belatedly and (for many readers) ineffectively, the determining role she had previously assigned to the financial plot. This imperfect effacement exacts its most obvious toll in the notorious fairy-tale ending of the novel, in which brother and sister drown in the flood that sweeps the mill downstream. As this conclusion suggests, Eliot left herself few options other than such a contrivance within the sentimental plot, for she had completely abandoned the constitutive tension that animated the first six books of the novel—the tension between imperfectly visible factors that transcend individual agency and individuals' struggles to thrive within a society governed by such impersonal forces. If she abandoned verisimilitude at this point in the novel, however, Eliot did not betray the conventions of realism. The embrace that links Maggie and Tom at novel's end has been foretold throughout the novel, and may be said simply to have been postponed by the worldly necessities of getting money and finding a mate.

The kind of exploration Eliot provides in this novel is typical of the contribution other Victorian realist novels made to contemporaries' experiences of the culture of investment. The vast majority of British novels published between the late 1840s and the end of the century use financial plots as Eliot does: as thematically central but formally marginal elements of a narrative system that creates a formal consensus among the novel's variety of events and characters. This formal consensus simultaneously enabled readers to experience imaginatively the dynamic by which Britain's financial institutions generated monetary value and to reflect upon the affect this dynamic created. Any reader of these novels would have encountered this affect in the reading experience itself, as the excitement that sustains suspense and the frustration that ensues when plots or characters disappear at the narrative's end. Readers might also have experienced it if they engaged in the investment opportunities offered in greater numbers in Victorian Britain, in the anticipation that feeds a speculative mania and the incomprehension that follows a crash. Having experienced this affect in an arena in which they might reflect upon it, readers might even have been encouraged to wonder if the dynamic of disclosure and secrecy that financial journalism sought to normalize was quite as natural as journalists wanted it to seem.

## Parting Thoughts

Let me acknowledge in parting that this essay contains two theoretical paradigms that some readers may consider incompatible. On the one hand, I have used a historical model to explain the constitutive relationship between disclosure and secrecy, which appears in nineteenth-century financial writing, the period's financial institutions, and the interplay of plots in *The Mill on the Floss*. I have argued that this relationship was constitutive for two reasons: because the market economy, which developed in a specific way in nineteenth-century Britain, required both that information be available to the public and that certain details and practices remain secret; and because realist novels liberally called upon this dynamic to prolong suspense and sustain their characteristic unity. On the other hand, however, I have used a Derridean model—the supplement—to explain both the internal dynamics of the system of financial writing and the contribution literary texts made to the culture of investment. The logic of the supplement, I argued, enables us to understand the fantasy about perfect writing that animated hopes for publicity and accounting and the way that replacing presence with representation could generate the kind of value I associated with literary texts like *The Mill on the Floss*.

I want to make two observations about this uneasy theoretical alliance. The first is that the logic of the supplement could be worked out historically, from the various references to accounting that we find in financial journalism and even in novels like *The Mill on the Floss*. For that novel does invoke the fantasies associated with accounting. It does so in book three when Mr. Deane tells Tom that he needs to learn bookkeeping in order to earn a place in the business firm of Guest & Co. In this very brief section of the novel, Eliot represents accounting as precisely the kind of disciplined writing that would negate the excesses she associates with Maggie's storytelling and correct the sentimentalized dealings in which Mr. Tulliver has indulged (228, 230, 234). Even though she invokes the fantasy that such a mode of writing might exist, however, she immediately rejects bookkeeping because it is inadequate to engage her readers imaginatively. Even though Tom does eventually gain mastery of the mill, she associates this recovery not with careful business practices but with Tom's un-narrated, but twice mentioned (367, 397), heroic race to disclose the failure of Pelley's bank to Mr. Guest. And even though Tom does pay off his father's debts, Eliot links this feat not to judicious record keeping but to some unspecified speculative investments in foreign trade that the packman Bob Jakin instigates (311). In other words, Eliot reveals to the careful reader both the nineteenth-century fantasy that accounting constitutes an absolutely certain and effective kind of writing and the limitations of this fantasy for the kind of imaginative longing that only heroism and daring can satisfy. In tying Tom's financial success to such sentimental exploits, Eliot rejects the idea that mere precision could be morally effective for a kind of writing that asks readers to do what accounting could not: evaluate the moral dimension of decisions made and actions taken.

My second point about yoking a historical explanation to one that seems to be ahistorical or even anti-historical is that the analysis I have offered really does need both. Even though I think I could generate something like Derrida's description of the supplement from a reading of the scattered references to accounting in financial journalism and novels like *The Mill on the Floss*, I don't think I would have been likely to notice or assign much importance to these references if I had not already been alert to the possibility that fantasies about some kind of perfect writing might haunt the system of financial writing. Thus I was able to enhance and extend an essentially historical analysis only because of the presence, within our own critical lexicon, of an analytic paradigm that is essentially ahistorical. As I have suggested in this essay, the relationship between these two theoretical paradigms is as constitutive as was the relationship between disclosure and secrecy in the development of nineteenth-century financial institutions and in the kinds of financial writing and the dominant novelistic genre developed in the period. One cannot think historically without the assistance of modern theoretical paradigms because these paradigms constitute the interpretive lenses through which we know the past—through which we create what counts as knowledge about the past for us. But our inevitable reliance on such paradigms also means that what we know of the past—what we know *as* the past—can never precisely recover or reproduce that past, but always signals the negotiation that is our attempt to know. When nineteenth-century Britons struggled to find out about the culture of investment emerging around them—so that they could write about it or deal with its influence imaginatively—they too engaged in such a negotiation. This negotiation—between the paradigms by which one can know and what one can know—was similarly intensified because the financial institutions Victorians sought to understand were only partially willing to disclose their secrets.

## Notes

1. For a helpful overview of prevailing trends in literary treatments of economic matters, see Woodmansee and Osteen, "Taking Account." My treatment of genre draws on the work of Cohen and Siskin. See also O'Gorman.

2. One could also argue that business writing began with *Circular to Bankers,* the weekly periodical begun by Henry Burgess in 1828. Because this was a publication of the association of country banks, however, and not primarily addressed to London bankers, I do not discuss it here.

3. I call these plots "sentimental" because this is a term that Eliot uses to describe business transactions motivated by emotion and to distinguish between these and the business practices of Guest & Co., which are presumably motivated solely by economic considerations. In book three, chapter seven, the narrator refers to "the cautious firm of Guest & Co., who did not carry on business on sentimental grounds" (243-44). By implication, Maggie and the rest of the Tullivers do conduct "business" on "sentimental grounds."

# 3   The First Fund Managers

## Life Insurance Bonuses in Victorian Britain

*Timothy Alborn*

Life insurance companies absorbed a large amount of the surplus capital that became increasingly dispersed throughout British society in the nineteenth century. In this they joined a number of other institutional investors, including building societies, savings banks, fire and marine insurers, commercial banks, and trust companies, each of which performed different social and economic functions. Socially, these institutions catered to people from all classes, ranging from the working man who paid a penny a week to his burial club to the aristocratic spinster who converted her inheritance into a comfortable living wage with help from a trust company. Economically, they were split between those that existed primarily in order to pass along most of the interest they earned to their customers, and those for which investment was secondary to the task of insuring against contingent outcomes. Within this range of investors, life offices occupied a middle ground socially and economically. Their main customer base was middle class, with the exception of a small number of "industrial" offices that sold working-class funeral benefits. In economic function, they sat somewhere between the straightforward investment role of banks and trusts and the subordinate role of investment that existed in other forms of insurance. The basis of this hybrid status was the companies' practice, prevalent by the mid-nineteenth century, of periodically dividing surplus income or "profit" among policyholders. Unlike purchasers of fire or marine insurance, who were satisfied to receive claims on damaged property and let the company keep whatever remained of their invested premium income, Victorian life insurance customers demanded a share in the interest earned on their collective savings in addition to financial protection against premature death.

If this sense of rightful participation in the fruits of investment set life customers apart from their fire and marine counterparts, other qualities distinguished them from bank patrons and members of trust companies. Most obviously, life office funds were less available for withdrawal by the person contributing the funds.[1] Consequently, policyholders participated in their company's investment activities in a strictly prospective sense: they could vicariously watch while their policies increased in value, but only the beneficiary could use that added value as a means of monetary exchange. Life offices offered three varieties of solace to customers who were tempted to choose the easy access of the bank balance over the distant disbursement of the life fund. First, as Charles Babbage noted, locking up funds in a life policy diminished the chances of sacrificing that savings to meet "any temptation of luxury, or any unexpected expense" (34). Second, because the funds were locked up, they could take full advantage of the power of compound interest; this "great wizard" guaranteed that even people who exceeded their expected term of life would earn more for their heirs than they paid in (*Insurance Record* 4 [1866]: 218; *IR* hereafter). And if these two arguments failed, the life office redirected its customers' attention away from its relative merits as a fund manager to the basic advantage which set it apart from the bank: even if the customer died an hour after paying his first premium, the full value of the claim would be paid (see Lawrance 11–12). These arguments were enough to convince most middle-class Victorians—especially those whose continued survival mattered financially to their dependents or creditors—to divert at least some of their surplus wealth from bank accounts or trust funds into insurance policies. In 1880, British life offices held £150 million in invested capital compared to £470 million in bank deposits; by 1914, life office funds stood at £530 million, half of the billion pounds held by banks and roughly six times the amount held by trust companies (Alborn, *Conceiving Companies* 142; Cassis 163; Supple 332).

Despite attracting less wealth than banks, life offices were better than banks at attracting attention to investment as a social practice. Interest on a bank deposit was fixed, and it accrued in increments that were so small as to pass unnoticed by all but the most fastidious customer. The money life offices added to their policyholders' stipulated claims, in contrast, was not fixed across time, nor did it accrue in increments that were unworthy of note. Since life offices had to balance their declared bonus against the continued security of the life fund, they periodically adjusted the level of surplus that they returned to policyholders. And since the task of calculating a safe and fair bonus was hugely labor intensive, most offices waited at least five years between declarations. These two factors turned the life insurance bonus into a significant event, to be first anticipated and then experienced with either gratification or disappointment. Although life offices did not originally intend this outcome, the bonus meeting would eventually become a potent marketing device, attracting customers' attention to a firm's underwriting efficiency and investment savvy. When a company's savvy was lacking or its luck ran out, on the other hand, the public spectacle of the bonus meeting threatened to exaggerate its deficiencies in the eyes of its customers and competitors.

Most economic historians have thoroughly appreciated the important contribution of life insurance to the Victorian capital market. Few, however, have heeded the more subtle sense in which life offices, through their bonus declarations, publicized money's reproductive powers. This relative lack of curiosity about the companies' social role as fund managers dates back to Victorian times, when financial writers (if not the companies themselves) subordinated investment matters to the quasi-sacred task of aiding widows and children. Sound portfolio management appeared in such accounts as playing a necessary but supporting role in the working of a life office. In this regard the Equitable Society, founded in 1757 as the first "modern" mutual life office in Britain, casts a long shadow on the subsequent history of insurance. Managed by William Morgan from 1776 to 1830, the Equitable invented the system of sharing surplus income with policyholders, hence popularizing the practice. Yet for all his apparent encouragement of bonuses, Morgan condemned competing firms and his own policyholders if they viewed life insurance in that way, and his suspicion of mammon established deep roots in the moral economy of Victorian life insurance (Ogborn 114–65).

Recent historians have noticed exceptions to this general story without altering its main features. They have pointed to the rash of life offices that formed during the Napoleonic Wars, mostly as vehicles for shareholders to enrich themselves by pocketing the difference between fixed death benefits and inflation-leavened reserves (Pearson). They have also aptly described the policyholders in these offices (who paid more than their life risks were worth and only rarely participated in the inflationary windfall) as dissolute aristocrats who had no choice but to pay usurious rates for life insurance as security against their debts. Yet even these early "investment clubs" are typically held out as exceptions that prove the rule of subsequent Victorian moralism, since their financial success could not last forever (it ended once prices fell after the war) and since they preyed on a self-limiting market (even Regency England eventually ran low on spendthrift aristocrats) (Trebilcock 1: 624–43).

The same assumption regarding the relative status of underwriting versus investment informs historians' views of British life insurance at the end of the nineteenth century, when the industry moved explicitly in the direction of fund management. The most popular policy on the market after 1890 was endowment insurance, which combined term-life coverage (typically for twenty years) with an annuity that took effect once the term ran out.[2] Unlike the whole-life policies they largely replaced, endowment policies encouraged customers to take a direct interest in their office's asset performance. Actuaries at the time resisted the innovation for as long as they could owing to its apparent departure from Victorian tenets of "thrift" (see A. K. Rodger 25–26), while outside critics suggested that customers in search of a pension plan would be better off letting a higher-yielding trust company handle their money (Trebilcock 2: 87–88). Most historians have split the difference, presenting endowment insurance as an inefficient transition between traditional Victorian life business and the industry's present-day focus on pension management and financial consulting (Supple 253–56).

By viewing Victorian life insurance as a half-century of prudence sandwiched by emphases on investment that were either irresponsible or inefficient, these accounts ignore the constant presence of portfolio management as a very public side of the industry throughout the nineteenth century. Specifically, they minimize both the central debates that agitated life offices in the 1830s as they formulated competing bonus schemes, and the subsequent impact of bonuses on management and marketing. Most such schemes gave most British policyholders a tangible reason to pay close attention to the investment performance of their office. And since most bonuses were not payable until after the policyholder's death, it was even possible for insurance companies to display a heartfelt interest in such matters without relinquishing their reputation for thrift. As the *Economist* claimed in 1846, life insurance made "the rate of interest—against which, under the name of usury . . . torrents of obloquy are sometimes poured out—a subject of far greater importance to social welfare than is generally supposed" (4: 1589).

Victorian investment straddled what Viviana Zelizer has identified as a division in the moral economy of risk taking between "[r]ational speculation that dealt with already existent risks" and "pure gambling which created artificial risk" (86). British life insurance mainly occupied the latter side of this divide for much of the eighteenth century, infamously fueling the morbid aristocratic pastime of wagering on the demise of at-risk strangers, until the Gambling Act of 1774 intervened by requiring all beneficiaries to have a legitimate financial interest (either as a dependent or creditor) in the life insured. As Geoffrey Clark has argued, this law did not "signal the death of life insurance's 'gambling phase' and the birth of its 'prudential phase,'" since it "could not uniformly segregate" prudence from speculation (*Betting on Lives* 22, 26). Efforts to effect just such a segregation continued throughout the nineteenth century, however, first in a series of common-law rulings that defined permissible levels of "insurable interest," then more subtly with the extension of bonuses. These efforts arguably rendered middle-class life insurance (if not its working-class equivalent) safe from the cultural designation of "pure gambling" by the final quarter of the nineteenth century (Alborn, "A License to Bet"). But as I argue below, bonus declarations introduced a new tension into life insurance's moral economy, this time between the prudent social practice of well-regulated investment and the choreographed drama of public spectacle. Ironically, the bonus declaration's public status colored each side of this Janus face: while subjecting customers and shareholders to manipulative display, it also provided them with the information they needed to be able to hold companies to basic (albeit imperfect) standards of accountability.

## Life Insurance Bonuses: Criticisms and Evolving Justifications

Asset management has traditionally been a trade in which a special premium is placed on the possession of accurate information. The investor with the most current knowledge about the present and prospective position of the widest range of stocks will outperform the market to the greatest extent. It is hence ironic that life offices, which prospered as institutional investors from the late eighteenth century, owed so much of their initial prosperity to actuarial ignorance and failed foresight. Lack of accurate vital statistics led the Equitable and succeeding firms to set premiums that erred substantially on the safe side; this, together with an excusable failure to anticipate the inflationary windfall during the Napoleonic Wars that would pad the face value of their reserves, meant the price of a typical policy far exceeded what was needed to meet their claims. As life offices watched their surpluses grow, they realized that part of this excess could be safely added to the value of policies, in the case of a mutual society, or to shareholder dividends, in the case of a "proprietary" (or joint-stock) society. As news of the Equitable's largesse to its policyholders surfaced, market pressures led many of the latter firms to share at least some of the wind-fall with policyholders as well.

The first life insurance bonus, in the modern sense, was a cash distribution by the Equitable in 1776, two decades after it had been established. Its actuary, William Morgan, calculated an available surplus of £25,143, out of which he divided £11,000 among the society's members. Further divisions followed—five between 1781 and 1795—but these, unlike the first, came as additions to the value of the policy and were payable, like the policy itself, upon the member's death (Raynes 134). By 1809, a £1,000 Equitable policy taken out in 1770 had increased almost four-fold in value to £3,900 (Ryan, "Early Expansion" 171). From the individual policyholder's perspective, such impressive gains needed to be taken with a grain of salt, since they mainly compensated beneficiaries for forty years' worth of overcharges and for the reduced purchasing power that came with inflation. From the perspective of the Equitable as an institutional investor, however, the advantages of the reversionary bonus were less ambiguous. Since the transfer of funds was only on paper, the office could declare a substantial bonus without sacrificing its ability to make long-term investments. Hence bonuses did not detract from one of the leading financial advantages of life insurance, namely that its precisely calculable, long-term liabilities opened up investment options (such as municipal bonds) that were closed to firms with more pressing liquidity issues.[3]

By 1810, the Equitable's bonus policy was having two effects, neither of which Morgan savored. The first was that the prospect of sharing in its substantial wartime gains led to a dramatic increase in membership. To most life office managers this would have been gratifying enough—but Morgan was concerned, to the point of paranoia, that its new members would endanger the society's solvency by voting themselves extravagant surpluses. He dealt with this threat in 1816 by convincing a majority of the existing members of the society (numbering 9,500 at the time) to restrict the bonus to the 5,000 members who had been with the society the longest (Ogborn 156–57). The first effect of the Equitable's financial success directly led to the second, which was that several life offices formed in order to compete with its unique combination of insurance and fund management. Some of these, like the Norwich Union (est. 1808), copied the Equitable's purely mutual constitution; others, like the Atlas and the Globe, retained the entire surplus for the benefit of their shareholders. Morgan did the Norwich Union a huge favor when he restricted the Equitable's bonus in 1816, the same year the newer office announced its first bonus of 20 percent on all premiums paid. New premium income at the Norwich Union nearly tripled from £304,000 in 1815 to £815,000 in 1818, while new Equitable customers declined from 600 to 200 per year between 1816 and 1841, as customers shrewdly flocked to the office where they would not have to wait decades for their bonus to start accruing (Blake 25; Morgan 67).[4]

Initially, strictly "proprietary" offices were content to let mutuals lure middle-brow customers with the prospect of profit sharing, and focused instead on the numerous upper-class customers who took out life policies as security against personal debts. Since many of these policies terminated with the loan, accumulated bonuses would seldom have been large enough to be a priority in such customers' choice of office. Indeed, the very idea of customer choice was often irrelevant in their case, since such policies were usually arranged by attorneys who had social or financial incentives to steer clients to a non-bonus office (De Morgan 258–59). Under this system, policyholders got what they paid for (a license to borrow), even though what they paid was demonstrably excessive. The obvious winners were the shareholders, who received in higher dividends what the fortunate 5,000 policyholders in the Equitable were getting as bonuses. This started to change after 1820, however, when a wave of new proprietary companies pressed against the built-in limits of the aristocratic market. Attracting shareholders to these new companies was easy, given the phenomenal dividends and rising share prices of the 1810s; attracting customers was not, and without customers there was no hope of surplus premium income being siphoned into shareholders' pockets.

An obvious strategy for joint-stock life offices in search of new customers was to imitate the Equitable and Norwich Union, and return part of the excess premiums to their policyholders. Hence emerged a new sort of "profit-sharing" company in which set proportions of the surplus were periodically distributed as bonuses to policyholders as well as shareholders. The Rock and the London Life pursued this strategy from their commencement in 1806; others switched over to profit sharing once they recognized its potential for increasing market share. When the Eagle decided to divide 80 percent of its surplus among policyholders in 1826, its directors presented the scheme as "something to be done in these days of competition to obtain public patronage" (Eagle Insurance, *Board Minutes* 3 Jan. 1826). Although not all shareholders were happy to part with such a large proportion of their dividend, the directors prevailed, and within a year they proved the malcontents wrong by announcing an eight-fold increase in business since making the change (Eagle Insurance, *Board Minutes* 6 Feb. 1826, 31 Aug. 1826). By 1840, more than fifty of the sixty-four proprietary British life offices were returning at least a third of their surplus reserves to policyholders (Saint-Clair 56–60). By 1860, most large proprietary offices were dividing upwards of four-fifths of their profits with customers. The only time these levels of profit sharing conflicted with shareholder interests was when a company bore unduly high levels of paid-up capital, and hence had to stretch a smaller surplus over a wider surface.[5] This problem sank the Globe, which could no longer deliver satisfactory dividends on its £1 million in paid-up shares once it started sharing two-thirds of its profits with customers in 1859. Five years later it was forced to merge with the recently established Liverpool and London (Walford 5: 428–31).

If the ease with which life offices accumulated surpluses between 1780 and 1820 led many companies down the path of profit sharing, it inspired others to isolate the main source of these surpluses—unduly high assumed mortality— and offer, as an alternative to bonuses, lower up-front premiums based on more accurate vital statistics. The Equitable's rates, which nearly all life offices copied prior to 1820, had been based on Richard Price's investigation into mortality records from a Northampton parish between 1735 and 1780 (Ogborn 110). A new table published in 1815 by the Sun's actuary, Joshua Milne, based on birth and death records from Carlisle between 1779 and 1787, offered a closer approximation, with premiums between 22 percent and 28 percent lower (depending on age) than rates based on the Northampton data (Sturrock 16). Such data did not automatically translate into a new set of lower premiums, however. Some new companies did offer reduced rates, together with effusive arguments defending the superior justice of their approach, but few of the older offices followed suit. Since the older firms could no longer defend the bonus as an artifact of actuarial uncertainty, they redefined it as a useful savings mechanism that was unavailable to policyholders who tried to invest money on their own. With this response, which mostly succeeded in staving off the cheaper companies, the Victorian life office went from being a fund manager by default to taking on asset management as a central feature of its business.

Of the new low-premium offices, the most popular were the Scottish Provident (est. 1837), which charged between 19 percent and 22 percent less than the Equitable up to the age of forty-five, and the Economic (est. 1823), which offered 14 percent lower rates at younger ages (Saint-Clair 56–60). A different set of firms, including the London Life and the Metropolitan, charged standard rates up front but reduced premiums once surpluses had been calculated (Conder 51–52, 213).[6] Although these all offered lower rates without wholly abandoning bonus payments, others offered lower still non-profit rates: from 23 percent to 29 percent less at the Argus (Saint-Clair 62). Defenders of such firms closely identified their lower premiums with recent scientific and social progress. Charles Morton, a Scottish Provident director, noted in 1842 that bonuses had been "engrafted" to the original system of life insurance "as a device . . . to palliate the errors arising from their rates being founded on old and exploded tables of mortality" (Scottish Provident 8). John Sturrock, in his *Principles and Practice of Life Assurance* (1846), similarly called bonuses "stumbling-blocks in the way of the provident and frugal" who wanted to insure their lives but could not afford an added contribution to a mutual fund (24).

Bonus offices fended off such charges by invoking two new justifications for profit sharing, both of which subordinated their "insurance" to their "investment" function. The first presented the reversionary bonus as a guarantee that even those members whose paid-in premiums exceeded the nominal value of their policy would come out ahead in the end; the second pointed to the life offices' ability to achieve higher yields on their members' combined savings than policyholders could earn individually. The first of these justifications marked a clear, if cautious, retreat from the altruism that lay at the heart of all forms of insurance. This was evident in a sales brochure's appeal to the bonus as an effective answer to the customer's objection that "I like my money to be making money for myself, not for other people" (Eagle Life Insurance, *Gift to the Uninsured*); and in the consulting actuary Arthur Scratchley's observation that the bonus "removes the only selfish objection to which that beneficent invention of science was formerly open: *viz.,* that those, who *live,* pay for those who *die* beforehand," since it tended "continually to restore the balance of advantage to those members, who survive each division of profits" (9).

To deliver on its appeal to the selfish policyholder, the bonus office needed to deliver a superior level of asset management. Otherwise policyholders would just deposit the extra money charged by a bonus office in a bank or play the market on their own. The Commercial Life's prospectus echoed numerous others when it urged that life offices "possessed . . . much more ample opportunities of investing Capital advantageously and safely than usually occur to an individual," and an extensive promotional literature contrasted the investment record of life offices with the more sluggish performance of banks (for contrasts with banks see, for example, Rhind 10; Saint-Clair 33–35). Life offices also argued that insurance policies, unlike bank deposits or company shares, represented a more *prudent* form of investment, since by locking up a person's money they guaranteed its future availability. A policyholder could cash in his or her policy, but only by accepting a "surrender value" that was seldom more than half its face value; and since the life office could hold onto most of its customers' funds for the duration of their lives, it could advantageously invest them at compound interest (A. Low 28–29; Nisbet 5).

By varying their emphasis on these new justifications for profit sharing, life offices evolved a bewildering diversity of bonus schemes between 1820 and 1850. At one extreme were the tontine offices, which steadfastly reserved the lion's share of the bonus to those whose premium payments had subsidized losses arising from premature claims. The Equitable and Norwich Union achieved this by restricting participation in the bonus to the five thousand members who had been insured for the longest period. Others, including the Gresham and Standard, paid bonuses in proportion to the number of years each member had been insured at the time of each division (*IR* 14 [1876]: 370; Standard 8). At the other extreme were offices that started adding value to their customers' policies as soon as they were purchased, treating the surplus as an investment fund that was wholly separable from the insurance side of the contract. Most life offices steered a middle course between tontines and immediate bonuses by requiring policyholders to survive a short period (usually three to five years) before becoming eligible to share in the surplus.[7]

Several tontine offices, especially the Gresham and Standard, enjoyed considerable success through the 1860s.[8] Over time, however, tontine divisions on the Standard's plan suffered from an actuarial Achilles' heel, which ultimately detracted from their popularity. As members of these offices grew collectively older, the surplus was spread over a wider surface, which diminished average bonus levels in proportion to policy value (Ryan, "Early Expansion" 187, 196). The Norwich Union, for its part, suffered the same difficulty attracting new business in the 1840s as the Equitable had fifty years earlier, when its privileged class of 5,000 bonus-receiving members forced the newly insured to wait many years for their first bonus. Competing offices, like the Scottish Widows' Fund, relentlessly drew attention to these failings, and one after another the tontine offices switched over to new division schemes starting in the 1860s (*IR* 3 [1865]: 136; Ryan, "History" 371). Tontines underwent a brief revival after 1870, when American firms like the Equitable and New York Life introduced their popular "deferred bonus" policies into the British market, but most British offices had learned from the Standard's example and refused to follow the trend. Instead, they increasingly turned to endowment insurance as a means of providing some of the benefits of tontines without endangering bonus levels over time.[9]

In their wider battle against the lower-priced firms, the bonus offices more than held their own. Although the Scottish Provident and Economic did very well in the race for business, a much larger number of offices offering comparably low premiums (including the Argus, East of Scotland, Active, Experience, and New Equitable) struggled to survive. The dramatic failure of one of these, the infamous Independent West Middlesex in 1841, provided bonus offices with all the arguments they needed to stress the danger of sailing too close to the wind in the matter of setting rates (A. Low 10–11). Other signs of the enduring popularity of bonuses abounded throughout the Victorian period. In the many proprietary offices that, from the 1830s, offered customers a choice between paying higher with-profit rates and lower non-profit rates, the proportion who picked the second option seldom exceeded 30 percent and sometimes was as low as 10 percent.[10] Also telling was the fact that when offices gave policyholders a choice between taking a reversionary bonus or the equivalent in reduced premiums or cash, most chose the first option.[11] By the 1850s, the surviving low-cost firms were assured of a secure hold on a niche market, but they could not expand that market any further without resorting to expensive sales tactics that would have forced them to increase premiums.[12]

## Days of Reckoning

If the life offices' various methods for distributing bonuses sometimes struck contemporaries as arcane, substantially more interest greeted the offices' periodic announcements that sums ranging from 5 percent to 20 percent of the premiums paid or amount insured would be added to the value of each policy. The complicated nature of most division schemes indirectly added to the drama surrounding the declaration, since it meant that life offices could only afford to deploy the clerical manpower needed for such calculations every several years.

Hence what might have been a frequent, and relatively small, addition to policy values emerged as an anticipated event for customers, shareholders, and the interested public. With all eyes watching, the bonus declaration became the primary occasion for public evaluations of the performance of life offices. As such, it embodied two contrary impulses of Victorian market culture, one tending toward display and the other toward discipline. The first tendency exhibited "a rhetorical mode of amplification and excess" that framed much of Victorian life (T. Richards 54). The second attempted to moderate such representational excess by subjecting it to the discipline of transparent "facts" (see Poovey, *Making;* Wiener, "Market").

The ability of life offices to declare substantial bonuses on a regular basis—not to mention meeting their more basic obligation of paying claims—depended on their ability to keep a step ahead of the changing Victorian capital market. Clive Trebilcock has tracked four phases of "enterprising" insurance investment during the nineteenth century. The first relates to the opportunistic war years of 1790–1815, when life offices lent money at high rates to an "embattled Government." The second runs from 1815 to 1835, when the favorite investments were loans secured by the estates and annuities of the "fading landlord interest," who were willing to pay high rates to preserve their social status. The third covers the period 1835 to 1870, when "proliferating towns and cities" generated a demand for personal loans to middle-class professionals (many of whom were also policyholders) and for municipal bonds (1: 742). And after 1870, life offices began to follow other British institutional investors into the market for "gilt-edged" foreign stocks (755). Although the performance of life offices tended to fall short of the average interest earned by capital in nineteenth-century Britain, it also steered relatively clear of the worst dips in the Victorian business cycle.

Bonus declarations dramatically altered the rhythm of the Victorian life office. A year before the declaration, companies formed special committees to calculate the amount of surplus that could be safely divided. Those directors with experience at property valuation worked with the actuary to determine the present value of the company's assets. The actuary determined the proportion of actual to expected claims over the bonus period to make sure that premium income was still sufficient to meet the claims that had yet to fall in, and considered whether to value by a new mortality table, either because a more reliable table had appeared since the last valuation or because of the changing age structure of the office. These activities were laborious enough, but they paled before the task of dividing the bonus equally among the members. To do this, every policy had to be separately valued based on age, policy size, and accumulated interest. Determining these individual policy values required massive work even in medium-sized offices—"upwards of 75,000" calculations for the Clerical, Medical & General's 1867 valuation (*IR* 5: 3). Actuaries postponed their retirement, office cricket teams' scoring averages dipped, and clerks—armed with little more than inkwells, logarithm tables, and slide rules—put in countless hours of overtime (Norwich Union Board Minute Book, 11 May 1886; *Ibis* 15 [1892]: 251). The Prudential, already huge in 1886, "had the whole of [its] staff on for double the usual office hours," performing thirty-two million calculations on seven million policies (*Parliamentary Papers* 1889 [10]: 226); the chair of the smaller Law Life office merely reported that his staff "became elastic on occasions of this kind" (*IR* 13 [1875]: 149). As a reward for this elasticity, clerks received between 10 percent and half of their annual salary for valuation work, and actuaries often took home double their usual salary during bonus years.[13]

The Olympian drudgery that bonus valuations entailed prompted most offices to wait several years (typically five or seven) between each declaration. Although the initial impetus for such long intervals had more to do with manpower than with marketing, life offices were quick to capitalize on the sense of anticipation that came to surround their periodic divisions.[14] Immediate bonus offices spread the word in the weeks leading up to the bonus meeting that new customers could add several pounds to the value of their policy if they signed up before the declaration. And at annual meetings preceding the bonus, actuaries and directors hinted that the "secrets of the prison-house" (*IR* 13 [1875]: 196) would likely prove "very satisfactory" at the upcoming division (39 [1901]: 575). Predictions tended to be coy in tone, to avoid raising expectations too high. The chair of the Scottish Equitable forswore any "attempt to lift the veil of the future and give any opinion" regarding the upcoming 1902 bonus (*IR* 40 [1902]: 324); it was, in the event, 10 percent lower than in 1897 (Chatham 1905). The importance of avoiding hubris was on display at the Briton Medical and General's bonus meeting in 1874, when its consulting actuary Arthur Scratchley delivered the bad news that there would be no bonus that year (*IR* 13 [1875]: 107). Policyholders (and agents, who had spent the previous months dutifully raising their customers' hopes) were outraged; not least because earlier that year the *Post Magazine* had reported Scratchley's promise that the bonus "would be equal [to] if not in excess of that declared in 1867." Scratchley denied the charge, offering "a reward of £20 to anyone who would bring him the shorthand writer's notes containing those words in his speech," but the damage had been done (110). By 1875 the Briton's new business declined 37 percent, nearly landing it in Chancery (276).

At the bonus meeting itself, directors and actuaries expressed cautious self-congratulation (if the surplus equalled or exceeded the previous declaration), or tried to make the best of a bad situation (if it fell short of expectations). The most typical way to mix good news with caution was to combine a decent bonus with an assumed interest rate that erred very much on the safe side. In 1874, the Scottish actuary James Macfadyen argued for valuing at the then low rate of 3 percent. Assuming more than that, he claimed, would force the company to state clearly how much of the resulting higher surplus it intended to withhold as a down payment on acquiring new business. As he concluded, it would "generally be found impracticable to thus dangle a surplus before the eyes of policyholders . . . and then put it back into the till" (*IR* 12: 406). A second reason for assuming a low rate was that it would make it easier to continue paying the same level of bonus over time if yields subsequently fell. Policyholders, claimed Macfadyen, preferred "a somewhat less present and future increasing profit" over "a somewhat higher present and a diminishing future" (*IR* 12: 406). As of 1878, many, if not most, British life offices appeared to be following Macfadyen's advice. Half of a sample of fifty offices valued at 3 percent, eight more assumed 3.5 percent, and the rest valued at 4 percent (Bailey, "Pure Premium" 123). By the end of the century, when the anticipated "diminishing future" came to pass, the proportion of life offices valuing at 3 percent, or even lower, steadily climbed. At the same time, lower assumed rates became easier to justify, since more aggressive marketing had produced in many offices a majority of recently insured lives. Such people were likelier to be sold on the idea of a "future increasing profit" than policyholders who might not live to see the next bonus (Ryan, "History" 612–13).

The problem of how to protect a life office's assets in times of prosperity must have seemed enviable to managers who came to the bonus meeting empty-handed. In such a case there were two choices: declare a bonus anyway, and pretend all was well; or declare no bonus, and come up with good reasons for doing so. It is difficult to say how many life offices took the former path—especially before the Life Assurance Companies Act of 1870, when only the declaration, not the accounts, were made public. Only a few brave companies took the latter tactic. The Norwich Union did it twice, in 1836 and again in 1866, and the circumstances of its two non-declarations shed light on the changing status of the bonus within the life office. The first time, the office (under the direction of Samuel Bignold) found itself stuck in a commercial crisis with too much cash and too few prospective mortgagees. In presenting this diagnosis, Bignold revealed that the "magic" of compound interest depended on a sufficiency of willing debtors: "Do you gentlemen imagine that I can find alternative securities for reinvestment just as it pleases me from day to day? . . . I am no wizard or magician" (Blake 31). Neither this stern admission, nor Bignold's rather weak appeal to the recent cholera epidemic, satisfied the members. Angry policyholders vented their spleens in pamphlets and in the Norwich papers for the following year, until order was finally restored when Daniel O'Connell—who held over £10,000 in Norwich Union policies and had political ties with its Irish sales staff—brokered a peace accord. In exchange for its members' continued business, the company agreed to open its board to six "outer circle" directors, and submitted to reforms suggested by outside consultants (Ryan, "History" 301, 312–34).

Thirty years later the Norwich Union executive committee again came to the bonus meeting with no value to add to members' policies. The excuses they gave were similar to those in 1836: the need to write down securities owing to a recent financial panic in London, and higher than expected mortality from tuberculosis. This time, however, they could legitimately claim that the non-declaration, while a necessary caution, did not signify a deeper crisis. Their consulting actuary, Samuel Brown, promised that the company would be in "good financial position" if it waited five more years for a bonus, and suggested that his own office had likewise gone through a period of exceptionally costly claims (*IR* 5: 118–19). The Norwich Union's executive did not escape without any rebuke, however; several of its outside directors succeeded in restructuring the board to create greater accountability. These reformers had been pushing for such changes for years, and the members' heightened sense of disappointment in 1866 was just what they needed to accomplish their goals (Ryan, "History" 370–72).

The real advantage in the Norwich Union's handling of its second nondeclaration appeared in subsequent decades, when it successfully repackaged its apparent managerial lapse as the first stage of a long-term plan to put the company on firm actuarial foundations. In 1886, after declaring a good bonus despite moving to a lower assumed rate of interest, a director, Isaac Coaks, took time out to praise "[t]he Board of 1866" for having "the courage of its convictions to do what was right" (Norwich Union Board Minute Book, 24 Nov. 1886). Coaks's tribute to the earlier board was ironic, since he had been one of the ringleaders who had exploited members' resentment against that board to reform the company. As vice president in 1887, Coaks brought in a new actuary, J. J. W. Deuchar, who took only fifteen years to lift the Norwich Union from the middle ranks of life offices to the second largest in Britain. The 1901 president, Thomas Blofeld, celebrated its new stature at that year's declaration, then led the gathered throng across the street, where the mayor of Norwich laid the foundation stone for its new head office building. At the subsequent dinner, held for 120 local worthies and staff members at the Maid's Head Hotel, Deuchar "expressed his pride and satisfaction that they had that day completed the long struggle they had been making . . . to place the Norwich Union Life Office in the very front rank of life insurance institutions." He finished by toasting the policyholders who "would experience great satisfaction in having received a really excellent bonus" (4 Nov. 1901).

In *The Commodity Culture of Victorian England* (1990), Thomas Richards identifies six elements of "a semiotics of commodity spectacle," among them "an autonomous iconography for the manufactured object; the use of commemoration to place objects in history; the invention of a democratic ideology for consumerism . . . and the invention of the myth of the abundant society" (58–59). All of these apply to the life insurance bonus, which in its own way was as much a "manufactured object" as any product of the Industrial Revolution.[15] The bonus was autonomous in the sense that both its embodied clerical labor and its dependence on arbitrarily chosen actuarial parameters were withheld, for the most part, from recipients; all they saw was the addressographed slip of paper announcing itself as so much new wealth. The bonus's commemorative side was clear at the Norwich Union, where fund management figured heavily in the repackaging of that company's past; and its emerging reputation as a prudent investment option helped to clinch the industry's "carefully cultivated image of . . . security," which, as Geoffrey Clark has indicated, "masks a past in which life insurance served as a vehicle for gaming" ("Embracing Fatality" 80). Life offices also applied a rich language of democratic ideology to their various methods of equitably dividing profits, allowing them to elevate the profane play of profit and loss into the more rarified sphere of political justice. Finally, by repeatedly associating bonus declarations with "*larger income* and *bigger Funds*" (Rock 50), the life office joined in what Thomas Richards has called "the vanguard of permanent prosperity" (66).

## Accountability

If life insurance bonuses were commodities that were spectacularized every five to seven years, they simultaneously performed a regulatory role in the Victorian money market by transmitting information that, in theory, rendered companies more accountable to their customers. These two functions were not fully complementary, any more than tabloid journalism is synonymous with government regulation. Still, in most cases some accountability was better than none at all, and the close attention paid to bonuses meant that these occasions (as with the Norwich Union) often sparked internal reforms. And significantly, when outside regulation did come to the industry with the Life Assurance Companies Act of 1870, its reporting provisions were closely modeled on the existing pattern of quinquennial valuations. The effect of the law was to strengthen policyholders' ability to discern the financial status of a life office without substantially detracting from the recurring spectacle of the bonus declaration.[16] Only in an indirect sense did the 1870 act assist in the eventual decline of the bonus's status as spectacle, by pushing companies in the direction of increasingly conservative investment practices.

As instruments of accountability, bonuses ranged from unwieldy to woefully ineffective. Their unwieldy side was apparent in the spectacular demise of the Albert Life Assurance Company, which went from declaring a large bonus in 1861 to declaring bankruptcy in 1869. Burdened by heavy expenses from a series of misguided acquisitions of smaller life offices, the Albert only avoided a non-declaration in 1864 by altering its interval between divisions from three to five years, then refused to offer any explanation for its lack of a bonus in 1866. The resulting anxiety, together with mounting rumors in the City, led shareholders and customers to demand an investigation into the company's affairs (*Times* 21 August 1869: 6). Added pressure came from members of the recently acquired companies, for whom the Albert's non-declaration came as a rude shock. Hence a *Times* correspondent, signing himself "Sixty-Six," contrasted the fate of his policy after it was transferred to the Albert with his experience at his old office, where "[e]ach returning five years saw a distribution of bonuses among the insured, and all went merry as a marriage bell" (25 August 1869: 10). The Albert's directors, in refusing to distribute sham profits to members of a concern that was fast approaching insolvency, had acted prudently. But their failure to communicate the severity of the situation in any other way, either before or after 1866, made a bad situation worse for shareholders and policy-holders alike once the collapse finally came in 1869 (Walford 1: 46–49).

The spectacle of the Albert crash paled before the even more disastrous failure of the European Assurance Society, which continued to declare bonuses right up to its bitter end in 1872. Like the Albert, the European's problems started when it acquired the business of a series of failing concerns, culminating with the large British Nation office in 1865. That year, with barely enough funds to meet its claims, the European divided £70,000 among its policyholders and shareholders (*Times* 4 October 1869: 11); the British Nation, for its part, had paid a 30 percent bonus out of largely wishful assets as recently as 1863 (Walford 1: 387). Until 1872, when a winding-up order was finally issued, the European managed to avoid bankruptcy by taking advantage of Chancery's stubborn refusal to comprehend the uniquely long-term nature of a life office's liabilities. Just as policyholders had accepted their bonus in 1865 as a sign of continued strength, the vice chancellor ruled in 1869 that no insurance company could be deemed insolvent until the day it failed to pay its first claim (Walford 3: 48–54).

By the early 1870s it seemed clear, as Cornelius Walford urged in his *Insurance Cyclopaedia,* that "bonus" was "a word bearing in the eyes of most policy-holders . . . the greatest signification of any word in the ins[urance] vocabulary" (1: 331). Exactly what any given bonus might signify, however, had been cast into serious doubt by the failures of the Albert and European. One of the central tasks of the Life Assurance Companies Act, which passed amid spiraling concerns about accountability, was to stabilize the meaning of the bonus by enabling actuaries to conduct informed public discussions of life offices' component assets and liabilities. Although other sections of the act addressed start-up companies, mergers, and winding-up procedures, its centerpiece was the requirement for life offices to submit to the Board of Trade annual balance sheets and revenue accounts, and to issue a full valuation of assets and liabilities every five years (Ryan, "History" 243–44). From the outset, the act was the creation of actuaries, who praised its "general principles of requiring full information from the companies in a stated form, with full liberty as to the management of their own affairs" (*Report* q. 479).

The 1870 act was far from perfect (especially regarding asset reporting), but it did draw attention to the need to reserve a sufficient fund for long-term liabilities, and it forced companies to divulge how much money they were spending on new business (Sprague). Initially, conservative offices took advantage of the law to accuse competitors of squandering bonuses in the imprudent pursuit of customers. Arthur Bailey, of the ancient London Assurance Corporation, issued a widely circulated pamphlet in 1874 revealing a clear link between low bonuses and high costs (as reported in the new Board of Trade returns), and a few "pushing" offices nearly went to the wall in the ensuing debate over bonus levels (Bailey, "Expenses"). Over time, however, well-managed growth-oriented offices like the Norwich Union could promise better bonus performance over the long run than would be possible with a more sluggish firm by appealing to the superior strength of their reserve fund. Again, such comparisons were only possible due to the industry-wide returns that the Life Assurance Companies Act had made available for the first time. Each of these developments added new shades of meaning for those policyholders who were inclined to ponder the deeper significance of the bonus when it was declared.

Actuaries encouraged such pondering, but only within carefully monitored limits. Although the intended beneficiaries of the 1870 act were policyholders (and to a lesser extent shareholders), actuaries used the act to bolster their own authority within the industry to determine proper valuation and bonus-division methods. Imposing such authority required the confidence of company directors, a reasonable level of consensus within the profession, and sufficient political clout to prevent the Board of Trade from countering their vision with its own conception of standards. Actuaries achieved the first of these conditions by wielding the social status that came with Royal Society membership and academic appointments (in England) and close ties with the financial clout of the accountancy profession (in Scotland) (Alborn, "Calculating Profession"; Walker). They achieved the latter two conditions through organizations like the Institute of Actuaries in London and the Faculty of Actuaries and Associated Scottish Life Offices in Edinburgh, which hammered out a consensus on many technical issues and (in the latter case) achieved notable success as a cartel. Actuaries forestalled legislative efforts in 1869 to allow customers to call for government audits of insurance companies, arguing that this "power of inflicting injury . . . would be a dangerous weapon in the hands of disaffected Policyholders";[17] five years later they forced the Board of Trade to retreat from early attempts to offer public advice on valuation methods (Associated Scottish Life Offices 29–33; *IR* 12 [1874]: 405–407).

The new regulatory regime after 1870 allowed actuaries to modify the meaning of the bonus without impeding its parallel development as a type of late Victorian public spectacle. Actuaries were quick to press the Life Assurance Companies Act into service as they retold their industry's past history and mythologized its endless accumulation of wealth. They referred in 1910 to "the pre-historic days of the business, before the Act of 1870" (Andras 94) and identified 1870 as the year when "modern Life Assurance may be said to have commenced" (Ecroyd 40); the branch secretary William M'Ilvenna praised the "welcome publicity of the Blue-books" that had "witnessed enormous accretions of wealth." Although he churlishly added that some of those accretions "might justly enough have been distributed as bonuses" (M'Ilvenna 6), most insurance managers took the lessons of the Albert and European more thoroughly to heart. In this regard the Provident's 1875 annual report was more indicative of the newly cautious discourse that surrounded insurance bonuses under the glare of the 1870 act: "the light now let in upon life insurance by the reports of the Board of Trade will, in due time . . . [show] clearly to the public that their true interest lies in solid security rather than in showy income, in the substantial nature of their bonuses rather than in new-fangled schemes for their payment" (*IR* 13: 34). This preference for substance over show would ultimately contribute to the diminishing relevance of bonus *declarations*, if not the bonus itself, in the post-Victorian life insurance industry.

### The Waning of the Bonus

In 1906, five years after the Norwich Union's proud moment, the *Saturday Review* published an article on "the decay of the bonus system" in Britain. Focusing on a new non-participating scheme advertised by the Law Union and Crown, the magazine reported that the life offices' superior "power of accurate prevision" had allowed them to rescue their policyholders from "paying too much at first and having the surplus returned to them later on" (102: 41). The idea was that since bonuses had originated out of the need of ignorant actuaries to reserve an excessive surplus to pay for possible errors in judgment, an improved ability to foretell the future would make the surplus, and hence the bonus, unnecessary. But in attributing the apparent resurgence of non-participating policies to advances in actuarial science, the writer was only half right. Companies had possessed the ability to reduce premiums safely for decades, and most had long offered their policyholders this option as an alternative to receiving a bonus. Of greater significance was the declining relevance of the bonus as a means of selling life insurance. The writer was hence closer to the mark when he suggested that there was something "quite attractive" about paying lower premiums for the same coverage, and at the same time being "free from possible disappointments caused by the decrease or absence of bonuses" (102: 41). The occasions for disappointment had increased since 1895, when little hope remained that yields would ever return to their pre-Victorian levels, and when increased competition from institutional investors made it harder for life offices to outpace even their most pessimistic forecasts. Of the forty biggest life offices at the turn of the century, twenty-two declared lower bonuses than they had twenty years earlier, only eleven had managed to improve from the 1880s, and two failed to pay any bonus at all (Chatham). As the *Times* noted, a policyholder would be justified in feeling let down under these circumstances: since "premiums are deliberately loaded in order to produce certain rates of bonus," the policyholder effectively got "no return for that part of the premium" in such an event (2 April 1913: 15–16).

The *Saturday Review* was also only half right about the demise of the bonus. It was wrong insofar as with-profit insurance policies remained more popular than their lower-priced non-participating equivalents well into the twentieth century (Trebilcock 2: 544–45). But it was right to sense that the bonus was starting to lose its central role in the management and marketing of life insurance. Not only did companies have a motive to downplay the significance of the bonus under market conditions that could not be counted on to produce consistently satisfactory yields, many were starting to move in the direction of removing the traditional ritual of the quinquennial declaration from the public stage. The decision, in this case, was less a calculated effort at concealment than a mundane response to rising labor costs. As the volume of life business grew, the interruptions and expense caused by periodic bonus calculations led many of Britain's largest insurers to examine alternative ways to divide their surplus. One option was to reduce the interval between bonuses to twelve months, and to treat the valuation process "as little more than an incident in the actuarial routine" (Todhunter 1). New office technologies like adding machines and arithmometers, and organizational improvements like card systems, made such routinization possible to an extent that could only have been dreamt about a century earlier. The Prudential, which by the 1890s was spending as much time preparing for its quinquennial bonus as it spent on normal business, was the first to make the switch. Having done so, it soon discovered that dividing its surplus more regularly vastly improved both internal and state-mandated accounting practices—not a minor point in an era when many life offices were merging with fire and accident companies, and when the Board of Trade was asking for more details in companies' yearly balance sheets. As one manager argued in 1906, switching to a yearly bonus kept "management on the button of expenses, knowing full well what it will mean every year" (*Report* q. 824).

As more offices followed the Prudential down this path, the bonus lost its value as spectacle and became a matter of routine—for customers as much as for clerks. Yearly additions to policies were smaller in an absolute sense and less liable to fluctuation than bonuses that were divided every five or seven years. Both in perception and reality, they were closer to the regular additions that appeared in a bank depositor's passbook. And if bonus declarations became less declarative after 1900, bonus recipients were less likely to react to the spectacle of their company's investment performance with the same sense of novelty that had once been the case. Not only was that performance less spectacular during the long decline that had commenced in the 1870s, the novelty of investment was also beginning to wear off. As mentioned in the introduction, most twentieth-century policyholders bought endowment insurance, which supplemented the vicarious pleasure of the bonus declaration with the more immediate thrill of a growing pension account. And many policyholders after 1900 had at their disposal a wide range of other, even more immediate, ways to watch other people play with their money. As trust companies boomed and stockbrokers spread from London to the provinces, Britain's first fund managers gave way to full-time speculators and retired to the more mundane task of preparing families for retirement and premature death.

## Notes

I wish to thank Nancy Henry, George Robb, and Cannon Schmitt for their helpful comments on previous drafts of this paper, and Sheree Leeds at Aviva, Isabel Syed at Zurich Financial Services, Chris Morgan at the Faculty of Actuaries, and the staff of the Guildhall Library for their valuable archival assistance.

1. This statement (and the focus of this essay) mainly applies to customers of life offices, as distinct from insurance company shareholders (a relevant group in all but the dozen or so mutual offices in Victorian Britain). These shareholders experienced investment in ways that more closely resembled shareholders in other moderately regulated industries, including banks and railways (for which see Alborn, *Conceiving Companies*)—although, as will be discussed in the text and in notes 14 and 16 below, they both influenced and were influenced by the development of profit sharing among policyholders.

2. Nearly two million new endowment policies were sold in Britain between 1890 and 1913, in contrast to only 330,000 whole-life policies. By 1910 endowment assurance had surpassed whole-life policies in terms of volume of policies in existence, cutting the latter's share of total policies in half from 80% in 1890 to 40% in 1910 (Supple 221).

3. Fire offices' need to maintain liquidity (to cover catastrophic conflagrations) was the main reason why bonuses never became a popular option in that sector, following a trial period between 1820 and 1850 when many companies offered them. See Trebilcock 1: 616, 645–46.

4. The Norwich Union copied the Equitable's restriction of the bonus to the oldest 5,000 policies, but since business did not reach that level until after 1820, this had no effect on its fortunes between 1816 and 1820. Partly for this reason, and partly due to mismanagement, its business receded after 1818 (Ryan, "History" 235).

5. As mutual offices were fond of pointing out, relatively little (if any) paid-up capital was necessary in a well-run life office, since annual liabilities were so easy to predict and since premiums would accumulate with interest for a generation before most claims started to fall due. Most offices established after 1825 had nominal capitals ranging from £500,000 to £1 million, but only called up a fraction of that (typically 10%).

6. Since the Northampton table undercharged older entrants, the main beneficiaries of the newer offices' lower prices were those who bought their insurance prior to age fifty. The London Life and Economic were among the top seven UK offices in premium income in the 1850s, a position that the London (but not the Economic) still held in the 1870s (Trebilcock 1: 745); and the Scottish Provident, with over £1 million in premium income, was the fourth-leading life office in that category in 1874 (*IR* 13 [1875]: 176–77).

7. For examples of "immediate bonus" offices see Albion and City of Glasgow prospectuses (both from 1849), pamphlet collection, Zurich Financial Services Group Archives. The same collection contains several examples of offices requiring a waiting period prior to bonus participation.

8. The Gresham and Standard Life were among the top four life offices in premium income in 1870, as was the Scottish Provident, also a tontine office, although its primary attraction was its low premiums (*IR* 13 [1875]: 176–77). Much of the Gresham's business came from its branch offices in Germany, Austria, and France.

9. A second response to the American threat was the "compound bonus," which calculated each reversionary bonus as a percentage of the sum insured plus all previously accumulated bonuses. These had existed since the 1820s but increased in popularity after 1890.

10. The proportion of Alliance non-profit policyholders ranged between 17.2% and 31.7% between 1863 and 1903 (Alliance Assurance Co., Reports); that in the Eagle de-

clined steadily from 32.7% in 1857 to 14.6% in 1893 (Eagle Insurance, *Board Minutes*); and that in the Commercial Union was 21.5% in 1870 (Walford 2: 20). Proportions closer to 50% were recorded by the Pelican and the Palladium, which were among the last to start offering with-profit policies (Eagle Insurance, *Board Minutes*; Trebilcock 1: 589).

11. Only 10.5% of Economic customers took their 1854 bonus in the form of a reduced premium (Downes 10), and 36.2% of Gresham policyholders between 1848 and 1865 (Gresham Life Assurance Soc.).

12. The lower middle-class market that the mid-century low-premium offices failed to reach was eventually exploited by industrial offices like the Prudential, which could add the task of selling ordinary insurance to their agents' daily rounds without substantially increasing overhead. Significantly, premiums on these ordinary whole-life policies, payable in monthly installments for coverage ranging from £50 to £300, were usually "loaded" to allow for reversionary bonuses (Dennett 118–19, 126; Ryan, "History" 249).

13. See English & Scottish Law Life Assurance Association (Board Minutes vol. 8, 13 July 1866; vol. 9, 23 June 1871, 23 June 1876; vol. 10, 20 May 1881; vol. 11, 21 May 1888, 19 March 1891, 19 March 1896; vol. 13, 28 Feb. 1901), Star Life Assurance Society (Board Minutes vol. 7, 26 March 1874; vol. 17, 21 Feb. 1894), and Eagle Insurance Company (*Board of Directors' Minute Books* vol. 11, 1 Oct. 1847; vol. 14, 8 Aug. 1862; vol. 16, 9 Aug. 1867; vol. 17, 9 Aug. 1872; vol. 18, 15 Aug. 1877; vol. 20, 28 March 1883; vol. 21, 14 March 1888; vol. 23, 5 April 1893; vol. 24, 13 April 1898; vol. 25, 1 April 1901), ESL 1/5/1/1, ST 1/5/1, EA 1/5/1, Zurich Financial Services Group Archives; and University Life Assurance Society (Board Minutes vol. 11, 2 June 1880; vol. 12, 10 June 1885; vol. 13, 11 June 1890; vol. 14, 5 June 1895; vol. 15, 23 May 1900), Church of England Fire and Life Assurance Society (Board Minutes vol. 1, 23 June 1848; vol. 3, 17 June 1853; vol. 4, 17 June 1858; vol. 5, 25 Oct. 1863; vol. 6, 13 June 1868), and Alliance Assurance Company (Board Minutes vol. 3, 27 March 1839; vol. 4, 8 May 1844, 11 April 1849; vol. 5, 31 May 1854; vol. 6, 30 March 1859; vol. 7, 20 April 1863; vol. 9, 10 March 1869; vol. 10, 25 Feb. 1874; vol. 11, 5 Feb. 1879; vol. 12, 13 Feb. 1884; vol. 14, 6 Feb. 1889), Guildhall Library Mss. 24,933, 12,160D, 12,162.

14. Since the bonus valuation also established the level of dividend for life office shareholders, the longer interval similarly enhanced the level of anticipation for that group—although these dividends were then typically paid out in equal annual installments leading up to the next declaration. Even in other types of companies, which paid fluctuating annual or semiannual dividends to their shareholders, the element of spectacle was seldom far from the surface: see, for example, George Elgar Hicks's 1859 painting *Dividend Day at the Bank of England* (I am grateful to George Robb for this reference).

15. The other two are "the transformation of the commodity into language [and] the figuration of a consuming subject," both of which also apply to the life insurance bonus, but would require more space to illustrate than is available here.

16. Bonus declarations and the 1870 act similarly improved access to information for insurance company shareholders, although they were starting from a relatively privileged position (e.g., power to elect auditors, to examine share lists, and to ask questions at annual meetings). The 1870 act required life offices to provide their shareholders with more information than any other type of mid-Victorian company barring railways.

17. Association of Scottish Life Offices Minute Book, vol. 2, 31 May 1869 (excerpt from a petition "unanimously adopted" by a meeting of London actuaries 1 June 1869), Faculty of Actuaries Ms. 1/1/2/2 Edinburgh. Revealingly, one of the "dangerous" scenarios envisioned by the actuaries under the proposed law was that "a diminution in the rate of bonus, disappointing sanguine Policy-holders, might lead many from various motives to concur in an application to the Board of Trade" for an audit.

# 4    Limited Liability, Market Democracy, and the Social Organization of Production in Mid-Nineteenth-Century Britain

*Donna Loftus*

The reform of the laws relating to limited liability in the mid-nineteenth century marks a significant intervention in the history of Victorian finance. The
Partnership and the Limited Liability Acts (1855) and the Joint Stock Companies Act (1856) recognized a form of business organization in which any
group of seven or more persons wishing to pool their capital could do so simply
by signing a memorandum of association. By the terms of the 1856 Act, individuals were no longer liable for the debts incurred by a company beyond the
value of the shares bought. As business and economic historians have noted, together these acts gave England one of the most permissive frameworks for business in Europe (Cottrell; Shannon, "Coming"). Debates preceding these acts
also provided for one of the most wide-ranging considerations of the market
and the community in Victorian England in which promoters of reform put
forward a vision of the market as open and democratic. Such narratives attempted to confer moral legitimacy on the market by making it fit with the political ideals of laissez-faire liberals and radical critics of industrial capitalism.
But, as this essay will show, such a vision was open to challenge by perspectives
that emphasized the separate qualities, skills, and duties of capital and labor.

Undoubtedly, the question of limited liability demonstrates the way that a
market culture was aligned to the process of community definition in the mid-
nineteenth century. Timothy Alborn's studies of early joint-stock companies
and coinage have demonstrated how questions about finance and commerce
in the nineteenth century also involved complex debates about the community
and the nature of the market in a "civilized" nation ("Coin" 252-71; *Conceiving*
1–81). In novels such as Charles Dickens's *Our Mutual Friend* (1864–1865) and
Anthony Trollope's *The Way We Live Now* (1874–1875), the very term "liability"
was seen to raise a series of expectations about individual and community responsibility for economic activity that involved considerations on the nature
of society (Feltes 356-69). This association between economic activity and
community building was a feature of early debates on the benefits of limited

liability. Mary Poovey has argued that limited liability, by severing the link between business failure and personal ruin, also helped to abstract the economic (*Making* 23). As debates on limited liability moved on in the nineteenth century, they helped to conceptualize the economic as a space subject to its own laws of political economy (N. Rose 102–103). This space, free from moral values and disabused of class, was promoted by a number of liberal reformers as a key site for the free and equal exchange of contracts in the market. At the same time, this abstraction of the economic was premised on a conceptualization of the social as an aggregate of self-regulating individuals, itself a highly political supposition. In this vision of society the separate claims of capital and labor were eclipsed by notions of free and fair exchange in the market.

As such, limited liability involved broader questions about market freedom and social relations, but this aspect of the question has not received much attention from historians. There are, perhaps, clear reasons why this is the case. The process of limited liability reform helped define the market as "free" from the biases and constraints of social and political life and subject to the laws of political economy. The economic history of limited liability has unpacked the legal and financial complexities of reform, but the social and political aspects of the question—in particular, the vision of a market democracy composed of working- and middle-class men—have been marginalized or considered separately in the social history of English labor. Recent scholarship has, however, acknowledged the importance of economics as a form of storytelling and invited perspectives that reintegrate economic, social, and cultural histories of markets and men (see Woodmansee and Osteen, *New*). Following this view, this essay shows how the broader issues encompassed in limited liability can be understood by considering the financial and legal aspects of reform in the context of the social and political environment in which they took place. The Duke of Argyll, a member of the cabinet that passed the Act of 1856, writing a history of political economy in 1893, recalled the question of limited liability as "one almost purely economic." Yet he also noted that the question could not be thoroughly probed without "considerations which concern metaphysics, jurisprudence, politics, morals, and even religion" (557). Following Argyll's assessment, I will view debates on limited liability as part of attempts to rethink the nature of the economy and society in the 1850s. The question of "liability" took place in the early 1850s against the background of Chartism, the ten hours question, and the "condition of England" debates—in years interrupted by debates over the political definition of the nation. In this context, limited liability was taken up by reformers as a panacea for social ills, able to accommodate the conflicting interests of capital and labor in the free market. Moreover, it was mobilized as a strategy of ethical governance, capable of manufacturing character through the sharing of capital in local communities.

Despite its potential for the promotion of market democracy, limited liability confirmed the separate interests of capital and labor. In exploring why this was the case, I will demonstrate how debates emerged out of working-class politics of the 1840s and middle-class responses to it. The permutations of debates through official inquiries, organized public opinion, and voluntary associations will be explored to demonstrate the slippage between narratives of the free market and class prejudice. Such slippage could be accommodated through a careful policing of the boundaries of investigation and inquiry, but as debates widened to include working-class men themselves, the limits of the free market were exposed.

### Markets and Men: The Background Debates on Limited Liability

Locating debates about limited liability in post-Chartist narratives of society may explain how far-reaching reform was passed quite suddenly in the 1850s. As Philip Cottrell has stated, "[t]he total reform of English company law during the years between 1855 and 1862 marks a sudden and sharp break; change both before and subsequently was a long drawn out, gradual process. Not only was the pace suddenly quickened, but also the law itself was turned upside down, with all the barriers in the way of company formation being removed" (54). Campaigns for the legal sanction of limited companies had emerged intermittently throughout the early nineteenth century. While debates overwhelmingly focused on fears of fraud and speculation, the issue of the social organization of capital was closely associated. This hitherto ignored aspect of the question—the potential of limited liability to reform the social arrangements of capital—contributed to changing attitudes to limited liability.

The Bubble Act of 1720, which had attempted to end speculation by forbidding joint-stock companies, was repealed in 1825 but incorporation was expensive. The limits of privately owned capital in an expanding economy were nevertheless soon recognized. For example, the Companies Act, passed in 1837, granted the Board of Trade the power to confer certain rights, including the regulated liability of individuals and the right to sue and be sued, on companies involved in hazardous practices or schemes beyond the capital of a few such as mining or railways. Despite this legislation, the 1837 report of the legal reformer Bellenden Ker, for the Select Committee on Joint-Stock Companies, has been seen as reflecting the majority view in the first half of the century through its emphasis on the necessary superiority of the privately owned and managed business, where individual owners were liable for all debts incurred (Saville, *Christian* 418). Anxiety was also expressed over the separation of ownership and management; with responsibility so diffuse, the market and the community, it was feared, would suffer ("Report"). To protect against fraud, the Joint Stock Company Registration and Regulation Act was passed in 1844. This allowed the Board of Trade to appoint a Registrar of Joint Stock Companies with the power to grant limited liability to registered companies with twenty-five or more men trading together whose capital was divided into transferable shares (Amsler, Bartlett, and Bolton 777). It also compelled all joint-stock companies to incorporate, register, and publicize their accounts.

Against this background of piecemeal and gradual reform, historians have attempted to explain the "sudden" passage of legislation in 1855 and 1856. Such a task is made more difficult by the great contrariety of opinion on the matter of reform that the 1854 Royal Commission on Mercantile Law noted. Despite the range of opinions, a number of studies have interpreted reform as an expression of transition in contemporary conceptualizations of the economy and the role of capital. One such study interpreted reform as a reflection of the growing influence of a "body of capitalists not directly engaged in trade" who sought an outlet for their profit (Jeffreys 9). A further study by Boyd Hilton has, rather famously, interpreted reform as the superceding of the "evangelical and retributive" version of free trade with more "optimistic and expansionist" visions (262–65). More recently, Robert A. Bryer interpreted reform as a struggle between two competing systems of political economy: on the one hand, modernizers in favor of limited liability emphasized the "enfranchisement of capital" and "freedom of contract" while, on the other, traditionalists justified unlimited liability as founded on the natural justice of individual responsibility for one's debts (37–39). Such explanations have focused largely on the issue of capital. But limited liability was also part of a wider transition in liberal attitudes to the working classes, a transition rooted in questions of the respective roles of capital *and* labor and the place of the "market" in the community (Biagini and Reid 1–19).

As recent work has shown, changing conceptions of the economy cannot be divorced from the discourse that produced knowledge about the market and society (T. Richards 33). The first half of the nineteenth century saw the creation of new metaphors, stories, and concepts that imaginatively described the market. New forms of writing, from financial journalism to the popular political economy of Harriet Martineau, intended to make the market knowable and accessible (Freedgood 210; Poovey, this volume 45). Such writing drew on existing forms of social description. Visions of community, fostered by market exchange, a shared moral code, and a unity of interests, were often articulated as a basis for a more optimistic outlook on social and economic relations (Ermarth, *English* 125). At the same time, such visions intended to register and record changing environments in a way that allowed for new subject positions. In this case, notions of mutual interests in the free market exchange could replace separated notions of class with stories of free and equal exchange between individuals in the marketplace.

Many mid-century promoters of limited liability reform argued that the organization of capital had become ossified and out of step with progress in social relations, a situation that threatened the rationale of liberalism and political economy. Supporters of limited liability were keen to demonstrate the emergence of a male working-class individualism that needed to be reflected in the reform of institutions and agencies. Looking back on the changes from the vantage point of 1872, the political economist Leone Levi, himself a late convert to the cause, argued that reform of the economy in the form of limited liability was needed because "society" itself had developed (Levi 333). Such sentiments were enshrined in the two major reports on partnership law commissioned by Parliament in 1850 and 1851, both of which contained this assertion:

> The great change in the social position of the multitudes from the growth of large towns and crowded districts, rendered it more necessary that corresponding reforms in the law should take place both to improve their condition and contentment, and to give additional facilities to investments of the capital which their industry and enterprise were constantly creating and augmenting. ("Investments" iv, "Law of Partnership" v)

The *Quarterly Review* considered evidence of working-class savings example enough of self-improvement, which it then considered the duty of the state to secure by providing scope for investments. Indeed, savings and investment, the *Quarterly Review* argued, propelled working men beyond their ranks into that of the capitalist, a status that required recognition from the state.

Limited liability was taken up within and outside Parliament by social reformers and liberals such as John Stuart Mill, Nassau Senior, Richard Cobden, John Bright, Robert A. Slaney, and the Christian Socialists, who saw it as a panacea that could further plans for working-class improvement while promoting, or at least not challenging, the ideals of enlightened laissez-faire political economy. These two designs were intertwined in campaigns. As Poovey has noted, the promotion of laissez-faire depended on the articulation of a social domain composed of similarly minded self-regulating individuals who in turn required freedom in the market (*Making* 22, 178).

These ways of seeing were a direct response to the politics of the period. Working-class political movements in the early to mid-nineteenth century had intermittently exposed the contradictions of industrial capital in which "class-based legal prejudice was combined with the supposedly value-free operation on the market" (Johnson, "Class" 147). But in the 1840s specifically Chartism and the ten hours movement produced alternative descriptions of economy and society that demonstrated the disenfranchised and unequal status of labor (see Finn, *After* 2–11). Such critiques did not disappear in the mid-century. They were absorbed into a reform agenda articulated by a rough alliance of radicals and liberals who sought to justify the free market and, at the same time, invigorate the economy by encouraging savings and investments from a broader range of people (M. Taylor 46).

Limited liability was also about politics; specifically, the role of the state in relation to working men. The late forties have often been associated with a sea change in legislative attitudes to reform, reflected in part in the passing of the 1847 Ten Hours Act (see Robson). Although the 1847 act sought to address itself to the protection of women and children's labor, thus upholding laissez-faire theory in relation to working-class men, there was, nevertheless, some uncertainty about the role of the state in improving the lives of working-class men. In the context of continuing campaigns for the franchise, limited liability emerged as a reform that addressed the political grievances of working-class men. When asked if he perceived reform as political, Mill responded that there was hardly anything greater that the legislature could do given the "present state of society and the present feelings of the working classes" ("Investments" 82). The Christian Socialists John M. F. Ludlow and Edward V. Neale echoed Mill's notion of "justice" and spoke of the consequent social peace "if the people found that the Legislature were willing to give them fair facility to try these schemes" (10, 17). For liberals like John Stuart Mill, limited liability would show that the legislature was interested in the state of working-class men by providing a framework for social mobility. Here the state could facilitate the emergence of the free market as a space for exchange in which social and political differences were "eclipsed" (Feiner 197). However, this way of seeing the market was merely suggestive and as such it was open to challenge. While the liberal discourses could argue in the abstract about shared capital and interests, representatives of capital and labor came forward offering differing perspectives of the market that drew limits to the vision of inclusion.

## The Social Panacea: Limited Liability and Social Reform

Limited liability was promoted in the early 1850s as a mechanism for social reform that would not require state intervention and would actively promote laissez-faire political economy. The persuasiveness of this vision can be seen in the way it was taken up in the periodical press. One contributor to debate in the House of Lords stated that no journal in the country except the *Leeds Mercury* would allow an article against limited liability (Carleton Hunt 132). The *Quarterly Review* and the *Westminster Review* took up the issue of limited liability in the early 1850s with a particular vigor. Both clearly perceived the issue of proposed reform as a social one, one which bore on the past, present, and future of community relations and national progress. Avoiding any discussion of the complex legal arrangements necessary in reform, both interpreted the law as an institutional framework that reflected the scale of a nation's advancement. As the *Westminster Review* noted, the present partnership law was "perplexing," "barbarous," and "oppressive and obstructive of progress" ("Partnership" 357). Reform would allow for communities to flourish around the sharing of capital with little intervention from the state.

The *Quarterly Review* noted that limited liability provided a means of reform that would not interfere with the fundamental laws of political economy:

> It combines all the requisites and avoids nearly all the prohibitions which mark out the legitimate path of philanthropic aid. It interferes with no individual self action: it saps no individual self-reliance. It prolongs childhood by no proffered leading strings: it valetudinareses energy by no hedges or walls of deference, no fetters of well-meant paternal restriction. (406)

It would build community by redrawing the "trenchant line of demarcation" between capitalists and laborers that was commonly presented as the root of all conflict (408). The working man, through investment and saving, would become "a tranquil and conservative citizen" (407). Likewise, the *Westminster Review* noted that reform would enable the building of schemes requiring large investment such as roads, ships, and commerce, all enabling men to "associate with one another":

> Independently of the commercial worth of industry fostered, labor abridged, enterprise encouraged, and genius rewarded;—independently of necessities cheapened, comforts augmented, luxuries put within the reach of all;—independently of the market value of knowledge increased, ideas developed, and character invigorated,—feelings of good will, sympathy, and friendship, would inevitably spring from laws which placed men in relations of mutual dependence and reciprocal benefit; and the happiness which such institutions would bring to individuals, and the strength they would give to the social fabric, are beyond estimation. ("Partnership" 414)

Capital was at the center of liberal visions of community in these debates. The social reform argument for limited liability imagined local communities tied together by capital investments, a potent example of mutual interests. As such, limited liability was a way to build communities both literally and metaphorically with the investment of capital and commitment. But this also premised a vision of local communities in which the laboring classes were initiated into the duties and responsibilities of citizenship through their engagement with the free market under the tutelage of more experienced men of capital.

Writing in the periodical press was undoubtedly part of, or at least influenced by, a broader campaign orchestrated by Christian Socialists and their supporters in Parliament, in particular Slaney and Frederick John Robinson (Viscount Goderich), to explore the possibilities of limited liability for reinvigorating social reform projects. Slaney had long pursued an interest in the health of towns, associating working-class improvement with environmental reform and "social peace" or class conciliation. Slaney promoted schemes to bridge gaps between capital and labor in the form of parks and model housing (P. Richards 85–101). Meeting with little success by the late forties, Slaney used the issue of limited liability to promote his causes further. There was a good deal of sense in this association: larger schemes of improvement were beyond the financial resources of personal wealth, so limited liability could be used to encourage investment for an urban infrastructure. Mapped onto this was also the question of a safe outlet for the modest savings of the poor. The Report on Joint Stock Companies (1844) and the Joint Stock Company Registration and Regulation Act of the same year had acknowledged a constituency of small investors interested in security rather than speculation (Hilton 265). Slaney used the cause of limited liability to draw a number of his reform interests together.

In 1849 Slaney received sanction for a *Select Committee on Investments for the Savings of the Middle and Working Class*. The Christian Socialists joined with Slaney to promote their own schemes of improvement in the form of worker co-operatives through the 1850 inquiry. What both had in common were visions of the unification of capital and labor through forms of joint investment in the local community. The local nature of these schemes was important in the provision it afforded for networks of trust based on personal knowledge. But the local nature of schemes also placed middle-class men, men of capital, in the driving seat, offering advice guidance and support to working-class men wishing to use capital. But it was less certain whether working men would invest their modest capital or their "labor" in such schemes. Evidence from the self-claimed "social improver" Samuel Bowley provided the strongest indication that working men might benefit from reform as shareholders, able to contribute to the building of their communities. Bowley spoke of a thwarted scheme for improved dwellings for working men in his locality. Despite the enthusiasm of local working men, and their willingness and ability to buy shares in the buildings, the expense and difficulty of obtaining a legal charter for a limited company prevented Bowley's plans ("Investments" 40–41). While the report highlighted the obstacles present in existing law to "benevolent projectors of a useful undertaking" ("Investments" iii), it was rather vague on whether or not working men could benefit from limited liability as shareholders or as partners in production. The category "shareholder" appeared to hover uncomfortably between capital and labor. Aside from Bowley, it would appear that few of the supporters of limited liability saw reform as providing an outlet for working men's capital.

Although in support of limited liability, Mill was clear in his evidence to the committee that the working classes would not, or could not, benefit as investors from large schemes of improvement. Mill's belief in the need for reform came from a different perspective:

> A limitation of the responsibility, so far as it related to the working classes themselves, might not be essential; . . . I think that the great value of a limitation of responsibility, as relates to the working class, would be not so much to facilitate the investment of their savings, not so much to enable the poor to lend to those who are rich, as to enable the rich to lend to those who are poor. ("Investments" 80)

In this view, Mill echoed the Christian Socialists that the benefits of limited liability lay in a greater capacity afforded to men of wealth to give loans to working men that would enable them to set up in business. The concern of the Christian Socialist movement at this time was in procuring loans from benevolent gentlemen of means to fund cooperative workshops, a principle enshrined in Kingsley's novel *Alton Locke* and in the various *Tracts of Christian Socialism* (Backstrom 29–53). These models for the organization of production were premised on the clear distinction between middle-class leadership based on a superior knowledge of the managing capital and the working classes. Limited liability was discussed almost exclusively in terms of *en commandite* partnership in the 1850s, a form of organization in which shareholding did not extend to having a say in the management of the concern (Saville, "Christian" 422). Slaney's committee made much of the work of middle-class trustees in promoting thrift, and the patronage of well-disposed gentlemen seemed central to the Christian Socialist vision of cooperative workshops ("Investments" vi;

Johnson, "Class Law" 150). The extent to which this patronage converted into authority and ownership of profits was an issue not taken up.

It would appear from the 1850 report that, as Johnson has noted, the "free market was reined in" as it was on the verge of considering working-class men, and a "protective equity" held out over newer forms of individualism (Johnson 149). Mill's arguments, in particular, demonstrate the slippage between class prejudice and a belief in free and equal exchange in the market place that circulated around mid-century liberalism. Mill acknowledged that the law as it stood presented an obstacle to working men wishing to set up cooperative production with their own, or borrowed, capital: "if they invest anything we are pretty sure that they invest nearly all they have, if they lose that they lose everything." However, Mill also suggested that such failures were due to the working classes being unable to establish "a proper control over one another, and over the managers" (Mill 407). For Mill, the successful investment of capital was closely tied to skills and qualities he did not recognize in the working classes. Despite this, he was aware that the concept of a free market required that all should have the opportunity to invest on the same terms as the rest of the community. Reform was about instructing the working classes in the intricacies of the market and skills associated with capital; ultimately Mill saw mid-century working men as unable to make sense of market knowledge.

In the 1850 report, limited liability was considered a gesture to an improved stratum of the working classes, an "experiment" that would both affirm the equality of the market and rule on the ability of an improved working class to work within it. Reform might democratize the market by allowing anyone of "recognized integrity and capacity for business" to obtain capital. Whether or not working men were capable of such qualities was quite a different matter. As Mill argued, limited liability would remove a major cause of discontentment by freeing up the market, and "even if such experiments failed, the attempt to make them succeed would be a very important matter in the way of education to the working classes, both intellectually and morally" ("Investments" 85). Failure would reveal to the working man the real skill and qualities required for successful business and, thereby, legitimize the profits of the capitalist and capitalist forms of production. In this way, failure would be just as instructive in the ways of the market as success (Alborn, "Useful").

The range and focus of the parliamentary inquiry brought many of the ambiguities about current understandings of the organization of capital and production to the fore. While the "cultural competence" of different publics affected the way they interpreted and articulated arguments, slippage in the language of reform revealed different expectations of the market (Gray 11). There was, as stated, considerable elision over issues of management, authority, and control but there were moments when the story of equilibrium broke down. The evidence of Walter Cooper to the 1850 Select Committee was revealing of this point. A journeyman tailor, Cooper was a manager of the Working Tailors Association, recently established by the Christian Socialists. Formed with borrowed capital from prominent Christian Socialists, the association included men who were paid wages and a share of profits after the interest of the loan and expenses were deducted ("Investments" 52–54). When questioned by a member of the committee, Cooper uncovered the many tensions over the practical meaning of association and the figures that represented a corporation:

> Do you not wish to give to the working men by means of association a share in the profits of the masters? We wish by association to see the masters and workers combined.
>
> Does that mean really anything else than that the workmen shall have a share, in proportion to his work, of the master's profit, as well as his wages? I do not clearly understand. In association there is no master; each man has a fair share of his own earnings. That which the master in ordinary cases would take to himself is divided amongst the workers.
>
> Does that mean anything else than that the association in its corporate capacity represents the masters? I have no objection to that; and the workmen too, they are combined. (54–55)

Such tensions over the extent to which capital conferred right to represent a trade, an association, or a corporation were never far from the surface of debates on the market and the organization of capital and production.

Perhaps because of such tensions, Slaney's report was not discussed in Parliament, but a second select committee report was commissioned in 1851 to inquire more specifically into the law of partnership. Again chaired by Slaney, the committee was appointed to consider the "expediency of facilitating the limited liability with a view to encourage useful enterprise and the additional employment of labor" ("Law of Partnership" iii). The report recommended, like the first, that charters for the establishment of limited companies be cheaper and easier. It also repeated the recommendation that a local and accessible framework for the prevention and remedy of fraud be provided through the full publication of the accounts of limited companies and through the transfer, to magistrates' courts, of the authority to deal with commercial disputes. Although reaffirming the conclusions of the first report, the second was more cautious, noting that "the best authorities are divided on the subject." Given the repetition of conclusions, the need for this second report warrants some attention. The 1850 inquiry demonstrated some uncertainty about the boundaries of debate on company law. Slaney had been criticized for being vague in his proposals for the inquiry of 1850 (Tyson 18). He was, after all, interested in a range of social reform measures; the social languages that Slaney employed involved broader issues about the role and authority of capital over labor and the conflicting notions of a free market based on contract in a hierarchical society. Slaney's second committee established more precisely the boundaries of debate.

The 1851 inquiry into the law of partnership may well have confirmed the conclusions of the 1850 inquiry, but it did so in a very different way. A language of social reform and democratization was replaced with a discourse that contained a greater emphasis on property and skill. The report claimed an interest in gradually removing restrictions on "the power which everyone has in the disposal of his property, and to remove those fetters on commercial freedom which long prevailed in this country" ("Law of Partnership" v). The beneficiaries of such legislation, the inquiry suggested, were "cautious persons, of moderate capital, and esteemed for their intelligence and probity," who would be enabled to use limited liability for "public benefit and private profit" in "useful enterprises" such as houses, clubs, roads, and bridges (vi). The inquiry report did suggest that "the middle and even the more thriving of the working classes" might benefit as shareholders along with their richer neighbors (vii). But, on the whole, the economy that was imagined and described was less accessible, less comprehensible to ordinary working people. This partly reflects the kinds of witnesses that were called to give evidence to the committee and who were overwhelmingly drawn from the legal and commercial professions with a few contributions from established political economists like Mill, Levi, and Charles Babbage. As such the market matters were presented as complex and requiring a certain kind of knowledge and expertise to manage. In this forum, William Cotton, an ex-governor of a bank and thus "well acquainted with commercial and monetary affairs," emphasized the professional qualities of capital, noting that the working classes by definition would lack the knowledge, intelligence, and experience of the market to invest their capital successfully. But, unlike Mill, Cotton recommended that the present system should be safeguarded until workers were more "intelligent" ("Law of Partnership" 96).

The inquiry into the law of partnership recast the market as complex, legal, and technical beyond the capabilities of the majority of the working classes (for whom moral and social languages were deemed more appropriate). Perhaps the most significant conclusion of the report was the recommendation that a royal commission of "adequate legal and commercial knowledge" be appointed to consider the issue of partnership law further (viii). This shift was confirmed by two developments. Firstly, the issue of working-class capital and investment was tackled separately in the Industrial and Provident Societies Act of 1852. Introduced by Slaney, this act freed co-operative societies from the provisions of 1844 requiring partnerships of twenty-five plus to register as joint-stock companies. The issue of limited liability was avoided and privileges such as the free transfer of shares still restricted. Secondly, the question of limited liability was taken up in terms that made little reference to the investments of working-class men. This latter point was in part a consequence of the former. With Slaney and other social reformers satisfied with the 1852 act, there was little to challenge the legalistic and formulaic definition of the market that was to emerge in further inquiries into limited liability. In official debates, visions of a market democracy involving working men as investors in community projects began to give way to older, more traditional notions of capital and labor.

The Royal Commission on Mercantile Law, 1854, reflected the full complexity of the issues that had become entwined with limited liability and the range of perspectives on reform. The inquiry was divided into two sections: the first dealt directly with partnership law, and the second with the question of how far mercantile law, in the different parts of the United Kingdom, could be advantageously assimilated. The second report was a dense legalistic document that reflected a broad range of opinion including chambers of commerce, law societies, commercial men, and senior legal figures mostly in favor of assimilation, with differences mainly framed around which law should take precedence. Within this report, partnership law was examined as one aspect of a range of issues including sale of goods, bankruptcy, and bills and notes, all of which were exposed to the minutiae of legal reasoning.

The Royal Commission report noted that the commissioners "have been much embarrassed by the great contrariety of opinion" on the matter and voted by five votes to four that the law should not be changed (Hilton 257; Royal Commission, first report 5). Its reasons for rejecting reform reproduced older conservative perspectives on the market that focused less on local trade and civic reform and more on national conceptualizations of a British market and with it questions of trade: "There is on every side such abundant evidence of satisfactory progress and national prosperity, it would be unwise to interfere with the principles which, in their judgment, have proved beneficial to the general industry of the country" ("Mercantile Law" Royal Commission, first report 7). On the contrary, the conclusions noted that reform would in effect damage British trading, leading to fraud and speculation, which in turn would damage British mercantile reputation. As to questions of market democracy, the report concluded that the occurrences of men of talent denied capital for investment and business had been "greatly over-rated" (6).

In response to such definitions of the market, supporters of limited liability could present reform as democratic while critiquing opposition as an unfair defense of privilege. Arguing in support of reform, G. W. Bramwell argued that those who failed to support proposals for limited liability were for the most part gentlemen engaged in trade who were "maybe somewhat influenced by their natural satisfaction with things as they find them" (23). Despite such asides, it became clear as debates unfolded around the 1856 Royal Commission that the wealthy were most likely to benefit as shareholders. As Bryer has argued, "although genuflections were made towards the idea that the working class and the middle class might have more opportunities to invest, many were careful to point out that the biggest beneficiary of limited liability would be the very wealthy" (Bryer 53). The links that limited liability was seen to inspire were between the gentry and trading class (Bryer 55). When the Limited Liability Act of 1855 was passed, the values of shares were set at £10, a figure well beyond the capabilities of most working-class men (Tyson 23). The 1856 Royal Commission presented limited liability as a matter for the financial and commercial elite over the conceptualizations of the free market. Whether in support of reform or not, parties to the debate rarely saw reform as a matter for the working classes, nor did they see it as a matter that bore on the social relations of production.

## The Royal Society of Arts and
## the Conference of Capital and Labor

The debate about limited liability exposed a range of languages used to describe the economy in the mid-nineteenth century from narratives that emphasized equilibrium and balance in communities of individuals bound together by shared investment to those that described complex financial markets requiring skill and expertise to manage. These narratives emerged from different parties to debate: political economists and social reformers, bankers, businessmen and lawyers. Despite differences and disagreements, the abstracted nature of discussions enabled the narratives to consider possibilities for an economic reality based on the combining of capital or the exchanging of contract for mutual benefit. But when debate involved participants embedded in the most contentious forms of economic and social relations in the period—the relationship between employer and employee—the terms of debate were not easy to contain.

This potential of limited liability to transform the organization of capital and labor emerged out of a post-Chartist and ten hours politics that had done much to present industrial relations as inherently unfair and unequal. In the context of the glaring publicity given to damaging strikes in the North of England, social reformers mobilized the question of limited liability as a means to manage the relations of capital and labor by bringing them out of the workplace and into a civilized public space (Dutton and King 72–73; Loftus 185–89). In this respect, reform represented attempts by members of the liberal bourgeoisie to replace popular radicalism with popular liberal notions of respectable citizenship by offering alternative visions of the market as equal and inclusive (James Vernon 270). Outside of Parliament, agencies such as the National Association for the Promotion of Social Science, in their strand on "Social Economy," and the Royal Society of Arts took up the cause of limited liability as a means of reflecting and promoting social improvement through economic and legal reform (*Transactions* 1860 127–50, 760). These agencies saw themselves as actively creating a dialogue between capital and labor. Such an exchange was made possible by the belief that all men were potentially like-minded. But narratives of similarity often co-existed with a belief in the separate qualities of capital and labor.

The Royal Society's involvement in the issues of the market would seem appropriate given its status as the "oldest and most powerful voluntary association" (*Journal* 221). Certainly, by the 1850s, the society had established a reputation for encouraging and promoting the industrial arts and sciences, not least through its association with the Great Exhibition of 1851 (Hudson and Luckhurst 234–40). Its turn to focus on the social arrangement of capital in the 1850s was, nevertheless, unusual but entirely in accordance with the narratives of civilization and reform that the Great Exhibition had facilitated. The Great Exhibition was presented to the public as a symbol of the triumph of laissez-faire capitalism, evidence of all that capital and labor could produce in concert.

Reflecting and emphasizing these narratives of social improvement, the good behavior of the working classes on shilling days was interpreted in newspapers and periodicals as evidence of their increasing civility (Gurney 115–16). To further promote these "civilizing tendencies," the society proposed a working man's exhibition as an offshoot of the exhibition of 1851. Echoing a cultural concept of work as unifying national identity, such a theme was deemed to be appropriate for a society of working men "from the Prince next to the throne and the minister in the cabinet, to the manufacturing operative and the agricultural labourer" (*Journal* 7).

The council of the Royal Society first called for an "exhibition" of working men in 1853, as a collection of issues around improvement for the laboring classes. In addition to promoting limited liability, the exhibition proposed to display model dwellings, clothing, and food from working men from different countries (*Journal* 7). A number of employers and trade associations were invited as well as those who, not engaged directly in the labor question, "have studied and mastered its various bearings" (7). The conference was well attended under the chair of Lord Robert Grosvenor, and the secretariat of Peter Le Neve Foster, on February 3, 1854, in the Societies House in London. The attendance list itself gives some indication as to the framework of the conference. Over 140 individuals attended, including key members of the Christian Socialist movement, a number of members of Parliament, lawyers, and reformers, such as Slaney, Sidney Smith, and Henry Tufnell, as well as persons of known radical repute such as Robert Owen and Ernest Jones. Forty-nine trade associations were represented, thirty-four of which were from London and three of which were working co-operatives. Representatives of the working classes were largely from the artisan trades. Only three chambers of commerce were represented and, apart from William Ainsworth, John Henderson of the firm Fox, Henderson, and Co., Caleb Wright, and a few other smaller manufacturers, employers were largely conspicuous by their absence (*Supplement* 189).

The theme and proposed exhibition were part of the society's strategy to demonstrate confidence in the improvement of working-class men by introducing them into public life, and what the society considered the conventions of debate and association. The society expressed the hope that the conference would provide this "neutral ground" within which parties could "fairly and temperately" discuss the causes of strikes and the means to prevent them (*Journal* 113). As the opening statement from the chair suggested, the aim of the conference was "to promote the peace and harmony of those whose interests . . . are so entirely the same and completely bound up together" (191). Disputes and unrest were presented as the result of the separation of capital and labor into entrenched enclaves in the local community; thus the value of limited liability in linking the two was explored. Yet, in the context of industrial unrest, the discussion of limited liability questioned the very boundaries of the market and the ability of political economy to act as a guide.

The significance of working-class improvement was presented by the Royal

Society of Arts in the drawing of a respectable working class into a disciplined and rationalized public space for private negotiation, behavior essential to the process of exchange in the marketplace. Reflecting these aims, the conference was minutely organized, with each speaker asked to address predetermined questions on combinations, strikes, and wages. In the interests of avoiding "acrimonious argument," speakers were allowed only ten minutes to address well-defined topics. Digression and the proposal of resolutions were expressly prohibited, and "demonstration, by way of applause or otherwise," expressly discouraged (*Supplement* 189). Four issues were posed to consider the impact of the social arrangements of capital on industrial relations: whether combinations, as composed of employers or laborers, were objectionable; whether a law of limited liability would render combinations unnecessary; whether limited liability would re-configure the private arrangements of trade as public concerns; and, finally, whether the right of association should be legislated against if operating to the detriment of the wider community. Despite the chair's optimistic appeal for dispassionate debate, the conference was immediately plunged into dispute over the ability of various parties to represent the claims of capital and labor. The first speaker, C. Sturgeon, expressed the opinion that the conference would find itself unfit to debate the issue of limited liability, lacking, in his opinion, the necessary knowledge of commerce and business. In direct contradiction, Ernest Jones called for legislation to enable the working classes to become their own employers and share in profits by abolishing the monopoly on land and opening up credit for laborers to manufacture on their own account (192). These first two speakers highlighted the core debate of limited liability: on the one hand, Jones asserted the right for workers to own the profits of their labor; on the other, Sturgeon denied the ability of men not involved in business even to discuss the issue. Presented in this way, and set alongside the wider questions of combinations, limited liability became an issue of knowledge of, and authority over, prices and profits in local communities.

Political economy produced a narrative about the market that was supposed to be true. The disputes that were aired at the conference revealed that the working men present were not persuaded that there was a market, subject to the laws of political economy, for the free and equal exchange of capital and labor because such a notion had no bearing on their experience. A London cabinet maker demanded to know what the "value of labor" was, given that the product for which he was paid no more than £3 could sell on the market for £20 (198). Likewise, a London baker noted that there were, in his trade, no standards in prices and conditions, leaving men subject to the "will and caprice of individual employers" (201). In such circumstances, the conference felt workers had no way of knowing how wages were decided and that political economy was no guide. Aitken, a working man from Ashton-under-Lyne, equally juxtaposed the public nature of working men's combinations compared with those of employers. Aitken illustrated his point with an anecdote of six Manchester manufacturers, employing 24,000 between them, who would make a resolution to reduce wages while traveling to London on the same train. Aitken's point was simple but significant: "the employers, being comparatively so few in number, could make their arrangements withdrawn from the public gaze" (196).

If political economy was no guide to the employment relation, neither was the assertion of mutual interest. While Slaney reflected the argument of reformers that limited liability, by reflecting the true and identical interests of capital and labor, would do away with the need for strikes (193), others, such as R. Fort of Read Hall, argued that the difficulty for limited liability lay in "determining terms of management" precisely because the interests of masters and men were necessarily different. As a result, he argued that limited liability would not work: "It would be to the master's interest to keep the divisible profits down, and that of the men to raise the divisible profits" (194). McNaughton Dickie of the Rational Reformers' Confederation argued that "everyday life" proved the opposite of the assertion that the interests of the employed and the employer were identical, "as it was the interest of the masters to get labor for the lowest possible price, and that of the men to get as much for their labor as possible" (204). This observation led the Rational Reformers to a different conclusion: that the only way forward was for a system of limited liability to enable men, like those on strike in Preston, to become co-operative owners rather than shareholders.

Slaney's vision of capital and labor, united in interests through the mechanisms of limited liability, was challenged in a debate that highlighted the real existence of combinations on both sides. For Slaney, complex issues of knowledge and authority were contained within the assertion of mutual interests. The laws of political economy, bolstered by the realization of mutual interests, would guide in decisions of management. However, worker powerlessness in the face of employer combinations was a recurring theme. Such criticisms did not come from workers alone. The MP Charles Hindley spoke of his own short experience as a manufacturer and the attempts by associations of local employers to fix prices and wages in the region. As Hindley said, in the simple inability to fix his own wages his career in political economy was finished. Workers were, in Hindley's experience, pawns in the employer's schemes (204). Despite correspondence to the conference from the Master Manufacturers of the Hyde District noting that employers were not in the habit of combining to fix prices, the overwhelming conclusion of the conference was that they did, albeit informally and in private (208).

The conference revealed that the value of limited liability for the working men present was less in schemes of share ownership and loans for business and more in the availability of information on wages and profits. In the majority of contributions from working men, limited liability was presented as ameliorating conflict by allowing access to accounts. The greatest contention centered less on the monopoly of capital and more on the monopoly of knowledge, particularly of business prices and profits. In this sense, a number of working men argued that combinations were necessary because accounts were not available for examination, thus leaving workers subject to reductions in their pay without knowledge of the figures (198).

Access to such knowledge represented democratization and a challenge to privilege for the working men present at the Royal Society of Arts conference. Perhaps the correspondence from the secretary of the Master Manufacturers of the Hyde District best illustrates the tensions invoked by the discussion. Declining an invitation, the secretary challenged the notion that the successful management of conflict was a duty of capital, declaring the conference itself as an "invitation to the invasion of the rights of property" (208). This issue highlighted the boundary between private ownership and public interest and the tension between individual action and community responsibility that was at the heart of debates about limited liability. But these issues were about more than fraud and speculation; they involved wider questions about the social organization of production and the ability of a market, structured by human agency, to regulate itself in the interests of the community. Despite the powerful argument put forward by working men that the employer in combinations, rather than the speculator, represented the moral pitfalls of the economy, there was a clear reticence on behalf of reformers to challenge the power and authority of capital (Poovey, *Making* 156).

## Conclusion

Despite the great contrariety of opinion on the question of limited liability both within the official inquiries and in wider debate, legislation was passed with little opposition. Bouveries, vice president of the Board of Trade, and Henry Palmerston introduced two bills in 1855. One opened up the privilege of limited liability to joint-stock companies, and the other amended the law of partnership to allow loans to companies on condition of a share in profits without formal and legal partnership. The latter failed on a technicality, but both were effectively replaced in 1856 by the Companies Act, which reestablished the law in broader terms. The act made limited liability more freely available, the only requirement being a "memorandum of association" to be signed by shareholders. Significantly, previous legislation, which set the value of shares at a minimum of £10, far beyond the capability of most working men, was overturned by this act. Indeed, in the Companies Act, there was no prescribed limit set on share prices. Advocates presented reform as democratizing the economy and unfettering trade, an attack on privilege that would allow social mobility to the talented, regardless of birth. In this way, limited liability was presented as the logical extension of laissez-faire economy, extending its privileges to the laboring classes (Hunt 116). The act was introduced in February 1856 by Robert Lowe, then vice-president of the Board of Trade, as a matter of principle, the principle being "freedom of contract and the right of unlimited association—the right of people to make what contracts they please on behalf of themselves" (*Hansard* 140: 129). As such, Lowe argued it mattered little how many took up the opportunity of limited liability; it was simply a just and logical extension of laissez-faire to the poor.

Lowe was skeptical about the success of schemes of co-operative production, perceiving the importance of reform more in terms of opportunity for social mobility (*Hansard* 140: 127). He saw reform as a scheme of education and improvement, an "experiment" that might include the poor in matters of trade. Limited liability could recognize working-class men's improvement by incorporation into the market with all the characteristics this was seen to imbue, such as independence and respectability, without the need for political reform. The slippage between economic and political references was a striking feature of Lowe's speech in the House. Speaking of the limited liability company as a representative democracy, Lowe reflected on the role of the Board of Trade: "having given them a pattern the state leaves them to manage their own affairs and has no desire to force on these little republics any particular constitution" (134; see also Hunt 135). Lowe, who rejected calls for the extension of the franchise, nevertheless presented company reform as the right to freedom of contract. The passing of the 1856 Act symbolized the privileging of "free market" narratives and the marginalization of working men's political claims (Somers 608).

The little social history available on limited liability has perceived the debates and reforms of the early 1850s as reflecting the "transitionary nature" of these years (Tyson 29). Hilton has argued that the reforms mark the giving way of an evangelical and retributive model of economics to one that was expansionist and cosmopolitan. As such, limited liability was a sign of the move in the mid-century to a more optimistic type of liberalism (Hilton 261). Support for limited liability represented a more positive attitude to social mobility and, in particular, the incorporation of skilled and improved working men into a "society" of self-regulating individuals. Few, however, were willing to imagine this society as composed of shareholders in the market. The political economist Levi made his views quite clear in a response to the proposed conference of the Royal Society of Arts:

> Even in a limited partnership commandite partners may inspect accounts, attend meetings, and exercise a certain amount of control, which it seems to me is incompatible with the character of an operative. . . . I believe that any attempt to abolish the relation of masters and servants must prove fruitless, as it is a divine institution, upon which the whole structure of society is founded. (*Journal* 170)

When a public debate on industrial co-operation reemerged in the 1860s, largely under the aegis of the Social Science Association, a distinction was clearly drawn between worker share ownership and having knowledge of, and a say in, the management of business. Similarly, the National Association for the Promotion of Social Science, formed in 1857, was not party to early debates on limited liability, but it is illuminating that the association's later promotion of schemes of profit sharing were premised on the clear separation of management and labor. Though working men might be incorporated into the market, there were clear limits set on the form this would take.

The association of limited liability with the democratization of the market enabled reformers to attach their cause to longstanding attacks on defenders of privilege that emerged in the radical politics of the early nineteenth century. In so doing, they presented the market as an arena that would absorb class differences and open up the possibility of free exchange between self-regulating individuals. Through limited liability capitalism could take the form of a partnership. As Alborn has noted in his study of banking, joint-stock companies employed democratic syntax in presenting the corporation as a body that represented the community (Alborn, *Conceiving* 85; Revill 208). Such narratives implied inclusivity and fairness while legitimating the power and authority of capital. But such perspectives required a careful policing of the debate.

The debates around limited liability provided a platform for one of the most wide-ranging public discourses of the relationship between (male) labor and capital. Emerging out of the politics of the 1840s, limited liability was promoted as a mechanism for reforming society through the sharing of capital. Reformers attempted to establish a preferred way of talking about the market as "free and equal," but the expansion of free market narratives failed to dislodge visions of society founded on the separate rights and duties of capital and labor. Tensions between equality and difference in the market could be accommodated in concepts of shared interests, but fissures opened as debate was broadened to include representatives of capital and labor. Despite the circulation of free market narratives, there was little to challenge the view expressed by those opposing reform in the Royal Commission of 1854 that the management of capital required skills working men did not have. By 1856, the debate was about the complicated legal position of shareholders and limited companies and not the social organization of capital. As it was, financial legislation that had the potential to transform the social fabric represented a retrenching of capital's financial and political power.

# 5 Fair Enterprise or Extravagant Speculation

## Investment, Speculation, and Gambling in Victorian England

*David C. Itzkowitz*

> When I was young, people called me a gambler. As the scale of my operations increased I became known as a speculator. Now I am called a banker. But I have been doing the same thing all the time.
>
> —Sir Ernest Cassell, banker to Edward VII (qtd. in Chancellor ix)

As Cassell's humorous observation suggests, the line that separates gambling from other forms of financial risk has never been easy to draw, but that has not stopped people from trying to draw it. The economic historian Roger Munting, for example, devotes several pages of his study of British and American gambling to an examination of the question of whether market speculation should be defined as gambling, finally concluding, for very technical reasons, that it should not (Munting 1–3). But the need to draw that line has been more urgent at some times than others, and the choice of just where to draw it has varied as well. There seems to have been little urgency during the eighteenth century, for example. The English State Lottery, which operated from 1694 to 1826, combined, in its earliest years, the features of a lottery and a government bond to almost no one's distress (Ewen; R. Richards). On the other hand, drawing the line between gambling and other forms of financial risk had particular urgency during the Victorian period. The great expansion of the commercial economy that characterized the nineteenth century and particularly the developments that followed the passage of the Limited Liability Act of 1855 and the Companies Acts of 1856 and 1862 led, by the late Victorian period, to middle- and upper-class England becoming, in the words of George Robb, a "nation of shareholders" (Robb, *White-Collar* 3). By the end of the century, roughly two-fifths of the national wealth was invested in company shares, and large numbers of upper- and middle-class people lived off dividends and interest from shares and other securities (Robb, *White-Collar* 91, 181). But as G. R. Searle has argued, this great expansion was accompanied by a desire that capitalism possess a moral component, and for many Victorians gambling was of questionable morality at best, even though a gambling industry flourished in late Victorian England (Searle xi, 22). In her study of nineteenth-century American gambling, Ann Fabian has argued that the construction of the nineteenth-century capitalist economy required the exclusion of those who gambled from what came to be seen as legitimate economic activity. Paradoxically, however, this process led to the legitimization of a new kind of gambling. "Gambling," she writes,

> was marginalized only to be domesticated at the end of the century, when risk and rapid gain reappeared as essential ingredients in rational capitalist speculation. The "new" gamblers, who profited from the operations of stock and commodities exchanges, presented themselves as virtuous, rational citizens by delineating their differences from the "old" evil gamblers. . . . For the speculation to stay, the gambling had to go. (Fabian 3, 61)

This essay argues that a similar, but not identical, process was occurring in Victorian England. As was the case in America, speculative trading would only be accepted once it was purged of an association with gambling. This purging was essentially accomplished by the 1860s, and, henceforth, speculation increasingly came to be seen as a reputable economic activity and speculators as respectable economic actors. But the situation in England was to be complicated by the development, in the 1870s, of two new industries—one financial, the other sporting—that created a renewed convergence of gambling and speculation and that called into question the separation that had been so carefully drawn. A new breed of speculative brokers, known pejoratively as "bucket-shop keepers," using language, advertising techniques, and appeals that were suspiciously like those being touted by a new breed of sporting bookmakers, offered a growing public the opportunity to become engaged in the world of speculative finance at relatively little cost and seemingly little risk.

The new speculative business was aided by the development of new forms of communication, including the popular press and the electric telegraph. But its existence was also made possible by the fact that speculation had already been legitimized earlier in the century by its separation from gambling. The new brokers and their clients no doubt saw themselves as participants in an activity whose legitimacy had been firmly established. But, in the eyes of many, they were turning the world of financial speculation into a new form of popular entertainment whose morality was ambiguous at best. The moral anxiety surrounding the intersection of speculation and gambling that had apparently just been put to rest was reawakened by the late 1870s, as it would continue to be reawakened from time to time down to our own day. The need to redraw the line that separated gambling from legitimate commerce once again took on a renewed urgency. In the end, the line was redrawn, though it was never more than a fairly permeable boundary. While new forms of speculation would remain legal and would not disappear, they continued to operate only in a state of marginal respectability.

Paradoxically, however, the fact that the new speculation could be branded as gambling only emphasized, by contrast, the legitimacy of other forms of speculation. By allowing the new speculation alone to carry the moral opprobrium that had once applied to all speculation, late Victorian society ensured that speculation in general would remain legitimate.

## The Domestication of Speculation

Conventionally, Victorians viewed gambling and investment as lying at opposite ends of a continuum of financial risk, with speculation lying somewhere in between. *Investment,* usually defined as the holding of property for the income it provided, was clearly seen as legitimate. With its resonance of both aristocratic landed wealth and middle-class prudence, investment had the cultural power to retain its legitimacy through changing paradigms of economic activity. *Gambling,* on the other hand, was increasingly viewed as an illegitimate form of financial risk. The Gaming Act of 1845 (8 and 9 Vict., c. 109), which made it a criminal offence to keep a gaming house, also made "wagering contracts"[1] unenforceable at law, thus excluding gambling from the world of respectable commerce. From at least mid-century, if not before, most respectable opinion would have agreed with the assertion of the anti-gambling activist J. Malet Lambert:

> The wealth and possessions of man are made by labour and by industry, money does not grow of itself, wealth is not for men if they are lucky enough to get it, but comes from the labour of men. The gambler looks upon the world as a place where wealth is open to him without patient labour, by luck or by chance. But his theory is demonstrably false. The mass of men must labour for wealth itself to exist.... If all men were to turn gamblers for a living, they would become like wolves searching the wastes of the earth without a living being to prey on, and forced to turn cannibals, or be honest, or die. (8)

Unlike either investment or gambling, whose moral connotations seemed relatively clear, the morality and legitimacy of *speculation,* which was usually defined as the buying or selling of commodities in order to benefit from changes in price, was more ambiguous. Controversialists on various sides of economic and moral debates could feel it in their interest to equate gambling and speculation. Critics of speculation, not surprisingly, found it a useful rhetorical device. "A great deal of condemnation was cast in England on the gambling that went on in Monte Carlo, and had taken place in Hamburg and other towns on the Continent," wrote one of them,

> but there at least the play took place on the green table, and was within sight of the public. In England, however, where no such public gaming was allowed, gambling on the price of stocks took place out of sight of the public for much larger sums, and, perhaps, with more mischievous results. (Meason, *Sir William* v)

Identical comparisons issued from the pens of gamblers eager not to condemn speculation but to defend gambling. "Having seen a good deal of gambling during the last few years," wrote the celebrated plunger Ernest Benzon, "I am unable to dissociate in my mind the man who plays regularly from the fellow who employs his time in dealing in stocks and shares, or earns his living buying articles which he hopes to sell at a profit" (Benzon 98).

This conventional rhetorical equation of speculation and gambling never disappeared; examples of it can be found in every decade of Queen Victoria's reign, as, for that matter, they can be found today. "Railway speculations . . . like all other gambling, is a fascinating, but delusive passion," wrote Henry Wilson in his 1845 pamphlet *Hints to Railroad Speculators* (5). "I cannot restrain myself from pointing out that there is a Gambling which hides its hideous features under the less offensive description of Speculation," agreed the Rev. Joseph Parker in his pamphlet *Gambling in Various Aspects,* which appeared over fifty years later (12).

But though the equation of gambling and speculation remained a constant of nineteenth-century discourse, it seems to have carried less and less practical force as the century progressed, except in the case of the new forms of speculation that will be described below. As early as the mid-1820s, a period marked by a noted speculative flurry, the London banker Alexander Baring had begun to articulate what would come, over the course of the century, to be the dominant view. "The evil" of speculation, he admitted,

> was certainly one which deserved to be checked; though he hardly knew how the check could be applied. The remedy would be worse than the disease, if, in putting a stop to this evil, they put a stop to the spirit of enterprise. That spirit was productive of so much benefit to the community, that he should be sorry to see any person drawing a line, discriminating between fair enterprise and extravagant speculation. (qtd. in Chancellor 109–10)

The difficulty of drawing the line between "fair enterprise" and "extravagant speculation" was to prove so great that most people stopped trying to draw it except for increasingly empty rhetorical purposes. By 1860, a member of the Palmerston government, defending the repeal of Sir John Barnard's Act, which had outlawed futures trading in certain securities, could declare that speculative trading was "the regular and ordinary form under which the whole of that vast and beneficial business of dealing in the funds was conducted" (3 *Hansard* 157: 1710).

By the end of the century, commentators as diverse as Francis Hirst, editor of the *Economist,* and W. W. Duncan, a speculative broker, were arguing that there was no real distinction between investment and speculation, and therefore, by implication, that both were distinct from gambling. For Hirst, the only thing that distinguished speculation from investment was the amount of risk involved. "The difference between investment and speculation cannot be defined accurately," he wrote, "but everyone has a rough idea of a line which divides safety, with the certainty of a reasonable interest, from risk, with all its possibilities of loss or profit" (Hirst 137). Though in the end, for purposes of discussion, he was willing to accept the conventional distinction between investment and speculation, he nonetheless observed that "even in an old and conservative country like England the average investor is a speculator" (180–81, 164). Duncan, as befitting his profession, was blunter. "As a matter of fact," he wrote, "investment and speculation are words with but slightly different meanings. . . . The investor receives his interest; the speculator his profit. Again a distinction without much difference" (Duncan 6–7).

In the end, the only separation that could be made was between legitimate speculation, no matter how difficult it might be to define legitimate speculation, and out-and-out gambling. Baring's reference to "extravagant speculation" is a hint of what was to come. As participants in the debates found themselves increasingly unable to distinguish between legitimate commerce on one hand and speculation on the other, all that remained to mark the difference were observations about the motive of the individual speculator. Gamblers and illegitimate speculators were somehow "extravagant" or "fevered," and the perceived absence of these traits could often be seen as one of the markers of the legitimate financial operator. As the speculative broker E. C. Maddison, no disinterested observer to be sure, put it in 1878, "speculation may, perhaps, be defined as enterprise carried to excess; it is only when the excess is extreme, and when speculation attains the form of mania, that it can be really hurtful in its results to the community generally" (Maddison 5; for a further elaboration of this point, see Jaffe in this volume, 151–52).

Speculation, to use Fabian's language, was becoming "domesticated" because people came to believe that, like investment and unlike gambling, it was a legitimate way to risk money. The clearest indication of this can be seen in the way that, beginning in the middle of the nineteenth century, the growth of legal restrictions on gambling was accompanied by the removal of most legal restrictions on speculation.

Limitations of space prevent a detailed discussion of these legal developments, but a brief examination of one aspect of the law is necessary to understand some of the later parts of this essay. The Gaming Act of 1845, it will be recalled, had, among other things, made "wagering contracts" unenforceable at law. In the words of one judge, a wager was made "a thing of a neutral character; not to be encouraged, but not to be absolutely forbidden; it leaves an ordinary betting debt a mere debt of honour, depriving it of legal obligation, but not making it illegal" (Stutfield 29).

Futures contracts, under which a party to a contract agrees either to buy or to deliver a commodity at some time in the future for a price agreed to at the time of the contract, are at the heart of speculation. But it could also be argued that they are a form of wager because the parties to the contract may be said to be betting on what the price will be at some future time. Were the commonest sort of speculative transactions, generally referred to as "time-bargains" or contracts for "differences," to be voided as wagering contracts?[2]

Though they had made wagering contracts unenforceable, Parliament seemed to have little difficulty accepting the legitimacy of speculative contracts. Sir John Barnard's Act (7 George II, c. 8), for example, which had outlawed futures trading in certain kinds of securities since 1734, was repealed in 1860 at the urging of the Palmerston government, many of whose members had also been in government at the time of the passing of the anti-gambling acts of 1853 and 1854. Though the repeal of Barnard's Act was attacked in the House of Commons as an encouragement to gambling, even the most prominent opponent of repeal, William Bovill, later Chief Justice of Common Pleas, declared that he "quite understood that it might be right and proper, in ordinary transactions on the Stock Exchange, that there should be contracts made which might be completed at a future day, and that contracts should be entered into by persons who at the moment might not be possessed of the stock which they contracted to sell" (3 *Hansard* 158: 914).

After the repeal of Barnard's Act in 1860, attempts to interfere through law in what was coming to be seen as the legitimate business of speculation virtually came to an end in the nineteenth century. There was one last flurry of activity in 1867, when, after several highly publicized bank failures, Parliament passed what came to be known as Leeman's Act, which prohibited the speculative trading of bank shares, but Leeman's Act was largely ignored in practice (Coldridge and Hawkford 218). The respectable members of the stock exchange could thus continue to enter into speculative bargains largely undisturbed by the laws of commerce. Instead, the greatest legal threat to speculative dealing came not from the laws that regulated commerce but from the laws that regulated gambling. Courts were to be confronted with the question of whether one or another instance of speculative dealing was to be construed as a wagering contract under the Gaming Act of 1845.

Shortly after the passage of that act, the decision in the case of *Grizewood v. Blane* (1851) seemed to pose precisely this threat to speculation. In this case, the parties had entered into a typical speculative agreement respecting the future price of some shares. The judge directed the jury that if they found, as a matter of fact, that, at the time of the original transaction, both parties understood that no actual delivery of shares was to take place, the transaction was void under the Gaming Act. The jury found that this was precisely the case and the contract was therefore voided (Stutfield 88).

But commenting on this case in 1886, G. Herbert Stutfield, a well-known expert on the law both of gambling and the stock exchange, wrote:

> This finding of the jury upon the facts of this case have been questioned in later cases, probably through the Courts being in possession of more complete information as to *the true nature of transactions on the Stock Exchange*. . . . From the cases to which we are about to refer, it would appear that in point of fact transactions never do take the form of contracts for the mere payment of differences. (Stutfield 88–89; emphasis added)

Stutfield's reference to the "true nature" of transactions on the stock exchange reflects what had emerged as the dominant view by the 1880s, a view that was actively promoted by professionals on the stock exchange and that came to be enshrined in court decisions and other official pronouncements. For purely technical reasons, transactions on the stock exchange were to be seen as legal, even if they might have the appearance of gambling. "The final result [of the typical speculative transaction] to the outside speculator is a gain or a loss," wrote a legal commentator in 1913:

> The result to the speculator may be the same as if he had entered into a mere difference transaction. But he has employed a different machinery, and has utilized separate legal obligations, which could have been specifically enforced, or for a breach of which damages of an ascertainable amount could have been recovered. (Coldridge and Hawkford 210)

This view also informed the report of the Royal Commission on the London Stock Exchange of 1878. Though the appointment of the commission had been prompted by claims that the exchange "was haunted by adventurers—Jews, Greeks, and so on" (*Times* 21 March 1877: 7), it included a number of sympathetic exchange members, including Nathaniel Mayer de Rothschild and S. R. Scott, chairman of the exchange's governing committee, who managed to diffuse any attacks on the morality of the exchange (London Stock Exchange Commission, *Report*). Although the question of gambling and speculation was not the major concern of the commission, a parade of carefully chosen exchange insiders all assured the commission that what looked to outsiders like gambling transactions were, in fact, something different and that the exchange was a vital part of the British economy. As long as the rules of the stock exchange required that all sales and purchases of stock obligated the parties to the transaction ultimately to deliver the stock that had been purchased, they claimed, there was no way to distinguish between a speculative bargain and an ordinary one.

This claim was disingenuous at best. Members of the exchange, whose rules barred them from transacting speculative business for clerks in public or private establishments without the knowledge of their employers, had no difficulty distinguishing speculative trading in that case. But when this point was raised during testimony, sympathetic members of the commission quickly distracted the attention of their colleagues (London Stock Exchange Commission, *Minutes* 275–76). Subsequent witnesses argued that there was, in fact, no difference at all between speculative transactions and other transactions, and one even argued that the only mark of an "illegitimate" speculation was the customer's knowledge that he could not afford to pay his obligations (313).

In the end, the commission had little choice but to accept what their witnesses had told them. "We do not think it is practicable to make bargains entered into for the purpose of speculation or gambling any more illegal than they are at present, and we do not propose any change in the law," they concluded (London Stock Exchange Commission, *Report* 21).

Thus, the conclusions of the Royal Commission harmonized nicely with the decisions rendered by the courts in the years following *Grizewood v. Blane*. As summed up by Stutfield in 1886, the general principle that was used by the courts was that though bargains for "mere differences" were wagers within the meaning of the act of 1845, for various technical reasons, speculative bargains transacted with brokers who were official members of the exchange were almost never considered "difference" bargains and hence were considered legitimate commercial transactions (103). The willingness of the commission, the courts, and other representatives of official opinion to accept this view is significant. There is, after all, no significant *moral* distinction between difference transactions and the kinds of transactions that had been legitimized by the 1880s. Speculation, its attendant risk, and its possibility of rapid gain had, to use Fabian's words, come to be seen as "essential ingredients in rational capitalis[m]" (3). The technicalities so eagerly seized upon by the spokesmen for official morality allowed those ingredients to be utilized without saddling speculation with the moral taint of gambling.

Despite their expression of confidence in the members of the exchange, the commission had gone on to note that they had no doubt that "gambling to an enormous extent" did exist in securities, leading to misery and bankruptcy on the part of those of "very limited means, who are not in such circumstances as to justify a broker in speculating for them" (London Stock Exchange Commission, *Report* 21). The commission, following the lead of their witnesses, blamed this state of affairs on the younger members of the exchange, who, presumably, needed the business. In fact, however, at precisely the time that the commission was issuing its report, speculative business was rapidly becoming the province of brokers who were not members of the exchange at all.

## The New World of Speculation

The late 1870s and 1880s saw the beginning of a new form of speculation that once again threatened the carefully constructed separation from gambling that had moralized and domesticated speculation. This new form was characterized by the appearance of a new group of speculators who were served by a new kind of broker. The new brokers resembled, in methods, style, and appeal, the professional bookmakers who had also come to prominence at about this time (Itzkowitz). Like the bookmakers, the new brokers called themselves to the attention of the public through aggressive advertising.

Promoting speculation through advertising was not in itself new. During the railway boom of the 1840s, railway promoters did not shrink from advertising their projects in their search for capital. New financial newspapers like the *Railway Courier and Stock Exchange Price-Current,* which began its brief life in 1845, carried advertisement after advertisement trumpeting the wonders of one or another projected railway line and soliciting for those who wished to invest their capital. These initial public offerings, as we would now call them, were, of course, highly speculative because there was no guarantee that the projected railway would ever be built, much less that it would be profitable. In fact, there did not need to be any relationship at all between the actual building of the railway and the profits to be gained by the investors, provided they were smart or lucky enough to sell their shares at a profit before the project collapsed. The anonymous author of *The Railway Investment Guide,* a one-shilling pamphlet published in 1845, openly advised prospective speculators that they could profit even if the railway was never built at all. All that was needed was for other investors to believe that it would be built (8). The *Guide* was, of course, a wholehearted puff for speculation. "The general rule is here suspended," it proclaimed, less than twenty years after the state lottery was abandoned in 1826,

> that what one wins, another must lose—and for this reason; additional capital, or what represents capital, has been, as it were, created and diffused, *from nothing....* Railway investment has in fact become a lottery (for it very closely resembles one in the uncertainty of the amount of profit) in which the chances are reversed, the prizes exceeding the blanks in number by as much as the latter are usually more numerous than the former. (5)

There were, to be sure, those who were somewhat less sanguine about the possibility of everyone "winning" in the great railway "lottery." Cautionary tales of speculative projects in railway building and in the floating of other, possibly fraudulent, "business opportunities" flourished from at least the late 1830s (among them, see MacFarlane; Meason, *Bubbles, Sir William;* Sinclair). Anthony Trollope's *The Way We Live Now* (1874–1875) is perhaps the best known and the most bitter of them, but it is hardly alone. For virtually all of these writers "speculation" referred to investing in new companies, and the great danger to be guarded against was fraud, rather than the moral dangers of gambling. There was a reason for their emphasis; these new ventures were a major outlet for speculative capital in the first half of the century.

A different form of speculation, buying existing stocks for an anticipated rise or fall in prices, was certainly not unknown in the early nineteenth century, but it became far more common after the passage of the Limited Liability Act of 1855 and the Companies Acts of 1856 and 1862 (Robb, *White-Collar* 11). Speculation in existing stocks and shares was facilitated by the particular rules of trading on the London Stock Exchange. Stocks bought or sold on the exchange did not, in fact, have to be delivered or paid for at the time of purchase. Instead, they could be held until the settling day, which occurred every two weeks for most securities and once each month for sales of the highly stable government securities known as "consuls." For that reason, virtually all transactions on the exchange were what we would now refer to as "futures," though the time between sale and delivery was relatively short.

By the middle of the nineteenth century, however, dealers and speculators had developed a mechanism to allow speculative purchases to be made in anticipation of a time frame longer than the single settling period. As the practice developed, *bulls,* those who had bought hoping for a price rise, could postpone having to accept, and pay for, the stock they had contracted to buy until the following settlement period—or the next "account" in the language of the exchange—but they had to pay a fee, known as a "contango," for the privilege. *Bears,* those who were hoping for a fall in prices, could also postpone delivery of stock they had contracted to sell until they could buy it at a lower price, and they, too, had to pay a fee, known as a "backwardation."[3] In theory, a speculator could "carry over" a transaction for as many accounts as he or she was willing to pay for.

By the 1870s, "speculation" was increasingly coming to refer to the speculative trading of existing stocks and shares. In 1874, "Dun Brown," a regular contributor to the *City Argus,* one of the mushrooming number of financial newspapers that began to appear in the 1870s, complained lightheartedly that brokers encouraged gambling in shares and stocks in order to increase their commissions. He and a friend, he wrote, had received contradictory advice about the same stock from the same broker. As a result, he claimed, he and his friend had given up buying stock altogether, and, instead, had taken to betting informally with one another on the performance of various stocks, thus saving the broker's commission. In the end, he called, not too seriously, for the establishment of a "bull and bear betting house" (10 January 1874: 4).

"Dun Brown's" suggestion was not, in fact, far off the mark. By the end of the 1870s, a number of enterprising brokers were establishing a business that came very close to being precisely that "bull and bear betting house." The progress of this new business can be followed in the increasingly strident advertisements that the brokers placed in the popular press, advertisements that in their form and their claims looked increasingly like those placed at the same time by bookmakers and horseracing tipsters.

Although members of the stock exchange were barred by its rules from advertising, there were many brokers who were not members of the exchange, and they were under no such restriction (Morgan and Thomas 166–67). As early as the 1840s, discrete advertisements from brokers had appeared in the financial press, but by the late 1870s, the nature of the advertising and the business began to change. "For reliable information on Foreign Stocks as well as Home Securities consult our MONTHLY PRICE LIST," advertised John Abbott and Company in 1878, "January Edition ready (post free) on application. . . . *Speculative Accounts opened on favorable terms*" (*City Mercury* 14 January 1878: 4; emphasis added). In that same year, Maddison and Company, which announced that it, too, was prepared to open "speculative accounts" for "responsible parties . . . for the bi-monthly settlement on favorable terms," issued a small pamphlet containing hints and advice for new speculative investors (Maddison, inside back cover).

The pamphlet was notable for admitting openly that "speculative investment" meant more than simply buying or selling stock in anticipation of price changes. "Speculative bargains," it stated,

> are those in which there is no intention to pay for or deliver the stock bought or sold, but where purchases will be closed by sales, and sales by purchases, at some

future time. Speculative purchases may therefore be made by persons not possessing sufficient money to pay for the stock bought, and speculative sales may be made by persons who are not possessed of stock. (9)

It is worth noting that Maddison and Company's pamphlet appeared in the same year that the Royal Commission on the Stock Exchange was hearing a parade of witnesses testify that all bargains on the exchange had to be closed by the actual delivery of stock.

Abbott and Maddison were among the pioneers of the new breed of "outside brokers" (so-called because they were not members of the stock exchange) or "bucket-shop" proprietors, as they were pejoratively named, who carried the business of speculating in stocks and shares to a wider public. By the standards of the next two decades, they were to appear staid. Over the course of the 1880s and 1890s, newspaper advertisements became more and more prominent and flamboyant. The small advertisements that had occupied no more than a few column inches gave way to quarter-page, half-page, and full-page advertisements touting the large profits to be earned by successful speculators.

Among the most prominent of the advertising brokers were Thomas Thompson, John Shaw, and George Gregory, who shared a verve and audacity that remains striking even in the opening years of the twenty-first century (see Fig. 1; readers who looked "below" found a third of a page of small print detailing the wonders of the Colon mine).

It was not just the use of advertising that marked the similarity between the new brokers and the bookmakers and tipsters who characterized the betting industry that flourished in late nineteenth-century England (see Clapson; Itzkowitz; McKibbin, "Working"). The two new industries resembled one another in style and appeal and probably in their customer base as well, though the latter is difficult to judge except by inference.

Like the large firms of credit bookmakers that advertised in the sporting newspapers, the outside brokers almost certainly dealt with middle-class clients rather than the poor, whose betting was done through illegal street bookmakers. The £5–10 required to open a speculative account with brokers like Gregory and Company was certainly beyond the reach of the poor. On the other hand, it seems likely that the outside brokers introduced speculation to a much wider audience than had been the case previously.

What may be most striking is the conflation of language between the two industries, which may be seen both among the brokers and among the bookmakers. Some brokers' ads adopted the language of betting directly. Thompson invited readers to consider "THREE GRAND MINING PRIZES" (*Society Herald* 15 October 1888), and H. Halford and Company, the "UP TO DATE BROKERS," who somehow managed to make a profit despite charging no fees, also capitalized on the language of sport and betting, advising their clients that "anyone can speculate and LOSE. We use all our skill and experience on speculating to WIN" (*Money and Trade* 30 January 1895; Fig. 2).

In a parallel development, bookmakers and sporting tipsters adopted the

THE OLDEST ESTABLISHED WEEKLY NEWSPAPER IN THE WORLD.

FOUNDED 1719 A.D. ENTERED AT STATIONERS' HALL.

# The Critic.

A Weekly Review of the Drama, Literature, Music, Art, Finance, and Other Things of Social Interest.

Edited by GEORGE EASTHALL WILLIAMS.

Offices for Advertisements and Publication, 9, 10, & 11, Cursitor Street, Chancery Lane, E.C.

VOL. CCCXLV., No. 4883. (VOL. III. No. XLIV.—NEW SERIES.) LONDON, SATURDAY, FEBRUARY 1, 1890. ONE PENNY.

# THOS. THOMPSON,

## STOCK AND SHARE DEALER,

## ANGEL COURT, LONDON, E.C.

AND

## MINING EXCHANGE, OLD BROAD ST., LONDON, E.C.

Telegraphic Address: "REMEMBRANCE," LONDON. Telephone No. 509.

*Bankers*:—CITY BANK, Limited, and METROPOLITAN AND BIRMINGHAM BANK, Limited.

Mr. THOMPSON transacts business in all classes of Securities, Bonds (Foreign and Colonial), Banks, Railways, Insurance, Telegraph, Tramway, Gas, Water, and all Miscellaneous Shares.

Shares sold at special prices for forward delivery (one, two, or three months) on deposit of 20 per cent.

A GIGANTIC RISE.—COLON GOLD SHARES, recommended originally in Mr. THOMPSON'S Circular at 3s., and now at 7s. 6d. to 8s. 6d., appear now on the eve of a big rise, possibly to £4 or £5.

*SEE BELOW.*

135,000 PER ANNUM.—See Notes on COLON MINE SHARES, recommended in MR. THOMPSON'S Circular at 3s, now at 7s. 6d. to 8s. 6d., and apparently on eve of great rise, possibly to £4 or £5.

*SEE BELOW.*

A BIG BOOM.—COLON MINE SHARES, recommended in MR. THOMPSON'S Circular at 3s., now at 7s. 6d. to 8s. 6d., and apparently on eve of great rise, possibly to £4 or £5.

*SEE BELOW.*

*"Nature is made to open her own Store-house."*

COLON.—The time is now close at hand—indeed, within a month or so—when all the preliminary work in connection with bringing a sufficiency of water on to the mines will be completed, and when the "hydraulic monitor" will be turned on with a view to washing and extracting the large quantities of gold which are believed to be lying dispersed over this great property. The time has accordingly arrived when we may begin with advantage to look over past reports and calculate for ourselves what may be the results which may be obtained.

Mr. Anderson, a well-known American Mining Engineer, wrote in a report published last year:

| | Dol. |
|---|---|
| From the results obtained from the two points opened we can form some idea of the nature and value of the ground, and its adaptability for hydraulic operations on a large scale. It appears from these two small prospects 105·80oz. coarse gold were obtained, value | 1937·7 |
| Cost of producing same by handwork, using 4in. to 6in. of water | |

with 500 inches, but this will shortly be augmented by a further 200 inches, and by the remaining quantity later on. But £270 (1,350dol.) profit in half a day! £540 in one day!! £135,000 profit over a year of 250 days!!! A dividend of 13s. each on shares now at only 7s. 6d. in the market!!!! Surely Colon gold shares ought to be bought at once.

Mr. W. S. Welton, Assoc. M. Inst. C.E. (the respected superintendent of the Gold Gravel Company, whose works, now being carried out, are about the largest of their kind in the world, Engineer to the Colombian Hydraulic, and who planned and laid out the enormous pipe of the Orita Company), writes in a report published about the same time as Mr. Anderson's:

The Colon deposit was worked by the Indians before the Spaniards arrived in the country, and the fame of the gold mines was so great that a special expedition was formed by the Spanish Government to gain possession of them. See "Historia General de los hechos de los Castillanos en las islas y tilna fume del mar oceans, 2nd edicion, Madrid, 1729." "Descrubemiento I fundacion de la Provincia de Sabandiga par el coronel Heraan Banegos, 1543." The only water then used was obtained from

500in. of water would do as much as 1,000in. at mines like the Colombian Hydraulic or Orita Company's mines. Estimated returns: From my personal experience of the deposit, I have no doubt that from 10,000dol. to 15,000dol. returns could be obtained per month, with a water supply of 500in. at a cost of 2,000dol., and I have every confidence in recommending this as a safe investment for capital.

Mr. Welton is cautious, but from his "personal experience" he puts the profits at from £1,800 to £2,800 per month, with 500in. of water, or, say, £3,600 to £5,600 with 1,000in., the smaller of which rates would be equal to an annual dividend of 4s. 4d., and the larger to about 6s. 9d. per share—a dividend which would probably bring the value of the shares up to £3 to £5.

By the way, the latest report is as follows:

Contractors work on Cristilina ditch—Lineal feet of ground cleared, 1,925; length of embankment excavated, 1,339ft. by 12ft. 6in. average width by 21ft. average height; length of ditch excavated and finished, 5,438ft.; number of workmen employed, 240. Company's account as per summary enclosed; Nature of

Figure 1. From the *Critic* 1 February 1890: 1. Courtesy the British Library.

language of trade and finance. Bookmakers called themselves "commission agents" and "turf accountants," as they strove for respectability (Itzkowitz 18). For bookmakers and their customers, bets increasingly were "investments" or "speculations," odds were referred to as "the state of the market," and winnings were "dividends," as they continue to be to this day for those who "invest" in the football pools. Robert Davey, a well-known bookmaker and sometime racing journalist, informed his clients in 1870 that he was willing to "negociate [sic] investments at starting prices on all races" (*Sporting Times* 24 September 1870: 312). By 1870, *Sporting Life*, the most important of the racing papers, had

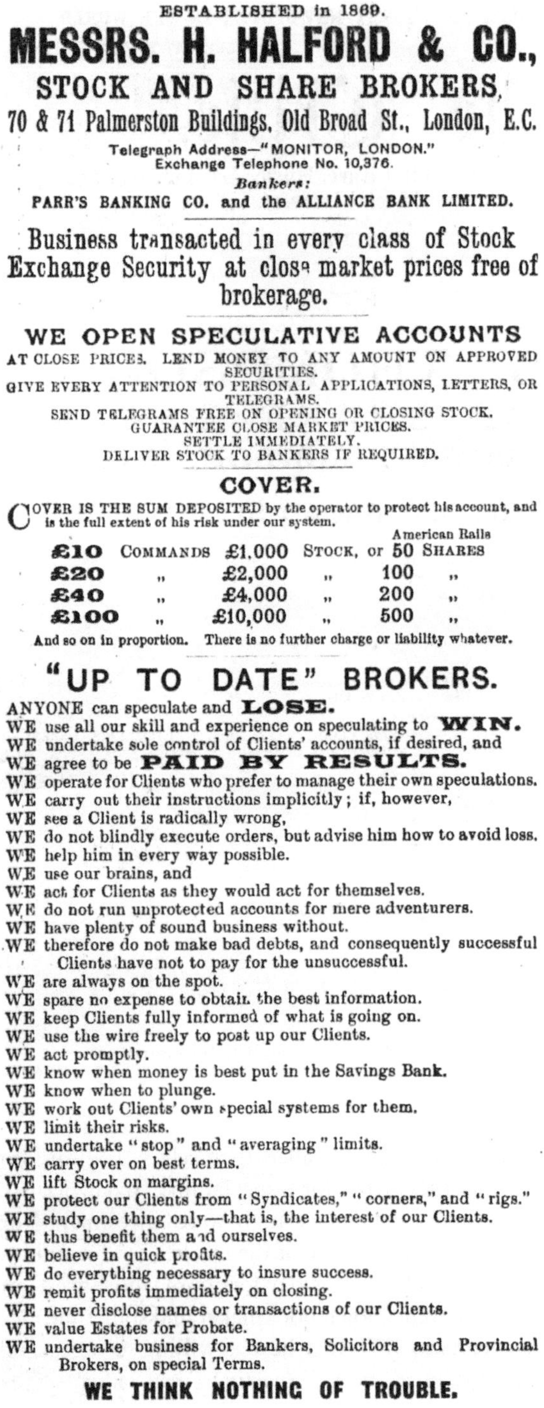

ESTABLISHED in 1869.

# MESSRS. H. HALFORD & CO.,

## STOCK AND SHARE BROKERS,

### 70 & 71 Palmerston Buildings, Old Broad St., London, E.C.

Telegraph Address—"MONITOR, LONDON."
Exchange Telephone No. 10,376.

*Bankers:*
PARR'S BANKING CO. and the ALLIANCE BANK LIMITED.

**Business transacted in every class of Stock Exchange Security at close market prices free of brokerage.**

## WE OPEN SPECULATIVE ACCOUNTS

AT CLOSE PRICES. LEND MONEY TO ANY AMOUNT ON APPROVED SECURITIES.
GIVE EVERY ATTENTION TO PERSONAL APPLICATIONS, LETTERS, OR TELEGRAMS.
SEND TELEGRAMS FREE ON OPENING OR CLOSING STOCK.
GUARANTEE CLOSE MARKET PRICES.
SETTLE IMMEDIATELY.
DELIVER STOCK TO BANKERS IF REQUIRED.

## COVER.

COVER IS THE SUM DEPOSITED by the operator to protect his account, and is the full extent of his risk under our system.

| | | | | American Rails |
|---|---|---|---|---|
| **£10** | COMMANDS | £1,000 | STOCK, or | 50 SHARES |
| **£20** | " | £2,000 | " | 100 " |
| **£40** | " | £4,000 | " | 200 " |
| **£100** | " | £10,000 | " | 500 " |

And so on in proportion. There is no further charge or liability whatever.

## "UP TO DATE" BROKERS.

ANYONE can speculate and **LOSE.**
WE use all our skill and experience on speculating to **WIN.**
WE undertake sole control of Clients' accounts, if desired, and
WE agree to be **PAID BY RESULTS.**
WE operate for Clients who prefer to manage their own speculations.
WE carry out their instructions implicitly; if, however,
WE see a Client is radically wrong,
WE do not blindly execute orders, but advise him how to avoid loss.
WE help him in every way possible.
WE use our brains, and
WE act for Clients as they would act for themselves.
WE do not run unprotected accounts for mere adventurers.
WE have plenty of sound business without.
WE therefore do not make bad debts, and consequently successful Clients have not to pay for the unsuccessful.
WE are always on the spot.
WE spare no expense to obtain the best information.
WE keep Clients fully informed of what is going on.
WE use the wire freely to post up our Clients.
WE act promptly.
WE know when money is best put in the Savings Bank.
WE know when to plunge.
WE work out Clients' own special systems for them.
WE limit their risks.
WE undertake "stop" and "averaging" limits.
WE carry over on best terms.
WE lift Stock on margins.
WE protect our Clients from "Syndicates," "corners," and "rigs."
WE study one thing only—that is, the interest of our Clients.
WE thus benefit them and ourselves.
WE believe in quick profits.
WE do everything necessary to insure success.
WE remit profits immediately on closing.
WE never disclose names or transactions of our Clients.
WE value Estates for Probate.
WE undertake business for Bankers, Solicitors and Provincial Brokers, on special Terms.

**WE THINK NOTHING OF TROUBLE.**

Figure 2. From *Money and Trade* 30 January 1895. Courtesy the British Library.

a regular column detailing the "latest market movements" (29 January 1870: 2), and, in 1875, the editors of *Sporting Opinion,* a racing newspaper that was little more than a tip sheet, informed their readers that "investments on First Favourites are modes of outlay much approved of by persons interested in Systematic Speculations" (1 June 1875: 4). To add to the confusion, an advertisement headed "profitable Speculations," inserted among ads for racing tipsters in *Sporting Life* in 1870, touted a mining stock. "It has this advantage, also, over betting," it read, "that what one gains it is not necessary another should lose" (26 March 1870: 1). One firm, A. E. Aston and Co. of Harrowgate, advertised both as "turf accountants" and as "stock and share brokers" (*National Sporting League Journal* June 1911: n.p.).

There was more going on here than just a conflation of language; there was also a conflation of practice and attitudes on both sides of the divide that separated gambling and speculation. The conflation allowed participants in both activities to view themselves simultaneously as sporting "men of the world" and as rational, calculating capitalists. Though horse racing was, traditionally, the pastime of the hearty sporting aristocrat, the mass betting industry centered on horse racing that flourished in England by the 1870s had created a new kind of bettor. Anti-gambling activists liked to claim that gamblers were enslaved by passion and sought an "unhealthy craving for continual excitement" (Carter 27), but, in fact, most of those who bet on horses believed, with some justification, that they were not simply throwing themselves on the winds of chance. The bettors, who followed the progress of their favorite horses in the sporting press and who risked their spare sixpence or shilling on the latest hope, looked for ways to calculate their best chances of winning. That is why the sporting press was able to flourish; it provided the information necessary to make rational choices (Itzkowitz 27).

Like those who bet on horse races, the new speculators, too, thought of themselves as rational actors and sought the advice of "experts" who could provide them with the sort of information that could make them winners. "It is a mistake to look upon speculation as a mere matter of 'luck,'" advised one of those experts in 1891. "Dame Fortune may, if kind, and you woo her with judgment, enlarge your profits, but *to win or not to win* is entirely a matter of play" (Ursa Minor 21).

At the same time, speculation was, by the 1880s at the latest, also becoming a form of entertainment and was entering into the same raffish bohemian world that was described by sporting and theatrical journalists. Although financial newspapers, like sporting ones, date from at least the eighteenth century, it was in the 1870s and 1880s that both really began to flourish. Some of the new financial papers were staid affairs that existed to provide information to serious investors and market professionals. Others, often short-lived, clearly existed for the new breed of speculator or those who liked to follow their doings vicariously. Like those sporting papers that were published by a particular bookmaker or tipster and that served to promote their primary business, some of the new financial newspapers were, themselves, little more than house organs for one or another broker. Others were independently owned but were dependent on the advertising of outside brokers, whose ads were often repaid by warm endorsements (*Capitalist* 26 January 1889: 644, 652).

Like the racing papers, the financial newspapers also employed their own tipsters to advise prospective speculators about one "good thing" or another. Even papers that tried to ignore the speculative market were forced by competition to come around. The *Financial Adviser: A Weekly Journal for the Protection of Investors and Sound Enterprises,* which had claimed to stand for the interests of serious investors, not speculators, sheepishly pointed out that it was "rather against our original intentions that we find ourselves in the position of successful tipsters" (23 October 1886: 49).

One of the most striking examples of the transformation was the case of *Barker's Trade and Finance.* From its beginnings, in 1886, it attempted to be a serious publication. It regularly carried an advertisement, inserted by its owners, the banking and brokerage firm Barker and Company, condemning speculation as "a new form of gambling" (4 January 1888: 18). Though Barker and Company continued to attack speculation in its advertising, Barker's newspaper began to carry a new feature in 1888, a column entitled "Our Indicator," which promised to give an opinion "as to the probable rise or fall of certain stocks and shares *during the next few days*" (emphasis added). The tips, it informed its readers, would be based on "*reasons known to us, but which cannot be published*" (19 September 1888: 16; emphasis added).

Like racing tipsters, financial tipsters traded on supposed inside information. As Mary Poovey has argued, a "tension between the imperative to disclose facts about finance and the incentive to keep aspects of the financial institutions hidden was essential to the [Victorian] financial system's success" (Poovey, this volume 49). Would-be speculators were well aware of the fact that, as outsiders, they were at the mercy of those with inside information and looked to the financial tipsters to even the playing field. Ironically, of course, the search for inside information highlighted the suspicion that the financial system might not be entirely on the up-and-up. The tipsters were not just providing information; they were, in the minds of their readers, helping to keep the system honest. Like racing tipsters, financial tipsters also trumpeted their successes. "We last week anticipated a 'bullish' market, and its course has completely confirmed our prediction," wrote "Our Indicator." "Without exception as will be seen below, the stocks and shares we named for a rise went up" (26 September 1888: 16).

The addition of "Our Indicator" was not the only step taken by *Barker's Trade and Finance* to survive in the competitive market. In the same year that it added its tipster, it also announced the addition of "new features," which included free gifts, prize competitions, and a certificate that guaranteed the purchaser of the paper a free fourteen-day life, disability, and partial disablement insurance policy (28 March 1888: 4). Though it continued to carry serious financial news, *Barker's Trade and Finance* also added jokes and gossip, and changed its name, first to *Barker's Trade, Finance, and Recreation* and then simply to *Trade, Finance, and Recreation.* It was joined on the newsstands by journals with such titles as the *Associator: A Monthly Journal of Fact, Fiction, and Finance;* the *City Mercury: A Journal of Finance, Society, Literature, Sport, and the Drama;* the *Critic: A Weekly Review of the Drama, Literature, Music, Art, Finance, and Other Things of Social Interest; Mammon: A Sunday Paper for Investors, Speculators, and Sportsmen;* and the *Society Herald: A Weekly Record of Social, Political, Theatrical, Literary and Financial Events.* These papers, which printed a mixture of gossip, jokes, anecdotes, reviews, and contests, were indistinguishable in tone and barely distinguishable in content from the organs of sporting Bohemia like the raffish *Sporting Times,* better known as *The Pink 'Un* for the tinted paper on which it was printed. *Mammon,* the third newspaper to carry that evocative title between 1889 and 1907, described itself as "written by men of the world, for men of the world" (16 June 1907: 7), and carried advertisements for bookmakers as well as financial news. One short-lived "financial" paper, *Stock Exchange Answers,* blurred the lines between speculation, gambling, and entertainment even further by running what it trumpeted as "the latest thing in financial journalism . . . our 'bull' and 'bear' competitions." The competition invited readers to compete for a £10 prize by predicting the stock that would have the greatest rise or fall in the coming week (8 December 1892: 8). "Skill competitions" of this sort, so-called to disguise the fact that they were lotteries of dubious legality, were a regular feature of a number of late nineteenth-century papers and magazines. One of them, *The Prize Winner,* which was published by the management of *The Pink 'Un,* consisted of nothing but "skill competitions." The extent of the "skill" needed to win may be gauged by the fact that its short-story competition could be entered simply by sending in a story clipped from the pages of a book or magazine.

The new world of speculation was, therefore, blurring at least two lines, one that separated gambling from legitimate financial risk and one that divided serious economic activity from frivolous amusement. Neither of those lines could easily be drawn again. Nevertheless, Victorian society did attempt, however imperfectly, to redraw at least the first of them.

### Redrawing the Line

> Stretched upon the stones with a step for a pillow, the bloody form lay—pallid, motionless, *dead.* Poor Boxer had closed his account!
>
> —*Lost in a Bucket Shop: A Story of Stock Exchange Speculation* (Scotter 77)

The great innovation of the brokers of the 1880s was what came to be called the "cover system," which was advertised as a great advantage to speculators, though in fact it was of greater benefit to the brokers. A prospective client could deposit a sum of money, known as "cover," with a broker and the broker would then use that money—usually only a tiny fraction of the face value of the stock that was being speculated in—to speculate on the client's behalf, and the client was guaranteed that losses in the market could not exceed the sum that had been deposited as cover.

"The system of a Broker guaranteeing his Clients immunity from loss beyond a certain fixed amount in an ordinary speculative account . . . [was] practically unknown until we introduced [it] to the public," boasted W. Gutteridge and Company in 1882. "We are prepared," Gutteridge declared,

> to buy or sell any amount of either Railway or Foreign Stocks (from £500 nominal value), upon a deposit cover of Two per cent (£20 per £1,000), with a guarantee of no further liability to the operator beyond the amount deposited.
>
> The comparative safety to a client by the adoption of this plan can readily be seen when dealing in highly fluctuating stocks, we taking the risk of closing the stock when the cover is run off. All we require you to do is to select the stock you wish to operate in, no matter how speculative in character, and forward us cover to the extent you wish to Bull or Bear it, and we will guarantee to do the business at close market price of the moment, and immunity from further loss beyond your deposit. (Gutteridge 8)

Precisely what "risk" Gutteridge and Company was taking in closing the account when the limit of the cover was reached is not clear. In fact, the broker was guaranteed to make money from his commission whatever happened to the stock, and the cover system was a greater protection for the broker than for the client, because the broker never had to take the risk of the client being unable to come up with the full extent of his losses. In addition, because the broker immediately closed the account the moment that the price of the stock fell enough to exhaust the cover, the investor would lose everything even if the price of the stock went up again before the settling day. Since the cover charged by most brokers was no more than 1 or 2 percent, it did not require much of a downward movement for the cover to be exhausted (Poley 265).

By the end of the 1880s, some brokers had even managed to figure out a way to advertise that they not only limited the client's risk but also took no commission. "Our business," announced George Gregory and Company in 1889,

> was established some months prior to any other institution of a similar nature, in order to enable the public to avoid the onerous commissions charged by Brokers upon Stock Exchange transactions. . . . The price at which we deal with Clients is the close market quotation of the moment; for example, Consols being quoted 99¾ to ⅞, we sell at 99⅞, or buy at 99¾, and the difference between such buying and selling prices invariably constitutes our only profit. (Gregory 9; Fig. 3)

Critics of outside brokers often accused them of never actually buying the stocks at all but simply acting as stock exchange bookmakers. The fact that Gregory charged no commission on "speculative accounts" but did, in fact, charge commission on "investments" (purchases where the client actually wished to hold the stock for the purpose of income) and that they advertised that they would "act as Brokers if required," raising the question of just what they were doing when they opened speculative accounts, suggests that the critics may well have been right (20).

Figure 3. George Gregory. Cover of pamphlet *Hints to Speculators and Investors in Stocks and Shares*. London: George Gregory, [1889]. Courtesy the British Library.

Gregory even suggested to its clients that the absence of commissions made it possible for them to take small profits by closing and opening their accounts in a particular stock "once or twice, even in a single day," anticipating the practice of "day-trading" that achieved such notoriety in the 1990s. Most important, of course, was the assertion that while losses were strictly limited by the cover system, the "profits [were] not limited" (10).

The new brokers, or bucket-shop keepers as they were known, were vilified and ridiculed by anti-gambling activists and defenders of "legitimate" speculation alike. C. J. Scotter's novel *Lost in a Bucket Shop: A Story of Stock Exchange Speculation* (1890) was perhaps typical in its depiction not only of the bucket shop but also of the grotesque characters that frequented it. "We get all the riff-raff," observed one bucket-shop regular in the novel. "It's strange but true, that if a man can't hold his head up in any other part of the City, he'll find himself perfectly at ease about the stock markets" (28). But, as this passage suggests, even the attack on the bucket shops and their customers was often framed not as an attack on speculation per se, but as a commentary on the moral weaknesses of those who engaged in this particular kind of speculation.

The members of the stock exchange, of course, expressed contempt for the outside brokers, though many members were not above doing business with them. In 1894 the exchange forced the Exchange Telegraph Company, the firm that ran the telegraphic stock ticker, to remove their machines from the offices of the outside brokers. But many outside brokers were able to receive the latest prices in other ways, including paying members of the exchange to provide them (Kynaston 102–103).

The appearance of the bucket shops had the effect of drawing a new line between legitimate and illegitimate speculation. They allowed even ardent anti-gambling activists like the members of the National Anti-Gambling League to soften their tone toward other forms of speculation, which could now be seen as at least quasi-legitimate because they did not involve the obvious gambling that characterized the bucket shops. In 1893, for example, the League drafted and unsuccessfully proposed a bill that would have declared the offices of brokers who were "not subject to the limitations as to advertising and other rules of the stock exchanges" to be common gaming houses (*Bulletin* November 1893: 75). Similarly, in the important collection of anti-gambling essays edited by B. Seebohm Rowntree in 1905, A. J. Wilson, author of the essay on "Stock Exchange Gambling," felt the need to absolve the "legitimate" brokers of blame for the gambling that went on. The great majority of the members of the exchange, he assured his readers, were men "as upright, as humane and high-principled as could be found among any body of merchants in the world. It is not their fault but their misfortune that the spirit of unbridled lust after unearned wealth should so continually strive for the mastery and so often become dominant in their business" (Rowntree 45–46).

Most importantly, the law, which by now protected the speculative business that was done on the official exchange, withheld that protection from the outside brokers. Like bookmakers, outside brokers were at the mercy of unscrupulous clients who could refuse to pay their obligations on the grounds that the contracts that they had entered into were wagering contracts and hence void under the Gaming Act of 1845. It was often cases arising out of this sort of circumstance that wound up in the courts, and, typically, judges instructed juries to ascertain whether the contracts were, in fact, pure wagering contracts. To protect themselves, outside brokers often inserted language in their contracts specifying that the bargains were, in fact, bona fide ones, under which the buyers of stock were obligated to accept the stock and sellers were obligated to deliver it (Poley 266, 269–70), but judges ruled that such language was irrelevant if the facts of the case supported the conclusion that the contract was a wagering one. John Shaw, for example, who sometimes needed more than a full page of newsprint to lay out his past successes and current recommendations (*Financial Adviser* 23 October 1886: 64–65), found himself in court in 1899 under his real name, Gieve, as former clients fought for a share of his possessions following his bankruptcy. In ruling on the validity of one claim, the judge pointed to Gieve's contracts, which specified the price for a certain transaction "plus 1/8th if stock is taken up." "The expression, 'if taken up,'" he wrote, "shows plainly that the parties do not intend that the stock shall be taken up; that the buyer need not take it up unless he chooses, but that if he does he is to pay the extra one-eighth. This is not, on the very face of it, therefore, a bargain for sale or purchase at all" (Poley 269–71).

Court decisions like this one did not put the outside brokers out of business. Like bookmakers, some of them flourished, though others eked out only a marginal living (Kynaston 62). But, like bookmakers, they could not always count on the law to protect them against unscrupulous clients, which is one reason why they needed the protection of the cover system.

Law is, of course, based on making fine distinctions between one kind of behavior and another, and there were clear technical differences between the kinds of speculative dealings that were done inside and outside the official exchange. But the significance that is assigned to those technical differences is another matter altogether. By making those technical differences the crux of the distinction between legitimate speculation and gambling, the Victorian authorities did more than leave the outside brokers on the outside, legally, morally, and institutionally. They also created a set of definitions that not only delegitimized the activities of the outside brokers and their clients but relegitimized the activities of the members of the exchange.

## Conclusion

In the end, late Victorian society reaffirmed the distinction between fair enterprise and extravagant speculation, between legitimate commerce and illegitimate gambling. But though the categories—commerce and gambling—remained the same, and though they remained on opposite sides of the line that divided the legitimate from the illegitimate, the contents of the categories had changed. Some forms of speculation had become respectable, others had become disreputable, but the artificiality of the distinction and the difficulty in asserting it became sharper as a result. The historical actors we have looked at could not always grasp the distinction themselves. The outside brokers and their customers, like the horseracing gamblers they resembled, did not believe that their activities transgressed against the mores of their culture. In the end, society told them that they were wrong.

It might be tempting to believe that it was simple snobbery and class prejudice that accounted for the distinctions; that it was individuals who were seen as respectable or disreputable, not their activities; that society legitimized the respectable members of the stock exchange and excluded the "riff-raff." No doubt there is some validity to this explanation, but it is not sufficient to understand what was happening.

The "domestication" of speculation that had characterized the first half of the nineteenth century, necessary as it might have been for economic reasons, was still too new for people to be fully comfortable with it. Anxieties about the infiltration of the commercial system by gambling never totally disappeared. They lingered, often just beneath the surface, and were at least partially responsible for the continued existence of the discourse that equated speculation and gambling.

The development of what I have called the new speculation allowed those anxieties to come to the surface once again just at the moment that speculation had become respectable. The activities of the bucket shops looked too much like gambling for comfort, and the "regular and ordinary form of that vast and beneficial business of dealing in the funds" (3 *Hansard* 157: 1710) could again be tainted by association. Speculative capitalism could retain its moral status only by differentiating itself from its sporting near-relative. By the end of the century, it was no longer possible to eliminate the bucket shops and their customers. But by ensuring that the new brokers continued to operate in a world of only semi-respectable legality, the late Victorians reassured themselves that they were, in fact, moral people even as they continued to reap the profits of "fair enterprise."

## Notes

Research on this paper was supported by grants from the National Endowment for the Humanities and the De Witt Wallace Research Fund of Macalester College. I would like to thank Daniel Itzkowitz, Vicki Itzkowitz, James Brewer Stewart, the editors of the special issue of *Victorian Studies* on "Victorian Investments," and the anonymous reviewers for their careful reading of the manuscript and their helpful suggestions.

1. A wagering contract is a contract with two essential characteristics: "First, an unascertained event; secondly, the parties to the contract must stand respectively either to gain or lose, according as the uncertainty shall be determined in the one way or in the other. The consideration for the contract consists in the mutual promises to pay made by the parties one to the other, according to the event of the uncertainty" (Coldridge and Hawkford 1).

2. There is a legal distinction between a *time* bargain, which is simply a bargain

to be settled at some future time, and a *difference* bargain, in which one party pays the other the difference between the buying and selling price of a speculative commodity. Nineteenth-century commentators, particularly those who were not lawyers, often used the terms interchangeably. Though the legality of time bargains seemed uncertain at the beginning of the nineteenth century, the legality of most of them was established in 1839 by the decision in the case of *Hibblewhite v. M'Morine* (Fellows 10).

3. The *Oxford English Dictionary* cites the first use of *bull* and *bear* to refer to those who speculate for the rise and fall of prices, respectively, in 1714; it cites the first use of *backwardation* in 1850, and *contango* in 1854, though Ranald Michie traces the practice back into the eighteenth century (Michie 22).

# 6   Ladies of the Ticker

## Women, Investment, and Fraud in England and America, 1850–1930

*George Robb*

Traditional assumptions of women's absence from business activity during the nineteenth century rest on very little evidence. Is it really likely that the well-documented profusion of eighteenth-century women shopkeepers and traders (the "she-merchants" of Georgian London and Colonial America) simply vanished with the Industrial Revolution?[1] Yet even the presumed absence of women entrepreneurs is only part of the picture. The industrial economy of the Victorian period was fundamentally different from the mercantile economy of the seventeenth and eighteenth centuries, and women could participate in it in ways that have largely gone unstudied.[2]

The new economy was dominated by joint-stock companies, which were financed by the investments of the faceless thousands—women as well as men. The period between the Railway Mania of the 1840s and the Great Depression of the 1930s was one of almost continuous commercial expansion in both Great Britain and the United States. The rise of banking, insurance, and an active market in stocks and bonds created important investment opportunities for the propertied classes (Poovey, *Financial*). Shareholding had special appeal for middle-class women, who were denied access to the professions and largely excluded from entrepreneurial activities but who might still have a need to make money, especially if they were unmarried.[3] Yet, while the corporate economy welcomed capital investments from women, it offered them little protection from unscrupulous promoters and managers.

Throughout the nineteenth century laissez-faire economics reigned supreme on both sides of the Atlantic. Anglo-American company law enshrined the principle of caveat emptor, placing few obstacles in the paths of aggressive entrepreneurs. There were no legal specifications as to the keeping of proper books and accounts, nor was there a mandatory audit for most joint-stock companies. The guidelines for prospectuses and advertisements were equally vague so that the public had little information on which to base its investment decisions. The proponents of classical economic theory in both England and America argued that the market was self-regulating, that good reputations would drive out bad, and that government oversight would undermine individual responsibility (Robb, *White-Collar* 147–68).

Although all investors suffered under this regime, women were especially vulnerable to its abuses, as they were usually much less knowledgeable about business matters than men and had less access to good sources of financial information or advice.[4] From childhood a gendered educational system emphasized polite accomplishments and domestic skills for girls, while boys were more likely to read works of political economy or to learn bookkeeping and the rudiments of accounting (Burstyn 48–69; Turnbull). Many men who invested in shares were themselves businessmen or professionals whose work brought them into contact with financiers, bankers, and lawyers. These men dined and drank together in pubs, coffee houses, and restaurants in urban business districts, and they socialized together in clubs and fraternal lodges. Such exclusively male spaces often contained trade journals like the *Railway Times* or the *Bankers' Magazine* and other important sources of financial advice such as the *Economist* or *Financial Times*. More importantly, clubs and coffee shops were places where business deals were cemented and information was shared and traded about all manner of investment opportunities. Women were largely excluded from these circles and sources of information (Preda 210–20; Rotundo 194–221). The fact that so many Victorian and Edwardian women's magazines published articles explaining the rudiments of finance also presupposed an ill-informed audience, though one that was hungry for such knowledge (see, for example, Field; Green, "Why"; and "How May").

This period of a burgeoning and largely unregulated share market coincided with intense debates over women's "nature" and their proper role in society. While the Victorian era is usually characterized as a restricted time for women, it also saw the birth of an organized women's movement in both England and America. Middle-class women in particular sought greater political participation, more control over their own property, and new educational opportunities to free themselves from economic dependence on men. Feminists were quite critical of an economic system that marginalized women and provided few protections against exploitation or abuse (Caine 27–42; Levine 82–101). Traditionalists countered that female emancipation would undermine the foundations of a stable society by destroying women's essential purity and by exposing the domestic realm to the corrupting influences of the marketplace. Financial chicanery and the dangers of speculation were invoked by both conservatives, who cited them as evidence that the business world was too insecure for women, and reformers, who saw fraud as proof that an economic system in which men held most of the cards was untenable.

This study is one of the first to look at British and American women's financial activities together, rather than as distinct national cases. As I have tried to argue, there are important similarities in the economic development of Britain and America during the nineteenth century. Both nations shared similar traditions of common law and company law, both were strongly influenced by the principles of classical political economy, and both experienced the same international trade cycles and financial crises. The British and American women's movements also shared many grievances and goals, including a strong concern for women's property rights and economic independence from men. A common language also meant that economic and cultural debates, and their attendant literatures, moved easily across the Atlantic. For example, the same financial advice manuals were often published simultaneously in London and New York (Atwood; Cromwell). Of course there were also differences in British and American business culture. As this chapter will point out, in the United States, unlike in England, it was sometimes possible for a woman to manage a bank or act as a broker. This might be attributable to less rigid gender roles in the States, though it could also be due to a more libertarian and freebooting American economic system that allowed a few enterprising women to operate at its margins.

\* \* \*

The Victorians frequently noted the prevalence of women investors. As an American stockbroker observed in 1880, "On almost any bright day, when stocks are rising, a dozen or more showy carriages may be seen drawn up in front of the offices of prominent brokerage houses, waiting for the gorgeous dames who ride in them to come out, when they have transacted their business with their brokers" (Fowler 449). An 1893 article in *All the Year Round,* the journal founded by Dickens, also noted with surprise the large number of women converging on the Bank of England on "Dividend Day":

> One does not associate youth and beauty with the sweet simplicity of the three per cents . . . but here they are, nevertheless, and giving the asthmatic old annuitant the go by in the race to the Bank counters. Lady Lackpenny was a little surprised when her pretty housemaid asked for a morning's leave to go and "draw her dividends," but she acceded with gracious alacrity. And the governess element is well represented, pale faces growing paler and more faded year by year, but brightening up in the reflection of the pink dividend warrant. ("Dividend" 462)

While both writers poke fun at women investors, they also clearly acknowledge their significance to the economy. Economic historians, however, have only begun to recognize that women made up a substantial portion of those with financial resources. For example, a pioneering study of the backgrounds of Victorian shareholders, L. E. Davis and R. A. Huttenback's *Mammon and the Pursuit of Empire,* found that women represented about 8 percent of their sample of eighty thousand British shareholders (195–220). This figure alone would account for hundreds of millions of pounds invested by women. This general cross-section, however, probably underestimates the even greater role women had in financing certain key sectors of the economy, such as government bonds, banks, railways, utilities, and debentures (loan securities)—which were often recommended to women as safe, low-risk investments. Indeed, the 1852 House of Lords Select Committee on the "Better Government of Her Majesty's Indian Territory" may have been startled to learn that half of the East India Company's Court of Proprietors (who elected the company's directors) were women (Henry, "Ladies" 117).

Railways were one key business that eagerly sought female investment, and women proved vital in raising railway capital. In his study of British railway shareholdings, M. C. Reed found that women investors in the Great North of England Railway grew from 9 percent of shareholders in 1836 to 13 percent in 1845. Women shareholders in the Newcastle and Carlisle Railway increased from 6 percent in 1825 to 12 percent in 1844, and the total sum of their share capital more than quadrupled, from £3,900 to £16,200. At the height of the Railway Mania in 1847, women held almost 18 percent of the £25 shares in the Great Eastern Railway. Women's share of railway loan capital (debentures) was even more significant. For instance, women made up 22 percent of the lenders to the Great North of England Railway, and their average loan was more than £1,500. Over 30 percent of the debenture holders for the Liverpool and Manchester Railway were women during the 1840s (Davidoff and Hall 211; Reed 183–90, 256–57). Yet even these impressive figures probably underestimate the full measure of women's capital investment, since they only count shareholders designated as "widow" or "spinster." In England, married women's shares would have been listed under their husbands' names until the 1880s.[5]

Women frequently comprised the majority of both depositors and shareholders in Victorian banks (Anderson and Cottrell 598–615). For instance, during the 1850s, women accounted for 50 percent of the shareholders in the Northumberland and Durham Bank in the North of England. Returns from the London joint-stock banks in 1856 similarly showed that women comprised a high proportion of the banks' shareholders ("London"; "Northumberland"). A recent study of Philadelphia savings banks during the 1850s also found that 58 percent of depositors were women. Women held the majority of the banks' shares as well (Alter, Golden, and Rotella). Bankers certainly recognized the importance of women as sources of capital, and many banks maintained special facilities for "ladies." By the 1890s, the mark of a discriminating institution was its ladies' entrance and ladies' department. A surviving photograph from 1906 shows one such location, the ladies' parlor of the New Amsterdam National Bank in New York City. Here elegantly dressed women write checks at mahogany desks or rest on plush chairs, surrounded by gilt mirrors, Turkish carpets, and potted palms. In the background, a uniformed black maid pours out tea from a silver service (Byron plate 100; see Fig. 4).

During the speculative boom of the 1920s, a number of brokerage firms also established special "ladies rooms." A magazine article in the *North American Review* described one such establishment in New York, where women could take "a hand in man's most exciting capitalistic game." Nestled "among the smart specialty shops" on Fifth Avenue,

[i]t might almost have been a club. The same discreet lighting, the cavernous davenports, an occasional bronze. In deep Florentine armchairs a dozen women lounged and smoked. But at one end of the room their gaze was transfixed by a wide moving ribbon of light. "PAK—3/4 . . . BDLA—1/2"—the cabalistic symbols glided across the magnified ticker tape. At the blackboard two blue-smocked girls, their leather

Figure 4. Ladies Department, New Amsterdam National Bank, 1906. Museum of the City of New York, the Byron Collection.

belts bulging with cardboard checks, sprang nimbly about, changing the posted stock prices to correspond. (Barnard 405)

A "sprucely tailored woman manager" supervised a cadre of "young assistants, smartly turned out as so many mannequins." Adjoining the trading room was "a miniature beauty salon ... to raise the spirits in time of loss." Apparently few resented the sex-segregated quarters. "'Men,' said a woman broker, 'do not want us in their board rooms. And I am sure,' she added, surveying her interior-decorated domain, 'we do not want a lot of men smoking cheap cigars in here'" (405–406, 410).

As advertisements in women's magazines attest, brokerage houses and banks frequently sought out women investors. In June 1913, the feminist journal the *Awakener* carried a full-page ad announcing the opening of Farrow's Bank for Women in London, purportedly the first bank exclusively for women, where "ladies find a courteous and obliging staff of their own sex, ready to assist them in any and every detail of Banking and Finance." The ad asserted that "the woman of today occupies a far different position in the sphere of influence and activity than did even her own mother, so rapid has been her advance. With her entry into business life and the professions fresh needs have arisen." Farrow's Bank not only provided women premises in which to conduct business but also touted a room "set apart as a Rendezvous," in which they might "keep appointments of a personal and professional nature, conduct correspondence and peruse newspapers, magazines and other literature" ("Farrow's Bank for Women" 11).

Although women played an important role in financing the industrial economy, they had very little control over their assets. In the United States, New York became the first state to give married women rights to their own property in 1848. In England, married women's property was under their husbands' management until 1870.[6] In those rare cases where a wife's property was held in trust for her, the trustees were usually male relatives who frequently used her capital to further their own economic interests (Davidoff and Hall 209). Yet even single women were hard-pressed to negotiate the world of investment. Bourgeois notions of gentility required that women remain ignorant of money matters. Some writers, like Harriet Martineau and Jane Marcet, tried vainly to reverse this trend by penning novels for young women that illustrated principles of political economy, banking, and investment. Marcet's *Conversations in Political Economy* (1816) went through six editions by 1839. Martineau's *Illustrations of Political Economy* was serialized in monthly parts from 1832 to 1835, selling as many as ten thousand copies a month. Many parents and educators, however, still felt that these subjects were not suitable for girls. Oscar Wilde later satirized this attitude in *The Importance of Being Earnest,* where Cecily's governess, Miss Prism, warns her to omit "the chapter on the Fall of the Rupee" from her political economy text, as "it is somewhat too sensational. Even these metallic problems have their melodramatic side" (276).

Suburban living and separate spheres ideology meant that women were (or were supposed to be) a rare sight in the City or on Wall Street, at banks, or at the stock exchange. Even their attendance at shareholders' meetings was frowned on. For instance, at the Great Eastern Railway's annual meeting in 1889, only one female shareholder, Fanny Hemsley, was present, although numerous women held shares in the company. As late as the 1920s, women still attended these meetings in very small numbers (Great Eastern Railway, company records). An American stockbroker facetiously defended women's exclusion from business premises: "It is well, however, that women rarely come in person into the stock-market to look after their interests. One can easily imagine the effect produced by several hundred women interested in stocks, being present at a panic and giving way with feminine impulsiveness to the feelings of the hour" (Fowler 456). Women were presumably too prone to hysterics and lacked the equanimity and levelheadedness necessary to conduct their own business dealings.

As Davidoff and Hall emphasize in *Family Fortunes,* the rise of the business corporation "shifted the world of women even further from the power of the active market." The structure of the new corporate economy was based on the separation of ownership and control. The rising scale of organization increased the distance between the nominal owners, the shareholders, and the active directors and heightened the impersonality of this relationship. The active money managers (bankers, brokers, trustees, directors) were always men. Women were more likely than men to be "the beneficiaries of 'passive' property yielding income only: trusts, annuities, subscriptions and insurance" (272–79). The passive nature of company investment seemed especially appropriate for women, whose dependence on men was increasingly underscored by both gender ideology and the structure of the new economy.

Since women of property were denied access to most professions and barred from active participation in economic matters, one could argue that they were dependent on the riskiest and most vulnerable kind of economic activity: "gambling" on the stock market. Single women were especially at risk in the game of speculation, as large numbers of them made up the ranks of the genteel poor—people who by birth or position were members of polite society, but whose incomes were so low that they were hard-pressed to maintain social standing. Often all that stood between such women and financial ruin was a small annuity or the yearly dividends from joint-stock investments (F. Low 405–17). Widows and spinsters were often tempted by risky and speculative promotions that promised them large returns for their modest capitals. The plight of such women was captured with feeling by an article in *Blackwood's* in 1876:

> Take a mother who has been left a widow with £5,000 and a rising family. "Put the money safely away in the funds; it would be sheer insanity to do anything else with it," says one friend of the family when she asks for advice as to its disposal; and he steps complacently into his carriage and is driven smilingly away. Another gentleman, a shade less scrupulous, is disposed to admit of first-class railway debentures, although he takes care to dwell on possible fluctuations to the extent of two to three percent. Very good! The lady acts on the advice of one or the other. But she finds that with her £150 to £220, she is not only embarrassed as to providing food, clothing, and houseroom for her growing family, but that she is compromising their future beyond remedy, from better fortunes. She is falling out of the circle of family acquaintance where her boys would be likely to find helpful friends and her girls to make happy marriages. She is unable to give them the education indispensable to their taking advantage of future opportunities. If she is to persevere in pinching, she condemns them to sink to an inferior grade of life, unless something in the nature of a miracle comes to save them. So, sorely against the grain, and at first in mortal apprehension, she has recourse to some of those more highly priced stocks which are the refuge of the widow, the clergyman, and the reckless. (Shand 294–95)

Impecunious investors like this imaginary widow were also easy prey for swindlers and frauds. As a London detective wrote in the 1870s, "it is a curious reflection that people who have the least money to spare are those from whom the professional swindler derives in many instances the largest revenue" ("A Detective" 37).

Considerable evidence exists that women were sought out as victims by frauds and embezzlers who well understood their vulnerability. During the 1860s, for example, the shady company promoter Albert Grant compiled lists of widows, spinsters, and other small investors to whom he sent circulars advertising his dubious speculations. Not only were these women lacking in business experience and acumen, but they were ill-placed to fight him in court should it come to that (Meredith 113). Many could not afford to pay for a prosecution and others were too ashamed to have their business dealings or failings publicized. Some observers wondered if the large number of female shareholders in certain companies might even encourage fraud. In the aftermath of the 1878 City of Glasgow Bank collapse, one businessman lamented that so many of the shareholders were women, who could offer no check to directorial malfeasance. The *Economist* also contrasted the few "really solid men" who held shares in British banks with the "incredible . . . number of spinsters and widows" who were so easily duped (qtd. in Alborn, *Conceiving* 135).

A typical fraud from the period involved the stockbroker William Lemon Oliver and his client Caroline Dance. In 1858 Oliver was found to have fraudulently converted to his own use £5,000 of Canadian government bonds left in his safekeeping by Dance. She never suspected that her bonds had been sold, since Oliver regularly paid her the accustomed amount of dividend, and the crime was only discovered when Dance asked for the securities and Oliver absconded (Robb, *White-Collar* 92). Significantly, it was Dance's impending marriage that precipitated this crisis, as she intended to turn over her financial affairs to her husband. Dishonest trustees were the bane of women investors, who were not expected to be active economic agents or even to be knowledgeable about their own property.[7]

Women often had no information about the investments made by their trustees, which further rendered them vulnerable to fraud. In a famous case from the 1840s, an unmarried woman, Ann Slack, had £3,500 in government securities "invested for her by her trustee, who died suddenly without fully informing her as to her affairs." Since Miss Slack was completely unaware that she owned any shares, a clerk in charge of "unclaimed stock" devised a scheme for defrauding her in alliance with an unscrupulous broker. The clerk forged a death certificate in Ann Slack's name and then fabricated a will leaving all her fortune to her niece Emma. The clerk then had "a pretty milliner" impersonate the niece. "All worked admirably. The stock was retransferred and sold, the broker who carried out the transaction identified Emma Slack as a pure formality, and the money was drawn and divided." Although the fraud was later exposed, it dramatized how dependent women were on the honesty of those men who managed their money ("Dividend" 465).

Before trust laws were tightened in the twentieth century and before the emergence of professional trust companies, most trustees did their work badly, though more problems were caused by careless and sloppy management than by outright fraud. Another issue usually downplayed by contemporary commentators was the fact that a woman's trustees were usually relatives or close family friends (Stebbings). Most writers, however, preferred to scapegoat villainous strangers (bankers and confidence men) than to question the power dynamics of the patriarchal family.

Trustee fraud proved a favorite theme of Victorian novelists like Anthony

Trollope, whose *The Three Clerks* (1857) recounts how Alaric Tudor, as trustee for the young Miss Golightly, embezzled £10,000 of her government bonds to pay calls on his own railway shares. The great harm of such crimes, Trollope reasoned, was that they undermined "that trust which the weaker of mankind [read: women] should place in the stronger" (492). Catherine Gore told a similar story of fraud in her novel *The Banker's Wife* (1846), where the nefarious banker Richard Hamlyn brought ruin on widows and orphans through his malfeasance. In a bizarre case of life imitating art, Gore herself lost some £20,000 in a fraudulent bank failure ten years later (Russell 70–71).

Women's magazines often printed warnings to their readers about business frauds directed against women, and the recounting of such cases became a staple of the Victorian and Edwardian press. During the 1870s, the American suffragist Victoria Woodhull's newspaper, the *Weekly,* exposed numerous fraudulent business schemes that preyed upon unwary women investors. In March 1871, for example, the paper condemned a "persistent disregard of the rights of the widow" by life insurance companies intent on fraudulently refusing claims ("Insurance" 8). In 1912, the British feminist journal the *Eye-Opener* alerted its readers to an insurance fraud being perpetrated against domestic servants:

> The method adopted is for the man to call at a house, in the absence of the occupier, and make representations to the servant that, not having insured her life in a recognised society, she is liable to a fine of £10. Her fears having been worked upon, she is induced to sign a paper of whose contents she remains in ignorance, and to part with a certain sum of money as a settlement of the supposed claim on her. ("A Warning" 2)

The Farrow's Bank advertisement mentioned earlier was itself later exposed as a fraud. Farrow's was in a complete state of insolvency when it opened its Women's Bank, which was merely a desperate attempt to pull in more money. The bank was only kept open through an elaborate system of accounting fraud that was finally exposed in 1920. The bank's losses were over £2 million, and many of its shareholders, including a large number of women, were impoverished.[8]

Women as victims of an unregulated economy became a cliché of Victorian newspapers, novels, and plays, and as such reinforced the prevailing image of women as weak and passive. Some women who lost money in the stock market or in other investments embraced the role of victim, as this afforded them a measure of public sympathy and absolved them of responsibility for bad financial decisions. When a Liverpool woman sued the Refuge Insurance Company in 1903 after paying £82 on two policies worth £72, she argued that the agent had told her "it would be all right—she could draw the money." The judge agreed that this was tantamount to fraud on the company's part. Alice Crosty used the same argument to win £53 back from the Scottish Temperance Life Office in 1909, on a policy she had taken out on her aunt's life. Were these women really dupes, or, as insurance companies suspected, seasoned veterans at demanding back premiums when the life they had "gambled" on refused to die in a timely fashion?[9] Women and their lawyers certainly capitalized on the assumption that pushy salesmen habitually took advantage of their female customers' naiveté (Alborn, "A License").

The trope of female victimhood was very well established and can be observed, for example, in the "begging letters" many women wrote to the Liberator Relief Fund, established in 1892 to assist small investors who had lost their savings in the Liberator Building Society, which had failed amid allegations of fraud and mismanagement. One applicant for relief, a schoolmistress and "sister of a clergyman," wrote:

> Every penny of my money was in the Liberator, £1,200. The interest paid my rent and taxes, and with the help of that I was able to get my living in a small private school. I am 55 years of age, and have worked as hard as any woman could since I was 17. I was straining every nerve to save a little more to pull my income to £100 a year, that I might cease from my labours at 60 and live at rest and in peace to the end. . . . Unfortunately for me this trouble with its sleepless nights of racking anxiety has so crushed me—some days are dragged through in agony—my future is dark enough, I know not in the least what will become of me. I can only sob out in the night (the only time I can allow myself the luxury of crying) Oh God, I have worked so hard, and looked forward to my little home with my books, so longingly, save me, oh save me from the workhouse. (R. Watts 4)

This was the language of melodrama, which, in its evocation of imperiled feminine virtue and domesticity, helped shore up the separate spheres and warned women away from the market economy and speculative investments.

A major theme of Victorian literature and political discourse was the inappropriateness of women in the public sphere, especially in the competitive world of business. Writers and journalists particularly chided women for their participation in speculative manias. In his *Life of George Stephenson* (1858), Samuel Smiles cited women's involvement in the Railway Mania of the 1840s as one of its most reprehensible features. He argued that the mad frenzy of railway speculation would not have been possible without the ignorance and credulity of shareholders such as "the widow and spinster of small means, who had up to that time blessed God that their lot had lain between poverty and riches, but were now seized by the infatuation of becoming suddenly rich" (Smiles 433–34). The less women concerned themselves with such matters the better.

A great deal of popular literature pitted virtuous women against an amoral marketplace. For example, in George Henry Lewes's melodrama *The Game of Speculation* (1851), adapted from a Balzac play, the wife of a crooked stockbroker is the play's voice of morality. At the climax, she confronts her husband's partner in crime, prevailing upon him to abandon a scheme to cheat creditors:

> The part my husband wishes you to play is a disgraceful one—give it up . . . you and my husband—you are going to ruin each other. Do not you understand that debts dishonour no one, when they are avowed? We can but work to pay them. You have

before you your whole life; and you have too much intelligence, if not too much heart, to wish to disgrace that life for ever, by a scheme which justice would repudiate, if not punish. (90)

Domestic fiction also served to warn women away from the world of commerce and investment. Sophia Vernon Somerset's evangelical novel, *A Good Investment, or, For Love of Money* (1891), contrasted false (financial) investments with a woman's true investments—love of God and family. The plot centers on Ellen Wright, a domestic servant, whose love of money leads her to make reckless investments. Not content with the steady 3 percent interest of a savings bank, she turns over her money to a shady lawyer who promises her an outlandish 15 percent return. The lawyer then decamps with her capital, leaving her broken in health and spirit.

An 1894 short story in *Demorest's Family Magazine*, "A Woman's Romance in Wall Street," further encapsulates the unease that women's involvement in business usually generated. The story follows Elinor Alvis, the orphaned daughter of a businessman, as she leads her cousin Grace on a tour of the mysterious offices and byways surrounding the New York Stock Exchange. The story is narrated in a mode reminiscent of an adventure tale, since, for women, the financial district is as foreign and perilous as "darkest Africa." There is also an air of impropriety about the visit, as "the thought of a woman being precipitated into that headlong struggle and rush for fortune [must] strike the mind as incongruous and peculiar." Elinor's familiarity with the stock exchange has to be justified as the actions of a dutiful daughter whose father's untimely death forced her to settle his business affairs and to invest her inheritance in such a way that she is able to save the family home. Primarily intended to educate female readers about the stock market, "A Woman's Romance in Wall Street" clearly cautioned women to avoid the market, which was best left in the more capable hands of men. As Grace concludes at the end of her tour, "I think it will be a long time before the average woman will make up successfully as a 'bull' or a 'bear.' The majority will be well content to let the Jasons go forth and do battle for the Golden Fleece" (Field).

Within the safe confines of the home, women might experience the excitement of the stock market vicariously through newspapers and novels. Some women writers like Catherine Gore and Charlotte Riddell even specialized in novels about finance and big business. At mid-century, Gore, a British merchant's daughter, wrote a series of novels on the theme of capitalism and social mobility that bore titles such as *Men of Capital* (1846) and *Mammon, or The Hardships of an Heiress* (1855). She often focused on how women's lives were shaped by the vicissitudes of the market and economic forces over which they had little control. Gore herself had lost a small fortune in the famous 1855 collapse of the Strahan, Paul, and Bates Bank. A generation later, Riddell, known as "the novelist of the City," dramatized the turbulent world of commerce in popular works like *Mitre Court* (1885) and *The Head of the Firm* (1892).

Two of the nineteenth century's most popular and prolific novelists, Ellen (Mrs. Henry) Wood and Emma Marshall, were themselves bankers' wives who took up writing out of financial necessity when their husbands' businesses failed. Henry Wood's bank collapsed in 1856 under mysterious circumstances. Hugh Marshall was manager of the West of England Bank, which failed in 1878 amid allegations of fraud. Thereafter, both women supported their families with their writing. Not surprisingly their works often dealt with domestic happiness threatened by financial problems and commercial impropriety. For instance, Wood's novel *The Shadow of Ashlydyat* (1863) follows the career of George Godolphin, who ruins his family's banking business through embezzlement. The ubiquity of financial themes in so much domestic fiction invalidates a too rigid imposition of separate spheres.[10]

Other domestic leisure activities also came to incorporate financial themes in unexpected ways. In the 1880s, for example, a new type of board game emerged whereby players achieved success through competitive capitalist behavior. In "Bulls and Bears," players move tokens around the board as they speculate on the rise and fall of shares. In the card game "Commerce," players attempt to corner the market in certain commodities by yelling out bids to other players. That some of these games were marketed to women can be seen in the box cover for "Commerce," which depicts a pretty, stylishly dressed "Gibson girl" energetically raising her arm in a "commodities deal" (Fig. 5). These games allowed women to feel like brokers and bankers, if only for a time, and if only in the seclusion of their homes (Hofer 78–91).

To actually allow women to plunge headlong into the frenzy and excitement of the stock market would surely undermine the tranquility of the home, and might even unleash the presumed darker qualities of feminine nature—capriciousness, frivolity, passion. As Catherine Ingrassia has demonstrated, as early as the South Sea Bubble of 1720 the unpredictability and instability of the new financial system were represented as feminine. "Speculative investment—financial ventures that depend on stocks, credit and fluctuations of the marketplace" came to be associated with "hysteria, disorder and enthusiasm, distinctly transgressive impulses typically associated with females" (Ingrassia 191). This viewpoint was expressed by a Victorian stockbroker, who concluded that women "are not only frequent, but daring speculators. They encounter risks that would appall the stoutest Wall Street veteran, and rush boldly into places, where even a Vanderbilt would fear to tread. The female character is, in many respects, suited to a life of speculation.... Speculation derives its food from excitement, and women often feed on excitement. Speculation comes from fancy, and women are much given to fancy" (Fowler 448). Of course this was a sarcastic assessment, as the very qualities that supposedly attracted women to the share market doomed them to failure. Men's more moderate, sober, and intellectual natures, it was believed, would allow them safely to navigate the turbulent waters of speculation, while women's essentially emotional character would offer them few protections against the dangers of the marketplace.

Figure 5. "Commerce," J. Ottman Lith. Co., ca. 1900. Collection of the New York Historical Society.

Outside the protective, or restraining, influences of the home women might prove even more reckless than men. Certainly lone, unprotected women were seen as easy prey for charlatans and swindlers. As Sherlock Holmes maintained in "The Disappearance of Lady Frances Carfax," "One of the most dangerous classes in the world . . . is the drifting and friendless woman. She is the most harmless, and often the most useful of mortals, but she is the inevitable inciter of crime in others" (Doyle 816). Lady Carfax falls under the spell of a criminal couple posing as missionaries. They defraud her of her wealth and attempt to murder her, until she is rescued by Holmes.

By the turn of the century there were numerous warnings to women about the potential dangers of the marketplace in all manner of writings: novels, plays, journalism, advice books. Although these narratives about investment have many similarities, we should also be sensitive to differences peculiar to genres or to the ideological perspectives of writers. Novels and other fictional accounts might well employ financial disasters for dramatic effect as they would natural disasters like floods or earthquakes. Such sensationalism seldom makes for balanced discussion. Novelistic representations were also more prone than other kinds of writing to depict women's interactions with investment as wholly undesirable. After all, most novelists were unconnected to the business world and often reflected the prejudices of the professional middle class against the entrepreneurial middle class.[11] On the other hand, financial journalists and business writers took women's interest in investment for granted. Such writers rarely demonized the City or Wall Street per se, but usually warned women against reckless speculation or too active management of their own resources, recommending instead certain safe investments and the services of an expert (male) advisor.

All cautionary tales aside, the industrial economy craved women's capital, and as the nineteenth century progressed, increasing numbers of women became more and more active in the share market. Negotiating the dilemma between domestic needs and the needs of business became increasingly difficult for both women and the agents of the marketplace. This ambivalence can certainly be seen in the late nineteenth-century memoirs of two American stockbrokers, William Fowler and Henry Clews. Both men devoted separate chapters to women speculators, whom they treated with a mixture of chivalry, humor, and disdain. Fowler began by noting the incongruity of women dreaming of stocks and bonds when they should "sit embroidering golden bees and butterflies on black velvet." Fowler then tells of a group of young ladies who pooled their resources, made a quick profit in railway shares, and finally made "heavy investments in moiré antique, Mechlin lace, and India shawls." Fowler is clearly charmed by these women, who are not seriously interested in business matters but in fashion and dress fabric. He is less charitable in his description of other women investors he has known, such as "Miss M"—a "strong minded" investor whose "face is that of a goshawk." Her preoccupation with the market has rendered her ruthless, predatory, and unfeminine (Fowler 449–50).

Henry Clews is less satirical than Fowler, and more matter-of-fact in his assessment of women's business sense. He asserts categorically:

Women do not seem to have the mental qualities required to take in the varied points of the situation upon which success in speculation depends. They are, by nature, parasites as speculators, and, when thrown upon their own resources, are completely helpless. Although they are able, through craft and subtlety, to rule the male sex to a large extent, yet, when obliged to go alone, they are like a ship at sea in a heavy gale without compass, anchor or rudder. They have no ballast apart from men, and are liable to perish when adversity arises. (Clews 437)

Clews, like most Victorian brokers and businessmen, certainly welcomed women with capital, but denigrated "strong-minded," independent women who refused to be guided by male advisors and intermediaries. Women were simply "too impulsive and impressionable" to make good business decisions on their own. He concludes that a woman's most successful "investment" was to marry a wealthy man. "It is probably only in the matrimonial line that women can become successful speculators" (444). As late as the 1920s, the spectacle of the woman investor continued to be treated in a comic and condescending manner. A 1929 article from the *North American Review*, "Ladies of the Ticker," is a case in point: "Aggressive and guttural dowagers, gum-chewing blondes, shrinking spinsters who look as if they belonged in a missionary-society meeting, watch, pencil in hand, from the opening of the market till the belated ticker drones its last in the middle of the afternoon" (Barnard 406).

Active businesswomen even more than women investors were in danger of becoming perverted by the public sphere, for, having abandoned their "natural" vocation as wives and mothers, corruption and crime were sure to follow. An 1880 article from *Bankers' Magazine* gleefully exposed frauds at the Woman's Bank of Boston, a business run by women for women. Of course, "all sane persons" knew the bank's ruin "to be inevitable" since women were incapable of managing complex financial affairs. Nor was the magazine surprised by the embezzlements of the bank's president, Mrs. Howe, who was described as "totally unbalanced and unscrupulous." According to the article, she had been "at different times a thief, a procuress, a swindler, a lunatic, and always a desperate adventuress. Her age is given at sixty, and she is described as short, fat, ugly, and so illiterate as to be unable to write an English sentence, or to speak without making shameful blunders." In other words, the businesswoman was regarded as so monstrous a creature that her degenerate nature was written on her body ("The Woman's Bank of Boston" 351–52).

There were very few opportunities for women within the upper levels of finance and business during the nineteenth century, and those rare cases received the harshest criticism. The most famous example from the United States concerned the "notorious" Victoria Woodhull, a prominent spiritualist who, early in 1870 and along with her sister Tennessee Claflin, opened a brokerage firm on Broad Street, not far from the New York Stock Exchange. According to Woodhull, she and her sister began the business to prove "that woman, no less than man, can qualify herself for the more onerous occupations of life" (Clews 442). Their patron in this endeavor was the great financier "Commodore" Cornelius Vanderbilt, who was much impressed with the sisters' spiritual gifts but who also hoped to tap into the vast reserves of female capital. Woodhull, Claflin and Company proved quite successful in garnering publicity and investments. When the firm opened, the streets of the Financial District were

Figure 6. Cartoon from New York *Evening Telegram* 18 February 1870.

clogged with people who came to gaze at the extraordinary sight of women brokers. Numerous women, from society hostesses to shopkeepers, schoolteachers, and housewives, entrusted the sisters with their savings, modest or otherwise. The press, initially supportive, dubbed them the "bewitching brokers" and the "queens of finance." In an attempt to provide an alternative to the usual masculine business office, Woodhull and Claflin's rooms were furnished to replicate the feminized space of a cozy parlor or drawing room, with plush furniture, lacy pillows, a piano, and religious-themed artwork (Goldsmith 191–92).

The firm nonetheless aroused considerable apprehension about women breaching the male bastion of finance. The stockbroker William Fowler was appalled at the very idea of women brokers, since this would require the gentle sex to "change her tender heart into stone" and "to crush out her human sympathies with the unfortunate and the distressed" (Fowler 456). A cartoon in the *Evening Telegram* depicted the sisters driving a chariot pulled by bulls and bears over the bodies of investors (Fig. 6). When Victoria and Tennessee adopted new business attire consisting of a man's jacket, tie, and waistcoat over a simple black skirt, their assault on male privilege seemed abundantly clear. Alarming rumors spread that the women profited from secret information supplied to them by prostitutes and mistresses of the city's leading businessmen. Victoria Woodhull's advocacy of women's suffrage and her presidential candidacy in the Equal Rights Party led to an avalanche of conservative attacks against her.

Revelations of her divorce and allegations that she supported "free love" only seemed to confirm presumed links between businesswomen and immorality. When Woodhull, Claflin and Company closed its doors in 1871, most in the business community concluded that this was "evidence how unsuited to woman's nature is such a field of enterprise" (Goldsmith 192–94, 304).

Almost thirty years later, Tennessee Claflin, in her new incarnation as Lady Cook, the wife of an English aristocrat, became the first woman to operate as a stockbroker in Great Britain when she opened business offices at St. Mildred's Court in 1898. In an interview with the *London Daily Chronicle*, Lady Cook claimed, "I have started my present business to show women that they are quite as capable of undertaking such work as men are" ("Lady Cook and Co." 7). Either the British press was unaware of her earlier career as a broker in the United States, or they chose to ignore it.[12]

The most successful businesswoman of the nineteenth century was undoubtedly Hetty Green, the heir to a New England whaling business.[13] In the decades following the Civil War she parlayed a modest fortune into a vast one through shrewd investments, principally in railway shares. A fearless speculator, she made millions in the stock market by buying at times of financial panic. With typical Yankee understatement, Green downplayed her own success: "All you have to do is buy cheap and sell dear, act with thrift and shrewdness and be persistent" (qtd. in Chancellor 166–67). She carefully kept her wealth separate from her husband's, whose business judgment she little trusted, but still experienced difficulties operating in the male-dominated financial sector. In an article Green wrote for *Harper's Bazaar* in 1900, she asserted:

> I believe that woman is quite as capable as man in conducting business affairs. A good business woman is often sharper than a good business man. She seems to have an intuitive perception which man lacks, and the diplomacy to shape affairs to her will. Mentally, I do not believe woman to be inferior to man, save as she has become so by a mistaken course of training. ("Why Women")

Unfortunately, women's second-class education had left them "handicapped in the business world, as men are usually afraid to deal with them, or else, knowing their weaknesses, take advantage of them." Green warned women that they were "just the prey the sharpers are looking for" ("Why Women"). On another occasion Green lamented, "I wish women had more rights in business and elsewhere than they now have. I could have succeeded much easier in my career had I been a man. I find men will take advantages of women in business that they would not attempt with men. I found this so in the courts, where I have been fighting men all my life" (Sparkes and Moore 231). If the "richest woman in the world" felt disadvantaged by her sex, how much more so the average female investor (Green, "Words" 123)?

Hetty Green was clearly an exceptional case, but many commentators still felt the need to minimize her achievements as a woman. One stockbroker attributed her success to "a powerful masculine brain" (Clews 441). Most press accounts depicted her as "the Witch of Wall Street"—a ruthless, grasping hag whose success was achieved at the expense of feminine modesty and grace (Drachman 69–73). When Green foreclosed on the mortgage for a Chicago church in 1903, the minister denounced her in a sermon on "the differences between Hetty Green and Jesus's friends, Mary and Martha" ("Pulpit Attack"). Like Victoria Woodhull, Green was demonized for breaching the boundaries of proper womanhood.

By the early twentieth century, as more women sought entry into the public sphere, the virtues of feminine modesty and domesticity were contrasted even more emphatically against the values of the marketplace. For example, in Beatrice Harraden's novel *Where Your Treasure Is* (1918), the First World War transforms the hard businesswoman Tamar Scott into a compassionate and self-sacrificing being. Abandoning the competitive "male" world of commerce, she finds a higher purpose aiding Belgian refugees. Likewise, in *The Enchanted April* (1922), Elizabeth von Arnim suggests that women's unbusinesslike qualities are a decided advantage. When the stuffy Mrs. Fisher asks her prospective travel companions for references, they are taken aback: "I don't think references are nice things at all between—between ordinary decent women.... We're not business people. We needn't distrust each other" (41–42).

Good women should avoid the market place and its corrupting influence. They were encouraged to rely on male relatives or friends to manage their business affairs and to advise them on financial matters. Numerous financial advice books for women also sought to protect them from "that army of sharks and rascals which, unfortunately, must be permitted to exist, and to which a defenseless woman of means presents a golden opportunity" (Cromwell vi). This advice literature was inevitably written by men, and usually employed a patronizing tone. Women were urged to be cautious and moderate in their investment choices, to avoid high-yield, but risky, speculations, and to favor "safe" investments such as government securities, public utilities, and established railroad companies ("How May" 7149–50; "A Woman" 413–14). Of course, such "conservative" investment strategies for "ladies" were open to multiple interpretations. They may have represented genuine attempts to protect women from potential risks and fraud, but they also served to exclude women from the most profitable investment opportunities. A money article from 1913 claimed that most legitimate brokerage houses would not offer to women clients "highly speculative securities, in which either the profit or the loss is likely to be large." The article endorsed this paternalist policy since most women "know nothing of the science of investment" ("A Woman's" 144).

As we have seen, the dangers of investment, both real and imagined, were constantly invoked during the Victorian and Edwardian periods in order to marginalize women's role in the economy. Yet, by the late nineteenth century, a number of feminists and other social critics drew upon this same picture of a corrupt business world to criticize male economic hegemony and to advocate women's moral mission to cleanse the marketplace. Elizabeth Cady Stanton, organizer of the first Women's Rights Convention, argued that women must rescue the nation from capitalist excess: "The need of this hour is not territory, gold mines, railroads or specie payments, but a new evangel of womanhood, to exalt power, virtue, morality, true religion, to lift man up into the higher realms of love, purity and thought" (Goldsmith 214).

Women's financial victimization was taken up by British and American feminists as a crucial part of their discourse on the economic and political empowerment of women.[14] Anna Dickinson's social critique, *A Paying Investment* (1876), contrasts men's investment in stocks and bonds with women's investment in their children and homes. She argues that men, in their greed to enrich themselves, have neglected to provide for the poor and weak and have allowed vice and crime to flourish in cities. Women therefore had a duty to "clean house" by reforming a corrupt system of business and politics: "A woman can only do her duty to her home,—to other people's homes,—if her own is safe . . . by going into the world . . . to do the work that no man is doing, the work that men are doing ill, the work that men are actually forbidding to be done" (112–13). In her feminist fable of 1894, "The Regeneration of Two," George Egerton proclaimed: "I see great monopolies eating away the substance of the people, and magnificent chapels built in memory of railway kings who ruined thousands of women and children, and I say, 'So much for the rulers'" (192). Florence Tuttle also criticized capitalism for seeking profit for profit's sake. In *The Awakening of Woman* (1915), she argued that women's entry into business, the professions, and politics would restrain the unfettered quest for riches that resulted in the "atrophy of inner qualities that racially count" (163–64). Here Tuttle draws on a strain of eugenic discourse that imagined women as the engine of human progress.[15]

Some critics contrasted an amoral, masculine world of business and finance with a moral, feminine sensibility that strived for justice and fair play. The British suffragist and Theosophist Frances Swiney made such an argument in her book *The Cosmic Procession* (1906):

> if the ability that dominated the fireside had been allowed free play in the outer circle of life's activities, we should not at the present day find every civilised nation groaning under National Debts, accumulated in their millions for human butcher bills, for military extravagances; we should not suffer from a system of finance, usury, and fraud that is so rotten, so corrupt, that it poisons and paralyses all industrialism, all social communal advance. . . . The Woman, with her children dying of hunger, asks why should such things be, when corn in plenty is garnered in other lands, only needing transport; and the answer of the men, that the dire situation is due to a corner in wheat, does not satisfy her logical common sense. (174–75, 178)

There are numerous other examples from late Victorian and Edwardian literature where a woman's moral viewpoint is contrasted with sharp business practice and financial fraud, including Henrik Ibsen's *A Doll's House* (1879), Oscar Wilde's *An Ideal Husband* (1895), George Gissing's *The Whirlpool* (1897), and Joseph Conrad's *Chance* (1913).

Perhaps most famously, in *A Doll's House*, Nora is shocked to discover that she has broken a law in signing her father's name to a loan security. The money financed a trip necessary to save her husband's life, and she didn't want to worry her father, who was himself dying at the time. When she is informed that "the law is not concerned with motives," she replies that "it must be a very stupid law. . . . Hasn't a daughter the right to protect her dying father from worry and anxiety? Hasn't a wife the right to save her husband's life?" (175). A similar viewpoint is voiced by Aunt Susan in H. G. Wells's novel *Tono-Bungay* (1908). As her husband's shady business collapses, she opines: "No woman has ever respected the law—ever. . . . It's too silly. The things it lets you do! And then pulls you up—like a mad nurse minding a child" (318). This seeming amorality of the law and government—which allowed a great deal of sharp business practice but which remained aloof from larger issues of social responsibility and welfare—struck a number of observers as hypocritical and indecent.

The whole premise of separate spheres—that the home should be a haven from the vicissitudes of the marketplace—appeared increasingly untenable. After all, an unregulated market continually menaced domestic security. Not only were women especially vulnerable to financial catastrophes and fraud, but, as the guardians of morality, they had a special duty to confront the problem. Men must be held to a higher standard, as Sir Robert Chiltern learns in Wilde's play *An Ideal Husband.* When Chiltern explains to his wife that he is withdrawing his political opposition to a fraudulent business scheme because "public and private life are different things . . . have different laws, and move on different lines," Lady Chiltern rejects this cynical view of the separate spheres. She insists that "they should both represent man at his highest. I see no difference between them" (176). Women and the domestic realm didn't need to be shielded from the marketplace; they needed to reform it. And yet here, as elsewhere in the Victorian debate over women's changing roles, we see the classic paradox of liberal feminism, described by the historian Mrinalini Sinha as "the simultaneous denial and assertion of sexual difference in women's claims of equality with, and difference from, men" (197). Women claimed the right to economic parity based on moral superiority. Even as they hoped to escape the restrictions imposed by separate spheres, women themselves re-inscribed the basic premises of the ideology, which defined them as essentially gentle and nurturing rather than aggressive and competitive.

The Victorian corporate economy depended heavily on the capital of women, who epitomized passive investment. So long as women entrusted their wealth to the stewardship of their male protectors they received public approbation and were likewise fitting objects of pity when their trust was betrayed by unscrupulous entrepreneurs. On the other hand, whenever women were seen as too actively or enthusiastically seeking their own fortunes on the stock market, they became the objects of scorn and ridicule, and their financial losses were seen as just desserts for having abandoned their modesty and domestic responsibilities. When, for example, Elizabeth Barrett Browning's close friend Mary Trepsack lost money in a financial investment, Robert Browning declared that this "should be a lesson to women not to take the administration of their affairs into their own hands" ("Dear Alibel" 5). As the century progressed and as some middle-class women longed to escape the Doll's House, they came to see economic empowerment and financial regulation as key to their liberation. By the late nineteenth century, there was a mounting feminist critique of investment capitalism and a belief that women had to reform an economy in which they were both marginalized and deeply implicated.

## Notes

1. For the history of eighteenth- and nineteenth-century businesswomen, see Burnette; Cleary; Dexter; Gamber; Murphy; Phillips; and Yaeger.

2. See, for example, the recent work on women's importance as consumers, including Finn, *Character;* Rappaport, *Shopping;* and Whitlock.

3. For pioneering work on Victorian women investors, see Henry, "Ladies"; and Rutterford and Maltby, "She Possessed" and "The Widow."

4. For a more optimistic assessment of women's access to financial information, see Rutterford and Maltby, "She Possessed."

5. Anglo-American law was vigilant about determining whether women investors were married or single. As one advice manual cautioned, "A stock in the name of a woman (unless the word 'Miss' is a part of the name on the face, and the certificate is so signed) must have a notary's acknowledgment showing that the lady is single, married, or a widow, as the case may be" (Atwood 14).

6. The English Married Women's Property Act of 1870 first recognized a wife's right to maintain property separate from her husband's control, but the 1882 act was a more comprehensive and far-reaching piece of legislation. See Holcombe; Shammus.

7. The problem of women as victims of white-collar crime continues to the present day. See, for example, Daly; Gerber and Weeks; and Szockyj and Fox.

8. Farrow's Bank fraud is discussed in Robb, *White-Collar* 77–79; "Farrow's Bank Failure"; and records of Farrow's Bank, PRO, BT31/18100. For other frauds directed against women, see "Male Vampires" and "Trappers of Women."

9. People sometimes bought life insurance policies based on the expectation that the insured life would die before they had paid very many installments.

10. For a more detailed discussion of Victorian women novelists and investment, see Henry, "Ladies."

11. For a general overview of the professional middle class's critique of entrepreneurial values, see Perkin, 252–70. For a discussion of writers' negative attitudes toward the business world, see Delany; Russell; and Westbrook.

12. For an account of contemporary sexual discrimination and harassment of women on Wall Street, see Antilla.

13. For a good overview of Hetty Green's life, see Slack.

14. Women's need for economic independence was crucial to Victorian feminism. See especially Vicinus.

15. For an introduction to feminist eugenics, see Robb, "Race."

# PART 3

*Fictions of Investment*

Trollope in the Stock Market

Irrational Exuberance and *The Prime Minister*

*Audrey Jaffe*

A television advertisement for CNBC, aired frequently before the late 2000 economic decline, features a digital stock ticker projected across the chest of a railway commuter, its numbers coursing around him in a continuous, moving ribbon (Fig. 7). Like an EKG, or some new kind of medical tracking device, this image—locating the numbers where the man's other ticker would be—captures the contemporary fascination with the stock market by identifying the movement of stock prices with life itself: physical and, especially, emotional life. The advertisement evokes the fantasy of connectedness that the stock market has become, as it pictures this commuter surrounded by—in effect, bound up in—a complex arrangement of digits that must, it seems, signify something crucial about him. The band across his chest registering both the intensity and banality of today's incessant market monitoring, the man with the ticker is a new every-man, a more intriguing version of the familiar workaday commuter, his internalization of the market (and the admiring gaze of his fellow commuter) singling him out as an enviable type: a vision of how connected we may all someday hope to become. In an age of such heightened attention to stock prices that they can be identified as vital signs, the man with the ticker is our better, more tuned-in self; watching the numbers, the ad intimates, we are simply watching ourselves.

But how, exactly, are those signs to be read? In both popular and academic discourse, the movement of stock-market prices, especially as represented by the jagged line of the stock-market graph, is amenable both to interpretation and to the failure of interpretation: it looks so much like a narrative, and yet no one can say for certain what it means. Or rather, everyone has something to say: an encyclopedia of "chart patterns" lists forty-seven variations, with such engaging names as "bump and run reversal," "hanging man," and "dead-cat bounce." The book also includes a chart identifying its own "failure rate": "Percentage of formations that do not work as expected" (Bulkowski 655). A writer on day trading cautions against selling on Mondays, with this caveat: "There is no pattern, relationship, or indicator in the market that will always be correct.... Now, getting back to the Monday pattern" (Bernstein 71). Nor does the graph's much-vaunted unpredictability, or "failure rate," inhibit interpretation; if its trajectory fails to confirm expectations, as it frequently does,

Figure 7. Ticker man.
Courtesy of CNBC.

that failure tends to be rationalized by the idea that the market knows us better than we know ourselves: more "sensitive" than any individual human being, it is said to respond to "unpredictable human impulses" (Carret 24). Indeed, most frequently, as the CNBC image suggests, the line's trajectory is assimilated to a narrative of feeling: universally apprehended as a picture of emotions—a snapshot of the national (or global) mood—it is understood as swinging between (for example) elation and depression, optimism and alarm. Looking to the numbers to see how we feel, we both personalize them—render them a projection of our individual and collective narratives—and depersonalize them, conceding our authority to know ourselves to an abstract system that seems to have captured this knowledge. Do the numbers emerge from within the man's chest, or are they projected from without? Is the market a projection of the man, or is the man a projection of the market? Making sense of the numbers, we seek to discover, in that familiar phrase that registers the identification of economic with emotional well-being, how we are doing.

The market must have some authority of its own, it seems—it can't be just us, writ large, and yet it appears to be. The idea of the stock market as emotional projection bears on the question, addressed by market theorists, of whether stock prices are determined by facts about companies or commodities or by opinions, as reflected in the activity of investment. The contention that stocks in the dot-com economy of the 1990s were "overvalued" was tied to an assessment of investor emotion: "irrational exuberance" was Alan Greenspan's term for the relationship between the way companies were valued and the way investors felt about their stocks. According to Greenspan, investors used their positive feeling about the market as a basis for further investment, investing, in effect, in their own emotions. This phenomenon drove up prices, leading to further exuberance, all of which tended toward the creation of a "bubble"—a term whose own implicit narrative, itself a rhetorical projection of the stock-market graph, stands as an answer to at least one of the interpretative questions the graph is said to pose.[1] For Greenspan, the irrationality of irrational exuberance lies in the absence of a connection between feeling and value: irrational exuberance is feeling based "merely" on feeling.

But the circularity that made Greenspan nervous (and along with him, eventually, everyone else)—the idea that the market affects feeling, and feeling affects the market—merely reconfigures a discomfort that has existed at least since Anthony Trollope's time: an uneasiness about the unpredictability of investing in shares and about the attenuated relationship between investors and the objects of their investment. Because investors usually operate at a distance from the companies or commodities in which they invest, possessing at best limited knowledge of them, they invest in something other than facts: in narratives about companies and commodities, for instance, and in their own hopes and wishes about those narratives. The term "irrational exuberance," referring both to the market and to the feelings of those who invest in it, seeks to ward off the danger of too much happiness by gesturing toward its unlikely sounding opposite, rational feeling: the idea that feeling could be an accurate gauge of value. But the attempt to separate rational from irrational feeling is only one of numerous futile attempts made during the course of stock-exchange history to remove instability from the market. Indeed, from Trollope to Greenspan, discussions about investment and the market have repeatedly sought to draw similar lines: between the solid and the ephemeral, between safety and risk—between, in general, value securely located in companies or commodities and value that is only imagined to be there—as a means of countering the uncertainty and unpredictability, indeed, the sheer uninterpretability, of the fluctuating value of shares.[2] In seeking to fix such lines, they merely point toward the uncertainties, and the movements of the heart with which we register them, that tie our identities to the market.

* * *

The CNBC commercial assimilates the movement of stock prices to the biological and metaphorical pulse, condensing in a single image—a videographic palimpsest—a connection that financial narratives from the Victorian period to the present have spelled out, and in doing so reinforced: that between money and the heart. Trollope's *The Prime Minister* (1875–1876) might be said to present an uncontroversial understanding of the way this connection works: one can read a man's character, the novel has it, in the way he manages his money. But *The Prime Minister* also offers other ways of understanding our own assimilations of feeling and the market and the lines we continue to draw in their name, perhaps most strikingly in its status as a precursor of today's stock-market dramas: those episodes, played out in the daily newspapers and the nightly news, in which a violation of financial rules (or merely a suspected one, since such cases do not always involve legal wrongdoing) registers as a general social violation, an offense against middle-class culture and feeling.[3] In offering up as villains stock-market characters whose particular forms of exuberance are routinely characterized as reverberating beyond the market, contemporary culture demonstrates the persistence and the usefulness of a Victorian master narrative within which matters not otherwise easily regulated may be placed.

Similarities between the contemporary stock market and the Victorian stock-market exchange are not hard to find. In both periods, an increase in the popular buying and selling of shares spurs widespread, vicarious interest in the movement of stock prices. Both periods are fascinated by the market's reverberations in everyday life: the potential for ordinary individuals to participate, via investment, in domestic and international commerce. New technologies—the railway and the Internet—allow for similarly phantasmatic relations between investor and investment: today's (or yesterday's) dot-com is the nineteenth-century's railway to Vera Cruz. But perhaps most relevant and least recognized are the Victorian foundations of the belief that the market as an institution depends on distinctions in emotion and character: distinctions vividly articulated in the Victorian novel.

The established, traditional families in Trollope's *The Prime Minister,* the Whartons and the Fletchers, rely on feeling as a means of gauging value, but the appearance of a new man—a man of the stock exchange—disrupts their ability to do so. Of the Whartons and the Fletchers, Trollope writes:

> As a class they are more impregnable, more closely guarded by their feelings and prejudices against strangers than any other. None keep their daughters to themselves with greater care, or are less willing to see their rules of life changed or abolished. And yet this man, half foreigner half Jew,—and as it now appeared,—whole pauper, had stepped in and carried off a prize for which such a one as Arthur Fletcher was contending! (662)[4]

It is precisely in relation to the feelings and prejudices of this class that the character Ferdinand Lopez poses a problem; about Lopez, throughout much of the first half of *The Prime Minister,* no one knows—though many suspect—what the appropriate feeling might be. Thus when trying to convince his daughter Emily, who has declared herself in love with Lopez, that the man is no gentleman, all Wharton can say with certainty is that "no one knows anything about him, or where to inquire even" (46). And while that ignorance, we are told, would be enough for Dr. Johnson, according to whom "any other derivation of this difficult word ['gentleman'] . . . than that which causes it to signify 'a man of ancestry' is whimsical" (10), what troubles Wharton's ability to make his case with conviction is the fact that, as the novel puts it, the nineteenth century admits exceptions. And Ferdinand Lopez is an exception: on the basis of his bearing, his clothing, his manner of sitting on a horse, and the lower half of his face (12), "It was admitted on all sides that Ferdinand Lopez was a 'gentleman'" (10).

The admission of Ferdinand Lopez as a gentleman—like Trollope's effacement of the quotation marks with which he briefly surrounds the term—constitutes an admission of the impossibility of keeping him out: like the markets, which cannot afford to invest only at home, English society is necessarily vulnerable to foreign charm.[5] What allows for Lopez's admission is this:

> We all know the man,—a little man generally, who moves seldom and softly,—who looks always as though he had just been sent home in a bandbox. Ferdinand Lopez was not a little man, and moved freely enough; but never, at any moment,—going into the city or coming out of it, on horseback or on foot, at home over his book

or after the mazes of the dance,—was he dressed otherwise than with perfect care. Money and time did it, but folk thought that it grew with him, as did his hair and nails. And he always rode a horse which charmed good judges of what a park nag should be;—not a prancing, restless, giggling, sideway-going, useless garran, but an animal well made, well bitted, and with perfect paces, on whom a rider if it pleased him could be as quiet as a statue on a monument. (12–13)

It is of course known by Wharton and others that not knowing anything about Lopez is the same as knowing something about him, and that the suspicions hovering around him are likely to resolve into knowledge of a specific kind. Indeed, we are told that his father is Portuguese, and we are invited to suspect that he is a Jew.[6] The novel's gentlemen intuit, as it is the business of gentlemen to do, Lopez's lack of gentlemanly status; what "a gentleman knows" (30) above all is how to identify another gentleman. However, the allowance of exceptions to the rule means that gentlemanliness must be determined in each individual case; once exceptions are admitted, each candidate becomes, in effect, a stock, his value a function of the assessment of the group. In this case, what a gentleman knows has no practical effect on what Ferdinand Lopez does, for his admission as a gentleman is an admission that nothing can be done about him. And once the doors to Wharton/Fletcher society, along with questions of gentlemanly identity, are thrown open, the identities of the Whartons and Fletchers—formerly held in place by their strong feelings and prejudices—are also in play.

If the nineteenth century admits exceptions, there is nothing to keep the Ferdinand Lopezes of the world from attending one's social gatherings, meeting one's family, running for Parliament, and marrying one's daughter. Victorian novels typically rely on narratives of romantic love to adjudicate the relationship between feeling and value, the love relationship absorbing and disseminating the codes of ideological discourses such as those of race, nationality, and class. It makes sense, then, that the crisis signaled by Lopez's admission into the world of the Whartons and Fletchers should take shape as the novel's romantic plot. But the relation between romance and finance in *The Prime Minister* is more complex than the model of ideological mystification allows, since for Trollope and his readers, as for twentieth- and twenty-first-century subjects of market economies and the narratives that circulate within them, the stock exchange has provided a compellingly coherent set of terms within which familiar cultural narratives, and indeed familiar cultural identities, have been rewritten and reconceived. In the cultural narrative of the stock exchange whose terms are *The Prime Minister*'s, for instance, Emily's feeling for Lopez may be understood as the characteristic attitude of the speculator: she must therefore be taught to invest her emotions, as she would her money, wisely. The terms of romance and those of finance are interchangeable, universalized by gender difference: if feeling is a woman's capital (and its signifier, since she brings her father's wealth with her), then speculating with love is understandable in relation to, or as an analogy for, speculating with money. Feeling here is a form of currency, and feelings about money are a template for feelings in general: the truth about a character, Trollope implies, can be learned from the way that character feels about money. Thus *The Prime Minister*'s calibration of feeling and value has as much to do with Lopez's financial dealings as it does with his romantic ones; indeed, the former serve as the hallmark by which the true character of the latter will be judged. The marriage plot *is*, in fact, the financial plot: the lesson Emily Wharton learns about Lopez is taught by way of her increasing knowledge of his financial dealings. His value—more precisely, his lack of value—emerges for her, as it does in the novel as a whole, in a series of demonstrations of the nature of his feelings about money.

After his failed run for Parliament, Lopez accepts payment for his electioneering expenses twice—once from the Duke of Omnium and once from Wharton—without telling the second that he has already been paid by the first. His thoughts on the subject are these:

> It was not as he sat at the breakfast table that Ferdinand Lopez made up his mind to pocket the Duke's money and to say nothing about it to Mr. Wharton. He had been careful to conceal the cheque, but he had done so with the feeling that the matter was one to be considered in his own mind before he took any step. As he left the house, already considering it, he was inclined to think that the money must be surrendered. Mr. Wharton had very generously paid his electioneering expenses, but had not done so simply with the view of making him a present of the money. He wished the Duke had not taken him at his word. In handing this cheque over to Mr. Wharton he would be forced to tell the story of his letter to the Duke, and he was sure that Mr. Wharton would not approve of his having written such a letter. How could anyone approve of his having applied for a sum of money which had already been paid to him? How could such a one as Mr. Wharton—an old-fashioned English gentleman,—approve of such an application being made under any circumstances? Mr. Wharton would very probably insist on having the cheque sent back to the Duke,—which would be a sorry end to the triumph as at present achieved. And the more he thought of it the more sure he was that it would be imprudent to mention to Mr. Wharton his application to the Duke. The old men of the present day were, he said to himself, such fools that they understood nothing. And then the money was very convenient to him. . . . By the time, therefore, that he had reached the city he had resolved that at any rate for the present he would say nothing about it to Mr. Wharton. Was it not spoil got from the enemy by his own courage and cleverness? When he was writing his acknowledgment for the money to Warburton he had taught himself to look upon the sum extracted from the Duke as a matter quite distinct from the payment made to him by his father-in-law. (376–77)

In a process that enacts the business it describes—"the more he thought of it the more sure he was"—Lopez provides himself with a rationale for keeping both sums. Gentlemanly behavior matters, to his way of thinking, only to others; it is a performance ("How could anyone approve?") relevant only insofar as it supports or interferes with his plans. And as he teaches himself to look upon two identical payments as distinct, differentiating himself in the process from "the old men of the present day," he displays a characteristic the novel defines elsewhere as an inability to perceive appropriate distinctions: he is a man who "wouldn't mind whether he ate horseflesh or beef if horseflesh were as good as beef" (141)—one who has, more generally, no feeling for "the lines which separated right from wrong" (373). The movement of his thought—choreographed by the movement of his feet and bounded by his trip from home to city—displays, indeed, not an observance of that line but rather a mental fluidity, an ability to justify the merits of the position he wishes to take.

Not possessing the sensibilities held by the old men of the present day—not knowing what it is that a gentleman knows, but aspiring nevertheless to gentlemanliness—Ferdinand Lopez is necessarily in the position of "teaching" himself "to look upon" things. When his partner, Sexty Parker, expresses concern that "the coffee and guano [in which Lopez has invested] were not always real coffee and guano," Lopez teaches him, daily after lunch, to see things in a different way:

> "If I buy a ton of coffee and keep it six weeks, why do I buy it and keep it, and why does the seller sell it instead of keeping it? The seller sells it because he thinks he can do best by parting with it now at a certain price. I buy it because I think I can make money by keeping it. It is just the same as though we were to back our opinions. He backs the fall. I back the rise. You needn't have coffee and you needn't have guano to do this. Indeed the possession of the coffee and the possession of the guano is only a very clumsy addition to the trouble of your profession. . . ." Coffee and guano still had to be bought because the world was dull and would not learn the tricks of trade as taught by Ferdinand Lopez . . . but our enterprising hero looked for a time in which no such dull burden should be imposed upon him. (377)

In fact, the world has since learned the tricks of the trade as taught by Ferdinand Lopez; for Trollope, however, Lopez's failure to distinguish between the guano that is not there and the guano that is further displays his status as a man who fails to make appropriate distinctions.[7] Repeatedly documenting Lopez's feelings about money, the novel illustrates in increasingly vivid detail the contention it finally makes explicit: "He knew how to speak, and how to look, how to use a knife and fork, how to dress himself, and how to walk. But he had not the faintest notion of the feelings of a gentleman" (497).

"Teaching to look upon," an activity that Trollope seems here to disparage, is also one whose necessity he admits—for despite the novel's insistence on the intuitive quality of gentlemanly knowledge, Abel Wharton no less than Trollope himself had to make his way to it. And Trollope's awareness of the necessity of such activity leads not to anarchy, or to *avant-la-lettre* deconstruction, or even to an excessively threatened social fabric, but rather and in several ways to the novel: that vehicle par excellence both for teaching the nineteenth century how to look upon things and, in Trollope's case as in others, for securing the admission of middle-class authors into gentlemanly circles.[8] Indeed, that Lopez's ambition is also his author's suggests the importance of the lines this novel attempts to draw. For if the speculator and the novelist are both seeking to rise in the world by telling stories—stories Trollope referred to in his own case as his "castles in the air" (*An Autobiography* 42)—then a certain strain accompanies the assertion that the true gentleman can be separated from the pretender by means of gentlemanly intuition.

In an atmosphere in which money seems to have appropriated the power to create gentlemen, Trollope makes it the business of his novels to delineate the distinctions in feeling that separate the gentleman from the non-gentleman: to refine and elaborate the code for an age in which that elaboration is, he believes, sorely needed. Revealing the contents of Lopez's mind in order to illustrate distinctions between gentlemanly values and their absence, Trollope both dramatizes the need his novels are designed to fulfill and seeks to affirm his own possession of the discourse, his solid grasp of the nature and texture of gentlemanly ideals. But his contribution to a history of the emotions lies, beyond this, in his ability to bring money into the realm of feeling, and more significantly, to demonstrate that it is already there. For the feelings within which Trollope discerns distinctions are feelings about money: money is the proving ground within which distinctions in feeling appear. In the context of wealth made rapidly and often mysteriously through the buying and selling of shares (a context in which respectability might be built on a foundation of guano, or, even worse, its absence), and in which discourses about money sought to maintain the possibility that respectability and the stock exchange could coexist by marking boundaries between legitimate and illegitimate ways of reaping investment's rewards, the distinction between what was regarded approvingly as investment and what was reviled as speculation turns out, not surprisingly, to be a distinction in feeling as well.[9]

\* \* \*

Trollope's emphasis on the role of gentlemanly feeling in financial matters informs his description of the way Wharton and Lopez came by their money. Wharton, we are told, "had begun his practice early, and had worked in a stuff gown till he was nearly sixty. At that time he had amassed a large fortune, mainly from his profession, but partly also by the careful use of his own small patrimony and by his wife's money. Men knew that he was rich, but no one knew the extent of his wealth" (*PM* 25–26). Here is the corresponding account of Lopez: "He had been on the Stock Exchange, and still in some manner, not clearly understood by his friends, did business in the City. . . . But nobody, not even his own bankers or his own lawyer,—not even the old woman who looked after his linen,—ever really knew the state of his affairs" (11). The difference between Wharton's gentlemanliness and Lopez's is, in keeping with Johnson's dictum, a difference in what is known of their ancestry, and the implication is that what this particular lack of knowledge signifies for Lopez's "use" of money is an absence of care. And the line between care and the absence of care is, in general terms (though not always in the manner one would expect), from the nineteenth century to the twenty-first, the line that separates the investor from the speculator.

If the stock-market graph is generally aligned with the movement of feeling, then a close attention to fluctuations of value suggests an identification with impulse itself. Thus while the investor is typically imagined as detached from his money, able to ignore its day-to-day movements, the speculator is viewed as a creature of unregulated impulse and unruly emotion, in thrall, day and night, to his greed. (Thus while the investor may make more careful "use" of his money, the speculator is a more active caretaker of his.) The investor, able to wait for his "emotional payoff" (Schott 25), is promised in the end an even greater reward, while the speculator serves as a useful embodiment of bad habits: mental depravity, idleness, deceitfulness, and greed.

But the image of the investor waiting patiently for his payoff should alert us to a certain wavering in conventional representations of the difference between speculators and investors—a difference that has long rested upon the premise that, when it comes to the business of making money from money, there is a right way and a wrong one. "Wealth accrues from generally right behavior," wrote a commentator in 1998, "not from trying to extract the maximum profit out of any situation" (Schott 24). "Generally right behavior," according to this formulation, refers not exactly to not trying to make money, but, as in Carlyle's formula for attaining happiness, to making money without appearing to try to make money—to making money, in effect, while looking carefully in another direction. "Speculation" routinely describes an energetic attention to fluctuations in value, as contrasted with the investor's long-term involvement with "safe" stocks; identified as the placing of money in the service of risky projects, speculation is associated with terms like "optimism," "hope," and "bubble." But if one seeks to define the term with any precision, and in particular to clarify the distinction between investment and speculation, what one discovers is not that distinctions cannot be made—on the contrary, everyone can make them—but rather that, in the context of Britain's economy in the nineteenth century no less than our contemporary one, there is hardly an investment that is not, according to the usual definitions, a speculation: "The practice of buying articles of merchandise, or any purchasable commodity whatever, in expectation of a rise of price and of selling the same at considerable advance" (S. Maunder, qtd. in Mottram 4).[10]

Distinctions between investment and speculation tend to be made on the basis of personal involvement: the investor is said to be more committed to the company or commodity to which he lends his money. But both activities posit an attenuated relationship to the substance or commodity being traded; neither investor nor speculator need ever see the coffee or the guano. Differences thus tend to be articulated as matters of degree, assessing the quantity and quality of such intangibles as duration (how long an investor plans to hold a stock before selling) and intent (is the investor primarily interested in building a railroad, or in making money from an expected rise in railway shares?). Moreover, the characteristic charge made against speculators—that their greed involves them in risky enterprises—is also a matter of degree, since the anxieties about risk and instability attached to the term "speculator" are simply amplifications or exaggerations of feelings that attend the buying and selling of shares in general. In the hair-splitting nature of these distinctions, and in particular the failure of academic discourse to arrive at any consensus as to the meaning of the terms,[11] it is possible to see that the two categories are characteristically distinguished from one another not by any precise definition of the activities themselves, where difference to this day remains at the level of name-calling (the annals of respectable financial activity include venture capitalists, investment bankers, stockbrokers—anything but speculators), but rather according to particular constellations of feelings and attitudes—and that the character called the speculator, whose qualities were rapidly assimilated to the villains of nineteenth-century fiction at the same time that investment (or speculation) became the province of middle-class novel readers, served for the Victorians, as he does for us, as a bogeyman whose function it is to make speculation safe for everyone else: to assume for the national psyche the risks of involvement in the market.[12] The term "speculator" marks a boundary between right and wrong that cannot quite be aligned with the wavering pattern of the stock-market graph; in particular, it insists on a distinction between respectable and illicit behavior in relation to what has traditionally been represented as the dubious practice of making money from fluctuations in value.[13] The opposition between investment and speculation serves to shore up the belief that the system of values defining gentlemanly behavior coincides with, and will be revealed through, an individual's feelings about money.

Describing the source of Wharton's and Lopez's money, Trollope provides no specific account of the "care" Wharton has taken. But care is evident in the novel's quiet mystification of Wharton's financial activity, since for neither man is the source of his money revealed. And though we are told repeatedly that Wharton keeps his financial status and that of his children secret, to their detriment, these details are hidden from readers as well. Given the attention the novel devotes to each man's thinking when it comes to Emily, to one another's faults, and to Lopez's financial dealings, its silence about Wharton's wealth may be said to echo Wharton's own: to participate in the mystification of money and power intended to secure the line between right behavior and wrong. Trollope's non-divulgence of details here—the silence of a novelist whose signature, critics often remark, is the precise specification of his characters' income and capital—underscores the point that the distinction between investors and speculators lies less in what they do than in how they are said to feel about what they do, and in how we are taught to feel about them.

\* \* \*

That Emily Wharton's feeling for Lopez resembles a speculator's hopes for his shares—that her feeling about him is irrationally exuberant—we, like her father, suspect but can do nothing about; such truths, like all speculations, can only be proved retrospectively, once the bubble has burst. While her initial feelings about him are supremely confident—"I do love him, and I shall never love anyone else in the same way" (46)—she must be taught to see that her feelings are as ungrounded as Lopez's own happiness upon receiving large sums of money. Indeed, for Emily, Lopez comes to personify the rapid fluctuations to which, living in the atmosphere of her father's apparently illimitable wealth, she has never before been subject: he proves to be the embodiment of fluctuating value, the man with a stock ticker for a heart. After receiving a requested loan of £3,000 from his father-in-law, for instance, Lopez is elated: "he was overjoyed,—so much so that for a while he lost that restraint over himself which was habitual to him. He ate his breakfast in a state of exultation" (224). And yet "almost immediately" he finds himself needing money again. Here is Emily's response: "She endeavoured to judge him kindly, but a feeling of insecurity in reference to his affairs struck her at once and made her heart cold. . . . surely a large sum to have vanished in so short a time! Something of the uncertainty of business she could understand, but a business must be perilously uncertain if subject to such vicissitudes as these!" (301). The pattern of feeling she begins to observe in her husband and in her married life—a pattern that causes her heart to grow cold, revealing it to be no less a ticker than her husband's—is that of the fluctuating value of shares, the pace of whose movement she cannot, though she tries, assimilate to the "better or worse" of her marriage vows (301). It is a pattern whose appropriate periodicity she has internalized in her father's house, along with the intuition that she need not—indeed, ought not—know the source of the money that supports her.

Lopez, we learn, is possessed of the power of compelling belief; to this is ascribed Emily's mistaken conviction "that she had found the good man in Ferdinand Lopez" (42). His financial success depends, as we see in his relationship with Sexty Parker, on perpetuating his beliefs: on selling himself. Thus his first order of business upon marrying Emily is to teach her to look as he does upon money: "She must be instructed in his ways. She must learn to look upon the world with his eyes. She must be taught the great importance of money." And, more seriously, "He had perceived that she had much influence with her father, and she must be taught to use this influence unscrupulously on her husband's behalf" (214). But she resists—indeed, recoils from—his teaching, which requires her to be the conduit of her father's wealth: "He demanded of her the writing of the letter almost immediately. . . . It seemed as though she were seizing the advantage of the first moment of her freedom to take a violent liberty with her father" (220).

That asking her father for money should resemble the "taking" of "a violent liberty" points toward the Oedipal nature of this scenario; in Emily's narrative the symbolic system that identifies money with guano includes sexuality among the categories from which respectability requires the keeping of a careful distance.[14] For Emily, knowing the source of her husband's money, and in particular having her father be that source, both demystifies and endangers the hygienic attitude toward money the Wharton/Fletcher class wishes to preserve. The atmosphere of wealth in which Whartons and Fletchers dwell—in which wealth *is* atmosphere, as in the "pretty things" with which Emily surrounds herself after her marriage—is transformed by Lopez into money: "she was told that her household gods had a price put upon them, and that they were to be sold"

(337). What Wharton keeps secret from his children is not, of course, that he is wealthy, but rather by how much: not the fact of wealth but the details, the numbers invested with the mystery of parental power. Thus Emily's growing sense of degradation involves not just her husband's financial failure but the fact that she cannot choose not to know about it; the book of life, once opened (and of course one may say this of Trollope as well), turns out to be the financial page: "Without a moment's hesitation he could catch at the idea of throwing upon her father the burden of maintaining both her and himself! She understood the meaning of this. She could read his mind so far. She endeavoured not to read the book too closely,—but there it was, opened to her wider day by day, and she knew that the lessons which it taught were vulgar and damnable" (338).

The irrationality of Emily's earlier exuberance is both confirmed and balanced by the otherwise inexplicable rush of degradation and self-loathing she experiences after Lopez's suicide: by her own account she is "the woman that he had thrust so far into the mire that she can never again be clean" (643). Her repulsion—and Lopez's Jewishness contributes here—viscerally reinforces the difference between speculator and investor. Moreover, the feelings about money embodied in each term take shape as paradigmatically different forms of masculinity and a lesson about manhood: "there would come upon her unbidden, unwelcome reminiscences of Arthur Fletcher. . . . She remembered his light wavy hair, which she had loved as one loves the beauty of a dog, which had seemed to her young imagination, to her in the ignorance of her early years to lack something of a dreamed-of manliness. . . . But now,—now that it was all too late,—the veil had fallen from her eyes." And once feelings about money take shape in this way—are embodied as two men—they can be "seen" with absolute clarity: "She could now see the difference between manliness and 'deportment'" (338). Indeed, money appears to make everything clear, as Lopez's increasingly bad luck with it seems naturally to accompany and support the revelation that he is a thoroughly bad character. Thus the stock-market narrative substantiates, in an altogether unsurprising way, the differences between Lopez's character and Fletcher's. And it also enables the drawing of another much-needed distinction: that between one's father and the "good man" who will be one's husband. In Emily's desire not to know, as in her feeling of repulsion toward her husband and herself, the narrative of speculation, with its moral baggage about greed and the defiling touch of money—and of the Jew—is intertwined with a necessary cultural narrative whose trajectory demonstrates, with the unmistakable clarity of a plunging line on the stock-market graph, the irrationality of her investment in Ferdinand Lopez.

Wharton's failure to stop his daughter's marriage has been ascribed both to a failure of his prejudice—he is not quite prejudiced enough—and to its success: so concerned is he about Lopez's "foreignness" that he fails adequately to scrutinize the man's character. But like other characters in the novel, including his daughter and Lopez, Wharton in fact blunders because he is overidentified with his investment: his ability to evaluate Lopez is clouded by his feeling for his daughter. Indeed, as he considers Emily's feeling for Lopez he is unable to maintain the distinction of which he had previously been so certain:

> But then was he sure that he was right? He of course had his own way of looking at life, but was it reasonable that he should force his girl to look at things with his eyes? The man was distasteful to him as being unlike his idea of an English gentleman, and as being without those far-reaching fibres and roots by which he thought that the stability and solidity of a human tree should be assured. But the world was changing around him every day. Royalty was marrying out of its degree. Peers' sons were looking only for money. And, more than that, peers' daughters were bestowing themselves on Jews and shopkeepers. Had he not better make the usual inquiry about the man's means, and, if satisfied on that head, let the girl do as she would? Added to all this, there was growing on him a feeling that ultimately youth would as usual triumph over age, and that he would be beaten. If that were so, why worry himself, or why worry her? (75)

Wharton's thoughts display not the unwavering certainty of the clear moral line but rather the jittery peaks and valleys of the stock-market graph; his willingness to entertain the possibility of Ferdinand Lopez as a son-in-law—to overlook a distinction he had previously considered vital—takes shape as a mental wavering, one not wholly dissimilar from that manifested by Ferdinand Lopez in the process of teaching himself to distinguish between two identical payments. Tracing the fluctuating movements of characters' thoughts as they wend their way from one side of a question to the other, Trollope gives narrative form and identity to those peaks and valleys. But the identity such thoughts suggest, as they cross and re-cross the lines that separate right from wrong, is not organized enough to take a stand on one side or the other: it is identity that, finding no solid ground but its own conclusions, is in the position of backing itself, of founding feeling on feeling. Indeed, the pattern of Wharton's thoughts here mimics the uncertain status of Ferdinand Lopez himself, whose admission into polite society threatens its solid values: not because that society doesn't "know," as a gentleman knows, what kind of a man he is, but rather because it cannot locate the line he has crossed, nor can it draw one that will keep him out. It is up to the novel, then—and not only Trollope's, but the entire genre of evil-speculator novels of the period—to do what novels do best, which is to draw that line: to harden suspicion into narrative, to fix the trajectory of Lopez's life into a recognizable pattern, to render vivid distinctions and differences in character and feeling.

The beginning of *The Prime Minister* keeps the status of Lopez's Jewishness mysterious: it invites characters and readers to wonder whether he is, in fact, a Jew. Suspicion, as in those "disagreeable matters" Lopez hopes will not come up for discussion, creates a distinction waiting to be made, an outline that requires filling in, a potential awaiting fulfillment. So too, it turns out, is his status as speculator; Lopez's careless treatment of his wife, deceitfulness, and commission of the actual crime of forgery invite not so much the conclusion that speculators are evil as the suspicion that perhaps they are not quite evil enough. The series of mishaps that leads Lopez to suicide suggests on the part of the novelist what market analysts call "magical thinking"—something is so because I have wished it to be: a kind of thinking distinguishable from the novelist's usual business, if it is at all, by the palpability of its need. Making Lopez a Jew and a criminal is the equivalent of wanting the guano to be real, the equivalent of narratives that attempt to explain what the market is doing: it is a stock-market story, an attempt to secure feelings and beliefs in something outside the self.

Just as Lopez's Jewishness functions simultaneously as a figure for the unknown (no one knows his background) and as an image of absolute predictability (reinforcing the suspicion that he will, and deserves to, come to a bad end), so too does the novel's final section substantiate the suspicions it has aroused about him and, at the same time, devote itself to annihilating his identity. Having lost everything in speculation, he throws himself under a train and is "knocked into bloody atoms" (520). But his clothes reveal no signs of identity: he carries no papers, and his handkerchief and collar bear no marks. "The fragments of his body set identity at defiance, and even his watch had been crumpled into ashes" (523–24). Hammering his point home, as another nail in the coffin, Trollope has it discovered five months later that Lopez has signed Sexty Parker's name to a bill, effectively ruining Parker's wife and children: "He had been all a lie from head to foot" (606). But Lopez is not exactly a lie. Like the stories periodically found to circulate in the market—stories, designed to move stock prices, whose authors must be discovered, punished, and never allowed to trade again—his is not so much a false story as it is a shadow story, a trope for the market itself, which retains a cultural function as a clearinghouse for the separation of true narratives from false ones. And it is a trope for Trollope as well, as he tells us the story of a man who looks, dresses, and sits on a horse like a gentleman but is not one. And we know he is not, we are told, because the stories he tells are not the right kind of stories.[15]

Veering between exuberance and self-loathing, Emily Wharton defines the boundaries between which, Trollope suggests, feelings about money characteristically waver; that her feelings appear spontaneous and visceral, and are mediated through men, naturalizes emotion whose financial bearing the novel elaborates more directly elsewhere. Intertwining personal drama and financial crisis, Emily's story incorporates money into the familial narrative: just as she recoils from herself in horror, as from the contents of her husband's mind, so too may the state of one's money seem to echo—or does it produce?—the state of one's emotions. Such narratives facilitate the transfer of identity into numbers that is the market's lifeblood; in the elation or self-loathing that attends the fluctuation of the numbers, we pursue our own self-regulation, an ideal self embodied in the fantasy of an ideal number. Exploring the painful consciousness that signifies a failure to keep one's proper distance from money, however, Emily's narrative in fact suggests how attending to the numbers may help us avoid such a consciousness, structuring our proper relation to money and the market. For the numbers, possessing the lure of authenticity and simultaneously refusing to give anything away, offer us the feeling that we know even as they tell us nothing, even as they serve as substitutes for whatever it is they might tell. Thus while keeping us focused on the drama of their movement—on, for instance, what we have designated the roller-coaster ride of the market's ups and downs—they allow us to keep our feet, or so it seems, out of the guano. After the narrative of Lopez's exuberance, of Emily's mistake, and of the degradation that results from their entanglement comes the embrace of what might now have to be called rational exuberance: the ordinary emotions of the married, middle-class subject, whose choice, shaped by life's hard lessons, is articulated by that narrative as a choice of investment over speculation. One might choose otherwise; in some cases, one has done so, and may do so again. To know this is to acknowledge the compelling quality of the line we have learned to straddle, and of the numbers we continue to look upon for what they can tell us about ourselves.

## Notes

1. This chapter was written toward the end of the "boom" of the late 1990s, before its end was officially designated. For what was then called the "slowdown" of winter 2000–2001 was a slowdown only in the context of the bubble narrative. Writes Robert Shiller: "The present stock market displays the classic features of a speculative bubble, a situation in which temporarily high prices are sustained largely by investors' enthusiasm rather than by consistent estimation of real value. . . . We need to know if the value investors have imputed to the market is not really there, so that we can adjust our planning and thinking" (xii). But a bubble only earns its name when most investors have ceased to put their money on those "overvalued" stocks—in other words, once it is perceived to have popped. Hence I tend to agree with Peter Garber that " 'Bubble' characterizations . . . are non-explanations of events, merely a name that we attach to a financial phenomenon that we have not invested sufficiently in understanding" (124).

Though this essay was inspired by the dot-com boom and the intense interest in the market that accompanied it, the issues and dynamics discussed here are not tied to, or limited by, any particular episode. (Indeed, as this volume goes to press, in 2008, the United States is at the end of another such cycle, this time involving the housing market: a bubble, again, defined as such after it is said to have popped.) My subject is the way stock market societies read prices as reflections of human emotions, at the same time attaching emotions to the supposed reality of stock prices. Such events as "booms" are, in this scenario, short-lived bursts of feeling in the context of a lengthy emotional narrative: episodes whose boundaries come into view only when prices are generally perceived to have become less "rational" than usual.

2. As Tatiana Holway observes, the problem is noted by Adam Smith: money "cannot adequately represent value, though the market, which trades on price, behaves as if it does, obscuring the distinction between the 'nominal' and the 'real.' " Holway goes on to discuss this distinction, writing that "speculation . . . served the interests of capitalism" (113). My point is that speculation *is* capitalism.

3. Contemporary examples include such figures as Ivan Boesky, Michael Milken, Martin Frankel, and Jonathan Lebed, the last discussed further below (note 15). Frankel's story is one of familial corruption and sexual debauchery as well as (the

always-cited) greed; Boesky notoriously expressed the extent of his corruption when he commented—at a commencement address, no less—that "Greed is all right." When Lebed's case came to light, his relationship with his family was of much interest to reporters. In such cases, the Securities and Exchange Commission appears (understandably) hapless, its job the regulation of an institution antithetical to regulation.

4. All references to *The Prime Minister* are to the 1994 Penguin edition edited by David Skilton. On Victorian participation in the market, see Hennessy 51.

5. Trollope uses the term "admitted" similarly in relation to Augustus Melmotte: "Mr. Melmotte was admitted into society, because of some enormous power which was supposed to lie in his hands; but even by those who thus admitted him he was regarded as a thief and a scoundrel" (*The Way We Live Now* 247; this quotation is from the 1994 Penguin edition edited by Frank Kermode). On Britain's exportation of raw materials and goods and importation of manufactured goods from the mid-1870s on, see Checkland, *Rise* 62–64.

6. The suggestion is that Lopez's open admission of his foreignness might deflect Wharton's attention away from other, still-unspecified problems: "He could not get over the fact that he was the son of a Portuguese parent, but by admitting that openly he thought he might avoid present discussion on matters which might, perhaps, be more disagreeable, but to which he need not allude if the accident of his birth were to be taken by the father as settling the question" (32–33). The "matters" remain unnamed: Lopez's financial activities and his Jewishness are, the implication is, equally and interchangeably disagreeable.

7. Thus while the definition of speculation is unstable, the insistence on a distinction between legitimate and illegitimate modes of investment is not. That stock-market discourse continues to insist on this difference even as the meanings of the terms shift (what Lopez does is now called options trading, for instance, and there is nothing illegitimate about it) both reveals the continuing presence of the nineteenth century in the twenty-first and explains why it is so easy not to see it. Any number of people today called "successful investors" are also contemporary versions of Ferdinand Lopez; Jim Rogers, for instance, who claims to "bet" on "whole countries," has this to say: "the only thing better is finding a country everybody's bullish on and shorting it" (Train 3). There is Michael Milken, said to have considered finance an art form, and Jonathan Lebed, discussed below (note 15)—both of whose activities, while widely considered immoral, were completely legal. See Lewis, *Money Culture* xiv. But perhaps the more salient point is that anyone involved in the market today is a Lopez figure in the sense that investment is the "backing" of opinion; our own Lopez-like qualities are obscured, however, by the speculator/investor dramas played out in public. When a good investment goes bad—as in the case of Enron, in December 2001—it becomes a speculation, and the search for culprits begins.

8. "My hope to rise had always been built on writing novels, and at last by writing novels I have risen" (Trollope, *An Autobiography* 169).

9. Trollope's attention to "the business of life" has been discussed by Collins, who notes that, when introducing a character, Trollope "specifies his or her income or capital" (297). But to say this much is only to suggest, as Trollope criticism typically does, that in his novels and in his life the author displays an amusing and eccentric—and thus wholly "Victorian"—obsession with financial detail.

10. Mottram dates the term "speculation" from "about 1850," although the point of his book is that "The thing itself is of immemorial antiquity." He offers his own, succinct definition: "Dealing in fluctuating values" (41). Writes Michael Guth, "A specu-

lator buys (sells) goods under uncertainty, with the intent to resell (repurchase) them after some anticipated favorable price change" (10).

11. Consider the fine shades of differentiation and judgment required by this definition: "The more a house purchaser weighs the capital gain potential of his investment, as opposed to wanting to capture the benefits from living in a house, the more he acts like a speculator *per se*" (Guth 10).

12. In Dickens's *Little Dorrit* (1855–1857), speculation is described as a "fever" and an "infection." Dickens thus seems aware that a speculator is an investor by another, less decorous name: he or she is an ordinary person with a "disorder." Says Pancks of Clennam, " 'It was my misfortune to lead him into a ruinous investment' (Mr. Pancks still clung to that word, and never said speculation)" (538; citation from the 1982 Oxford University Press edition edited by H. P. Sucksmith). The figure of the investor reinforces the characteristic Victorian division between work and home, while the speculator's imagined constant attention to his money attests to the unsavory nature of someone who has no "other" life. In this way, the speculator turns out to be a strangely unified figure, and Victorian discomfort about him reveals the undesirability of such unity in Victorian ideologies of identity. For another example, see Jaffe, "Detecting the Beggar."

13. This dubiousness is, of course, emotional and moral as well as practical. Identifying someone as a speculator is thus analogous to diagnosing that person as having an "eating disorder" or finding him or her to be a "compulsive shopper." Such diagnoses, classifying the psychological and somatic effects of capitalism as "disorders," simultaneously define and disavow the mechanisms on which capitalism depends; they gesture toward an ideal balance in relation to which individual subjects are measured.

14. My use of the term "Oedipal" refers to the way in which marriage invokes the specter of parental sexuality. Wharton's desire that Emily marry Arthur Fletcher—the candidate most like himself, and someone she has known her entire life—requires the drawing of a distinction between father and husband; this is accomplished, first by Emily's choice of an outsider as husband, and then by the association of that husband with everything illicit. Lopez is too close to the money, and that closeness is linked to racial and sexual impurity as well as moral degradation because marriage itself evokes the possibility of being too close to the money: to parental sexuality. (The intense odoriferousness of Lopez's chosen commodities—coffee and guano—figures in this symbolic constellation as well.) Emily's first marriage thus enables—requires—a return, in the second, to her father and her father's values; it allows for a marriage from which the dangers of illicit desire, whether imagined as involving sexuality or money, have been purged. Fletcher, it should be noted, is a lover on the investment model: he will wait for Emily indefinitely.

15. Here are some examples of the wrong kind of stories: "The stock price of Emulex, a maker of computer networking equipment, plunged early yesterday after a false negative report about the company was circulated" (Berenson). Also relevant is the story of Jonathan Lebed, a New Jersey teenager who made his avid attention to the CNBC numbers pay off by

attend[ing] high school by day and, according to securities regulators, manipulat[ing] stocks by night on his computer. When he was apprehended for his scheme of promoting obscure stocks on the Internet that he had recently bought himself, then selling the shares at higher prices to those who inexplicably acted on his anonymous tips, his response was "Everybody does it." In a world where analysts put outlandish price targets on stocks and money managers regularly promote the stocks they hold on CNBC, truer words were never spoken. (Morgenson)

(This article hands out the annual "Augustus Melmotte Memorial Prize," which Lebed won for 2000.) The false report works, of course, because it looks exactly like a true one, and the "hair-trigger" state of the market reflects investors' awareness of their inability to tell the difference. A profile of Lebed by Michael Lewis makes a number of relevant points, including the idea that the Securities and Exchange Commission was created because, "To the greater public in 1934, the numbers on the stock-market ticker no longer seemed to represent anything 'real,' but rather the result of manipulation by financial pros. So, how to make the market seem 'real'? The answer was to make new stringent laws against stock-market manipulation, whose job it was to make sure their machinations did not ever again unnerve the great sweaty rabble. That's not how the S.E.C. put it, of course" ("Extracurricular Activities" 32–33).

# 8 "Rushing into Eternity"

## Suicide and Finance in Victorian Fiction

*Nancy Henry*

> One can never punish any fault in the world if the sinner can revenge himself
> upon us by rushing into eternity.
>
> —Anthony Trollope, *The Prime Minister*

According to John Kenneth Galbraith, following "Black Thursday" on the New York Stock Exchange (October 24, 1929), the London penny press told of Wall Street speculators "hurling themselves out of windows; pedestrians picked their way delicately between the bodies of fallen financiers. The American correspondent for *The Economist* wrote an indignant column for his paper protesting against this picture of imaginary carnage" (128).[1] Galbraith observes: "In the United States the suicide wave that followed the stock market crash is also a part of the legend of 1929. In fact, there was none" (128). Citing statistics that show suicide rates were higher during the years of the market's recovery than in the immediate aftermath of the crash, he writes: "One can only guess how the suicide myth became established" (129–30).[2]

While we still do not know exactly how the tenacious legend of leaping financiers originated, Galbraith's tracing of the "imaginary carnage" to the London penny press is suggestive of transatlantic cultural exchanges and the seemingly irresistible convention of imagining financiers as suicides. Throughout the second half of the nineteenth century and into the twentieth, some British and American financiers and businessmen did kill themselves in response to collapsing markets, personal bankruptcy, or the exposure of fraud. But the ground for the myth of 1929 was prepared by Victorian novelists who used suicide repeatedly when representing a sphere of economic activity in which they were often implicated as active investors but about which they were morally ambivalent. Galbraith concludes about the 1929 myth: "The weight of the evidence suggests that the newspapers and the public merely seized on such suicides as occurred to show that people were reacting appropriately to their misfortune" (130). The combination of sensationalism and moral judgment evident in the image of ruined speculators splattered on the New York pavement has its origins in Victorian financial plots—in novels such as Charles Dickens's *Little Dorrit* (1855–1857), in which the financier Mr. Merdle slits his throat in a public bath, leaving the marble "veined with a dreadful red" (590), and Anthony Trollope's *The Prime Minister* (1875–1876), in which the speculator Ferdinand Lopez steps in front of an express train and is "smashed into bloody atoms" (II: 194).[3]

The suicide myth is part of a broader critique of capitalism that attended the crash of 1929 and that also has its origins in Victorian literature. Edmund Wilson invoked suicide to launch his bleak cultural analysis of the time: "The brokers and bankers who are shooting themselves and jumping out of windows have been disheartened by the precariousness of their profession—but would they be killing themselves if they loved it?" Who today, he asks, "can really love our meaningless life . . . ?" (527). Wilson's left-leaning literary set hated the Big Business era and resented its "barbarism, its crowding-out of everything they cared about." The writers and artists he knew "couldn't help being exhilarated at the sudden, unexpected collapse of that stupid gigantic fraud" (498–99). His outrage at "our meaningless life" and his society's "barbarism" is not only that of the socialist angry at economic inequalities under capitalism; it is the anger of the educated elite at bourgeois vulgarity, and in this it recalls Matthew Arnold's attack on the Philistine businessman.

In *Culture and Anarchy* (1869), Arnold invokes a newspaper article reporting "the suicide of a Mr. Smith, secretary to some insurance company, who it was said, 'laboured under the apprehension that he would come to poverty, and that he was eternally lost'" (115).[4] The conjunction of these two apprehensions supports Arnold's argument that a narrow Puritanism has reduced the concerns of the middle-class Philistines to the fate of their souls (rather than the quality of their lives) and confused that spiritual future with the present size of their bank accounts: "What havoc do the united conceptions make of our lives!" (116). For Arnold, as for Wilson over half a century later, the businessman's suicide is a predictable indication of the havoc and meaninglessness of our lives. Arnold had explored the Hellenic impetus to suicide in his poem "Empedocles on Etna" (1852). He is unwilling, however, to confer any dignity on the act of his contemporary Mr. Smith. The sense of familiarity Arnold experiences in reading about what he calls Smith's "violently morbid, and fatal turn" (116) reflects not only the occasional suicide reported in the newspaper but the prevalence of financial suicides in Victorian literature.

## Suicide and Finance in Victorian Fiction

[N]o ungentlemanly act on Mr. Merdle's part would surprise me.

—Charles Dickens, *Little Dorrit*

Suicide in response to financial loss began to emerge in British literature in the mid-1850s. It haunts the characters in Tennyson's *Maud* (1855), which begins with the invocation of an alleged suicide over failed speculations, and Elizabeth Gaskell's *North and South* (1854–1855) in which the industrialist John Thornton's career is overshadowed by his father's suicide following a similar failure. *Little Dorrit* initiated a tradition of resolving a financial plot with the dramatic suicide of the financier. In the 1860s and 1870s, Trollope developed the tradition, which continued, with variations, into the twentieth century.[5]

Literary critics have viewed the fictional suicides of financial men as either an inevitable moral justice or an allegory of modern society. In *Victorian Suicide*, Barbara Gates writes that "these once-monied ruins would, in being self-murdered, have seemed suitably self-judged" (69). In *The Hell of the English*, Barbara Weiss claims that suicide is part of the larger metaphor of bankruptcy in the Victorian novel—"the perfect representation of this shattered culture" (22). John Reed refers to suicide as "fiction's conventional ending for the wicked speculator" (190). Taking up the subject in early twentieth-century American novels, George M. Spangler argues that "self-destruction is one of the salient facts and an apt symbol of social conditions in Western Europe and the United States" (496).

I want to argue that the trope of suicide as a response to financial loss beginning in mid-Victorian literature was not only a denunciation of a corrupt financial culture, and was not even only a metaphor. Rather, it was part of an attempt to find the right language and images with which to represent a financial sector that had long been considered unsuited and inappropriate for fiction because of genteel and literary society's distaste for trade, business, and finance. Suicide in the financial plots of novels emerged when Victorian novelists were compelled to begin incorporating business and finance into literature. Their challenge was to create characters and plots that were at once realistic (because finance was becoming such a pervasive dimension of Victorian life), entertaining (because finance was dull), and appropriately moral without being simply didactic.

Critics have addressed the ways in which an emerging financial culture—new institutions, concepts, professions, and kinds of knowledge—affected narrative form and content especially in the realist novel. Tara McGann argues that understanding high finance required "new narratives, new narrative devices, new modes of narration, and a new narrative arc" (155). Audrey Jaffe suggests that the stock exchange provided "terms within which familiar cultural narratives, and indeed familiar cultural identities, have been rewritten and reconceived" (this volume 147). Mary Poovey has shown how the realist novel emerged in conjunction with financial journalism, arguing that mid-century novelists used financial plots to "enhance their genre's reputation for relevance and seriousness" and that novelists adapted "financial themes to the formal conventions of realism" (this volume 52). The financial plot and the realist novel evolved together.

When financial plots are resolved by the suicide of the financier, we often see traces of other, non-realist discourses—Gothic, Romantic, sensational—suggesting that novelists did not yet know whether "the City"—that square mile where London's financial institutions are located and its financial transactions conducted—should be portrayed as a foreign, exotic land of danger and adventure or an all too familiar English world of misplaced values where money was more important than life itself. In Trollope's *Can You Forgive Her* (1864–1865), even the evil George Vavasor, who started his career as a stockbroker, contracts a hatred for the City when no one there will honor the bills of exchange he has extorted from his cousin Alice: "George Vavasor cursed the City, and made his calculation about murdering it. Might not a river of strychnine be turned on round the Exchange about luncheon time?" (II: 209). Trollope's allegorization of the City suggests not only Vavasor's deranged state of mind but a general perception that the City had a separate, coherent identity and operated with its own logic. Decisions made there, for reasons mysterious to outsiders, nonetheless affected lives throughout the nation (see Checkland, "Mind").

The novelist Charlotte Riddell (1832–1906) was a lone voice protesting the failure of her contemporaries to represent businessmen realistically. In *George Geith of Fen Court* (1864), her narrator complains that the subject of trade "can find no writer worthy of it, no one who does not jeer at business and treat with contempt that which is holy in God's sight, because it is useful, and proves beneficial to millions and millions of His creatures" (98). Through her efforts to redress the literary bias against the world of business and finance, Riddell became known as "the novelist of the City," provoking one critic to ask whether her works "should be reviewed in the columns that are set apart for literature, or whether they would not more fitly receive a notice side by side with the works on foreign exchanges or the currency" ("Review of *The Senior Partner*" 375; see also Srebrnik).

Most literary men and women knew the financial sphere primarily through its representation in financial journalism. They read about foreign exchanges and currency and occasionally something more exciting: a smash or a suicide like that of Mr. Smith, which caught Arnold's eye in the *Times*.[6] It is not surprising that sensational accounts in the press often accompany the suicides in Victorian financial plots. Lack of first-hand knowledge about finance was a point of pride for the social and cultural elite, as an ambiguous compliment of Riddell's "fearful and wonderful knowledge of matters financial" suggests (Noble). Riddell's husband was a businessman in the City who at one point declared bankruptcy. She was unusual, especially for a woman, in having the opportunity to observe City life, and she was ahead of her time in seeing the potential of business as material for fiction. Neither her realistic representations nor her exhortations to other writers to give business its due changed the fact that most mid-Victorian novelists were still more likely to represent City men as players in sensational financial plots than as realistic characters whose lives were integrated with those of other professionals.[7]

In the figure of the financier-suicide, novelists took an occasional real-life event and turned it into a literary convention that satisfied readers' growing taste for violence and sensation, guaranteeing that the City remained separate and "other." The swindling financiers who commit suicide in the fiction of the 1850s–1870s—Merdle in *Little Dorrit*, Dobbs Broughton in *The Last Chronicle* of *Barset* (1866–1867), Augustus Melmotte in *The Way We Live Now* (1874–1875), and Ferdinand Lopez in *The Prime Minister*—established a pattern to which later authors self-consciously responded. Tracing the relationship between finance and suicide in the realist novel, we can see how the City (and later Wall Street) infiltrated the domestic sphere, specifically the lives of women. While Dickens's Amy Dorrit remained pure and free of the corrupting influences of Mr. Merdle, later financial plots represented the inevitable collapsing of the separate spheres and the adoption of City traits and tactics by women.[8] By the end of *The Way We Live Now*, Marie Melmotte has become an excellent "woman of business" and "her father's own daughter" (II: 448).[9] The plot of George Gissing's *The Whirlpool* (1897) is set in motion when Bennett Frothingham shoots himself in the City following the failure of his Britannia Loan, Assurance, Investment and Banking Co. Ltd. It concludes when his daughter Alma, who pursues her musical career with all her father's reckless energy, takes an overdose of a cordial to which she has become addicted. In Edith Wharton's *The Custom of the Country* (1813), Undine Spragg is the daughter of a Wall Street speculator whose ruthless social ambitions are compared explicitly to her father's financial dealings. Her relationship with the successful financier Elmer Moffat leads to the suicide of her patrician, financially inept husband, showing how Wharton adapted the Victorian novelists' use of suicide as moral critique to her own Gilded Age American context.

## Trollope's Financial Plots

Now for the man of money.

—Anthony Trollope, *The Way We Live Now*

In an 1863 letter to George Eliot, Trollope insisted that his novels were "not sensational" (*George Eliot Letters* 8: 313).[10] Aware of the market for sensation that emerged particularly in the 1860s and later satirized by him in the authoress Lady Carbury in *The Way We Live Now*, Trollope was self-conscious about his measured use of sensational scenes. *The Last Chronicle of Barset* opposes sensational fiction (with its origin in Byronic romanticism) and Victorian realism. The Byron-reading Miss Lucy Toogood would like to see a Corsair or a Giaour in Tavistock Square, but she resigns herself to current reality: "But all that is over now, you know, and young people take houses in Woburn Place, instead of being locked up, or drowned, or married to a hideous monster behind a veil" (396).[11] Taking houses in Woburn Place is just the sort of thing Trollope's characters would do.

Just as Miss Toogood contrasts the dullness of "taking houses" to the danger of being "locked up or drowned," Miss Madalina Demolines contrasts dull and dangerous forms of income. Her own money is invested in "a first-class mortgage on land at four per cent" because "land can't run away" (255), a phrase similar to that used by Dr. Grantly when advising his son: "Land is about the only thing that can't fly away" (605). But Madalina has a voyeuristic fascination with people who play the market and describes Dobbs and his wife as "living in the crater of a volcano" waiting for a "smash" to come: "These City people get so used to it that they enjoy it. The risk is everything to them" (390). In Trollope's financial plots, the financier/speculator is a type of Victorian Corsair—vital and bold—yet also often reckless and fraudulent, inhabiting the mysterious world of the City, whose values were foreign to the landed gentry, the genteel West End, and the literary intelligentsia.[12]

*The Last Chronicle*'s nouveau riche speculator Dobbs Broughton, recalling Merdle and anticipating Melmotte, is uncommunicative and impenetrable as he and his wife rise to social prominence on the impression of wealth, despite the skepticism of characters such as Johnny Eames: "I think they stink of money . . . but I'm not sure that they've got any all the same" (248). Their status and very identities are without foundation and destined to collapse. Eventually, Dobbs fails in his speculations with other people's money and becomes violent and monstrous with drink. Metaphorically cornered by creditors, he unromantically shoots himself in his City offices.

Following the event, Miss Demolines is drawn to the scene, determined to find out the bloody details of the tragedy, which she then uses to captivate Johnny, whom she coyly asks, "'Would you have me repeat to you all the bloody details of that terrible scene?' she said. 'It is impossible'" (777). And yet she does "so far overcome her horror as to tell them" and "with something more of circumstance than Eames desired": "'I shall see—that—body, floating before my eyes while I live,' she said, 'and the gory wound and—and—.' 'Don't,' said Johnny, recoiling in truth from the picture by which he was revolted" (777–78). Madalina's representation of Dobbs's suicide signals Trollope's awareness of how violence simultaneously captivates and revolts. Trollope's belief in the ultimately unsatisfying nature of sensation, which led him to insist on the realistic nature of his fiction, is suggested by the artist Conway Dalrymple when Johnny asks him whether he is shocked by Dobb's suicide: "Yes; it shocked us all at first; we are used to it now" (781).

The City offered a world full of potential for realist fiction, but as Riddell points out, most writers held themselves above the activities and perceived values of business and finance and found it virtually impossible to represent City life without contempt. While financial journalism may have been attempting to naturalize aspects of the City for its readers, cartoons in *Punch* mocked it and melodramatic plays demonized its inhabitants. Authors such as Trollope, Dickens, and Eliot negotiated their contracts and invested their profits in a business-like manner, and yet remnants of the prejudice against the perceived philistinism of business persist in their fiction.

Trollope's financial plots attempted to capture the reality of an expanding financial sphere but were unable to forgo the judgment that genteel society passed on business culture or the temptation to cast the financier as a "hideous monster" behind a veil of social respectability. In *The Way We Live Now*, Georgiana Longstaffe warns her parents: "you and papa must not be surprised if I take some horrid creature from the Stock Exchange" (I: 203). There was also something vulgar about possessing the kind of knowledge of business and finance that would allow a novelist to represent them accurately. Trollope repeatedly used suicide—with its Gothic, melodramatic, and sensational associations—to cut against the grain of his unsensational narratives. When he decided on suicide rather than a trial for Melmotte, he invited connections with John Sadleir—a real financier-suicide—but he also recurred to a convention that created intertextual connections to Dickens's Merdle and his own Dobbs Broughton, raising the question of whether the literary convention of the suicidal financier should be read as a representation of an infrequent but real part of Victorian life or as a shift into a melodramatic register that seemed appropriate to the resolution of financial plots. Trollope and later novelists seemed to be distinctly self-conscious about the religious, moral, legal, and literary discourses surrounding suicide so that the intertextual resonances complicate the financers' suicides, making them more than simply an apt punishment for financial crimes.[13]

## Body and Soul

> ... what punishment can human laws inflict on one who has withdrawn himself from their reach?
>
> —William Blackstone, *Commentaries on the Laws of England*

Trollope's financial plots emphasize the physical, rather than spiritual, fate of his men of money. His language implicitly contrasts the modern-day equation of money with life to religious and superstitious concerns about the afterlife. Matthew Arnold's Mr. Smith killed himself because he believed that he was eternally lost (as well as because he feared losing his money). Arnold objected to this Puritan preoccupation with the fate of the soul after death, viewing it as a misguided, modern obsession that went hand in hand with the Philistine emphasis on material wealth. Discussions of suicide in England, however, had always turned on the fate of the soul after leaving the body. In *Commentaries on the Laws of England* (1765–1769), William Blackstone observes that the spiritual offence of suicide lies "in invading the prerogative of the Almighty, and rushing into his immediate presence uncalled for" (937). Thus, in English law, the spiritual crime of suicide is constituted by the act of the soul after leaving the body.

The concept of the hereafter is invoked throughout Trollope, particularly in relation to suicide. In *Can You Forgive Her?*, George Vavasor, with a hideous scar down his face, fantasizes about murdering himself and those around him in addition to "the City." His ideal is the murderer "who had scoured his bosom free from all fears of the hereafter" (II: 125). Perhaps it is this fear for his soul that prevents Vavasor from murder and suicide, but it does not prevent him from imagining the ways in which he might kill himself. His fantasies anticipate precisely those suicides Trollope would represent in his later financial plots.

He thinks of poison (what Melmotte takes) and a pistol (what Broughton uses), and in a remarkable foreshadowing of Lopez's suicide, "He thought of an express train rushing along at its full career, and of the instant annihilation which it would produce" (II: 179). Later, finding himself hopelessly ruined, Vavasor speaks to his former mistress of the journey he plans to take. She asks, "But, George, where are you going?" He replies, "Wherever people do go when their brains are knocked out of them; or, rather, when they have knocked out their own brains,—if that makes any difference" (II: 325). And yes, given the distinctive crime of suicide, the means of death would matter to the destination of both body and soul.

Vavasor escapes justice by absconding to America. In later works, Trollope repeatedly takes up Blackstone's notion of suicide as a spiritual absconding—"invading the prerogative of the Almighty, and rushing into his immediate presence uncalled for." Describing the inquiry following Melmotte's suicide, Trollope's narrator refers to Melmotte as one who has "rushed away to see whether he could not find an improved condition of things elsewhere" (II: 356). Lady Glencora complains after the death of Ferdinand Lopez in *The Prime Minister*: "One can never punish any fault in the world if the sinner can revenge himself upon us by rushing into eternity" (II: 215).[14] By "rushing into eternity," Broughton, Melmotte, and Lopez evade punishment and achieve a kind of perverse revenge that Dickens recognized when he described Merdle as "the greatest Forger and the greatest Thief that ever cheated the gallows" (777).

Trollope's treatment of suicide is also self-conscious about the historical images surrounding the suicide's body. Blackstone asks "what punishment can human laws inflict on one who has withdrawn himself from their reach?" The answer is that in addition to forfeiting property, the suicide receives an "ignominious burial in the highway, with a stake driven through the body" (938). This gruesome safeguard against soulless bodies rising to haunt the living was still practiced in some parts of England until an 1823 law prohibited it (Gates 6).

In *The Way We Live Now*, Melmotte's corpse is kept under constant watch; his daughter hardly dared leave her room "lest she should encounter him dead, and thus more dreadful even than when alive" (II: 338). While many suicides in the Victorian period were spared having their possessions confiscated by a judgment of temporary insanity, Trollope's narrator asserts that "a Melmotte" would not be "saved by a verdict of insanity from the cross roads, or whatever scornful grave may be allowed to those who have killed themselves with their wits about them" (II: 356), and in the end Melmotte is judged "*felo de se*, and therefore carried away to the cross roads—or elsewhere" (II: 357).[15]

This tradition of burying at the crossroads was already obsolete in Trollope's time, but it was part of British cultural memory. In Gissing's *The Whirlpool*, Frothingham's suicide initiates and then haunts the plot. Hugh Carnaby, whose wife has lost her fortune in the failure of Frothingham's company, is pleased when Frothingham is declared *felo de se* rather than assigned "the foolish tag about temporary madness." The financier had escaped the wrath of his shareholders, who felt the typical frustration at not being able to punish the guilty. Hugh remarks: "It's a pity they no longer bury at four cross-roads, with a stake in his inside. (Where's that from? I remember it somehow.)" (54). His wife responds: "You're rather early-Victorian," the narrator adding that by this term she "was wont to signify barbarism or crudity in art, letters, morality or social feeling" (54).

The superstitious past is recalled in various vampiric images throughout Trollope's financial plots. Before Melmotte's suicide, it was said that "he was fed with the blood of widows and children" (I: 68). Broughton calls his business partner, Mrs. Van Siever, a "downright leech" (367–68). The blood-sucking Mrs. Van, who pushes Dobbs to suicide, and the sensationalizing Miss Demolines, whose name recalls the French Revolutionary Camille Desmoulins (guillotined in 1794) and who describes the suicide in the chapter called "Madalina's Heart is Bleeding," are part of the subtext through which Trollope infuses his financial plots with Gothic and sensational discourses.

The traces of superstition evident in the image of blood-sucking moneylenders contrasts an older benighted belief system to the modern religion of Mammon. The image of the Christian soul freed to rush away from the body and its sins, like that of money so insubstantial it can fly away in an instant, shows a late Victorian anxiety about the loss of the stability provided historically by religion and a social hierarchy based on landownership. Trollope's ironic inclusion of such images suggests that the immediate threat is less the souls of suicides invading the prerogative of the Almighty than stock market money becoming predominant over land-based wealth.

## The Last Chronicle of Barset

> Shot hisself in the City—laws!
>
> —Anthony Trollope, *The Last Chronicle of Barset*

For Trollope, overly sensitive, romantic thoughts of suicide are also remnants of the past, and are explicitly contrasted to the real thing. In identifying this dichotomy, he participated in a larger cultural conversation about representations of suicide from the late 1850s.[16] In his 1857 article, "Suicide in Life and Literature," G. H. Lewes objected to "the extreme discrepancy manifested between the literary conception of the causes of suicide, and the conception necessarily formed after a survey of the facts" (57). His article was partly a reaction against the influence of Romantic portrayals of suicide such as Goethe's *Sorrows of Young Werther* (1774), which Lewes argued "throw a sentimental halo over suicide" (77). In this article, which appeared shortly after the completed publication of *Little Dorrit,* he saw a lack of realism in recent novels that used suicide as "a clumsy contrivance for cutting a knot which the author cannot skillfully untie" (75).[17]

In her 1859 essay "Self-Murder," Harriet Martineau also objected to romanticized portrayals in literature, writing that "it would be a great blessing if the rude and disgusting truth were thoroughly known and appreciated that, in the great majority of cases, the self-destroyer has injured his brain by drink or other excess" (510). Olive Anderson concurs that the main route to suicide in the City in 1861 was not financial failure but alcoholism: "it is in the City that the link between suicide and alcoholism seems strongest in mid-Victorian London" (128). The connection between the City, alcoholism, and suicide is part of the factual discourse on suicide that co-exists with the romantic and melodramatic within Trollope's realist fiction. The opinion in the City is that Dobbs killed himself "rather through the effects of drink than because of his losses" (691), and Melmotte is drunk when he swallows poison.

Lewes and Martineau call on authors to provide less romantic, more realistic representations. In his financial plots, Trollope is aware of the alternative models available for representing suicides: the romantic, the sensational, and the realistic. In *The Last Chronicle* the realistic suicide of Dobbs is juxtaposed to the romantic fantasies of suicide indulged by the Reverend Josiah Crawley. This juxtaposition comments on the nature of the financier and the place such a character might have in fiction. In *George Geith*, Riddell's narrator argues that literature belittles business "solely because business has never yet learnt to be self-conscious; because it is in its very nature to work, rather than to think, to push forward to the goal rather than to analyze the reasons which induce it to push forward at all" (98). Matthew Arnold simply lamented "the entire subordination of thinking to doing" (113). Trollope stages this dichotomy between the thinker and the doer, using it to structure his two main plot lines. Throughout the novel, Crawley is all interiority and inaction, while Dobbs— especially after he "blows his brains out"—is all exteriority—unreflective, unexamined action.

Crawley's problems with money are far from those of Trollope's financiers.[18] He has been accused of stealing a £20 check, and vague and impractical as he is, he cannot remember whether or not he did take it. This state of uncertainty initiates an existential crisis for the brooding clergyman, who has never been able to support his family properly. Crawley's thoughts and language are learned and literary. Recalling Tennyson's poem "Mariana" (1830): "'Would that I were dead!' he repeated. 'The load is too heavy for me to bear, and I would that I were dead!'" (79). Throughout the novel, Trollope elaborates an association between money problems and a wish to die. Describing Crawley's condition, the narrator explains that "these are the pangs of poverty which drive the Crawleys of the world to the frequent entertaining of that idea of the bare bodkin" (92). But like Hamlet, Crawley only contemplates suicide. The idea of "making away with himself had flitted through his own mind a dozen times" (118–19).

Crawley is also associated with suicide through metaphor. When he considers giving up his position—committing "professional suicide" (404)—he plays out his abasement in detail, and Trollope describes him by simile:

> He was as a man who walks along a river's bank thinking of suicide, calculating
> how best he might kill himself—whether the river does not offer an opportunity
> too good to be neglected, telling himself that for many reasons he had better do so,
> suggesting to himself that the water is pleasant and cool, and that his ears would
> soon be deaf to the harsh noises of the world—but yet knowing, or thinking that he
> knows, that he never will kill himself. (403)

Crawley only dreams of suicide in his quiet, literary way. He has the heightened, complex consciousness that marks him as unfit for the real world, so that the matter of the check undoes him.

*The Last Chronicle* invokes both the Romantic tradition of representing suicide—the premeditated death of the sensitive individual to which Lewes and Martineau objected—and the alcohol-fuelled, bloody suicide that seemed appropriate for the City. Crawley's consoling thoughts of a bloodless drowning represent the Romantic strain. In contrast, Dobbs's suicide is unexpected and disgusting, as summarized by Johnny: "He blew his brains out in *delirium tremens*" (820). The contrast between the literary interiority of Crawley and the unexamined act of Dobbs represents the difference between genteel/intellectual and business cultures and dramatizes an assumption about the type of character who goes into business, that is, unintellectual, unreflective, unliterary, and therefore historically unsuited to literature. Complicating the realism of Dobbs's act is Madalina's determination to sensationalize it in the recounting. Romanticism, realism, and sensationalism are all self-consciously put into play, as they would be when Trollope brought both the financial plot and the financier's suicide to the forefront in his great financial novel, *The Way We Live Now*.

## The Way We Live Now

> Of course they had none of them as yet heard of the way in which the Financier
> had made his last grand payment.
>
> —Anthony Trollope, *The Way We Live Now*

S. G. Checkland notes that in 1875, the *Economist* identified "a new psychology of finance": "the new men were devoid of grace, culture, or intellectualism of a recognizable kind" (266). Tara McGann argues that *The Way We Live Now* is a new kind of financial novel that, rather than conforming to a "pre-scripted moral framework" of transgression and punishment, "attempts to account for the business cycle theory emerging during the late 1860s and 1870s" (136). Her argument is consistent with Checkland's claim that the City was beginning to understand downturns of fortune as an inevitable risk of the market's unpredictability (rather than as a failing of the financier). McGann claims that Melmotte is represented as a victim of these impersonal economic forces, rather than as a villain. Her reading suggests that Trollope's depiction of finance anticipates later attitudes to businessmen as victims of cycles rather than vampires to be staked at crossroads. This helps explain how *The Way We Live Now* naturalizes finance while self-consciously incorporating Romantic, Gothic, and sensational images that adhere particularly to the idea of suicide.

As he had with the Crawley/Broughton opposition, Trollope pits Romantic against realist sensibilities through the opposition of Roger Carbury and Melmotte. The narrator says of the landowning, backward-looking Carbury: "No man in England could be less likely to throw himself off the Monument or to blow out his brains" (74). Carbury is bound by tradition and the scruples of a gentleman; Melmotte is bound by nothing except, as McGann points out, the business cycle and the availability of credit. The American Mrs. Hurtle admires Melmotte as a man who "rises above honesty" and knows that "wealth is power and power is good" (245–46). For her, Melmotte is the antidote to the effete civilization that England has become, its weaknesses embodied in the likes of Carbury and even in her lover Paul Montague. Trollope's position lies somewhere in between Carbury's old-monied horror at and Mrs. Hurtle's approval of Melmotte's rise.

Melmotte's suicide is lonely and unsensational, though it creates a sensation in both the City and the West End. The great man, who gradually becomes more sympathetic as he takes over the novel and is granted a slight degree of interiority, chooses a silent, bloodless ending. While the death occurs offstage, it is much talked about afterward. Melmotte's butler emotionally recounts the scene: "I see him lay on the ground, and I helped to lift him up, and there was that smell of prussic acid that I knew what he had been and done" (II: 335). Although he is certainly a swindler and a forger, Melmotte is found after his death to be worth a great deal of money. His wealth was not a complete illusion: he was rather strapped for cash, unable to get credit, harassed and hounded by small cares that undermined his great ambitions. While his body may be metaphorically carried off to the crossroads, his reputation enjoys a "whitewashing" (357).

Preparing to leave for America, Marie Melmotte's fiancé, the American speculator Hamilton K. Fisker, asks her:

> "D' you think we're all going to smash there because a fool like Melmotte blows his brains out in London?"
> "He took poison."
> "Or p'ison either." (II: 394)

Getting the details wrong, Fisker evokes the cliché of blowing one's brains out, which Trollope used in all of these novels—so literally externalizing the internal. The point is that neither the means nor the fact of Melmotte's suicide makes any difference to the great international game of finance. Wherever the soul may pass eternity, the game of speculation will go on. The notion of punishment is meaningless, the suicide a futile act signifying nothing. And still the scene of the speculator's suicide drew Trollope, who returned to it again in his next novel.

# The Prime Minister

*It would kill me, I think, if I had to confine myself to Spanish bonds.*

—Anthony Trollope, *The Prime Minister*

In Trollope's novels, political and/or financial failure prompts the same questions, which are at once practical and existential. When Palliser's term as prime minister has come to an end, he asks: "What was now to come of himself? How should he use his future life . . . ? What was he to do with himself?" (II: 307). Similarly, when Lopez loses the election for Parliament and his duplicity in extorting money from both his father-in-law and the Duke is exposed, he wonders despairingly: "What should he do with himself . . . what should he do with himself;—where should he go?" (II: 126).

Palliser only jokes about suicide, suspecting that others will "think that I've thrown myself into the river" (II: 266). Like his aristocratic counterpart Roger Carbury, the Duke would be the last man to jump off the Monument. Similarly, when the very English Arthur Fletcher talks with Romantic despair about suicide—"The best thing to do would be to shoot myself" (I: 138)—we know he speaks rhetorically. In contrast, when Lopez wonders: "Would not a pistol or a razor give him the best solution for all his difficulties?" (II: 175), we have the weight of Trollope's past speculator-suicides to bolster the belief that he is in earnest.

Eschewing the more traditional pistol or razor, Lopez walks in front of a speeding train after wandering among the tracks and platforms at Tenway Junction. The scene is drawn out and entirely externalized, giving us no insight into the desperate man's thoughts. The presence of the railway "pundit" who observes, questions, and follows Lopez on the platform makes it tense and suspenseful. Having described the air at Tenway as "loaded with a succession of shrieks"—each a "separate notice to separate ears of the coming or going of a separate train" (II: 192)—Trollope builds the tension of Lopez's approach to the tracks: "At that moment there came a shriek louder than all other shrieks, and the morning express down from Euston to Inverness was seen coming round the curve at a thousand miles an hour" (II: 194). At the height of realism and suspense, the narrator undermines the reality with fanciful, breathless language—"a thousand miles an hour." The pundit, who has followed Lopez from one platform to another, "called to him, and then made a rush at him,—" but is too late.

Just as the representation of Dobbs's suicide by Miss Demolines constitutes a commentary on sensationalism, so the subsequent representation of Lopez's suicide becomes as important to the novel as the event itself. Anticipating the London penny press's accounts of splattered financiers on Wall Street in 1929, about which the American correspondent for the *Economist* complained, the journalist Quintus Slide sensationalizes Lopez's death, describing "those gory shreds and tatters of a poor human being with which the Tenway Railway Station was bespattered" (II: 206). Trollope's narrator reflects that "self-inflicted death caused by remorse will, in the minds of many, wash a blackamoor almost white" (II: 205), thus recalling the whitewashing following Melmotte's death. His solicitor father-in-law is also able to procure a verdict of temporary insanity, thereby saving the family name from association with a *felo de se*. Lopez, the great lie, whose splattered body "set identity at defiance" and whose premeditated "rush into eternity" left his victims and detractors without the satisfaction of punishment, was the last of Trollope's speculator-suicides.

## The Whirlpool

I know what to think when B.F. commits suicide.

—George Gissing, *The Whirlpool*

The motif of suicide runs through *Can You Forgive Her?*, *The Last Chronicle*, *The Way We Live Now*, and *The Prime Minister*. Vavasor, Lady Glencora, Johnny Eames, Crawley, and Fletcher all think of it, but it is the financier/speculators Broughton, Melmotte, and Lopez who do the deed. Even the act of self-murder represents an energy and initiative lacking in the atrophied, genteel culture with which the City is always contrasted. Gissing continued the realists' analysis of the nineteenth-century culture of speculation, capturing the genteel class's response to its overpowering force. Many elements of Trollope's financial plots may be found in *The Whirlpool*: the suicidal financier, the rentier disdainful of finance, concern about the effete gentility, and disgust with the vulgar man of action. Trollope and Gissing also employ imagery of market culture as a destructive natural force. Broughton lived in the crater of a volcano; Melmotte is described as one who had "rushed from one danger to another, till at last the waters around him had become too deep, even for him" (II: 345). After the suicide that begins the novel, Gissing's rentier, Harvey Rolfe, feels "as if we were all being swept into a ghastly whirlpool which roars over the bottomless pit" (48). And in *The Whirlpool* everyone seems swept up: Frothingham the perpetrator, Edgar Abbot the victim of the smash who takes an overdose of morphia and leaves a wife and two children behind, and Alma, who tries to make a life for herself in the shadow of her father's disgrace.

Rolfe lives off an inheritance from his father (a railway man), surrounding himself with books, and appreciating nature and quiet study. The ways of financiers are a mystery to him. Looking in from the outside at the life of the Frothinghams, he wishes ironically that "it were possible for him to watch and comprehend the business of a great finance-gambler through one whole day. What monstrous cruelties and mendacities might underlie the surface of this gay and melodious existence!" (39). Rolfe recurs to old images of the City as foreign (not to mention Jewish), almost boasting: "I know no more of finance than of the Cabala" (12). And yet for all this, he is oddly excited by

Alma. When he hears that the Britannia has been "shut up," he had "a singular sensation, a tremor at his heart, a flutter of the pulses, a turning cold and hot," suggesting an involuntary, physical response to the charge generated in the financial and the sexual realm represented by the Frothinghams, father and daughter.[19]

Alma, for her part, seems driven by undefined ambitions. Wanting to be a musician without loving music, she suffers socially by her father's fall, and, in the New Woman tradition, exiles herself to Germany to study music. After turning down a proposal of marriage and a proposal to live as a mistress with a wealthy Englishman, she marries Rolfe and thereafter fluctuates wildly between the desire for domesticity and for public acclaim, becoming entangled in relationships with men who might further her career. Attempting to support her desire to live in London, Rolfe becomes financially pressed, but: "To study the money-market gave him a headache. He had to go for a country walk, to bathe and change his clothes before he was at ease again" (208). His prospects for scoring on the stock market seem slight, making him seem obsolete if not impotent compared to his speculating friends.

Ultimately, Alma dissolves into hysteria. Near the end of the novel, feeling little affection for her husband or her son, she realizes that the world views her as "the daughter of a man who had set all on a great hazard; who had played for the world's reward, and, losing, flung away his life." She thinks how she would live her life differently and "like her father, play boldly for the great stakes" (419). She is also responsible for her own death when she takes an extra "draught of oblivion," saying to herself: "The last time" (447).

Bennett Frothingham's suicide is the primal scene in *The Whirlpool*. As with the suicides of Broughton, Melmotte, and Lopez, accounts of it after the fact are as significant as the act itself. Rolfe reads in the newspaper about the unused office in the building of Frothingham's paper, *Stock and Share*, where the body was discovered "at full length on the floor, in his hand a pistol" (46). Soon he tires of hearing the story: "And so on, and so on, in one journal after another, in edition upon edition. Harvey Rolfe read them till he was weary, listened to gossip of the club till he was nauseated" (48). Like Trollope, Gissing equated the sensationalism of the press with the mendacities of the finance-gambler and worried that the state of writing generally was declining beside the rise of the financial culture. The very notion of a paper called *Stock and Share* suggests a particular class of readers consuming the type of writing that made Rolfe feel unclean. Rolfe's physical symptoms—his racing heart, nausea, and sense of contamination when touched, even indirectly, by modern finance—are his reaction to the danger posed by the financial sector to his class and values.[20]

The three suicides in *The Whirlpool* combine the mid-Victorian demise of the monstrous financier with the notion that the financier's values have been transmitted to society generally, including to women. Gothic images like burying at the crossroads are invoked as antiquated, while the sensitive, literary rentier has little recourse against rising economic and social forces. Edith Wharton, whose fiction has so much in common with Trollope and Gissing, took both realism and suicide in relation to finance to new levels of self-consciousness and social critique.

## The Custom of the Country

In America the real *crime passionnel* is a "big steal"—there's more excitement in wrecking railways than homes.

—Edith Wharton, *Custom of the Country*

From her Victorian predecessors Wharton inherited a tradition of using suicide to advance her social critique and the realist novel. Suicide due to financial failure had its particular imagery and differed from the suicidal wish of the main characters in *Ethan Frome* (1911). Her reworking of the suicide convention as developed by Dickens, Trollope, and Gissing is a literary response to the increasingly dominant culture of finance in the United States.[21]

While Alma's overdose resembles that of Wharton's Lily Bart in *The House of Mirth*, Alma's ambitions and flirtations have more in common with Undine Spragg from Wharton's ruthless critique of New York high society, *The Custom of the Country* (see Collinson). Undine does not commit suicide, but her defeated husband Ralph Marvell, the parallel to Harvey Rolfe, shoots himself following a speculative failure brokered by Moffat, the Wall Street tycoon whom Undine eventually marries for the second time. Just as Alma wonders whether she should have played her life as boldly as her father, perhaps running off with one of her suitors, so Undine compares her decision to go away with a married man for two months to her father's financial enterprises: "It had been a bold move, but it had been as carefully calculated as the happiest Wall Street 'stroke'" (685). Alma and Undine marry men with independent incomes but little interest in finance. Both men are forced by their wives' style of living to enter a marketplace they neither like nor understand. Both women neglect their sons, leaving their husbands to assume the maternal role (see Simon J. James). The same bipartite structure that obtains in Victorian London applies to Wharton's New York: the West End and the City translated to Fifth Avenue and Wall Street. In Wharton's hands, it is the remnant of the old social order that is driven to suicide by the financial dealings and successes of brazen financiers.

Wharton's fiction may be read in an American realist/naturalist tradition with her contemporaries Crane, Dreiser, and London. But it is also revealing to read her international plots in light of the Victorian British tradition. Connections between Wharton and Trollope have been particularly overlooked. Like *The Prime Minister*, *The Custom of the Country* has at its heart an ill-fated marriage that ends in the husband's suicide after financial failure, accompanied by his recognition of absolute personal loss. The opposition between old and new money is clearly drawn and is central to both the disastrous marriages and the plots generally. In *The Prime Minister*, however, it is the upwardly mobile speculator Lopez who commits suicide, while in *The Custom of the Country* it is the old-monied Marvel.[22] Ralph is inhibited by "his inability to get a mental grasp on large financial problems" (617) and is ultimately the victim of his own incomprehension of the market. Just as Lily Bart had trusted Gus Trenor to speculate for her, Ralph places himself in the hands of Moffat, who promises an almost magical solution to his financial problems. Ralph tries to understand but can only daydream in the face of "the intricate concert of facts and figures" (745).

Ralph learns simultaneously that the speculation he had hoped would double his money will pay nothing and that this man he has trusted with a borrowed sum was once married to Undine. With these joint revelations, he feels that "the whole archaic structure of his rites and sanctions tumbled down about him" (756). His failure on the market and in marriage recalls Lopez's experience, and the scene of his suicide owes much to that of Trollope's speculator. Lopez sees a future that is "blank and black" (II: 188), while Ralph sees a future that is "bare and blank" (726). Whereas Emily Wharton realizes that Lopez had been "a lie from head to foot," Ralph realizes that in his marriage to Undine "there hadn't been a moment when she hadn't lied to him" (750). Ralph emerges from Moffatt's office and finds himself "at the corner of Wall Street, looking up and down its hot summer perspective" (750). The perspective is as dizzying to him as Tenway Junction was to Lopez, quite, as Trollope says of Tenway, "unintelligible to the uninitiated" (II: 191). Marvell then takes a subway from Wall Street to Waverly Place, "the nasal yelp of the stations ringing through the car like some repeated ritual wail" (755). The ritual wail reminds us of "the succession of shrieks" at Tenway. Ralph wanders to his old home in Washington Square, retreating to his room, and trying to avoid the old parlor maid, who would engage him in domestic chatter.

Although taking place in a private room rather than a public station—and focused internally on Ralph's thoughts to the exclusion of external reality—Ralph's suicide is similar in structure, suspense, and urgency to that of Lopez. Echoing Lopez's "What should he do with himself ... what should he do with himself;—where should he go?," Ralph asks: "'But the money—where's the money to come from.' ... The money—how on earth was he to pay it back?" (759). Whereas Lopez is hounded by the pundit, Ralph is hounded by the servant, the thought of whose return obsesses him: "He raised his head and sat listening for the sound of the old woman's step.... 'She's coming.' ... He didn't feel anything now except the insane dread of hearing the woman's steps come nearer" (759). So hounded, he takes a pistol from the drawer and puts it to his head. Though Wharton leaves the bloody explosion off stage, the scene is neatly contained, the pursuit of the desperate man and his ultimate suicide ending the chapter.

Newspapers and sensationalizing representations of suicides factor prominently in *The Prime Minister* and *The Whirlpool*. In *The Custom of the Country,* newspaper headlines track and announce the plot's actions. Ralph is mortified at having his wife's divorce and remarriage exposed in the gossipy social columns. At the end of the novel, their son Paul has all but forgotten his suicide father and searches for clues to his own identity in newspaper clippings collected by the manicurist and social hanger-on Mrs. Heeny. Paul hopes that the clippings "might furnish him the clue to many things he didn't understand" (830). Realist narrative and newspaper article are blurred in the text. Wharton's analysis moves beyond Trollope's and Gissing's concerns about the degrading effects of journalism: what Paul reads in the newspaper becomes his reality by providing a narrative account of things he never understood while they were happening. Wharton uses the newspapers as a way of reproducing the simulacra of the stock market on which Undine's success is built and also as a way of commenting on the relationship between representation and reality. Paul has forgotten his pedigreed father and headlines are as good as any other reality upon which to construct a narrative and an identity.

## Conclusion

Introducing business and finance into fiction brought about changes in its form and content. Victorian authors were self-conscious about the pressure these new subjects put on their novels and experimented with different discourses to represent the City and its people (Gothic, sensational, realistic). Trollope satirized the combined romance and money plots in the novel Lady Carbury is planning at the end of *The Way We Live Now,* "The Wheel of Fortune": "A young lady was blessed with great wealth, and lost it all by an uncle, and got it all back by an honest lawyer, and gave it all up to a distressed lover, and found it all again in a third volume" (366). The authoress contemplates her new work, so vague in its comprehension of money, while Melmotte's inquest is in progress: "Of course Lady Carbury was intent upon her book, rather even than on the exciting death of a man whom she had herself known" (II: 367). Her fictional money plot is already more real to her than Melmotte's suicide, the "exciting death" of Trollope's own financial novel.

Not surprisingly, Wharton was even more self-consciousness about the intersection of finance and literature than her Victorian predecessors. The motif of Ralph Marvell's unwritten novel runs through *The Custom of the Country,* raising the question: can the very thing that threatens to kill art become the subject of art? Must the realist novel, to survive, encompass the power and vitality of the financial sector? In this, Wharton was exploring an idea expressed and practiced by Charlotte Riddell—to show readers "what trade really is; what an excitement, what a pain, what struggle; and when honestly and honourably carried out, what a glory too" (97).

When Ralph is forced to join a real estate firm to support his wife, "he had come in contact for the first time with the drama of 'business'" and "he found a certain interest in watching the fierce interplay of its forces" (215). Later, in closer contact with Moffatt, Ralph wonders why the insight into intricate business matters "did not qualify every financier to be a novelist, and what intrinsic barrier divided the two arts" (262). Despite these flashes of insight into the dramatic potential of business, Ralph is pulled down by "the persistent mortification of spirit and flesh which is a condition of the average business life" (311). He never writes his novel, and his suicide is the triumph of the speculator Moffat and the speculator's daughter Undine over the genteel classes whose demise was foreshadowed in the fiction of Trollope and Gissing. Wharton seems to allegorize the very death of art, yet like her predecessors she saw the drama of the stock market and made fiction out of finance (see Preston).

Harold James argues that the "literary financier" served Victorian authors as a scourge for the corrupt aristocracy; once that class was effectively extinct, it was no longer possible to make "a morality tale out of the life and destiny of the man of business" (256) and the type disappeared from fiction.[23] Between the publication of *The Custom of the Country* in 1913 and the 1929 stock market crash, speculation became a craze fueling all aspects of the "roaring twenties." Speculators were no longer monsters inhabiting a strange world; they were ubiquitous. Reflecting a rather cynical view about the values and the power of Wall Street in 1929, "it was commonly said that the market was 'discounting not only the future but the hereafter'" (Chancellor 196). After the crash, however, Wall Street became "the principal villain in a national saga of guilt, revenge and redemption" (Fraser 414). The perceived greed of the speculator was such that, apparently, the populace was ready to accept a modern morality tale propagated by the press: financial success followed by absolute loss and suicide. That morality tale has persisted as a modern myth born of Victorian realist fiction.

## Notes

1. The correspondent writes: "Stories of the streets clogged with the bodies of suicides and of savings banks stripped of funds reveal modern journalism at its worst." He contends that "in New York City there were only two or three suicides that appeared to have been prompted by the *débacle* in stocks" ("Overseas Correspondence"). *Time* magazine reported: "To contradict rumors of a suicide wave, New York authorities showed that in Manhattan there were only 44 from Oct. 13–Nov. 15, as compared to 53 last year" ("Heroes, Wags and Sages").

2. Citing Galbraith, later historians debunk the myth without exploring it further. Charles P. Kindleberger and Robert Aliber write: "The picture of stockbrokers jumping from Wall Street windows in October 1929 as they faced bankruptcy is now believed to be a myth." They add that suicide following financial ruin "may be more usual in fiction" (173). Shachtman reports that a window cleaner was mistaken for a jumper and a British correspondent, taking the rumor for reality, "cabled his newspaper that Lower Manhattan was littered with fallen bodies" (147).

3. All references to *Little Dorrit* are to the 1999 Oxford University Press edition edited by Harvey Peter Sucksmith. All references to *The Prime Minister* are to the 2001 Oxford University Press edition edited by Jenny Uglow, which is internally divided into volumes I and II.

4. "Suicide in Cornhill" appeared in the *Times* on March 4, 1868. The brief article dwells more on Smith's disturbed mental state than on his financial affairs.

5. The *Oxford English Dictionary* defines a speculator as "One who engages in commercial or financial speculation" (first reference 1778) and a financier as "A capitalist concerned in financial operations" (first reference 1867). Suicidal money men appear in Charles Reade's *Put Yourself in His Place* (1870), Walter Besant and James Rice's *Ready-Money Mortiboy* (1872), and Joseph Conrad's *Chance* (1913).

6. On financial journalism, see Poovey's "Writing about Finance" in this volume.

7. Moody explains the coincident rise of financial and sensation plots on the Victorian stage, rightly pointing out that while the novel is generally considered to be the "definitve genre of capital," the mid-Victorian theater responded to changing financial conditions with equal if not greater energy (92).

8. On nineteenth-century women investors, see Henry, "Ladies"; Robb, "Ladies of the Ticker" (in this volume); and Rutterford and Maltby, "She Possessed."

9. All references to *The Way We Live Now* are to the 1982 Oxford University Press edition edited by John Sutherland.

10. On Trollope's financial plots especially in relation to women, see Rutterford and Maltby, "Frank."

11. On Trollope's relationship to Byronism and other Romantic discourses, see Swingle.

12. For an extensive treatment of this dichotomy in English culture, see Delany. See also Henry, "Ladies"; Robb, "Ladies of the Ticker" (in this volume); and Rutterford and Maltby, "She Possessed."

13. John Sutherland writes that Melmotte has "no identifiable single original" and is a "compound of literary and historical antecedents" (xvi). On Melmotte's suicide, see P. D. Edwards and Slakey.

14. On Trollope and the law, see Lansbury and McMaster.

15. "A *felo de se,* therefore, is he that deliberately puts an end to his own existence, or commits any unlawful malicious act, the consequence of which is his own death" (Blackstone 937).

16. Olive Anderson writes that in the 1860s, "the aura of want and destitution which had been made to surround suicide in the years of guilty concern about 'the Condition of England' was rapidly being replaced by one of maudlin sensationalism, and traditional explanations of suicidal behaviour in terms of worldly dishonour or disappointment in love" (213).

17. Part 17, in which Merdle commits suicide, appeared on April 1, 1857, four months before "Suicide in Life and Literature" was published. George Eliot had already criticized the early parts of *Little Dorrit* for lapses in realism in "The Natural History of German Life" (*Westminster Review,* July 1856).

18. On *The Last Chronicle* as Victorian culture's response to dramatic changes in economic practice and theory, see Michie. See also Franklin.

19. On associations between the stock market and the heart, see Jaffe in this volume.

20. On the proliferation of financial newspapers and journals, see Itzkowitz in this volume. Eitan Bar-Josef explores Gissing's self-reflexive portrayal of the literary marketplace: "an inability to adapt oneself to the laws of the business—an inability to appeal to the mass of Philistines—results in failure, even death" (186).

21. On Wharton's fiction in relations to Wall Street, see Westbrook. On suicide in Wharton, see Spangler.

22. In *The Writing of Fiction* (1924), Wharton praised *The Last Chronicle* (65). In 1934, she wrote to Bernard Berenson that she had "gone back to 'Can you forgive her?' & 'the Prime Minister'—& oh, how good they are!" (Wharton, *Letters* 12 Feb 1934).

23. J. Reed concludes: "With the turn of the century, literature presented a less dramatic view of finance and commerce. . . . The Victorian pattern of finance in fiction was over" (201–202).

# 9   Rumor, Shares, and Novelistic Form

Joseph Conrad's *Nostromo*

## *Cannon Schmitt*

On February 27, 2007, the U.S. stock market registered the largest drop in points since the first day of trading following the September 11, 2001, attacks on the World Trade Center and the Pentagon. The proximate cause, much to the surprise of many commentators, was a precipitous fall in the Chinese stock market the day before. David Barboza described the aftermath in an article for the *New York Times* business section that ran under the headline "A Shock Wave from Shanghai": "China's worst one-day tumble in a decade set off a tumult that rolled through markets around the globe, from Tokyo to Frankfurt to Brazil to Wall Street." Appearing on the front page of the *Times* the same day, Norris Floyd and Jeremy W. Peters's piece on the decline, "Slide on Wall St. Adds to Worries about Economy," was printed next to a chart labeled "Jitters Spread Around the World" that showed the damage visually: plunging lines indicated a loss of 8.8 percent for China's stock indexes, 3.3 percent for the United States, and 2.6 percent for Europe, while the placement of the chart, centered at the top of the page, conveyed the apparent gravity of the news.

In the subsequent widespread coverage, financial journalists could not determine how best to represent the story's import. Some thought it signified the fragility of world stock markets due to investors' complacency; others believed it pointed to underlying weakness in the U.S. economy; still others took the occasion to announce the arrival of the People's Republic of China (PRC) as an economic power to be reckoned with. In a contribution to the Op-Ed section of the *Times* on March 2, 2007, Paul Krugman went so far as to indulge in a kind of dystopian science fiction. Beneath the spurious date February 27, 2008, Krugman writes as though he were looking back on a global economic catastrophe—his title was "The Big Meltdown"—touched off by the market crash in China of a year before.

Many articles included the detail, although always only in passing, that the fall in China's market that had initiated the worldwide sell-off was due to the circulation of an unverified notion about Beijing's intention to intervene. In "A Shock Wave from Shanghai," Barboza pointed out that "the Chinese stock market was rife with rumors that the government was considering new measures to tame the world's hottest stock market before a bubble developed." The imposition of new taxes seemed imminent, either on capital gains or trading itself. Faced with such a prospect, Chinese investors acted in the most "rational" way possible: they dumped shares hoping to cash in on the astounding gains they had made to date—the value of stocks sold on the Shanghai and Shenzhen exchanges had increased more than 120 percent in 2006 alone—before a new tax ate into their profits. This in turn spurred investors in New York, Tokyo, London, Frankfurt, Toronto, and elsewhere to draw back. But the rumors turned out to be false. No new tax was announced, and the drop in value most indexes experienced was due to misinformation and widespread credulity, not simply among Chinese investors, so new to stocks that they might be expected to make a few missteps, but all across the world.

There can be little doubt that the events of February 27, 2007, had to do with everything journalists proposed they did: the increasing interconnectedness of economies, the globalization of stock markets, and the advent of the PRC as a player in the world of investment capitalism. Given that a false rumor precipitated them, however, they are just as importantly understood as a costly demonstration of the dictum that, in David A. Zimmerman's words, "Financial markets . . . are markets for information" (24)—as well as of the significant corollary that such markets often have difficulty distinguishing accurate from inaccurate information. As such, those events bear out the continuing existence in the present of the very culture of investment whose lineaments Mary Poovey traces in this volume. Seeking to differentiate the place of investment in mid-nineteenth-century Britain from its place in earlier historical moments, Poovey writes that "one sign of the novelty of the emergent culture of investment was the way that modern technologies combined with the professionalization of journalism to so completely confuse the distinction between rumor and [factual] information that even a seasoned financial journalist could not always tell whether what he reported was true or simply a cleverly planted tip intended to incite speculation" (50). The global stock sell-off of late February 2007, started by a rumor and exacerbated by the rapid dispersal of the news of Chinese investors' reaction via television, satellite, mobile phone, and the Internet, constitutes the latest testimony to such confusion. But it also, crucially, demands attention to a third possibility, no less consequential for being so obvious: that the information on which investors act may be neither true nor a deliberate falsehood but simply unfounded. Such a possibility marks the ineluctable effect of the aleatory in the formation and dissolution of investment value. And it invites closer consideration not only of the financial writing whose centrality to the culture of investment Poovey documents but also of the often untrustworthy, unverifiable, or otherwise errant language to be found in what might, on the principle of analogy, be referred to as financial talking.

In the case of February 2007, the vicissitudes of financial talking were compounded by the specific kinds of misprision that can occur when old and new systems, as well as "domestic" and "foreign" systems, become interimplicated. Rumors have long held an unusually prominent position in the public life of the PRC, a country in which the ruling party's commitment to secrecy and near-total control of the means of disseminating information forces the populace to draw conclusions from the merest hints or appearances.[1] Add to this a new financial market—the Shenzhen Stock Exchange was created in 1990, the same year that the Shanghai Stock Exchange was re-established following its suspension in 1949—that, like all such markets, rises or falls on the strength of what people believe, combined with the rapid dispersal of an apparently credible piece of news such as that of an impending tax increase, and the Chinese crash results. Add to this, in turn, the arrival on the world scene of an equities market in a "developing" country whose fortunes are suddenly and intimately connected with those of the already fully (or overly) industrialized and digitized nations and you get the shockwave effect seen on February 27—again, all flowing from a rumor that turned out to be false.

It is in the light of this sequence of events that I wish to consider Joseph Conrad's *Nostromo* (1904). As has often been observed, the novel takes a dim view of capitalist modernization, presenting the pursuit of wealth as destructive to the individual and revealing Europe's incorporation of new markets and the increasing economic interconnectedness of "developed" and "developing" worlds to be a kind of imperialism. Martin Seymour-Smith puts the matter most succinctly: "*Nostromo* is about nothing if it is not about 'material interests'" (11). Benita Parry offers a more expansive thesis when she writes: "Against the mystification of the profit motive and the idealism of economic activities . . . [*Nostromo's*] discourse mobilises a relentless attack, and the illegitimate joining of utilitarianism with idealism is condensed in the key phrase 'material interests'" (*Conrad* 115). And even as he pursues a somewhat different claim about the novel, namely that its "ultimate narrative message" has to do with the "disjunction between the movement of history and its enactment by individual subjects," Fredric Jameson encapsulates *Nostromo's* plot in the formulation: "So the act happens—capitalism arrives in Sulaco" (*Political* 278). So much is well established. What has been less appreciated is that, despite the overarching presence of the sort of industrial endeavor represented by the San Tomé mine, the silver concession at the novel's center, *Nostromo* chronicles the arrival in Latin America not of capitalism per se but specifically of finance capitalism. Moreover, and like the Chinese crash, in its treatment of that arrival Conrad's novel is about not only those "material interests" that constitute its most insistent verbal motif but also the immaterial foundation of such interests: speech, and more particularly speech's most uncontrollable incarnation, rumor. This has the dual result that *Nostromo* prosecutes a critique of the culture of investment as mandating a society at the mercy of misprision even as it exemplifies a development in novelistic form—call it modernism—that may itself be seen to derive its distinctive qualities from the function of language in such a society.

\* \* \*

Before turning to its modernism, it would be well to note that there is considerable "realism" in Conrad's treatment of Latin America, if by that term we mean not the conventions of a certain type of literary production but simply fidelity to historical fact. The Americas for Europe have always been the locus of treasure both actual and imagined, from the voyages of Columbus, Pizarro, Sir Francis Drake, and Sir Walter Raleigh to twenty-first-century petroleum ventures in Ecuador or bioprospecting in the Amazon River basin. Conrad himself alludes to this legacy in *Heart of Darkness* (1899) by saddling a group of rapacious European adventurers in central Africa with the name "Eldorado Exploring Expedition" (54). He rehearses it at more length in a late essay titled "Geography and Some Explorers": "And if the discovery of America was the occasion of the greatest outburst of reckless cruelty and greed known to history we may say this at least for it, that the gold of Mexico and Peru, unlike the gold of the alchemists, was really there, palpable, yet, as ever, the most elusive of the Fata Morgana that lure men away from their homes" (3). As it did for early-modern Spaniards, Portuguese, and Britons, for the Victorians and Edwardians Latin America served as the repository of just such equivocal treasure, at once "palpable" and "the most elusive of the Fata Morgana." From the 1820s on, British investors sunk millions of pounds into mines in Mexico and Central and South America (Bethell 6; Eakin 15). A host of travel narratives ranging from Sir Richard Francis Burton's *Explorations of the Highlands of Brazil; with a Full Account of the Gold and Diamond Mines* (1869) to Alexander James Duffield's *Peru in the Guano Age: Being a Short Account of a Recent Visit to the Guano Deposits with Some Reflections on the Money They Have Produced and the Uses to Which It Has Been Applied* (1877) offered the public vicarious participation in the discovery and excavation of the sort of found wealth that the region appeared to offer. Most of these schemes were financial catastrophes; J. Fred Rippy puts the number of mining companies in which Britons invested in the nineteenth century at around four hundred, of which fewer than twenty turned a profit (Rippy). But the occasional success proved sufficient to keep interest high. In the unglamorous case of guano taken up by Duffield, for instance, so profitable, for a time, was the house of Gibbs and Sons in importing it from Peru for use as a fertilizer on British fields that the wealth produced was memorialized in a doggerel quatrain once apparently well known in City of London financial circles: "Antony Gibbs / made his dibs / selling the turds / of foreign birds" (qtd. in Bethel 5; see also Cain and Hopkins 306–10; Mathew).

The guano boom was not lost on Conrad. Costaguana, the imaginary South American nation in which *Nostromo* is set, may literally be translated "Palm Coast" but also punningly evokes "Guano Coast." The latter moniker resembles names such as Ivory Coast and Gold Coast, acting as a signboard for a valuable regional commodity. In a more sardonic vein, it also gestures at the country's failings—its history of violent revolutions, string of caudillos or autocratic "strong man" leaders, and inability to provide security or stability for its citizens. This wry bit of nomenclature, however, is an anomaly in a novel characterized from the outset by a much darker register. *Nostromo* opens with a verbal map of Costaguana, like Colombia a South American nation possessed of both a Caribbean and a Pacific coast and riven down the middle by a rugged cordillera.[2] Cartography, however, quickly gives way to ethnography. In the first of many subtle transitions responsible for some of the novel's distinctive texture, the narrator leaves off in the midst of his mapmaking to ventriloquize a folk explanation for the killing barrenness of the peninsula of Azuera, an arid spit of land sticking out into the Pacific:

> The poor, associating by an obscure instinct of consolation the ideas of evil and wealth, will tell you that it is deadly because of its forbidden treasures.... Tradition has it that many adventurers of olden time had perished in the search [for them]. The story goes also that within men's memory two wandering sailors—*Americanos,* perhaps, but *gringos* of some sort for certain— ... stole a donkey to carry for them a bundle of dry sticks, a water-skin, and provisions enough to last a few days. (39–40)

Although they never return, these nameless and countryless gringos are reputed not to have failed but rather to have found what they sought: "spectral and alive, [they] are believed to be dwelling to this day amongst the rocks, under the fatal spell of their success. Their souls cannot tear themselves away from their bodies mounting guard over the discovered treasure" (40). An early instance of local color in a text long admired for its encyclopedic and thus thoroughly Borgesian documentation of Costaguanero life high and low, this story presages the fate of all the principal characters of the novel, who end up, like Charles Gould, the Costaguana-born Englishman in charge of working the San Tomé silver mine, imprisoned "within a circumvallation of precious metal" or, like Gian' Battista Fidanza, the Italian boatswain and factotum whose nickname gives the novel its title, "the slave of a treasure" (205, 432).

The mine itself, of course, functions as the primary site and symbol of New World treasure in *Nostromo.* A concession granted to Charles Gould's father by one of Costaguana's corrupt governments in payment of loans and as a pretext for exacting royalties on putative future profits, the mine lures Gould back to South America from a voluntary exile in Europe. Much of the novel's complexity derives from its deployment of two scales in which to render the consequences of this return: an intimate, interiorized, psychological scale for delineating the process by which each of the characters falls under the spell of the mine and its silver and a vast, historically and geographically panoramic scale for chronicling how the mine's successful working at once requires and enables the modernization of Sulaco, the coastal province in which it is located, including the building of railroads, the stringing of telegraph lines, the laying-down of undersea cables, the development of port facilities and shipping, and, finally, the province's secession from the rest of Costaguana, victory in a war of independence, and emergence as a sovereign nation, the Occidental Republic, so-called "Treasure House of the World" (402).

In these details Conrad adheres closely to the history of nineteenth- and early twentieth-century Latin America, known to him through his friendship with R. B. Cunninghame Graham; from source materials such as George Frederick Masterman's *Seven Eventful Years in Paraguay* (1869), Edward B. Eastwick's *Venezuela* (1868), and Ramón Páez's *Wild Scenes in South America* (1863); and no doubt from the more ephemeral journalistic accounts with which the British press was filled (Fleishman 167–71; Karl 542; Sherry 137–201; C. Watts, "Nostromo"). Just how carefully Conrad has modeled what takes place in Costaguana on the historical record becomes evident when one notes that Latin American mining in the period was usually conducted via concessions, and that extensive operations were typically in the hands of foreigners (Glade 27, 29); that large-scale mining required the building of additional infrastructure, often achieved by British funding for, expertise in, and oversight of railways, ports, utilities, banks, and technologically advanced means of communication, including telegraph lines and transoceanic cables (Bethell 6–8; Glade 40); and that, finally, struggles over mineral wealth in the region could lead to outright war and the redrawing of political boundaries, as happened most notably in the War of the Pacific.[3] Started by Chile in 1879 against Peru and Bolivia, it ended in 1883 with Chile's seizure of the nitrate fields under dispute and Bolivia's loss of an outlet to the sea (Sater).[4] Britain, although officially neutral, worked behind the scenes to ensure its interests would be provided for regardless of the outcome (Cain and Hopkins 308). In short, Conrad's novel, with a documentary impulse and a high level of accuracy, fictionalizes how, as William Glade writes, "Latin America became increasingly integrated, or, as it is more commonly expressed in Latin America, 'inserted,' into the overarching structure of articulation provided by the world market system" (7–8).

In contrast to the celebratory attitude taken toward that insertion by many economic historians, Conrad displays characteristic cynicism. As so often, of all the characters in *Nostromo*, Martin Decoud is closest to the narrator's—and hence arguably Conrad's—judgment in these matters. In a letter to his sister penned in the midst of the revolutionary violence in which he is a reluctant actor, Decoud, recently returned to his native Costaguana from Paris, comments laconically: "All the engineers are out, and have been for two days, looking after the property of the National Central Railroad, of that great Costaguana undertaking which is to put money into the pockets of Englishmen, Frenchmen, Americans, Germans, and God knows who else" (210). Despite their apparent offhandedness, these remarks constitute the leitmotif of Decoud's interpretation of the situation in which his country finds itself. The railroad, although a "great Costaguana undertaking," will benefit everyone except Costaguaneros. In this it resembles the San Tomé mine, the transoceanic cable, the expanded port facilities, and all the other "national" projects planned, executed, and funded by foreigners—including most ironically the Occidental Republic's "independence" itself, in this context an Orwellian term signifying the precise opposite of what it properly denotes.

And so at another moment in the novel, again prompted by the railroad (the "explosive noise of the railway trucks"), Decoud expounds at greater length on its meaning:

> "This sound puts a new edge on a very old truth.... Yes, the noise outside the city wall is new, but the principle is old.... [T]here used to be in the old days the sound of war trumpets outside that gate. War trumpets! I'm sure they were trumpets. I

have read somewhere that Drake, who was the greatest of these men, used to dine alone in his cabin on board ship to the sound of trumpets. In those days this town was full of wealth. Those men came to take it. Now the whole land is like a treasure-house, and all these people are breaking into it, whilst we are cutting each other's throats. The only thing that keeps them out is mutual jealousy. But they'll come to an agreement some day—and by the time we've settled our quarrels and become decent and honourable, there'll be nothing left for us. It has always been the same. We are a wonderful people, but it has always been our fate to be"—he did not say "robbed," but added, after a pause—"exploited!" (168)

This short paragraph adumbrates what *Nostromo* in its entirety takes nearly five hundred pages to establish: namely, that despite their declaration of various exalted motives—modernization, philanthropy, Christian mission, and so forth—the nineteenth-century Europeans and North Americans who work mines, build railroads, and open banks in South America are no different in essence from either Iberian conquistadors or Elizabethan privateers. Decoud places Gould and the others as merely up-to-date versions of their predecessors. Sporting new costumes, accompanied by the sound of railway cars rather than war trumpets, and expropriating treasure without recourse to outright violence, they expropriate it nonetheless.

Avrom Fleishman clearly perceived this aspect of *Nostromo* when he wrote that for Conrad "the ascendancy of foreign 'material interests' [in Latin America] is a form of conquest" (171). Developments in the history of imperialism have made it possible to be more precise about what that form is and how it functions. In 1953, John Gallagher and Ronald Robinson first suggested the existence of an "imperialism of free trade," and in 1977 D. C. M. Platt, addressing Britain's nineteenth- and early twentieth-century involvement in Latin America, published a study of what he called "business imperialism." But the most sustained and far-reaching version of this line of thought about what is now termed "informal imperialism" appears in P. J. Cain and A. G. Hopkins's two-volume *British Imperialism* (1993). Modifying and extending the case made by Gallagher, Robinson, and Platt, Cain and Hopkins attempt nothing less than a redefinition of empire *tout court*. They displace seizure of territory from its heretofore fundamental position, viewing it as a sometimes necessary adjunct to what they see as the indispensable aspect of Britain's expansion up through the middle of the twentieth century, namely the extension of the British service sector—which includes banking, transportation, communications, and insurance—over ever greater areas of the non-European world. Further, they aver that "Britain's relations with South America in the nineteenth century" provide "the crucial regional test" of their theory (276).[5]

Well before professional historians, Conrad in *Nostromo* treats capitalist modernization as a kind of imperialism that, however different from classic imperialist expansion in its workings, is similar in its results: in this instance, North Americans' and Europeans' economic exploitation of a Latin American country, which in turn requires the attenuation of that country's sovereignty. But there is more to be said. In the same extended passage quoted from above,

Decoud gives particular shape to his accusations: "No, but just imagine our forefathers in morions and corselets drawn up outside this gate, and a band of adventurers just landed from their ships in the harbour there. Thieves, of course. Speculators, too. Their expeditions, each one, were the speculations of grave and reverend persons in England. That is history, as that absurd sailor Mitchell is always saying" (168). Even as he continues to point to the continuity between early modern colonialism and nineteenth-century informal imperialism, Decoud's repeated use of the word "speculators" identifies investment as key.

Here, too, Conrad drew heavily on what he knew about Latin America, where Great Britain was the dominant investor for the entire hundred years between the successful Spanish American independence movements in the second decade of the nineteenth century and the First World War in the second decade of the twentieth (Stone 690–91). Some sense of the vast sums involved can be gained from Charles William Centner's quantification of the British stake in the region circa 1909, when "no less than £766,647,023 of British capital were invested in Spanish America, of which amount £343,318,713 were placed in railroads, £289,026,320 in national and municipal governmental bonds, and £18,171,457 in banks and shipping companies" (76). Were Centner to have included Brazil in his calculations, these figures would be considerably higher. Glade makes a related point in prose rather than numerals when, describing the same period of time as that in which most of *Nostromo* is set, he notes that "[t]he four or five decades before the First World War, the era of high capitalism, were a golden age for foreign investment in Latin America" (39)—as do Cain and Hopkins when they claim that nineteenth-century Latin America's most important economic role was as the "recipient of British capital" (283).

So frenzied had British overseas investment become as early as the 1870s that the House of Commons convened a Select Committee to investigate it and the abuses to which it was liable. Latin America loomed disproportionately large. John Sutherland points out that "[t]he principal objects of the Committee's attention were a series of South American schemes for which capital was raised mainly in London and Paris. Most notorious were the Santo Domingo Loan, 1869; the Coast Rica Loan, 1872; the Paraguay Loan, 1871–2; and, above all, the loan for the Interoceanic Railway in Honduras" (xix). Again, Decoud voices both his awareness of these facts and his interpretation of them as signaling Costaguana's exploitation by foreign powers when, in response to his country-man Don José Avellanos's suggestion that cables to the United States and Europe be sent with reassuring news about the fortunes of the mine during the revolution that threatens it and its supporters, the ruling Ribierist party, he mutters: "Oh, yes, we must comfort our friends, the speculators" (169).

If Decoud's cutting remarks alert us to the possibility that finance capital is at issue in *Nostromo*, that possibility is more than confirmed by the novel's ubiquitous references to investment. Several characters are themselves investors or proxies for investors. There is Sir John, the "head of the chairman [*sic*] of the railway board (from London)," along with another representative of a "friendly" foreign power, who "had come [to Sulaco] to countenance by their presence the enterprise in which the capital of their countries was engaged" (62).[6] There is Holroyd, San Francisco financier and devotee of a puritanical but conveniently capitalistic brand of Protestantism who, in Emily Gould's words, "looked upon his own God as a sort of influential partner, who gets his share of profits in the endowment of churches" (90). Holroyd's view of the world (and many nineteenth-century Europeans' and North Americans' view of Latin America) is neatly conveyed by his summary judgment on the land of Charles Gould's birth: "Now, what is Costaguana? It is the bottomless pit of ten-percent loans and other fool investments. European capital has been flung into it with both hands for years" (94). Finally, not individualized but standing palpably in the background, there are the nameless but numerous European and U.S. shareholders in the railroad, the port, the transoceanic cable, and so on—those "grave and reverend persons in England" and elsewhere otherwise known as "our friends, the speculators."

Still more significant, in ways that have hardly been noticed, each of the novel's pivotal events centers on investment. Holroyd's capital finances Gould, and thus the Ribierist party that promises to maintain conditions favorable to the operation of the mine. That party itself comes to power on a platform that gives equal weight to "attempt[ing] to save the peace and credit of the Republic"—"to establish[ing] the prosperity of the people on the basis of firm peace at home, and to redeem[ing] the national credit by the satisfaction of all just claims abroad" (145, 143). As Decoud says to the Frenchmen with whom he associates while still in Paris: "[T]hese Ribierists, of whom we hear so much just now, are really trying in their own comical way to make the country habitable, and even to pay some of its debts. My friends, you had better write up Señor Ribiera [the dictator whose installation Gould funds] all you can in kindness to your own bondholders. Really, if what I am told in my letters is true, there is some chance for them at last" (152). Further, General Montero, the Minister of War who defects from the ruling party and leads the revolution against it that gives *Nostromo* most of its plot, does so in the name of redressing the shame attendant on foreign ownership of Costaguana. Montero issues his call for "military revolt in the name of national honour" under the pretext (or perhaps because he actually believes) that the country's honor has been "sold to foreigners." Ribiera, acting in "weak compliance with the demands of the European powers—for the settlement of long outstanding money claims—had showed himself unfit to rule" (146). The so-called Monterist press that arises to provide the revolution's ideological arm deploys the same rhetoric, "cursing in every issue the 'miserable Ribiera,' who had plotted to deliver his country, bound hand and foot, for a prey to foreign speculators" (147).

Although the novel renders identification with Montero all but impossible, caricaturing him and his brother Pedrito as craven, stupid, greedy, and power-hungry, the convergence of his claims and those of the Monterist press with Decoud's indicates that *Nostromo* endorses his version of the history of Latin

America.[7] Moreover, given Conrad's relentless exposure of all actions and ideals as mandated by and subordinate to "material interests," Montero's embarrassing toast to Sir John early on turns out to have been simply prescient: "He hesitated till his roaming eyes met Sir John's face, upon which he fixed a lurid, sleepy glance; and the figure of the lately negotiated loan came into his mind. He lifted his glass. 'I drink to the health of the man who brings us a million and a half pounds'" (127–28). If there is little attempt to make anything but objects of scorn out of those who pursue revolution in the name of a national honor sold to foreign speculators, there is equally little effort to depict the modernization of Sulaco as anything but the successful speculation of certain Europeans and North Americans. Thus, to take only the most exemplary case, Gould's solemn declaration to Emily that "In Costaguana we Goulds are no adventurers" is reversed near the novel's end, when, faced with the prospect of having to dynamite the mine to keep it out of the Monteristas' hands, he has the following epiphany: "After all, with his English parentage and English upbringing, he perceived that he was an adventurer in Costaguana, the descendant of adventurers enlisted in a foreign legion, of men who had sought fortune in a revolutionary war, who had planned revolutions, who had believed in revolutions" (85, 311). This direct realization of the truth of Decoud's—and, it should again be noted, Montero's—recriminations converges with the entire novel's insistence on the complicity of investment in the supremacy of "material interests." And because it is cast in an indirect discourse that encourages no readerly questioning of its veracity, it carries the narrator's imprimatur as well. That, as Decoud tells us the absurd sailor Captain Mitchell would say, is history.[8]

Adventurers, thieves, speculators: these terms point the nature of the novel's analysis with particular clarity. For Decoud, in using "speculator" as if it were identical with "thief"; Montero and the Monterist press, in refusing to name the backers of foreign loans anything but "speculators"; and Gould, in referring to himself as an "adventurer"—all effectively redefine global finance capitalism as informal imperialism and investment as speculation.[9] In doing so they emphasize both investment's aleatory nature and the differential power relations that subtend it and that it perpetuates. European and North American investment in Latin America is revealed as a game of chance in which Latin Americans stand to lose most whether things turn out well for the speculator or not.

So it is that Mitchell has almost the last word. Describing in the iterative Mitchell's "more or less stereotyped relation of the 'historical events' which for the next few years was at the service of distinguished strangers visiting Sulaco," the narrator undercuts the sailor's version of the "betterment" of the country as tragicomically obtuse (394). The preceding several hundred pages show the human, environmental, and political costs of such betterment and identify its impetus in speculation from abroad and its rewards as mostly accruing to foreign investors. The final touch of grim humor comes with Mitchell's self-satisfied declaration at novel's end that he "hold[s] seventeen of the $1000 shares" in what has by this point grown to become "the Consolidated San Tomé mines":

"All the poor savings of my lifetime, sir, and it will be enough to keep me in comfort to the end of my days at home when I retire. I got in on the ground floor, you see" (396).

* * *

Conrad's critique of "material interests" in *Nostromo*, then, possesses a high level of specificity. It portrays the relation between the "developed" and "developing" worlds as an informal but nonetheless damaging form of imperialism, and it places particular stress on the role of finance capital in that relation. It also, however, does more, for in its expansiveness it enlists that specificity in a redefinition of investment itself such that all its forms fall under the rubric of speculation—as well as in a broad attack on the culture of investment. This side of the novel's critique is to be found not in the direct pronouncements of its characters or narrator but rather in its narrative form. Distinctive about that form, and the reason *Nostromo* has often been seen as an early instance of the sort of prose modernism iconically represented by James Joyce's *Ulysses* (1923) or Virginia Woolf's *Mrs. Dalloway* (1925), are its byzantine temporal structure as well as its focalization via, or outright narration by, a range of characters. Both of these innovative strategies, I want to argue, are entailments of the attempt to represent a world given over to the logic of the culture of investment, a world in which what is heard, suspected, or believed carries more weight than what is known or seen—in which value rises or falls not according to what *is* but, instead, according to what is *said*.[10]

To begin with time in *Nostromo*: in one sense it poses no problem at all, for the novel begins at the beginning—"[i]n the time of Spanish rule" are its first words—and ends at the end, with Nostromo's death in the now-prosperous late nineteenth- or early twentieth-century Occidental Republic (39, 465). In between these two concrete temporal markers, however, there unfolds a plot notoriously difficult to follow—so difficult, in fact, that no less eminent a critic than Cedric Watts found it worthwhile to offer benighted readers a chronology.[11] In his *Preface to Conrad*, Watts places Gould's return to Costaguana in 1884; the installation of the Ribierist government for which Gould and Holroyd provide financial backing in 1888; Montero's defection and revolution in 1889; Sulaco's subsequent war of independence between 1890 and 1891; and, finally, the building of the lighthouse on the Great Isabel, the island in the Golfo Placido where Nostromo is killed, in 1898. Less important than the specific dates, over which there is anyway some disagreement, is the perceived necessity to produce a chronology at all, a necessity that derives from Conrad's liberal use of analepsis and prolepsis, of various narrative frequencies, of the technique Ian Watt named "delayed decoding," of shifts from pronouncements about the sweep of centuries to myopic unfoldings of the events of a single day, and so forth.[12]

To place in evidence only the anachrony of the first few chapters: chapter 1 begins with the verbal mapmaking and tale of the gringo treasure hunters discussed above, then resumes the geography lesson to finish with a description of the harbor of Sulaco. Apart from the opening references to Spanish rule, the tense of the whole is the present—not an actual present, that of some specific moment, but the abstract, atemporal present of cartographic discourse: "On one side the short wooded spurs and valleys of the Cordillera come down at right angles to the very strand; on the other the open view of the great Sulaco plain passes into the opal mystery of great distances overhung by dry haze" (32). Chapter 2 begins with this same eternal present but quickly modulates, first into the iterative of Captain Mitchell's repeated recountings to various hapless visitors to the country of "hav[ing] been called upon to save the life of a dictator" from a violent mob (" 'Sir,' Captain Mitchell would pursue with portentous gravity"), then to the past tense and a particular day and time: "Early on the morning of that day the local authorities of Sulaco had fled for refuge" (44, 45). Then Nostromo is introduced and the role he played on "that day" begins to be detailed. Chapter 3 moves back into the past to tell the back story of Nostromo's attachment to Giorgio Viola and his family, then forward again to the instant on "that day" when Nostromo arrives to ensure the Violas' safety. Chapter 4 moves back in time once more, to the beginning of the day and Nostromo's having kept an eye on the Casa Viola, then forward to the moment of his arrival there, then to an iterative evocation of daily life in the Casa, then back again to the beginning of the same day focalized through Viola himself, then to his past fighting in South America and Italy under Garibaldi's command, then again to an iterative account of his family's life in Costaguana. Chapter 5 leaps back once more, this time very exactly to the moment "eighteen months before" when "the Excellentissimo Señor don Vincente Ribiera, the Dictator of Costaguana, had described the National Central Railway in his great speech at the turning of the first sod" as a "progressive and patriotic undertaking" (61). The occasion is the same one on which Sir John and the other representative of a foreign power come to lend approval to the work being financed by their countries' capital, and on which Montero makes his unfortunate toast. But the toast itself is not related until the end of chapter 8, when the narrator—suddenly and briefly, at the beginning of the same chapter, first-person limited ("as I am told" [108]) rather than, as for the rest of the novel, third-person omniscient—returns to the inauguration of the railway after having been diverted in chapters 5, 6, and 7 to Charles Gould's childhood, his courtship of Emily in Italy, his father's obsession with the mine that is foisted upon him, the brutal dictatorship of Guzman Bento, and so on.

Examples might be proliferated at much greater length, but these should be sufficient to establish the basic observation about *Nostromo* that its temporal experimentalism is marked by the kinds of complexity and difficulty associated with modernism. Events in themselves recede from view, replaced by characters' and readers' understanding of them in their kaleidoscopically changing relations to one another. The distribution of the narration across a range of voices, although a different technique, produces similar results. Because, again, instances are legion, I will simply refer to those that have already been mentioned: the ventriloquizing of the folk legend in the first chapter; the narrator's move from third-person omniscient to first-person limited and then back again; Decoud's letter to his sister, which takes up half of the seventh chapter of part 2, to which may be added the many sections of the novel where his speeches displace other discourse; and Mitchell's iteratives that almost but do not quite bookend the novel, appearing in the second chapter of part 1 and the tenth chapter of part 3. The consequence of these and other instances, and particularly the presence throughout of free indirect discourse, is a thorough-going perspectivism. It isn't at all that nothing happens in the novel, or that what happens isn't crucial in itself; it is, rather, that even more crucial is what is said and believed about what happens.

That these and other techniques deployed in *Nostromo* mark a shift away from nineteenth-century realism toward what would come to be modernist prose is a truism. So, too, is the further observation that Conrad understood the need for this shift to derive from what he saw as the exigencies of a higher realism.[13] As he wrote to Arnold Bennett in a letter dated March 10, 1902, not long before he began writing *Nostromo,* "You just stop short of being abso-lutely real because you are faithful to your dogmas of realism" (Conrad, *Collected Letters* 2: 390). What has not been recognized is that such techniques find both their necessity and their possibility with the ubiquity of the cul-ture of investment. Jameson has made the case for modernism as a response to the globalization of economic relations brought about in part by empire. Observing that "colonialism means that a significant structural element of the economic system as a whole is now located elsewhere, beyond the metropolis, outside the daily life and existential experience of the home country," he argues for "the emergence of a properly modernist 'style'" as a response to the impos-sibility of representing the society constituted by that system ("Modernism" 50–51, 59).[14] But just as I have claimed that there is something more at stake in *Nostromo* than the documentation of the arrival of capitalism *qua* capitalism, I believe that its narrative strategies, which is to say its distinctive style, spring from and respond to not simply empire but more specifically the increasingly dominant role of investment both at home and abroad. The novel's pervasive thematization of investment is matched by the pervasive effects the culture of investment has on its form. Nowhere is this clearer than in the place of speech, misinformation, and rumor.

To a degree remarkable in such a textual, writerly work, *Nostromo* fore-grounds speech. So, for instance, the folk tradition about the Azuera is intro-duced with the tag "The story goes" (40); we learn that Gould's nickname is the "King of Sulaco" from "the current gossip of the foreign residents" (106); and the narrator, commenting on the time he spent in Sulaco before the ar-rival of the railroad, relates: "The outward appearances had not changed then as they have changed since, as I am told, with cable cars running along the streets of the Constitution. . . . Nobody had ever heard of labour troubles then" (108). Less clearly marked but just as indicative of the privileged place of orality in the novel are its many passages of free indirect discourse, among the most instructive of which must be counted the narration of Gould's threat to

Pedrito Montero, who has occupied the Intendencia of Sulaco to await the arrival of his brother with more troops: "And Charles Gould had also said that the destruction of the San Tomé mine would cause the ruin of other undertakings, the withdrawal of European capital, the withholding, most probably, of the last installment of the foreign loan. That stony fiend of man said all these things (which were accessible to His Excellency's intelligence) in a cold-blooded manner which made one shudder" (341). The phrases "stony fiend" and "cold-blooded manner which made one shudder" are recognizably the thoughts of Pedrito; the parenthetical statement regarding "His Excellency's intelligence" recognizably a condemnatory aside from the narrator; the rest—the threatened loss of European investment should anything happen to the San Tomé mine—may well be an accurate representation of what Gould says, but the free indirect discourse in which the whole is cast makes confidence on this score impossible. The crucial thing for *Nostromo* is that this is what Pedrito believes Gould has told him, and that he acts on this belief.

The foregrounding of speech, the mediation of information by way of rumor and free indirect discourse, the confused temporal relations, the wide distribution of the narration: all these aspects of Conrad's novel render a world in which what is, although not quite disappearing, is overshadowed by what has been said.[15] This is why errant language and questions of interpretation are such major forces in *Nostromo*. Both are thematized as well as enacted in Mitchell's relation of his version of events, marked by the narrator as unreliable: "Unfortunately, Captain Mitchell had not much penetration of any kind; characteristic, illuminating trifles of expression, action, or movement, escaped him completely" (291). Although Mitchell appears to be an extreme case, none of the novel's characters is able to see a thing in itself; like the novel's readers, they are creatures of inference. So the English engineer-in-chief opines to Dr. Monygham, a Briton long resident in Costaguana: "Upon my word, doctor, things seem to be worth nothing by what they are in themselves. I begin to believe that the only solid thing about them is the spiritual value which everyone discovers in his own form of activity—" (275). Monygham retorts: "Bah!"— and the place of "material interests" in *Nostromo* may encourage us to believe that the novel as a whole speaks with him. But there is a way in which the engineer is precisely right: Conrad tells us of a place and time in which things are in effect what they are thought or said to be. It is not the instransigence of the natural world or even the impossibility of politics, then, that the novel represents as insuperable to human aspirations. In regard to the first, we have the narrator's casual comment on Sir John's "indifference of a man of affairs to nature, whose hostility can always be overcome by the resources of finance" (66). In regard to the second, Sulaco does after all become "independent" and "modern"; capitalism does after all arrive. The problem (and the promise) for value inheres, rather, in drift in meaning—which is why Gould takes such an obsessive interest in "abandonded workings": "They might have been worthless, but also they might have been misunderstood" (81).[16]

Whence, finally, the novel's title. Conrad's friends judged it a mistake and recommended "Costaguana" instead. But from the point of view of its diagnosis of the culture of investment, *Nostromo* makes eminent sense. Gian' Battista Fidanza upholds an apparently outdated notion of value, one based on reputation, on one's "name." "His prestige is his fortune," Monygham says of him, and Decoud in the letter to his sister writes similarly that he is a man "for whom the value of life seems to consist in personal prestige" (277, 221). Of course there is irony here: he is called "Nostromo" at all only because of Mitchell's mispronunciation of the Italian word for his former occupation, that of boatswain or bo's'n. The name of which Fidanza is so proud is not even his own. And of course, too, the events of the novel also seem to reveal the error of belief in names, for Nostromo's sterling one is both false—he ends up a thief—and without value—he feels betrayed by those whose approbation he sought. But in another sense they reveal a clandestine continuity between the old and the new, between Nostromo's nearly feudal notion of the power of names and the market's responsiveness to rumor. This, at any rate, is the lesson Nostromo pays for with his life. For it is a rumor that another man, Ramirez, intended to elope with one of his daughters that leads Viola to murder the man he treats as his son: "In one way or another a good deal of talk about Ramirez had reached him of late. . . . He slept very little now; but for several nights past . . . he had been prowling actively all about the island with his old gun, on watch over his honour" (452–53).

In a disparaging judgment, Gould says: "The words one knows so well have a nightmarish meaning in this country" (344).[17] *Nostromo* suggests, however, that the complaint applies not merely to Costaguana and the "developing" world for which it serves as synecdoche but to all societies given over to the culture of investment, societies in which talk with its unstable, unpredictable meaning determines value. To mount such a critique, however, Conrad must emulate the very things to which he objects. The techniques by means of which he gives shape to his fictional world, as well as their effects on the writing and reading of narrative, echo the functioning of language in an extra-fictional world in which information is both indispensable and unreliable: mediated meaning, the inaccessibility of fact, the rise or fall of value according to what is believed about what has been said.[18]

*   *   *

Writing about *The Way We Live Now* (1874–1875), an important precursor for *Nostromo* in several ways, Tara McGann comments on Trollope's use of free indirect discourse as well as the prominent place he assigns to rumor.[19] "By withholding from the reader a touchstone to assess the judgements received," she writes, "the novel forces a reassessment of assumptions and the discarding of empty conventions. As such, *The Way We Live Now* stands as the first realist novel about finance in the British novel tradition" (156). For McGann, the realist novel of finance is born when older conventions of representing high finance come under pressure. With Trollope's novel, she argues, the impersonality of the "business cycle" replaces older individualizing and moralizing accounts of financial crisis (134, 138).[20] One of the implications of my reading of *Nostromo* is that the realist novel may not have gone far enough in this regard. Business cycle theory depersonalizes economic failure, but it also continues to imagine failure (and success, for that matter) to be predictable. Bubbles and crashes, although limit cases of stock market performance, nonetheless illustrate the unpredictability and lack of control constitutive of the market. Rumor—as well as reputation, interpretation, misprision—constitutes value in the stock market and, consequently, in the larger world of which the market forms a part. As a novel of finance and much else besides, Conrad's *Nostromo* enlists narrative innovation in the service of representing a world in which even Trollopian realism is found wanting. It is, in other words, far from accidental that the first modernist novel (or one of the first, certainly) happens also to be the first modernist novel of finance.

But there is another side to this question of innovative form, of the old and the new. In the same recent collection in which McGann's essay appears, Nicholas Shrimpton reminds us of the degree to which many of the most influential Victorian critics of finance saw money values displacing older forms of connection or relation. Carlyle, Marx and Engels, Tennyson, George Eliot—all, Shrimpton writes, "directly juxtapose family or erotic relationship with monetary relationship" and see the latter as putting an end to the former (35). But *Nostromo* shows how older forms are not so much replaced as transformed and, hence, preserved. The novel emphasizes the continuities between the value Nostromo and the market place on a good name as much as or more than it emphasizes how, as with the Goulds, one set of values (conjugal love) is replaced by another (wealth).[21] The cryptic allegory for this dynamic may appear in the ships of the Oceanic Steam Navigation Company, Captain Mitchell's employer. Although named after classical mythological personages (Cerberus, Juno, Saturn, Ganymede, Ceres, Pallas [43, 405]), they transport decidedly modern cargo and bear visiting foreign dignitaries away from Costaguana to the "Olympus of plutocrats" (87). The modernity of the culture of investment does not render former systems and beliefs archaic and therefore irrelevant; it incorporates them—even if their continued existence often only takes the form of the capacity to introduce more error.

Which returns us to the Chinese crash of 2007. The rumored move by Beijing to rein in China's stock market did eventually occur. In May 2007, the authorities raised taxes on trades, tripling the previous rate. Writing in the *New York Times* on May 31, 2007, about the response, David Barboza observed: "When Chinese shares fell sharply at the end of February, markets around the world tumbled in tandem. . . . [But this time] major European share indexes ended down fractionally, and leading indexes in the United States gained 0.8 percent." The title of his piece says it all: "Tax Increase Batters Chinese Stocks, but There's Little Wider Damage." It is as if, having already reacted to the false rumor, global markets found no need to respond to the fact itself. Just as the Chinese crash provides a fine gloss on *Nostromo,* so the novel helps us understand the crash—again in the person of Captain Mitchell, who places notable occurrences into one of only two categories: "Almost every event out of the usual daily course 'marked an epoch' for him or else was 'history'; unless with his pomposity struggling with a discomfited droop of his rubicund, rather handsome face, set off by snow-white close hair and short whiskers, he would mutter: 'Ah, that! That, sir, was a mistake'" (121–22). Wrong as usual, Mitchell seems not to understand that, in the culture of investment, "history" and "a mistake" are often synonymous.

## Notes

For insightful responses to earlier drafts of this chapter I am grateful to Nancy Henry, Benita Parry, and Dana Seitler.

1. S. A. Smith's "Talking Toads and Chinless Ghosts: The Politics of 'Superstitious' Rumors in the People's Republic of China, 1961–1965," an examination of rumor in connection with the devastating but officially ignored famine of the early 1960s, contains a useful set of references to recent studies of rumor in the PRC and other nations under the rule of authoritarian regimes.

2. Fleishman points out that the parallels between Costaguana and Colombia are not only geographical: "[A]n [interventionist] outside force existed in both Colombia and Costaguana, and even the form of its intervention is somewhat similar. In the former, it was the European and United States' interest in building a mid-hemisphere canal which, with the encouragement and the active support of the nationalists by the United States government, led to the separation of the Province of Panama from Colombia.... In the fictional country, the outside force is the Gould concession, backed by European and American capital and the naval presence of the United States" (169–70). Moreover, he continues, the "connection between the historical and the fictional events lies not only in their parallelism; the United States intervention in Panama culminated in 1904, during the writing of the novel, and must be considered an active influence on its creation" (170).

3. The U.S. financier Holroyd refers directly to the War of the Pacific when he cautions Charles Gould about what might befall him should he succeed in making the San Tomé mine productive: "Let us suppose that the mining affairs of Sulaco are taken in hand. There would then be in it: first, the house of Holroyd, which is all right; then, Mr. Charles Gould, a citizen of Costaguana, who is all right; and, lastly, the Government of the Republic. So far this resembles the first start of the Atacama nitrate fields, where there was a financing house, a gentleman of the name of Edwards, and—a Government; or, rather, two Governments—two South American Governments. And you know what came of it. War came of it; devastating and prolonged war came of it, Mr. Gould" (93–94). In the background is surely also the example of Baring Brothers bank, which was nearly ruined when a revolution in Argentina stopped repayment of its loans there, as well as "the famous copper-ore trade between Swansea and the Chilian [sic] coast" in which, Conrad mentions in *The Mirror of the Sea*, Captain Edwin John Blake, under whom he served as second mate aboard the *Tilkhurst* in 1885 and 1886, "served his time" (Conrad, *Mirror* 144; Shrimpton 26).

4. Reclaiming access to the Pacific remains a nationalist watchword in Bolivia to this day. Writing in the *New York Times* on September 23, 2006, Simon Romero observed: "In a diplomatic push combining nostalgia and shrewd nationalist politics,

President Evo Morales has begun lobbying to regain a small part of that coastline [lost during the War of the Pacific] for Bolivia."

5. Jacques Berthoud enlists Cain and Hopkins's argument about "gentlemanly capitalism" in his reading of *Lord Jim* as "an exploration of chivalric gentlemanliness as the product of Victorian imperialism" (xvi). See also John Kucich's demonstration that Conrad's corpus articulates a "class-specific imperial ethos [that] wholly depended on professionals' capacity to negotiate masochistic fantasy and to mark their own imperial melancholia in redemptive ideological terms," an ethos for which chivalric gentlemanliness proved essential (199, 236). Vigorous debate continues over the accuracy and implications of Cain and Hopkins's conclusions. See Aguirre; Aguirre and Forman; Bowen; Dumett; Knight; Osterhammel; Robert Freeman Smith.

6. Norman Sherry argues that the character of Sir John was constructed closely on the model of Edward B. Eastwick, author of *Venezuela: or Sketches of Life in a South American Republic; with the History of the Loan of 1864* (London, 1868): "Eastwick went to Venezuela in 1864 as financial commissioner for the General Credit Company which had floated an immense loan for Venezuela"; he "was earnest in trying to impress upon the Government the necessity of fulfilling their obligations in the matter of the loan: 'I tried to impress upon every one in authority that any infraction of the conditions of the contract would strike a fatal blow at the national credit'" (172).

7. Jameson, pursuing the explication of *ressentiment* that forms one of the key strands of his argument in *The Political Unconscious,* observes that "the third and deepest ideological level" in *Nostromo* is "the theory of *ressentiment;* and the Montero brothers are described, and their motives explained, in terms that are the commonplaces of all the great counterrevolutionary nineteenth-century historians" (*Political* 270–71). This seems to me both indisputable and far from the whole story.

8. So while Edward Said seems exactly right when he notes in *Culture and Imperialism* that "Conrad *dates* imperialism, shows it contingency, records its illusions and tremendous violence and waste," the *way* he dates empire in *Nostromo* requires rethinking the centrality of territory and spatiality that forms such an important line of thought in Said's book (26; emphasis in the original).

9. On the vexed attempt to distinguish among investment, speculation, and gambling at the end of the Victorian period and beyond, see Itzkowitz, "Fair Enterprise," and Daunton, "Afterword," both in this volume.

10. Parry writes in this regard: "Rather than articulate the consensual consciousness of the upward development in history exemplified and implemented by the nation-states of Europe and North America, the novel's story line goes against the grain of convention to follow an errant path that circumvents the constraints of sequence and refuses the demand of imperialist ideology to map an itinerary of orderly ascent and splendid achievement. Hence the retardations, deferrals, digressions and temporal displacements, where significant effects precede any credible explanation of the generative circumstances to the phenomena recounted, countermand the official recitation of continuous progress and regeneration" (*Postcolonial* 139–40).

11. Said notes that "[i]n the confusion of its uncertain focus, *Nostromo* resembles many of Conrad's other tales in which the course of the narrative stream is unclear; because of this we are never really certain about the novel's time scheme" (*Beginnings* 121).

12. Apart from "delayed decoding" (a technique "to put the reader in the position of being an immediate witness of each step in the process whereby the semantic gap

between the sensations aroused in an individual by an object or event, and their actual cause or meaning, was slowly closed in his consciousness" [Watt, *Conrad* 270]), these terms are those used by Gérard Genette to describe various relations between "story"—the events on which a narrative is based—and "plot"—those events as they are narrated. Prolepsis (colloquially, "flash forward") occurs when an event is narrated earlier in the plot than it happens in the story, analepsis ("flashback") later. The varieties of frequency specify how many times an event is narrated in relation to how many times it occurred. See Genette, *Narrative Discourse* and *Narrative Discourse Revisited.* On anachrony in *Nostromo,* see Talib.

13. Among *Nostromo*'s modernist qualities should be included as well its densely "poetic" language, shaped by various motifs—the most easily recognizable of which is that of mineral wealth itself. The treasure hunt of the first few pages creeps into the narrator's language with, to select a few examples from a myriad, the phrases "emerald green wedge of land" and "opal mystery of great distances," place names such as Esmaralda (42–43), Antonia Avellanos's "forehead, priceless pearl" (441), and the novel's final sentence: "In that true cry of undying passion that seemed to ring aloud from Punta Mala to Azuera and away to the bright line of the horizon, overhung by a big white cloud shining like a mass of solid silver, the genius of the magnificent Capataz de Cargadores dominated the dark gulf containing his conquests of treasure and love" (465).

14. On realism, modernisn, and economics, see also Jameson, "Culture and Finance Capital," and Vernon, *Money and Fiction.*

15. Similarly, Gould himself knows that the entire success of the mine depends on his reputation. "The worth of the mine—as a mine—is beyond doubt," he tells Emily. "But its safety, its continued existence as an enterprise, giving a return to men—to strangers, comparative strangers—who invest money in it, is left altogether in my hands. I have inspired confidence in a man of wealth and position" (91).

16. Thus it is impossible to agree with Daniel R. Schwarz when he concludes that "*Nostromo* justifies the choice of personal fulfillment over political involvement because it shows politics as a maelstrom that destroys those it touches and shows, more importantly, that one inevitably surrenders a crucial part of one's personality when one commits oneself to ideology" (550–51). For not only does *Nostromo* show, instead, that "personal fulfillment" and "politics" are inescapably intertwined, in the influence it accords to rumor it definitively demonstrates each character's subordination to forces beyond the reach of individual or even societal control. How (paradoxically) inevitable, then, that when Conrad returns to the question of finance capital he does so in a novel titled *Chance* (1914).

17. Although my focus has been on rumor and misprision in *Nostromo,* the novel also features prominently the sort of deliberate falsehood Poovey considers. In an attempt to preoccupy General Sotillo, whose troops have occupied Sulaco's harbor in the name of the Monterist revolution, Monygham encourages him to believe that the latest shipment of silver, rather than having been sent away on a boat, was buried nearby (296, 368). Later, at Nostromo's instigation, he changes his story, telling Sotillo that the treasure has been hidden in shallow water to be recovered later (384). The first lie leads to the torture and murder of the Jewish hide-dealer, Hirsch (294ff.). The second, to the possibility of the successful defense of Sulaco by placing Sotillo's troops out of combat: "Sotillo, blind and deaf to everything, stuck on board his steamer watching the dragging for silver, which he believed to be sunk at the bottom of the harbour" (402).

18. In *Voice and the Victorian Storyteller,* Ivan Kreilkamp makes a similar point by

linking *Heart of Darkness* to the phonograph and disquiet surrounding its implications for the human voice: "For Conrad, the perception of disembodied voice pointed the way to groundbreaking innovations in literary style and form, but it also seemed to represent a grave danger to human agency and authorship" (182).

19. For example, *The Way We Live Now* features Hamilton K. Fisker, a San Francisco financier, and the grand undertaking of Trollope's swindler or businessman, depending on one's perspective, August Melmotte, is to be the "South Central Pacific and Mexican Railway" (276–77). See also Trollope's *The Prime Minister* (1876), featuring a swindler named Lopez who deals in those quintessentially Latin American commodities, coffee and guano. (Audrey Jaffe offers a sustained meditation on investment and *The Prime Minister* in her essay in this volume.) Karl notes that the "importance of Trollope in Conrad's literary development may come as somewhat of a surprise." But in an unpublished letter to A. N. Monkhouse, editor of the *Manchester Guardian,* Conrad revealed that he found Trollope "a writer of remarkable talent for imaginative rendering of the social life of his time, with its activities and interests and incipient thoughts. . . . I was considerably impressed with them [his novels] in the early eighties, when I chanced upon a novel entitled 'Phineas Finn'" (68n.).

20. Note the similarity here to Poovey's observation that the interplay of disclosure and secrecy in George Eliot's *The Mill on the Floss* (1860) as a "relationship between plots" allows the exploration of a "model of causation that transcends individual psychology" (54).

21. Writing itself provides no escape or antidote—as witness the proof pages of Don José Avellanos's *Fifty Years of Misrule* scattered through the streets of Sulaco; Decoud's work in *L'Avenir,* seamlessly enlisted in the Anglo-American dominance of the country; and Gould's father's letters warning his son never to return to Costaguana, not simply ineffective but in fact producing the opposite result from that intended.

# Afterword

## Martin Daunton

Mr. Gladstone famously remarked that he wished to allow money to fructify in the pockets of the people, an ambition that entailed rolling back the level of public spending and encouraging individual prudence and self-reliance. It meant a reduction in the level of government spending from about 23 percent of the gross national product during the Napoleonic Wars to 8 percent by 1890 (Middleton 90–91). It meant redemption of the national debt through rigorous use of sinking funds, balancing the budget, and diverting any surplus to repayment. The net liabilities of the state fell from £837.7 million in 1840 to £685.0 million in 1890 ("Return" 328–31). When Edward Hamilton, a leading Treasury official, published *Conversion and Redemption* in 1886, it was not a study of missionary activity and the saving of souls, but of the successful conversion of the national debt to a lower rate of interest in order to redeem it more quickly and to reduce the burden of taxes on productive wealth. The play on words was more than a private joke by the son of a bishop; economic policy *was* about sin and salvation, creating a moral and prudent society. Gladstonian financial orthodoxy and the Treasury view were based on the firm belief that state spending "crowded out" more efficient use of funds in the market. A high level of savings was personally desirable as a way of dealing with the risks of life and providing for dependents after death—and it was also desirable for society as a whole. A higher proportion of large incomes could be saved after meeting the needs of the family; and these savings were translated into investments that led to the erection of more factories and houses, to more employment and higher wages. As Keynes put it, in this orthodox Gladstonian or Treasury view, a dog labeled savings wagged a tail called investment (qtd. in Clarke 246).

On this set of assumptions, the higher the level of savings, the better it would be for everyone. Individuals should be encouraged to become more prudential and far-sighted in their use of their income, putting more money aside for a rainy day. Hence Mr. Gladstone created the Post Office Savings Bank in 1861 to allow workers to save small sums in a readily accessible network of offices across the country—and the money was all used to redeem the national debt and free resources for profitable investment. Personal morality allowed the state to free itself from debt and the economy to prosper (Daunton, *Royal* ch. 3). At the same time, social reformers mounted a campaign against the irresponsible and imprudent habits of the working class—their reliance on pawnshops with exorbitant charges, their use of credit to incur large debts with shop-keepers, their fascination with betting.

In the eyes of many commentators, there was an evolutionary development from primitive to sophisticated attitudes to consumption, mirrored by differences between men (cautious) and women (emotional) and working-class consumers (irresponsible) and middle-class families (responsible). Evolutionary theories stressed a movement from instinct and gratification (found among savages and working men who spent their wages on instant pleasure) to reason and prudence (found among middle-class families who could defer their desires). In the words of Samuel Smiles in 1861, "Wise economy is not a natural instinct, but the growth of reflection. . . . Thus the savage is the greatest spend-thrift, for he has no forethought, no tomorrow, and lives only for the day or for the hour. Hence the clever workman, unless he be trained in good habits, may exhibit no higher a life than that of the mere animal; and the earning of increased wages will only furnish such persons with increased means of indulging in the gratification of the grosser appetites" (qtd. in Johnson, "Class Law" 164). The aim of social reformers, expressed in legislation as well as in moral commentary, was to weaken visceral or immediate desire and to instill prudence and deferred gratification (see Finn, *Character;* McKibbin, *Ideologies;* Rappaport, "The Halls," "A Husband," and *Shopping*).

The literature discussed in this collection of essays was framed by the basic set of assumptions that were challenged by Keynes in the 1930s when he argued that a dog labeled investment wagged a tail called savings. As he pointed out, there was no reason why savings should be invested, and the result of a high level of savings might be to reduce consumption, so creating unemployment and depression. There was a gap between private virtue and social benefit: what was good for an individual might be bad for society. In Keynes's view, industrialists would only invest if they had a market for their goods, and if they needed funds for investment, they would attract savings. It followed that the government might stimulate the economy by spending more money than it received from taxes, so that an unbalanced budget was beneficial. The intellectual debates over these different attitudes were fought out in the 1930s, and there the matter is usually left by historians of economic thought (Clarke; Peden).

One of the many virtues of this collection of essays is that it complicates the narrative provided by the history of economic thought. The Gladstonian notion of the virtues of saving leading directly to beneficial investment was in fact problematical, for the distinction between visceral and prudential consumption applied equally to investment. Was all investment worthwhile and prudent? Could savings derived from careful management of household resources be wasted on speculation rather than converted into productive investment? Were investors careful and prudent or irrational and emotional? The relationship between investment and speculation or gambling was crucial. Broadly, investment was sound, whereas speculation was unwise or greedy. But the line between the two remained blurred and contested, and the authors of these essays do not entirely agree where it was drawn by contemporaries.

David Itzkowitz argues that by the 1860s speculation was purged of its association with gambling, and "speculation increasingly came to be seen as a reputable economic activity and speculators as respectable economic actors." His point is that wagers were not enforceable in law, whereas "time contracts" were enforceable from the repeal of Barnard's Act in 1860. The courts realized that there was no way of telling the difference between bargains on the stock exchange that speculated on changes in the price of shares and those that were ordinary bargains, and they decided not to make the attempt. Even when new forms of dubious speculation emerged in the 1870s, it proved possible to rebrand them as gambling, so making them illegitimate and legitimating other forms of speculation.

Other contributors differ from Itzkowitz's interpretation. Mary Poovey argues that financial journalism depicted the financial sector as law-governed and natural, seeking to naturalize financial institutions and show that investment was safe, whereas speculation was unwise. Audrey Jaffe stresses that Trollope continued to draw a distinction between investment and speculation, expressing unease about investing in shares because of the attenuated relationship between investors and the objects of their investment. This distance meant that they were investing in narratives about the companies rather than in facts, with a confusion between what was solid and what was ephemeral. Similarly, in his fascinating discussion of *Nostromo*, Cannon Schmitt suggests that Conrad did not define speculation as legitimate but rather that investment in general was speculation. To Conrad, investment implied unstable and unpredictable meanings, where what was suspected or believed had more significance than what was known or seen. The culture of investment entailed confusion, described in language that was untrustworthy and unverifiable, and where rumor was not differentiated from fact. As Poovey remarks, financial journalists were constrained from openly describing the workings of companies, for they could only operate if some of their dealings were hidden: rumor and information, secrecy and disclosure were confused.

Of course, the boundaries between legitimate investment and illegitimate speculation, between desirable entrepreneurship and reprehensible greed, continued to be contested, and still are. A significant strand in Labour thinking in the twentieth century argued that the stock market made irrational investments, driven by a search for short-term profits that fueled inequality in society. The solution was to take decisions away from financiers and hand them to managers in either nationalized industries or large, bureaucratic private concerns, who would invest in research and make long-sighted decisions. Labour policy after the Second World War rested on this distinction between poor decisions in the external capital market and rational decisions within companies, reflected in tax incentives to retain profits rather than to distribute them to shareholders. The Conservative government in the late 1950s and early 1960s was also concerned about speculators in the property market, fearing that their actions were bringing capitalism into disrepute: a tax on short-term capital gains was therefore introduced (Daunton, *Just;* Whiting). The line between investment and speculation continued to trouble politicians long after the Victorian period.

It would be interesting to consider the definitions of speculation and investment in the Victorian period in a more systematic way, not through a few major novels by Conrad or Trollope but through a much wider analysis of a variety of sources: stories in popular magazines, comments by judges, discussion in the financial press. Questioning the morality of a capitalist society did not come merely from social critics such as Ruskin or Marx, for many Victorian businessmen and political economists were concerned to reconcile morality with the market. The *Economist* was confident that commerce was intrinsically moral, an antidote to war and ignorance. In the words of the *Economist,* "Trade carries with it a rigid morality . . . it naturally inculcates punctual and rigid honesty" (qtd. in Searle 21). Not everyone went so far, and many commentators realized that the issue was more complicated, including that great promoter of self-help and ambition, Samuel Smiles. "He who recognizes no higher logic than that of the shilling," Smiles pointed out in *Self-Help,* "may become a very rich man and yet remain all the while an exceedingly poor creature. For riches are no proof of moral worth." The point of commercial life, he argued, was to rise above its moral dangers, for "if there were no temptations, there would be no training in self-control, and but little merit in virtue" (qtd. in Searle 46). Similarly, Herbert Spencer was more than the advocate of individualism and the survival of the fittest that he is often assumed to have been. He believed that society was evolving from egoism to altruism, and he looked to the creation of a society where "associated activities can be so carried on, that the complete living of each consists with, and conduces to, the complete living of all." He feared that "trade is essentially corrupt" as a result of "*the indiscriminate respect paid to wealth.*" Urban, industrial society should not collapse into an atomistic pursuit of self-interest, a war of all against all; it should be moral and co-operative (qtd. in Searle 98).

Some historians argue that moral checks were indeed imposed on the economy. As Geoffrey Searle remarks, "Intelligent middle-class Victorians, slowly, haltingly, acquired an appreciation of the complexity of the social and ethical codes upon which a market-driven economy ultimately relies for its success. Capitalism, they learnt, requires a particular balance between acquisitiveness and probity: tilt the balance too much in one direction, and social (even economic) disaster threatens" (274). The market had to be "moralized" if capitalism were to flourish.

At the heart of this debate was the nature of limited liability and the joint-stock company. Initially, unlimited liability appealed as a way of chastising illegitimate or speculative behavior that would be punished through personal insolvency—as the Presbyterian minister Thomas Chalmers pointed out, God would punish businessmen for their sins. But the Evangelical link between illegitimate trade and punishment was severed by the adoption of limited liability in 1856: speculation could now create profits without punishment. If the threat of financial ruin and retribution did not suffice, what did? Were the norms of

Evangelical morality internalized by businessmen, regardless of the coming of limited liability? Was there a widespread acceptance of the notion of altruism that Stefan Collini argues was at least as important to mid-Victorian intellectuals as a concern for self-interest? Or were these Evangelical and altruistic ideas confined to a small number of preachers and writers with little impact on the behavior of most businessmen? Paul Johnson argues that commercial norms became dominant, so that speculation and even fraud were tolerated in the late Victorian period to a much greater extent (rather as argued by Itzkowitz). Rather than commerce being civilized by Evangelicalism or altruism, Johnson argues that "the morality of Mammon . . . was exported to and enthroned in the wider world of law and politics" (Collini, 62; Hilton, ch. 4; Johnson, "Civilizing" 304–306, 314, 316–19; J. Taylor, "Commerical"). Of course, business scams and scandals are easily found, and some involved leading politicians such as the notorious Marconi scandal where cabinet ministers used inside knowledge. But Johnson's argument is too one-sided, ignoring the very real concern about the culture of a market society and the need to impose controls.

The approach of Jaffe to defining the boundary between investment and speculation has much to commend it. As she points out, Trollope was expressing unease about the unpredictability of investing in shares and the attenuated relationships between investors and the objects of their investments. Their investments were in stories about the companies or commodities, which confused the solid and ephemeral. An individual's character as a gentleman or non-gentleman was read from the way in which money was managed. In Jaffe's view, the distinction between what was approved as an investment and reviled as a speculation was a matter of feeling and personal involvement. The investor was detached from his money, ignoring daily fluctuations; the speculator was a creature of impulse and emotion, and was in thrall to greed—much as in the case of the distinction between visceral and prudential consumption. As we shall see, there was also widespread unease about the attenuated relationship between individual responsibility or morality and the actions of companies that were distinct from the owners of the shares.

Limited liability could offer a mechanism to reform society by allowing ownership to become more democratic. As Donna Loftus shows, radicals supported joint-stock companies as a way of bringing together the conflicting interests of capital and labor in a free market, encouraging the diffusion of share capital in local communities, and increasing investment by pooling small savings. Hence radical reformers argued that limited liability could tie communities together by capital investments. This view was developed by Joseph Chamberlain, who represented the corporation of Birmingham as a giant joint-stock company in which the citizens were shareholders (Jones). But such a view was far from being widely accepted, for suspicion of joint-stock companies and speculation was widespread in early and mid-Victorian Britain. Many novelists and social critics suspected that the temptation to speculate was often *not* resisted, a theme permeating early and mid-Victorian novels and plays. Joint-stock companies would threaten commercial morality by weakening any sense of personal responsibility. Whereas partnerships rested on character and reputation, corporations rested on a more casual relationship. Shareholders did not have the same close identity with the company, and were more concerned with their dividend, without personal engagement with the morality of its activities. Companies might lead to speculation and gambling through playing the stock market, leading to greed and mania; they might exploit the public through monopolizing gas and water, or by behaving irresponsibly in the pursuit of profit. Shareholders themselves might be exploited, seduced by misleading prospectuses and deceitful directors who drew lucrative salaries or manipulated share prices to make a killing before the company collapsed. Companies might rest on mere show and display rather than real worth, as in Dickens's account in *Martin Chuzzlewit* of the Anglo-Bengalee Disinterested Loan and Life Assurance Co. (J. Taylor, "Commercial"). Such fears posed the question of how these new corporate forms should be treated in order to prevent their subverting moral order and economic stability. Family firms and partnerships, for all their supposed moral virtues, could not operate railways or utilities with their large demands for capital. On what terms should the privilege of joint stock be granted, and how should companies be controlled? How should claims on companies' profits be adjudicated between directors, shareholders, customers, and workers? The issue was less one of Evangelical morality than of distributive justice and the power of companies over owners and the public.

In the first half of the nineteenth century, joint stock was a closely guarded privilege, confined to companies fulfilling some public purpose. Between 1844 and 1856, the status became more freely available. In 1844, the right to create a joint-stock company was granted by the state either by application to the Board of Trade or to Parliament, as yet without limited liability. The motivation was to prevent fraud. In the early 1840s, the railway mania and notorious frauds by insurance companies—above all the West Middlesex Fire and Life Insurance Co.—were assisted by their unincorporated status. Granting joint-stock status had much in common with Sir Robert Peel's imposition of strict monetary policy in the Bank Charter Act of 1844. This act was not a narrowly technical economic policy, for it had a moral dimension: to remove the temptation to speculate created by monetary laxity, and to ensure that those who gambled faced retribution. Similarly, free trade had a moral justification as a policy to purge the state of corruption and self-interest, and to benefit consumers with cheap food. By formalizing the status of joint-stock companies, they might be forced into respectability. Of course, the argument could be reversed: companies with a more secure legal status might be better able to exploit unsuspecting and naïve investors, so that the privilege should be more strictly controlled to ensure that only reputable businesses were granted joint-stock status. Despite these concerns, joint-stock status was liberalized in 1855–1856 to remove constraints on the economy by mobilizing capital and overcoming the threat of monopoly by encouraging competition. Liberalization of joint-stock status complemented free trade and freedom of contract: denial of joint-stock status would restrict trade, and the government was not competent to judge between moral and immoral, efficient and fraudulent companies. Companies were seen as generally in the public interest as agents of technical progress and investment. The legislation was consistent with the reform of tariffs and the state: in the same way that tariffs offered opportunities for corruption and the pursuit of self-interest, so did discretion in the award of joint-stock status; free trade and a more routine granting of corporate status purged the state of favoritism and corruption. Although fraud and business failure continued, as with the collapse of Overend Gurney in 1866, more emphasis was placed on stimulating the economy by encouraging investment than on preventing speculation (J. Taylor, "Commercial").

Initially, few industrial concerns took advantage of joint-stock status—something that is not entirely clear from the essays in this collection. Industrial workers were still largely employed by family firms and partnerships with unlimited liability. Between 1856 and 1865, 4,839 companies were registered, with the largest numbers in gas and water (469) and in coal, iron, lead, and copper mines (633). By contrast, there were only 20 in woolen textiles and 157 in cotton. Family and firm remained closely connected, fundamentally affecting the operation of the business. Over his career, a partner moved from an initial stage of indebtedness when loans were repaid and drawings out of the firm were low, to a point where loans were repaid and larger drawings were possible. Men in their fifties gradually moved from active involvement to unearned rentier income, making larger drawings out of the firm and removing capital to provide for sons who were not involved in the business, or to give marriage settlements to daughters. When a partner retired or died, he or his executors would take the equity out of the business in order to escape from the risks of unlimited liability and to provide for his heirs. These heavy cash withdrawals, and the need to buy out the equity on retirement or death, could impose immense strain on the firm. The remaining partners had to find the money to buy out the share, and they faced the difficult task of finding a successor from within the family, by tapping their social networks, or by recruiting an able employee. Succession and inheritance were not always handled with care, and the boundaries between family and firm were often blurred to the detriment of both. If assets were kept in the firm, the family might suffer from business failure; and if incompetent family members ran the firm, the business might face difficulties. In a joint-stock company, it was easier to dispose of shares on the stock market or to recruit a salaried manager. Manufacturing concerns only really started to take up joint-stock form on any scale from the 1890s, when one motivation was for the owners to float companies on the stock exchange in order to extract value by selling shares at inflated prices. Another motivation was to convert family firms or partnerships into private limited companies using new powers in the Company Act of 1907. But larger concerns also had an entirely legitimate need to turn to joint-stock organization to allow a more bureaucratic managerial style and to permit growth beyond the scope of families and partnerships (Hannah 61; Morgan and Moss; Morris; Shannon, "First" 422).

The separation of ownership and control posed serious questions for the morality of business. The repeal of the corn laws and free trade offered cheap food, but what if the flour was adulterated by an unscrupulous miller or the bread by a deceitful baker? Should they be monitored by public officials, or should the principle of caveat emptor apply? Of course, a customer could only beware if adulteration were detectable and if there were alternative suppliers. As John Stuart Mill pointed out, it was one thing to remove custom from a baker who charged excessive prices or supplied poor bread; it was quite another thing with gas and water, where the consumer was powerless and joint-stock companies could exploit the consumer, unconstrained by the sense of personal responsibility found in family firms and partnerships. As we have noted, most joint-stock companies were in this sector, creating particular problems of responsibility and morality. Herbert Spencer expressed a common view, that the corporate conscience of a company was inferior to the conscience of an individual, and a group of men might collectively undertake an act that each as an individual would find repellent (Atiyah 281). The monopoly powers of the East India Co., or the protection of West Indies sugar planters had ended; might not the new monopolists of the local gas concern simply take their place? The repeal of the navigation acts allowed merchants to use any ship, only to find that they were captives of railway companies able to charge high freight rates to move their goods between Manchester and Liverpool. Tariffs on raw materials might be abolished, only to place producers at the mercy of companies able to charge high prices for other vital commodities. The owner of a spinning mill or weaving shed in Lancashire might be faced with a high price for gas lighting, or for water to process the cloth. Mill was concerned that the utility companies were not accountable: in theory, shareholders had power over the directors of companies, but in practice their input was minimal. There were serious dangers, for Mill pointed out that "a government which concedes such monopoly unreservedly to a private company does much the same thing as if it allowed an individual or an association to levy any tax they chose for their own benefit, on all the malt produced in the country, or on all the cotton imported into it." What was needed, therefore, was strict regulation over private companies to control their prices and profits, or even to take the concerns into public ownership. As Mill saw it, any "delegated management" was likely to be "jobbing, careless and ineffective" compared with personal management by the owner, whose own reputation was at stake. Despite the dangers that a powerful state bureaucracy would keep citizens in a child-like condition, Mill felt that the threat posed by company control of gas and water was still more serious (Mill, *Principles* bk. 4, ch. 11). William Farr pointed out in 1873 that the East India Co. was, in effect, "nationalised" after the uprising of 1857 and the railway companies "have alike earned, and are destined to receive the same apotheosis—Absorption into the Sovereign Power" (qtd. in Alborn, *Conceiving* 51–52). Public ownership might therefore have its origins in individualism rather than in socialism, in an attempt to protect the consumer in circumstances where competitive capitalism was inappropriate. The contention that the "morality of Mammon" was exported to the wider world misses these debates and concerns.

Investment in railway and utility companies was not feasible unless they were granted power against the property rights of other parties, in order to cross land, demolish housing, break open streets, construct reservoirs. Parliament granted power to the companies and regulated them to prevent abuse of their position, in much the same way as the removal of customs duties and chartered monopolies ended the power of West Indian sugar planters or the East India Co. to exploit consumers. The politics of natural monopolies were formulated in the same way as the politics of taxation: electors and their representatives needed to pay close attention to the spending and taxing powers of the government, and consumers of gas and water needed to pay close attention to the ability of companies to "tax" through their charges for essential services. Far from democratizing investment, joint-stock companies might undermine democracy through giving power to a small number of shareholders to impose excessive rates on the larger number of consumers. In both the government and the companies, the "franchise"—the voice of the person purchasing or consuming services—should be carefully devised to provide effective controls, and to prevent the state or the companies from levying taxes or charges on one group to the benefit of another, or from creating sinecures for directors and politicians. As Mill put it, "The question is not between free trade and a Government monopoly. The case is one in which a practical monopoly is unavoidable; and the possession of the monopoly by individuals constitutes not freedom but slavery; it delivers over the public to the mercy of those individuals" (Mill, *Public* 434). The issue was how the government should best protect the public from the power created by network investment (on gas companies, see Daunton, "Material").

The politics of joint-stock companies did not end with making limited liability more easily available, for the rights of various stakeholders continued to be in tension. Companies operated in the public sphere and they were intrinsically political entities; their performance reflected their response to the interplay of different stakeholders. What power should directors have over the company; how accountable should they be to shareholders? Would the shareholders have large denomination shares and form an oligarchy, or would shares have low denominations and allow a more democratic franchise? Might consumers use their political voice to demand more or less stringent regulation; might they form an alliance with the shareholders against the directors, or join with the directors against the threat of workers to their profits and dividends? The directors opposed controls that threatened the dividend paid to shareholders, perhaps by presenting themselves as the guardians of managerial efficiency against the corrupting power of political authority. Workers might secure political voice, demanding protection of their welfare and safety. The politics of joint-stock companies were complex, and varied between sectors according to the constellation of interests and their interaction. The same language was used as in debates over the franchise and taxation: directors might be portrayed as corrupt sinecurists, unaccountable to the citizens; shareholders might strive to create a subscribers' democracy where they were coterminous with the consumers; or the utility might be taken into public ownership, as with telegraphs in 1869 and municipal gas and water concerns, so creating a unity of owner and consumer (Alborn, *Conceiving*).

These issues were much less pressing in manufacturing industry, where firms continued to be dominated by families and partnerships with unlimited liability right up to the end of the century. Investment in network industries was "lumpy" and large-scale, so that plowing back of profits was not feasible; in manufacturing industry, most investment came from this internal source, as well as the use of credit from suppliers and overdrafts from banks. In manufacturing, a single concern was not able to dominate the market and exploit the consumer to anything like the same extent. Here to Alfred Marshall was the basis of Britain's industrial success: a plethora of firms specializing in different branches of the trade secured all the benefits of concentration without the cumbersome organization of a large firm. Rather than joint-stock companies and limited liability diffusing capital through the community and removing conflict between labor and capital, as argued by some radicals, it would have the opposite effect. To Marshall, the associations of small family firms and partnerships supplied technical and commercial information, established a framework for contracts and arbitration, and helped to set wage rates for the industry—without impinging on the individuality of each firm that guaranteed dynamism and responsibility. Marshall stressed the virtues of industrial districts:

> so great are the advantages which people following the same skilled trade get from near neighbourhood to one another. The mysteries of the trade become no mysteries; but are as it were in the air, and children learn many of them unconsciously. Good work is rightly appreciated, inventions and improvements in machinery, in processes and the general organization of the business have their merits promptly discussed.

In Marshall's world, competition and individuality were moderated by "constructive co-operation," and the benefits of scale were achieved outside the firm through the associational life of the industrial district. Marshall argued that joint-stock companies would be less efficient than family firms, for salaried managers with delegated powers were inclined to opt for an easy life "of not striving energetically for improvement, and of finding excuses for not trying improvement until its success is established." Unlike individual owners, managers were more concerned with creating systems to monitor and control their workforce, an approach that "is necessarily wasteful of effort, and hostile to elasticity: and here lies a chief disadvantage under which a joint stock company lies in competition with a private firm." The result was a loss of initiative, "a tendency to ossification of the social organism . . . as the result of bureaucratic habits of shirking troublesome initiative." He presented a positive case for a fragmented, small-scale structure as peculiarly suited to the English:

What suits their character best is to have a broad and solid association based on many smaller associations, not controlling and directing them without absolute necessity, but acting as a common centre for help and advice; serving as a channel by which any member that is in special need may receive the aid of others, and taking perhaps an active part in administering aid and the wholesome advice by which it may perhaps be accompanied. . . . Broad-based, highly-organised freedom of action is characteristically English.

Indeed, Marshall argued that the organization of the wider urban or regional economy was becoming more sophisticated over time: trade knowledge was spread through newspapers or associations; technical progress depended on the pursuit of scientific knowledge for its own sake. Small and medium firms might secure all of these external benefits, without the costly internal management systems of large firms where bureaucracy would stifle change and creativity (Marshall, "Co-operation" 249; *Industry* 249, 324–25, 577–78, 582–84, 590, 605–608; *Principles* 138–39, 271, 279–80, 283–85, 304).

When Marshall was writing in 1919, the industrial district of Lancashire was undergoing transformation as many firms in the cotton industry were floated on the stock exchange in a speculative frenzy, which contributed to the difficulties faced by the industry for the rest of the interwar period. But his account provided a reasonably accurate picture of the cotton towns in the Victorian period, as well as a very well articulated normative vision. Industrialists did come together in the Manchester Chamber of Commerce to defend their interests; they did co-operate in setting wages. They also worked together in the civic life of the towns and in charities, building hospitals, universities, and art galleries. At a more private level, competing industrialists acted for each other as executors or trustees of marriage settlements (Rodger). Industrial investment was intensely social, a feature that is captured in the novels of Arnold Bennett more than in Trollope or Conrad.

The social character of industrial investment was particularly marked in the issue of inheritance and succession. As we have noted earlier, the needs of the family could require the withdrawal of funds from the firm that could threaten its viability; on the other hand, the accumulation of funds could exceed the needs of the firm and might be withdrawn. In some cases, the surplus funds were invested in a diverse range of assets at home and overseas—in railway shares, in government bonds, and so on (Lenman and Donaldson; Sigsworth). Of course, land offered one safe haven for investment. Land was at the opposite end of the spectrum from speculation on the stock exchange. Above all, Trollope saw wealth based on land as stable and moral, and he feared that society would be corrupted by stock market money (Nancy Henry). This is a view with a long ancestry—it goes back to at least the eighteenth century when land ownership was linked with "republican virtue" and distinguished from self-interested financial or industrial property. Landowners were seen as disinterested, with the time and income to serve the state and to bear arms in defense of the public (Pocock). By the nineteenth century, attitudes were changing. Virtue was now to be shown through dedication to business, and politicians indicated that they were "disinterested" by the care they took in handling the affairs of state and ensuring that they were above the narrow concerns of particular vested interests. Land started to lose its moral superiority as the basis of an incorrupt polity that was rather guaranteed by free trade, the gold standard, and the Bank Charter Act.

Nevertheless, land purchase remained appealing at least until the serious fall in price in the last quarter of the nineteenth century. Land purchase by "new men of wealth," or at least by their heirs, is seen by some historians as a retreat from trade and industry, an erosion of investment in production by a flight to status and gentrification encouraged—so it is claimed—by the disparagement of industry in English culture. But it is possible to make a different argument, that ownership of land was a device to reduce risks and to remain in business. In family firms, ownership of land could fulfill two functions. The first was to support members of the family who were not competent businessmen. The second was to withdraw money from the firm where it might tempt partners into over-expansion and risk. Investment in land was therefore not necessarily a means of opting out of industry (Rubinstein; Thompson "Life" and *Gentrification;* Wiener).[1]

Investment in land was also politically contested, for economists from David Ricardo to J. S. Mill and Henry George argued that land was far from the basis of republican virtue or of social stability and moral order as argued by Trollope. To these economists, landowners were the passive recipients of "unearned" increments created by active, dynamic businessmen who increased the demand for a strictly limited supply of land. On this view, landowners were parasitical on productive wealth, and they were the proper object for taxation or even expropriation. These radical sentiments were not widely shared by most politicians, but by the 1890s they had a stronger purchase in advanced Liberal circles, and fed into William Harcourt's graduated estate duty and Lloyd George's land campaign. It also connected with the introduction of differentiation of the income tax in 1907, when income from land and government bonds was defined as "unearned" and paid a higher rate of tax than "earned" income from employment and active engagement in trade and industry. The tax system was permeated with moral notions: as Winston Churchill remarked, the question now asked was not only "how much have you got" but "how did you get it." Passive investment paid more tax than active participation. Curiously, savings were encouraged as prudential and a route to independence and security—but the income was then taxed at a higher rate as passive. At the same time, capital gains from speculation escaped taxation entirely, for only regular, recurring forms of income were liable to tax (Churchill 377–78; Daunton, *Trusting;* Offer, *Property*). The moral and cultural assumptions behind these approaches in income from different sources suggest some of the complexities of attitudes to investment and savings.

The debate over differentiation of the income tax brings out some of these complexities. It was proposed when the income tax was reintroduced in 1842, and involved debates over the capacity of different forms of income and investment to bear tax. The income tax divided income into different schedules according to the nature of the underlying asset or source: whether bonds, dividends, land, or self-employed earnings from trade and business. The proponents of differentiation in the mid-nineteenth century argued that the income from land or bonds and shares continued regardless of the efforts or health of the owner, and left an asset to dependents and heirs after death. Hence there was no need to save. However, earned income from salaries, professional fees, or self-employment in trade and industry depended on energy and health, and ceased entirely on retirement or death. Hence there was a need to save and invest. On these grounds, the advocates of differentiation argued that "spontaneous" income should pay more tax than "industrious" or "precarious" income. Different forms of investment would be treated differently: a government bond or a railway stock produced unearned income; an industrial concern owned by a family or partnership produced earned income (Daunton, *Trusting*).

The danger of differentiation, in the eyes of Gladstone, was that it used the tax system to set one interest or class against another—and particularly landed wealth against industrial capital. In 1853, Gladstone contained the demand for differentiation by offering a tax break to one form of investment: life insurance. Differentiation defined one type of income and asset against another with potentially alarming consequences; and it offered a tax advantage to industrious income regardless of whether money was actually saved, so that it might be an encouragement to imprudence. By contrast, life insurance was available to all forms of income, derived from any source or investment, provided that they actually put money into a life insurance policy. This might seem highly prudential, far removed from the culture of gambling and speculation that had marked life insurance in the eighteenth century, when "bets" were placed on lives in the hope of a quick profit (Clark, "Embracing"). However, Tim Alborn shows that the practice of offering periodical "bonuses" on life insurance policies introduced an element of theater and ritual, with hopes of sharing in profits rather than merely receiving a fixed sum. The practice of offering bonuses appealed to customers as a halfway house between investment and contingency insurance. As Alborn points out, the bonus led to tension in the moral economy of insurance companies between prudence and public spectacle. The payment of the bonus allowed the companies to manipulate their customers, yet the public meeting to declare its level also offered them information that could bring the concern to account. The bonus offered some element of democratic accountability for the policyholders. Whether accountability was effective is another matter, for it was actually very difficult for policyholders to control the concerns.

As far as the companies were concerned, offering occasional bonuses at their own discretion made more sense as a device to attract customers in a highly competitive market than cutting premiums, which could not easily be reversed. The bonus was only transferred to the policyholder on paper so that companies did not sacrifice their long-term investments. The bonus was a useful saving device, offering an incentive to pay into a life insurance policy without allowing profits to be spent imprudently. Life insurance policies and the bonus offered commitment mechanisms to encourage long-sighted, prudential behavior and to check visceral or hedonistic consumption. Although a policy could be surrendered before it came to the end of its term, it would only pay about half of its value—a clear incentive to leave the policy to maturity or death.

Avner Offer, in his recent important book *The Challenge of Affluence*, has argued that visceral consumption and the satisfaction of immediate desires has increased in the second half of the twentieth century at the expense of prudential behavior and a concern for the future. The saving rate has declined, debt increased, and hedonistic desire for new goods and satisfactions accelerated. The balance between immediate and deferred gratification depended in part on intrinsic self-control, and in part on social norms and devices, such as the structure of life insurance policies. Offer is more concerned with their erosion in the second half of the twentieth century than their construction in the nineteenth. Nineteenth-century commentators constantly complained about the imprudence of the poor—their use of credit or hire purchase to buy goods that they could not afford, their reliance on pawnshops, or spending on drink and betting. Such attitudes informed legislation, such as controls on betting by the working class or the limitations to the opening hours of pubs, and the judgment of courts. They also led to institutional innovation such as the Post Office Savings Banks. Similarly, women and dependent children were seen as feckless and irrational, inclined to give in to their desires, and the legal system was careful to ensure that women could not pledge their husband's credit by buying inappropriate goods. Women shopped, acting as the agents of their husbands, who generally paid for and owned the goods, so creating fear among alarmed cultural conservatives that women's desires, and their manipulation by retailers, would corrupt the home and weaken the husband. Samuel Smiles feared women's passions would subvert society, for their "rage for dress and finery . . . rivalled the corrupt and debauched age of Louis XV of France" and would ruin both their husband and trader (qtd. in Rappaport, "Husband" 167). The legal right of a wife to pledge her husband's credit was uncertain. What would happen if women were seduced into buying goods, pledging their husbands' credit? Female desires could destroy their husbands if they were obliged to honor the debt, or could harm traders if they refused to pay. Both parties turned to the law for protection, and judges had to decide between the two claims. Generally, the courts favored husbands over the retailers, limiting men's responsibility for their wives' consumption. Mr. Sharpe, the Keeper of Records at the Guildhall, refused to pay for a sealskin coat purchased by his wife from Whitley's for £12; he argued it was extravagant and he should not be liable. His wife claimed to have warned him that if he did not supply money for winter clothes, she would buy them without consent—a threat that Mr. Sharpe denied having heard. The judge found for Sharpe against Whitley. The jacket, he opined, "may be perfectly 'suitable' . . . but it cannot be called necessary, and, if the husband is not generous enough or rich enough to indulge his wife in the luxury, she must go without" (Finn, *Character*).

The cultural distinction between visceral, immediate gratification and prudential deferred gratification in consumption and saving is reflected in the debate over speculation as unregulated emotion and greed, and investment as rational, calculating, and careful. As George Robb shows, women were seen as emotional, unable to cope with the market in a calm and calculating manner— tempted to buy shares as they might sealskin coats. Could women be trusted to buy and sell shares, for they might be gullible and emotional, taking risk by their lack of rationality and access to information? If they did succeed, they might then be criticized as being defeminized, abandoning their proper role as wife and mother. On the other hand, they might be pitied as the naïve victims of unscrupulous financiers, and the widowed victim of confidence men was a common trope.

A major issue in the nineteenth century, as in any industrial society, was the trade-off between private profit and social benefit. How far could the desire of investors to make a good return on their capital be limited by a concern for the social consequences? We have seen how the monopoly power of railways or gas companies was controlled by regulations to protect consumers, and similar issues arose over pollution and accidents to the public and workmen. Should chemical works or copper smelters be allowed to pollute rivers and the air, destroying crops and affecting the health of towns? Should they be forced to provide protective guards on machinery to prevent accidents? The problem, of course, was that regulations could reduce investment and harm employment, and the courts and Parliament constantly debated the boundary between encouragement to investment and protection of workers, consumers, and the public (Brenner; McLaren; Simpson, *Leading*).

The balance between private property rights and the public benefit was at stake in a leading case of the 1890s: Bradford (mayor of) versus Pickles. Edward Pickles owned land adjoining Many Wells spring, which was fed by water from his land. The spring was used by Bradford corporation to provide water to the growing industrial town, and Pickles's family and the corporation had long been in dispute. The corporation felt that it was entitled to the water without any payment under a private act of 1842 establishing the water company, which it had purchased, that made it unlawful for anyone to divert or appropriate water feeding the spring. When Pickles decided to build a tunnel to drain the land in order to quarry flagstones, so threatening the water supply to the spring and hence to Bradford, the corporation took legal action against him. The corporation suspected, and the court agreed, that Pickles's intention was not to produce flagstones but to force the corporation to buy him off. The corporation sought an injunction to stop him, arguing that he was committing a nuisance and that malicious behavior is always wrongful. The case was finally decided by the House of Lords, which found against the corporation, arguing that any notion of an abuse of rights did not apply to economic self-interest.

Lord Macnaghten took a robust line: Pickles had something to sell. "He prefers his own interest to the public good. He may be churlish, selfish, and grasping. His conduct may seem shocking to a moral philosopher. But where is the malice?" The issue, as Brian Simpson remarks, was whether the law recognized a doctrine of abuse of rights, where to set "the proper limits to the despotic dominion of the property owner, and the legitimacy of greed in a capitalist market based legal system." Different conceptions of property were at stake: a communitarian use of natural assets as argued by Bradford corporation, or the notion that the owner of land was a despot within his own realm. What the case established was that a lawful act was not made unlawful as a result of malice (Bradford; Getzler; Simpson, "General" vii–viii; Taggart 1–4, 155–66). Such issues were fought out in many cases of nuisance and pollution, testing the relationship between the private and social benefits and losses of any investment.

The issue did not apply only to pollution and nuisances: another concern was the impact of investment on workers who might suffer from accidents and loss of income or even life. Ian Baucom, in his essay on the infamous case of the drowning of slaves on the *Zong* in 1781, raises the issue of how ship-owners, insurers, and judges interpreted loss of life in fiduciary terms, and how justice and the courtroom were transformed into a scene of exchange. The matter turned on the interpretation of a contract of insurance: was it a necessity to throw "goods"—slaves—overboard in order to save the ship? Of course, the definition of slaves as "goods" posed an ethical question that was avoided: it was generally accepted that slaves were indeed goods. Rather, the case turned on the issue of whether the ship was in such distress that the action of the captain was justified. This case is deeply distressing to modern readers, and it might be thought that the issues posed in 1781 disappeared after the abolition of the slave trade in 1807. Could human life any longer be treated as goods? In fact, the interpretation of life in terms of cash did not cease, for workers in mines or mills or railways faced the prospect of loss of life and limb, with poverty and hardship for their dependents. What precisely was the responsibility of the owners and employers for the safety of their workers, and for compensating them in the event of accident? In the case of slaves, the loss was incurred by the owner; in the case of waged workers in a free labor market, the issue was more complicated.

The initial position adopted by the courts was that workers had the freedom to enter into a contract for employment so that they were assenting to the risks of the particular trade, which were compensated for in the wage offered by the employers. In this view, they consciously opted to work in dangerous coal mines in return for a higher wage. Under the English common law, a defendant (including an employer) could be held liable if he had a "duty of care" to the plaintiff (including a worker) and was in breach of that duty. The plaintiff could then sue for damages under the tort of negligence. However, workers were in a weaker position than other plaintiffs, given the assumption that workers had knowingly accepted the risks. Further, many accidents were caused by the negligence of fellow employees, and the principle of "vicarious liability" held that the employer could not be held responsible for the injury caused by one worker to another—a view that rested on the belief that workers had a high level of personal responsibility for industrial processes.

These interpretations started to falter from the 1870s. In part, the change reflected tighter control by employers over the workplace and the erosion of workers' control. The argument that risks were covered by the wage rate was also viewed with increasing skepticism: perhaps workers were bearing the costs of death and injury that should be passed to the employer or the consumer. In 1880, the Employers' Liability Act marked the beginning of a new approach. Employers were liable for their own acts and those of their supervisors, but workers could still be denied compensation if their own negligence contributed to the accident; and employers were not liable for the actions of all of their workers. The issue of responsibility was considered by courts, with the burden of proof resting on the injured person. Employers could also "contract out" of the act and use of the courts if they made alternative arrangements through a mutual fund or insurance policy. The act was soon criticized. Would contracting out lead employers to neglect safety? Was it leading to frequent legal disputes that workers could not afford, often denying any compensation or only making a small payment? The survival of contributory negligence and vicarious liability greatly weakened the position of workers. The courts started to draw a distinction between workers' being aware of risks and consenting to them, and the law was changed by the Workmen's Compensation Act of 1897, which applied to a number of dangerous industries. It was no longer necessary to prove the negligence of employers or supervisors, vicarious liability was abolished, and workers were compensated even if they had contributed to their injury, unless intentionally.[2]

Attitudes to risk therefore shifted for workers as well as investors. Workers, like investors, moved from unlimited liability for all the risks of work and investment. The risks of investors were reduced by the introduction of limited liability so that their loss was confined to the money actually invested in the joint-stock company; and workers were compensated as a matter of right. What was at stake was the relationship between the costs and benefits of investment. Could investors receive their return regardless of the impact on their workers, or was loss of life and limb a charge on the profits of the concern? The shift from family firms and partnerships with a sense of personal involvement to joint-stock companies with a large number of shareholders separated from direct control over the firm posed the danger of a lack of individual responsibility, and hence an undermining of commercial morality. The shift in corporate form was a continuing source of anxiety and was closely linked with the contemporary debates over the nature of democracy. This collection of essays starts on a much needed project of linking cultural history and economic history, showing how a highly commercialized, urban, and industrial society was imaginatively constructed and interpreted. Margot Finn's recent book on the culture of credit, and James Taylor on attitudes to companies, show what can be done by a careful reading of texts and images; this volume builds on and extends their approach with great success.

## Notes

1. For studies of land purchase and continuance in business, see M. Rose; Daunton, "Inheritance."

2. These comments on industrial compensation rest on the research of Julia Moses for her Ph.D. thesis at the University of Cambridge.

# Bibliography

Abraham, Nicolas, and Maria Torok. *The Shell and the Kernel.* Ed. and trans. Nicholas T. Rand. Chicago: University of Chicago Press, 1994.

Aguirre, Robert. *Informal Empire: Mexico and Central America in Victorian Culture.* Minneapolis: University of Minnesota Press, 2005.

———, and Ross Forman, eds. *Connecting Continents: Britain and Latin America, 1780–1900.* New York: Rodopi Press, forthcoming.

Alborn, Timothy L. "A Calculating Profession: Victorian Actuaries among the Statisticians." In *Accounting and Science: Natural Inquiry and Commercial Reason.* Ed. Michael Power. Cambridge: Cambridge University Press, 1994. 81-119.

———. "Coin and Country: Visions of Civilization in the British Recoinage Debate, 1867-1891." *Journal of Victorian Culture* 3.2 (1998): 252-81.

———. *Conceiving Companies: Joint-Stock Politics in Victorian England.* London: Routledge, 1998.

———. "A License to Bet: Life Insurance and the Gambling Act in the British Courts." *Connecticut Insurance Law Review* (forthcoming, 2008).

———. "'A Useful Lesson of Contentment': Pedagogies of Failure in Mid-Victorian Market Culture." In *Worlds of Political Economy: Knowledge and Power in the Nineteenth and Twentieth Centuries.* Ed. Martin Daunton and Frank Trentmann. London: Palgrave Macmillan, 2004. 95-114.

Alliance Assurance Company, Board Minutes. Guildhall Ms. 12,162.

Alliance Assurance Company, Reports . . . re Actuarial Valuations, Guildhall Library Ms. 14,980.

Alter, George, Claudia Golden, and Elyce Rotella. "The Savings of Ordinary Americans: The Philadelphia Savings Fund Society in the Mid Nineteenth Century." *Journal of Economic History* 54 (1994): 735-67.

Amsler, Christine E., Robin L. Bartlett, and Craig J. Bolton. "Thoughts of Some British Political Economists on Early Limited Liability and Corporate Legislation." *History of Political Economy* 13.4 (1981): 774-93.

Anderson, B. L., and P. L. Cottrell. "Another Victorian Capital Market: A Study of Banking and Bank Investors on Merseyside." *Economic History Review* 28 (1975): 598-615.

Anderson, Olive. *Suicide in Victorian and Edwardian England.* Oxford: Clarendon, 1987.

Andras, H. W. "Returns of Life Assurance Companies to the Board of Trade." *Insurance Institute Journal* 13 (1910): 93-120.

Antilla, Susan. *Tales from the Boom-Boom Room: Women vs. Wall Street.* Princeton, N.J.: Bloomberg Press, 2002.

Argyll, Duke of. *The Unseen Foundations of Society: An Examination of the Fallacies and Failures of Economic Science Due to Neglected Elements.* London: John Murray, 1893.

Arnold, Matthew. *Culture and Anarchy.* 1869. Ed. Jane Garnett. Oxford: Oxford University Press, 2006.

Arrighi, Giovanni. *The Long Twentieth Century: Money, Power, and the Origins of Our Times.* London and New York: Verso, 1994.

Associated Scottish Life Offices. *Regulations and Proceedings Selected from the Records of the Association and Printed for Use of Members*. Edinburgh: privately printed, 1895.

Association of Scottish Life Offices, Minute Books. 3 vols. 1840–1894. Faculty of Actuaries Ms. 1/1/2/1–3, Edinburgh.

*Associator: A Monthly Journal of Fact, Fiction, and Finance*. London.

Atiyah, P. S. *The Rise and Fall of Freedom of Contract*. Oxford: Oxford University Press, 1979.

Atwood, Albert W. *Putnam's Investment Handbook*. New York: G.P. Putnam's Sons, 1919.

Aytoun, W. E. "The National Debt and the Stock Exchange." *Blackwood's Edinburgh Magazine* 66 (Dec. 1849): 655–78.

Babbage, Charles. *Comparative View of the Various Institutions for the Assurance of Lives*. London: J. Mawman, 1826.

Backstrom, Philip. *Christian Socialism and Cooperation in Victorian England*. London: Croom Helm, 1974.

Badiou, Alain. *Being and Event*. Trans. Oliver Feltham. London: Continuum International Publishing Group, 2006.

Bagehot, Walter. "What to Buy—I: A Series of Popular Articles on Investment." *Economist* 24 (1866): 1449–51.

———. "What to Buy—II." *Economist* 25 (1867): 31–32.

Bailey, A. H. "The Expenses of Life Assurance Companies: How They Affect the Assured." *Journal of the Institute of Actuaries* 19 (1875): 1–11.

———. "The Pure Premium Method of Valuation." *Journal of the Institute of Actuaries* 21 (1878): 115–26.

Barboza, David. "A Shock Wave from Shanghai." *New York Times* (28 Feb. 2007): C1+.

———, et al. "Tax Increase Batters Chinese Stocks, but There's Little Wider Damage." *New York Times* (31 May 2007): C4.

Bar-Yosef, Eitan. " 'Let me die with the Philistines': Gissing's Suicidal Realism." *Literature, Interpretation, Theory* 13 (2003): 185–204.

*Barker's Trade and Finance*. London.

Barnard, Eunice Fuller. "Ladies of the Ticker." *North American Review* 227 (April 1929): 405–10.

Baucom, Ian. *Specters of the Atlantic: Finance Capital, Slavery, and the Philosophy of History*. Durham, N.C.: Duke University Press, 2005.

Belchem, John, and James Epstein. "The Nineteenth-Century Gentleman Leader Revisited." *Social History* 22.2 (1997): 174–93.

Benjamin, Walter. *The Arcades Project*. Trans. Howard Eiland. Cambridge, Mass.: Harvard University Press, 1999.

Benzon, Ernest. *How I Lost £250000 in Two Years*. London: Trischler, n.d. [1899].

Berenson, Alex. "On Hair-Trigger Wall Street, a Stock Plunges on Fake News." *New York Times* (26 Aug. 2000): A1+.

Bernstein, Jake. *The Compleat Day Trader II*. New York: McGraw-Hill, 1998.

Berthoud, Jacques. "Introduction." *Lord Jim*, by Joseph Conrad. Oxford: Oxford University Press, 2002. xii–xxxi.

Bethell, Leslie. "Britain and Latin America in Historical Perspective." In *Britain and Latin America: A Changing Relationship*. Ed. Victor Bulmer-Thomas. Cambridge: Cambridge University Press, 1989. 1–24.

Biagini, Eugenio F., and Alistair J. Ried. *Currents of Radicalism: Popular Radicalism, Or-*

ganized Labour and Party Politics in Britain, 1850–1914. Cambridge: Cambridge University Press, 1991.

Blackstone, Sir William. Commentaries on the Laws of England. 4 vols. Ed. George Chase. New York: Banks & Bros. Law Publishers, 1890.

Blake, Robert. Esto Perpetua: Norwich Union Life Insurance Society 1808–1958. Norwich, Engl.: Newman Neame, 1958.

Blanchard, Sidney Laman. "A Biography of a Bad Shilling." Household Words 2 (Jan. 1851): 420–26.

"Book-Keeping." Dublin Review 19 (Dec. 1845): 433–53.

Bowen, H. V. The Business of Empire: The East India Company and Imperial Britain, 1756–1833. Cambridge: Cambridge University Press, 2006.

Bradford v. Pickles, [1894] 3 Ch 53, [1895] 1 Ch, [1895] AC 587.

Brantlinger, Patrick. Fictions of State: Culture and Credit in Britain, 1694–1994. Ithaca, N.Y.: Cornell University Press, 1996.

Brenner, J. F. "Nuisance Law and the Industrial Revolution." Journal of Legal Studies 3.2 (1974): 155–221.

Brewer, John. "Commercialization and Politics." In The Birth of a Consumer Society: The Commercialization of Eighteenth-Century England. Ed. Neil McKendrick, John Brewer, and J. H. Plumb. Bloomington: Indiana University Press, 1982. 197–262.

Brown, Samuel. "On the Investments of the Funds of Assurance Companies." Assurance Magazine 7 (1858): 241–54.

Bryer, Robert A. "The Mercantile Laws Commission of 1854 and the Political Economy of Limited Liability." Economic History Review 1 (1997): 37–56.

Bulkowski, Thomas N. Encyclopedia of Chart Patterns. New York: Wiley, 2000.

Bulletin of the National Anti-Gambling League. London.

Burnette, Joyce. "Businesswomen in Industrial Revolution Britain." Essays in Economic and Business History 14 (1996): 387–408.

Burstyn, Joan. Victorian Education and the Ideal of Womanhood. London: Croom Helm, 1980.

Byron, Joseph. Photographs of New York Interiors at the Turn of the Century. New York: Dover, 1976.

Cain, P. J., and A. G. Hopkins. British Imperialism: Innovation and Expansion 1688–1914. 2 vols. London: Longman, 1993.

Caine, Barbara. Victorian Feminists. Oxford: Oxford University Press, 1992.

Capitalist: A Weekly Record of the Movements of Capital. London.

Carret, Phillip L. The Art of Speculation. New York: Wiley, 1930.

Carter, Henry. Facts and Figures for the Temperance and Anti-Gambling Campaign. Bristol, Engl.: Rose and Harris, n.d. [1906].

Caruth, Cathy. Unclaimed Experience: Trauma, Narrative, and History. Baltimore: Johns Hopkins University Press, 1996.

Cassis, Youssef. City Bankers 1890–1914. Cambridge: Cambridge University Press, 1994.

Centner, Charles William. "Great Britain and Chilean Mining 1830–1914." Economic History Review 12.1/2 (1942): 76–82.

Chancellor, Edward. Devil Take the Hindmost: A History of Financial Speculations. New York: Farrar, Straus, Giroux; London: MacMillan, 1999.

Chandler, James. England in 1819: The Politics of Literary Culture and the Case of Romantic Historicism. Chicago: University of Chicago Press, 1998.

Chatham, James. Report to the Scottish Union & National Insurance Company, April 1905. CGNU Group Archives, Norwich, UK.

Checkland, S. G. "The Mind of the City, 1870–1914." *Oxford Economic Papers*, New Series, 9.3 (Oct. 1957): 261–78.

———. *The Rise of Industrial Society in England, 1815–1885*. New York: St. Martin's, 1965.

Church of England Fire and Life Assurance Society, Board Minutes. Guildhall Ms. 12,160D.

Churchill, Winston Spencer. *Liberalism and the Social Problem*. London: Hodder and Stoughton, 1909.

*City Argus: A Chronicle of Finance and Investment*. London.

*City Mercury: A Journal of Finance, Society, Literature, Sport, and the Drama*. London.

Clapson, Mark. *A Bit of a Flutter: Popular Gambling and English Society, c. 1823–1961*. Manchester: Manchester University Press, 1992.

Clark, Geoffrey. *Betting on Lives: The Culture of Life Insurance in England 1695–1775*. Manchester: Manchester University Press, 1999.

———. "Embracing Fatality Through Life Insurance in Eighteenth-Century England." In *Embracing Risk: The Changing Culture of Insurance and Responsibility*. Ed. T. Baker and J. Simon. Chicago: University of Chicago Press, 2002. 80–96.

Clarke, Peter. *The Keynesian Revolution in the Making, 1924–36*. Oxford: Clarendon Paperbacks, 1988.

Cleary, Patricia. *Elizabeth Murray: A Woman's Pursuit of Independence in Eighteenth-Century America*. Amherst: University of Massachusetts Press, 2000.

Clews, Henry. *Twenty-Eight Years in Wall Street*. New York: Irving Publishing Co., 1888.

Clokie, Hugh McDowell, and J. William Robinson. *Royal Commissions of Inquiry: The Significance of Investigations in British Politics*. Stanford, Calif.: Stanford University Press, 1937.

Cohen, Ralph. "History and Genre." *New Literary History* 17.2 (Winter 1986): 203–18.

Coldridge, Ward, and Cyril V. Hawkford. *The Law of Gambling: Civil and Criminal*. 2nd ed. by Ward Coldridge and William F. Swords. London: Stevens and Son, 1913.

Collini, Stefan. *Public Moralists: Political Thought and Intellectual Life in Britain, 1850–1930*. Oxford: Clarendon Paperbacks, 1991.

Collins, Phillip. "Business and Bosoms: Some Trollopian Concerns." *Nineteenth-Century Fiction* 37.3 (Dec. 1982): 293–315.

Collinson, C. "*The Whirlpool* and *The House of Mirth*." *Gissing Newsletter* 16.4 (1980): 12–16.

Commercial Life Assurance Co., Prospectus, 1840. ESL 4/1/3/2/1, Zurich Financial Services Group Archives, Cheltenham, UK.

Conder, William S. *The Story of the London Life Associated Limited*. London: privately published, 1979.

Conrad, Joseph. *Chance: A Tale in Two Parts*. 1914. Oxford and New York: Oxford University Press, 2002.

———. *The Collected Letters of Joseph Conrad*. Ed. Frederick R. Karl. 7 vols. Cambridge: Cambridge University Press, 1983–.

———. "Geography and Some Explorers." 1924. In *Last Essays*. Garden City, N.Y.: Doubleday, 1926. 1–21.

———. *Heart of Darkness*. 1899. Harmondsworth, UK: Penguin, 1995.

———. *The Mirror of the Sea*. 1906. In *A Personal Record and The Mirror of the Sea*. Harmondsworth, UK: Penguin, 1998.

———. *Nostromo: A Tale of the Seaboard*. 1904. Harmondsworth, UK: Penguin, 1983.

Cottrell, Philip. *Industrial Finance, 1830–1914: The Finance and Organization of English Manufacturing Industry.* London: Methuen, 1980.

*Critic: A Weekly Review of the Drama, Literature, Music, Art, Finance, and Other Things of Social Interest.* London.

Cromwell, John Howard. *The American Business Woman: A Guide for the Investment, Preservation and Accumulation of Property.* London: G. P. Putnam's Sons, 1900.

Daly, K. "Gender and Varieties of White-Collar Crime." *Criminology* 27 (1989): 769–94.

Daunton, Martin. "Inheritance and Succession in the City of London in the Nineteenth Century." *Business History* 30.3 (1988): 269–87.

———. *Just Taxes: The Politics of Taxation in Britain, 1914–1979.* Cambridge: Cambridge University Press, 2002.

———. "The Material Politics of Natural Monopoly: Gas in Victorian Britain." In *The Politics of Consumption: Material Culture and Citizenship in Europe and America.* Ed. Martin Daunton and Matthew Hilton. Oxford: Berg Publishers, 2001. 69–88.

———. *Progress and Poverty: An Economic and Social History of Britain, 1700–1850.* Oxford: Oxford University Press, 1995.

———. *Royal Mail: The Post Office since 1840.* London: Athlone Press, 1985.

———. *Trusting Leviathan: The Politics of Taxation in Britain, 1799–1914.* Cambridge: Cambridge University Press, 2001.

Davidoff, Leonore, and Catherine Hall. *Family Fortunes: Men and Women of the English Middle Class, 1780–1850.* Chicago: University of Chicago Press, 1987.

Davis, Lance E., and Robert A. Huttenback. *Mammon and the Pursuit of Empire: The Political Economy of British Imperialism, 1860–1912.* Cambridge: Cambridge University Press, 1986.

De Morgan, Augustus. *An Essay on Probabilities, and on Their Application to Life Contingencies and Insurance Offices.* London: Longman, 1838.

"Dear Alibel." *TLS* (11 Feb. 2005): 5.

Delany, Paul. *Literature, Money and the Market: From Trollope to Amis.* Basingstoke, UK: Palgrave, 2002.

Denby, David. *American Sucker.* New York: Viking, 2004.

Dennett, Laurie. *A Sense of Security: 150 Years of Prudential.* Cambridge: Granta, 1998.

Derrida, Jacques. *Specters of Marx: The State of the Debt, the Work of Mourning, and the New International.* Trans. Peggy Kamuf. London: Routledge, 1994.

———. ". . . That Dangerous Supplement . . ." In *Of Grammatology.* Trans. Gayatri Chakravorty Spivak. Baltimore: Johns Hopkins University Press, 1984. 141–64.

"A Detective." *The Ways of Swindlers.* London: T.H. Sheppard, 1879.

Dexter, Elisabeth Anthony. *Colonial Women of Affairs: A Study of Women in Business and the Professions in America before 1776.* New York: Houghton Mifflin, 1924.

Dickens, Charles. *Little Dorrit.* 1857. Ed. H. P. Sucksmith. Oxford: Oxford University Press, 1982.

———. *Little Dorrit.* 1857. Ed. Harvey Peter Sucksmith. Oxford: Oxford University Press, 1999.

Dickinson, Anna E. *A Paying Investment.* Boston: James R. Osgood and Co., 1876.

"Dividend Day." *All the Year Round* (11 Nov. 1893): 462–64.

Downes, J. J. *Actuary's Report on the Seventh Quinquennial Investigation into the Affairs of the Economic Life Assurance Society.* London: n. p., 1859.

Doyle, Arthur Conan. *The Case-Book of Sherlock Holmes.* 1927. London: Wordsworth Classics, 1994.

Drachman, Virginia. *Enterprising Women: 250 Years of American Business.* Chapel Hill: University of North Carolina Press, 2003.

Dumett, Raymond E., ed. *Gentlemanly Capitalism and British Imperialism: The New Debate on Empire.* London: Longman, 1999.

[Duncan, W. W.]. *Duncan on Investment and Speculation in Stocks and Shares.* London: Effingham Wilson, 1894.

Dutton, H. I., and J. E. King. "The Limits of Paternalism: The Cotton Tyrants of North Lancashire, 1836–54." *Social History* 7 (1982): 59–73.

Eagle Insurance Company. *Board of Directors' Minute Books.* 31 vols. 1807–1947. Uncataloged Guildhall Mss.

Eagle Life Insurance Co. *A Gift to the Uninsured.* Uncataloged Guildhall Mss.

Eakin, Marshall C. "The Role of British Capital in the Development of Brazilian Gold Mining." In *Miners and Mining in the Americas.* Ed. Thomas Greaves and William Culver. Manchester: Manchester University Press, 1985. 10–28.

Eastwick, Edward B. *Venezuela; or Sketches of Life in a South American Republic; with the History of the Loan of 1864.* London, 1868.

*Economist.* 365 vols. London: Economist, 1843–2002.

Ecroyd, C. W. "A Superficial Survey of the Principles and Practice of Modern Life Assurance." *Insurance Institute Journal* 13 (1910): 35–70.

Edwards, P. D. "Trollope Changes His Mind: The Death of Melmotte in *The Way We Live Now.*" *Nineteenth-Century Fiction* 18.1 (June 1963): 89–91.

Edwards, Ruth Dudley. *The Pursuit of Reason: The Economist 1843–1993.* Boston: Harvard Business School Press, 1993.

Egerton, George [Mary Chavelita Dunne]. "The Regeneration of Two." *Keynotes and Discords.* 1893. London: Virago, 1983. 163–253.

Eliot, George [Marian Evans]. *The George Eliot Letters.* 9 vols. Ed. Gordon S. Haight. New Haven, Conn.: Yale University Press, 1954–55, 1978.

———. *The Mill on the Floss.* 1860. Ed. Gordon S. Haight. New York: Oxford University Press, 1996.

English & Scottish Law Life Assurance Association, Board Minutes. Uncataloged Guildhall Mss.

Ermarth, Elizabeth Deeds. *The English Novel in History, 1840–1895.* London: Routledge, 1997.

———. "Realism." *Encyclopedia of the Novel.* Ed. Paul Schellinger. Chicago: Fitzroy Dearborn, 1998. 2 vols.

Evans, David Morier. *Speculative Notes and Notes on Speculation, Ideal and Real.* 1857. New York: Burt Franklin, 1968.

Ewen, C. L'Estrange. *Lotteries and Sweepstakes: An Historical, Legal, and Ethical Survey of Their Introduction, Suppression, and Re-establishment in the British Isles.* London: Heath Cranton, 1932.

Fabian, Ann. *Card Sharps, Dream Books, and Bucket Shops: Gambling in 19th-Century America.* Ithaca, N.Y.: Cornell University Press, 1990.

"Farrow's Bank Failure." *Times* (7 June 1921): 19.

"Farrow's Bank for Women." *Awakener* (14 June 1913): 11.

Farrow's Bank Ledger Books (1920), PRO, BT31/18100.

Feiner, Susan. "A Portrait of Homo Economicus as a Young Man." In *The New Economic Criticism: Studies at the Intersection of Literature and Economics.* Ed. Martha Woodmansee and Mark Osteen. New York: Routledge, 1999. 193–209.

Fellows, Alfred. *The Law as to Gaming, Betting, and Lotteries*. London: Solicitors' Law Stationary Society, 1935.

Feltes, Norman N. "Community and the Limits of Liability in Two Mid-Victorian Novels." *Victorian Studies* 17 (1974): 355-69.

Field, Arthur. "A Woman's Romance in Wall Street." *Demorest's Family Magazine* 30 (Jan. 1894): 151-58.

*Financial Adviser: A Weekly Journal for the Protection of Investors and Sound Enterprises*. London.

Finn, Margot. *After Chartism: Class and Nation in English Radical Politics, 1848–1874*. Cambridge: Cambridge University Press, 1993.

———. *The Character of Credit: Personal Debt in English Culture, 1740–1914*. Cambridge: Cambridge University Press, 2003.

Fleishman, Avrom. *Conrad's Politics: Community and Anarchy in the Fiction of Joseph Conrad*. Baltimore: Johns Hopkins University Press, 1967.

Fontana, Biancamaria. *Rethinking the Politics of Commercial Society: The* Edinburgh Review *1802–1832*. Cambridge: Cambridge University Press, 1985.

Fowler, William Worthington. *Twenty Years of Inside Life in Wall Street*. New York: Orange Judd Co., 1880.

Franklin, J. Jeffrey. "Anthony Trollope Meets Pierre Bourdieu: The Conversion of Capital as Plot in the Mid-Victorian Novel." *Victorian Literature and Culture* 31.2 (2003): 501-21.

Fraser, Steve. *Every Man a Speculator: A History of Wall Street in American Life*. New York: HarperCollins, 2005.

Freedgood, Elaine. "Banishing Panic: Harriet Martineau and the Popularization of Political Economy." In *The New Economic Criticism: Studies at the Intersection of Literature and Economics*. Ed. Martha Woodmansee and Mark Osteen. New York: Routledge, 1999. 210-28.

Freeman, Mark, Robin Pearson, and James Taylor. "'A Doe in the City': Women Shareholders in Eighteenth- and Early Nineteenth-Century Britain." *Accounting, Business and Financial History* 16.2 (July 2006): 265-91.

Gagnier, Regenia. *The Insatiability of Human Wants: Economics and Aesthetics in Market Society*. Chicago: University of Chicago Press, 2000.

Galbraith, John Kenneth. *The Great Crash, 1929*. 1954. Boston: Houghton Mifflin, 1979.

Gallagher, Catherine. *The Body Economic: Life, Death, and Sensation in Political Economy and the Victorian Novel*. Princeton, N.J.: Princeton University Press, 2006.

Gallagher, John, and Ronald Robinson. "The Imperialism of Free Trade." *Economic History Review* 6 (1953): 1-15.

Gamber, Wendy. "A Gendered Enterprise: Placing Nineteenth-Century Businesswomen in History." *Business History Review* 72 (Summer 1998): 188-217.

Garber, Peter M. *Famous First Bubbles: The Fundamentals of Early Manias*. Cambridge, Mass.: MIT Press, 2000.

Gates, Barbara. *Victorian Suicide: Mad Crimes and Sad Histories*. Princeton, N.J.: Princeton University Press, 1998.

Genette, Gérard. *Narrative Discourse: An Essay in Method*. 1972. Trans Jane E. Lewin. Ithaca, N.Y.: Cornell University Press, 1980.

———. *Narrative Discourse Revisited*. Trans. Jane E. Lewin. Ithaca, N.Y.: Cornell University Press, 1989.

Gerber, J., and S. L. Weeks. "Women as Victims of Corporate Crime: A Call for Research on a Neglected Topic." *Deviant Behavior* 13 (1992): 325–47.

Getzler, J. A. *History of Water Rights at Common Law.* Oxford: Oxford University Press, 2004.

Gilbart, James William. *A Practical Treatise on Banking.* London, 1849. 3rd American ed. Philadelphia: G. D. Miller (from the 5th London ed., 1855).

Gissing, George. *The Whirlpool.* 1897. London: Hogarth Press, 1984.

Glade, William. "Latin America and the International Economy, 1870–1914." In *The Cambridge History of Latin America.* Ed. Leslie Bethell. 11 vols. Cambridge: Cambridge University Press, 1984–1994. 4: 1–56.

Goldsmith, Barbara. *Other Powers: The Age of Suffrage, Spiritualism, and the Scandalous Victoria Woodhull.* New York: HarperCollins, 1999.

Gray, Robert Q. *The Factory Question and Industrial England, 1830–1860.* Cambridge: Cambridge University Press, 1996.

Great Eastern Railway, Shareholders' Meeting 1889, PRO, Rail 227/216.

Green, Hetty. "Why Women Are Not Money Makers." *Harper's Bazaar* (10 March 1900): 201.

———. "Words of Wisdom from the Wealthiest Woman in America: The Benefits of a Business Training to Women." In *Looking Forward: Life in the 20th Century as Presented in the Pages of American Magazines from 1895 to 1905.* Ed. Roy Brousseau. New York: American Heritage, 1970.

Gregory, George. *Hints to Speculators and Investors in Stocks and Shares.* London: George Gregory, n.d. [1889].

Grenfell, H. R. "What Is a Pound?" *Nineteenth Century* 9 (June 1881): 937–48.

Gresham Life Assurance Society, Bonus List. Guildhall Ms. 17,926.

Gurney, Peter. "An Appropriated Space: The Great Exhibition, the Crystal Palace and the Working Class." In *The Great Exhibition of 1851: New Interdisciplinary Essays.* Ed. L. Purbrick. Manchester: Manchester University Press, 2001. 114–45.

Guth, Michael A. S. *Speculative Behaviors and the Operation of Competitive Markets under Uncertainty.* Avebury: Ashgate, 1994.

Gutteridge, W., and Company. *Speculation and Investment in Stocks and Shares with a Minimum Risk.* London: W. Gutteridge, 1882.

Habermas, Jürgen. *The Philosophical Discourse of Modernity: Twelve Lectures.* Trans. Frederick J. Lawrence. Cambridge, Mass.: MIT Press, 1990.

Hannah, Leslie. *The Rise of the Corporate Economy.* 2nd ed. London: Johns Hopkins University Press, 1983.

*Hansard's Parliamentary Debates.* 3rd series. London.

Harraden, Beatrice. *Where Your Treasure Is.* London: Hutchinson and Co., 1918.

Haskell, Thomas L., and Richard F. Teichgraber III. *The Culture of the Market: Historical Essays.* Cambridge: Cambridge University Press, 1993.

Hennessy, Elizabeth. *Coffee House to Cyber Market: 200 Years of the London Stock Exchange.* London: Ebury, 2001.

Henry, Nancy. *George Eliot and the British Empire.* Cambridge: Cambridge University Press, 2002.

———. "'Ladies do it?' Victorian Women Investors in Fact and Fiction." In *Victorian Literature and Finance.* Ed. Francis O'Gorman. Oxford: Oxford University Press, 2007. 111–31.

"Heroes, Wags and Sages." *Time* (25 Nov. 1929): 129–30.

Hilton, Boyd. *The Age of Atonement: The Influence of Evangelicalism on Social and Economic Thought, 1785–1865.* Oxford: Clarendon, 1988.

Hirst, Francis W. *The Stock Exchange: A Short Study of Investment and Speculation.* London: Williams and Norgate; New York: Henry Holt, n.d. [1911].

Hofer, Margaret K. *The Games We Played: The Golden Age of Board and Table Games.* New York: Princeton Architectural Press, 2003.

Holcombe, Lee. *Wives and Property: Reform of the Married Women's Property Laws in Nineteenth-Century England.* Toronto: University of Toronto Press, 1983.

Holway, Tatiana M. "The Game of Speculation: Economics and Representation." *Dickens Quarterly* 9 (1992): 103–14.

Horner, Francis. "Thornton on the Paper Credit of Great Britain." In *The Economic Writings of Francis Horner in the* Edinburgh Review *1802–6.* Ed. Frank Whitson Fetter. London: London School of Economics, 1957.

Houston, Gail Turley. *From Dickens to Dracula: Gothic, Economics, and Victorian Fiction.* Cambridge: Cambridge University Press, 2005.

"How May a Woman Invest a Small Sum?" *World's Work* (Feb. 1906): 7149–50.

Hudson, Derek, and Kenneth W. Luckhurst. *The Royal Society of Arts, 1754–1954.* London: John Murray, 1954.

Hunt, Bishop Carleton. *The Development of the Business Corporation in England, 1800–1867.* New York: Russell and Russell, 1963.

*Ibis Magazine and Journal of the Prudential Clerks' Society.* 90 vols. London: Prudential Insurance, 1878–1967.

Ibsen, Henrik. *A Doll's House and Other Plays.* London: Penguin, 1965.

Ingrassia, Catherine. "The Pleasure of Business and the Business of Pleasure: Gender, Credit, and the South Sea Bubble." In *Studies in Eighteenth-Century Culture.* Ed. Carla Hay and Syndy Conger. Baltimore: Johns Hopkins University Press, 1995. 191–210.

"Insurance Frauds." *Woodhull and Claflin's Weekly* (18 March 1871): 8.

*Insurance Record.* 113 vols. London: Tudor Press, 1863–1976.

"Investments for the Savings of the Middle and Working Classes: Select Committee Report." *Parliamentary Papers* 18 (1850): sess. 508.

Ireland, Paddy W. "The Rise of the Limited Liability Company." *International Journal of the Sociology of Law* 12 (1984): 239–60.

Itzkowitz, David C. "Victorian Bookmakers and Their Customers." *Victorian Studies* 32.1 (Autumn 1988): 7–30.

Jaffe, Audrey. "Detecting the Beggar: Arthur Conan Doyle, Henry Mayhew, and 'The Man with the Twisted Lip.'" *Representations* 31 (1990): 96–117.

James, Harold. "The Literary Financier." *American Scholar* 60.2 (Spring 1991): 251–57.

James, Simon J. *Unsettled Accounts: Money and Narrative in the Novels of George Gissing.* London: Anthem Press, 2003.

Jameson, Fredric. "Culture and Finance Capital." *Critical Inquiry* 24 (Aug. 1997): 246–65.

———. *Marxism and Form: Twentieth-Century Dialectical Theories of Literature.* Princeton, N.J.: Princeton University Press, 1972.

———. "Modernism and Imperialism." In *Nationalism, Colonialism, and Literature.* By Terry Eagleton, Fredric Jameson, and Edward W. Said. Minneapolis: University of Minnesota Press, 1990. 43–66.

———. *The Political Unconscious: Narrative as a Socially Symbolic Act.* Ithaca, N.Y.: Cornell University Press, 1981.

Jeffreys, James B. *Business Organization in Great Britain 1856–1914*. New York: Ayer, 1977.

Johnson, Paul. "Civilizing Mammon: Law, Morals and the City in Nineteenth-Century England." In *Civil Histories: Essays Presented to Sir Keith Thomas*. Ed. Peter Burke, Brian Harrison, and Paul Slack. Oxford: Oxford University Press, 2000. 301-19.

———. "Class Law in Victorian England." *Past and Present* 141 (1993): 147-69.

Jones, Linda. "Public Pursuit of Private Profit? Liberal Businessmen and Municipal Politics in Birmingham, 1865-1900." *Business History* 25.3 (1983): 240-59.

Joseph, Gerhard. "Producing the 'Far-Off Interest of Tears': Tennyson, Freud, and the Economics of Mourning." *Victorian Poetry* 36.2 (Summer 1998): 123-33.

*Journal of the Society of Arts*. London, 1854.

Joyce, Patrick. *Democratic Subjects: The Self and the Social in Nineteenth-Century England*. Cambridge: Cambridge University Press, 1994.

———. *Visions of the People: Industrial England and the Question of Class, 1848–1914*. Cambridge: Cambridge University Press, 1991.

Kant, Immanuel. "An Old Question Raised Again: Is the Human Race Constantly Progressing?" In *Kant: On History*. 1798. Ed. Lewis White Beck. New York: Liberal Arts Press, 1963. 137-54.

Karl, Frederick R. *Joseph Conrad: The Three Lives. A Biography*. New York: Farrar, Strauss and Giroux, 1979.

Kindleberger, Charles P., and Robert Aliber. *Manias, Panics, and Crashes: A History of Financial Crises*. Hoboken, N.J.: John Wiley and Sons, 2005.

Knight, Alan. "Britain and Latin America." In *The Oxford History of the British Empire*. Vol. 3, *The Nineteenth Century*. Ed. Andrew Porter. Oxford: Oxford University Press, 1999. 122-45.

Koselleck, Reinhart. *Futures Past: On the Semantics of Historical Time*. Trans. Keith Tribe. Cambridge, Mass.: MIT Press, 1985.

Koss, Stephen. *The Rise and Fall of the Political Press in Britain: The Nineteenth Century*. Chapel Hill: University of North Carolina Press, 1981.

Kreilkamp, Ivan. *Voice and the Victorian Storyteller*. Cambridge: Cambridge University Press, 2005.

Krugman, Paul. "The Big Meltdown." *New York Times* (2 Mar. 2007): A21.

Kucich, John. *Imperial Masochism: British Fiction, Fantasy, and Social Class*. Princeton, N.J.: Princeton University Press, 2007.

Kynaston, David. *The City of London*. Vol. 2, *Golden Years, 1890–1914*. London: Chatto and Windus, 1995.

"Lady Cook and Co." *New York Times* (21 Dec. 1898): 7.

Lambert, J. Malet. *Gambling: Is It Wrong?* London: Simpkin; York, UK: John Sampson, 1890.

Lansbury, Coral. *The Reasonable Man: Trollope's Legal Fiction*. Princeton, N.J.: Princeton University Press, 1981.

"Law of Partnership: Select Committee Report." *Parliamentary Papers* 18 (1851): sess. 509.

Lawrance, Frederick. *A Short Treatise on Life Assurance*. London: P. Richardson, 1843.

Lenman, B., and Kathleen Donaldson. "Partners' Incomes, Investment and Diversification in the Scottish Linen Area, 1850-1921." *Business History* 13.1 (1971): 1-18.

Levi, Leone. *The History of British Commerce and of the Economic Progress of the British Nation*. London: John Murray, 1872.

Levine, Philippa. *Victorian Feminism, 1850–1900*. Gainesville: University of Florida Press, 1994.

Lewes, George Henry. *The Game of Speculation*. 1851. In *The Lights O' London and Other Victorian Plays*. Ed. Michael R. Booth. New York: Oxford University Press, 1995.

———. "Suicide in Life and Literature." *Westminster Review* (July 1857): 52–78.

Lewis, Michael. "Jonathan Lebed's Extracurricular Activities." *New York Times Magazine* (25 Feb. 2001): 26+.

———. *The Money Culture*. New York: Penguin, 1991.

Loftus, Donna. "Industrial Conciliation, Class Co-operation and the Urban Landscape in Mid-Victorian England." In *Urban Governance: Britain and Beyond*. Ed. R. J. Morris and R. H. Trainor. Aldershot, UK: Ashgate, 2000. 182–97.

"London Joint-Stock Banks." *Economist* (15 March 1856): 290.

London Stock Exchange Commission. *Minutes of Evidence Taken Before the Commissioners: Together with Appendix, Index, and Analysis*. Parliamentary Papers. 1878 19 [C-2157-I].

———. *Report of the Commissioners*. Parliamentary Papers 1878 [C-2157].

Low, Alexander. *The Principles and Practice of the Life Association of Scotland . . . Founded on the Original Model of the London Life Association*. Edinburgh: Neill, 1843.

Low, Frances H. "How Poor Ladies Live." *Nineteenth Century* 41 (March 1897): 405–17.

M'Ilvenna, William Richard. "Life Assurance—Some Modern Aspects of Competition." *Journal of the Federated Insurance Institutes* 9 (1906): 1–12.

MacFarlane, A. *Railway Scrip; or, The Evils of Speculation. A Tale of the Railway Mania*. London: Ward and Locke, 1856.

Maddison, E. C. *Speculation on the Stock Exchange: An Explanation of the Various Methods of Operating in Stocks and Shares*. London: Effingham Wilson, 1878.

"Male Vampires." *Forum* (Feb. 1917): 183–94.

*Mammon: A Sunday Paper for Investors, Speculators, and Sportsmen*. London.

Marshall, Alfred. "Co-operation." 1889. In *Memorials of Alfred Marshall*. Ed. A. C. Pigou. London: Augustus M. Kelley, 1925.

———. *Industry and Trade*. London: Macmillan, 1919.

———. *Principles of Economics*. London: Macmillan, 1890.

Martin, Linda Carroll. "Live from New York, the Trading Day." *New York Times* (9 July 2000): C7.

Martineau, Harriet. "Self-Murder." *Once a Week* (19 Dec. 1859): 510–20.

Mathew, W. M. *The House of Gibbs and the Peruvian Guano Monopoly*. London: Royal Historical Society, 1981.

McGann, Tara. "Literary Realism in the Wake of Business Cycle Theory: *The Way We Live Now* (1875)." In *Victorian Literature and Finance*. Ed. Francis O'Gorman. Oxford: Oxford University Press, 2007. 133–56.

McKibbin, Ross. *The Ideologies of Class: Social Relations in Britain, 1880–1950*. Oxford: Oxford University Press, 1990.

———. "Working-Class Gambling in Britain, 1880–1939." *Past and Present* 82 (Feb. 1979): 147–78.

McLaren, John P. S. "Nuisance Law and the Industrial Revolution: Some Lessons from History." *Oxford Journal of Legal Studies* 3.2 (1983): 155–221.

McMaster, R. D. *Trollope and the Law*. London: Macmillan, 1986.

[Meason, Malcolm R. L.]. *The Bubbles of Finance: Joint-Stock Companies, Promoting of Companies, Modern Commerce, Money Lending, and Life Insuring. By a City Man*. London: Sampson, 1865.

———. *Sir William's Speculations or, the Seamy Side of Finance: A Tale of Warning Re-*

*specting the Joint Stock Company Swindles of the Day.* London: Sampson, Low, Marston, Searle & Revington, 1886.

Meredith, Hubert A. *The Drama of Money Making.* London: Sampson, Low, Marston and Co., 1931.

Michie, Elsie B. "Buying Brains: Trollope, Oliphant, and Vulgar Victorian Commerce." *Victorian Studies* 44.1 (Autumn 2001): 77–97.

Michie, Ranald C. *The London Stock Exchange: A History.* Oxford: Oxford University Press, 1999.

Middleton, Roger. *Government versus the Market: The Growth of the Public Sector, Economic Management and British Economic Performance, c1890–1979.* Cheltenham, UK: E. Elgar, 1996.

Mill, J. S. *Collected Works.* Vol. 5, *Essays on Economics and Society.* London: Routledge, 1967.

*Money and Trade.* London.

Moody, Jane. "The Drama of Capital: Risk, Belief, and Liability on the Victorian Stage." In *Victorian Literature and Finance.* Ed. Francis O'Gorman. Oxford: Oxford University Press, 2007. 91–109.

Morgan, E. Victor, and W. A. Thomas. *The Stock Exchange: Its History and Functions.* London: Elek, 1962.

Morgan, Nicholas J., and Michael Moss. "'Wealthy and Titled Persons': The Accumulation of Riches in Victorian Britain: The Case of Peter Denny." *Business History* 31.3 (1989): 28–47.

Morgan, Richard. *Familiar Observations on Life Insurance, and the Causes Affecting Population, etc.* Norwich, UK: Joseph Fletcher, 1841.

Morgenson, Gretchen. "Market Watch." *New York Times* (31 Dec. 2000): C1.

Morris, R. "The Middle Class and the Property Cycle during the Industrial Revolution." In *The Search for Wealth and Stability.* Ed. T. C. Smout. London: Macmillan, 1979. 91–113.

Mottram, R. H. *A History of Financial Speculation.* Boston: Little, 1929.

Munting, Roger. *An Economic and Social History of Gambling in Britain and the USA.* Manchester: Manchester University Press, 1996.

Murphy, Lucy. "Business Ladies: Midwestern Women and Enterprise, 1850–1880." *Journal of Women's History* 3 (Spring 1991): 65–89.

*National Sporting League Journal.* London.

Nisbet, Harry C. *Prize Essay on Life Assurance.* Uxbridge, UK: John Mackenzie, 1853.

Noble, John Ashcraft. Review of *Mitre Court. Academy* (5 Dec. 1885): 372.

Norris, Floyd, and Jeremy W. Peters. "Slide on Wall St. Adds to Worries about Economy." *New York Times* (28 Feb. 2007): A1, C6.

"Northumberland and Durham Bank." *Bankers' Magazine* (1857): 540.

Norwich Union Board Minute Book. 11 May 1886; 24 Nov. 1886; 4 Nov. 1901. NU 1395 and 1400, Aviva Group Archives, Norwich, UK.

Offer, Avner. *The Challenge of Affluence: Self-Control and Well-Being in the United States and Britain since 1950.* Oxford: Oxford University Press, 2006.

———. *Property and Politics, 1870–1914: Landownership, Law, Ideology and Urban Development in England.* Cambridge: Cambridge University Press, 1981.

O'Gorman, Francis. "Introduction." *Victorian Literature and Finance.* Oxford: Oxford University Press, 2007. 1–16.

Ogborn, Maurice Edward. *Equitable Assurances: The Story of Life Assurance in the Experience of the Equitable Life Assurance Society 1762–1962.* London: George Allen, 1962.

Oliphant, Laurence. "Autobiography of a Joint-Stock Company (Limited)." *Blackwood's Edinburgh Magazine* 120 (July 1876): 96–122.

Osterhammel, Jürgen. "Semi-Colonialism and Informal Empire in Twentieth-Century China: Towards a Framework of Analysis." In *Imperialism and After: Continuities and Discontinuities*. Ed. Wolfgang J. Mommsen and Jürgen Osterhammel. London: German Historical Institute/Allen & Unwin, 1986. 290–314.

"Overseas Correspondence." *Economist* (7 Dec. 1929): 1081.

Parker, Joseph. *Gambling in Various Aspects*. 5th ed. London: H. R. Allenson, 1902.

*Parliamentary Papers* 1889 (10), q. 5195.

Parry, Benita. *Conrad and Imperialism: Ideological Boundaries and Visionary Frontiers*. London: Macmillan, 1983.

———. *Postcolonial Studies: A Materialist Critique*. New York: Routledge, 2004.

Parsons, Wayne. *The Power of the Financial Press: Journalism and Economic Opinion in Britain and America*. New Brunswick, N.J.: Rutgers University Press, 1989.

"Partnership with Limited Liability." *Westminster Review* (1853): 374–415.

Pearson, Robin. "Thrift or Dissipation? The Business of Life Assurance in the Early Nineteenth Century." *Economic History Review* 43 (1990): 236–54.

Peden, G. C. "The 'Treasury View' on Public Works and Employment in the Interwar Period." *Economic History Review*, Series 2, 37.2 (1984): 167–81.

Perkin, Harold. *Origins of Modern English Society, 1780–1880*. London: Routledge, 1969.

Phillips, Nicola. *Women in Business, 1700–1850*. Woodbridge, Suffolk, UK: Boydell Press, 2006.

Platt, D. C. M., ed. *Business Imperialism, 1840–1930: An Inquiry Based on British Experience in Latin America*. Oxford: Clarendon, 1977.

Pocock, J. G. A. *Virtue, Commerce and History: Essays on Political Thought and History, Chiefly in the Eighteenth Century*. Cambridge: Cambridge University Press, 1985.

Poley, A. P. *The History, Law, and Practice of the Stock Exchange*. London: Sir Isaac Pitman, 1907.

Poovey, Mary, ed. *The Financial System in Nineteenth-Century Britain*. New York: Oxford University Press, 2003.

———. *Genres of the Credit Economy: Mediating Value in 18th- and 19th-Century Britain*. Chicago: University of Chicago Press, 2008.

———. *A History of the Modern Fact: Problems of Knowledge in the Sciences of Wealth and Society*. Chicago: University of Chicago Press, 1998.

———. *Making a Social Body: British Cultural Formation, 1830–1864*. Chicago: University of Chicago Press, 1995.

Porter, Dilwin. " 'A Trusted Guide of the Investing Public': Harry Marks and the *Financial News* 1884–1916." In *Speculators and Patriots: Essays in Business Biography*. Ed. R. P. T. Davenport-Hines. London: Frank Cass and Co., 1986. 1–17.

Preda, Alexander. "The Rise of the Popular Investor: Financial Knowledge and Investing in England and France, 1840–1880." *Sociological Quarterly* 42.2 (2001): 205–32.

Preston, Claire. "Creative Finance: Making Money and Making Fiction in Edith Wharton's *Custom of the Country*." *Q/W/E/R/T/Y* 10 (2000): 57–65.

Price, Bonamy. "What Is Money?" *Fraser's Magazine* 101 (Feb. 1880): 248–60.

*Prize Winner*. London.

"Pulpit Attack on Mrs. Green." *New York Times* (24 Feb. 1903): 1.

*Quarterly Review* (1852): 406–410.

Rae, George. *The Country Banker: His Clients, Cares, and Work from an Experience of Forty Years*. 1885. 7th ed. London: John Murray, 1930.

*Railway Courier and Stock Exchange Price-Current.* London.

*Railway Investment Guide: How to Make Money by Railway Shares; Being A Series of Hints and Advice to Parties Speculating in the Shares of British, Colonial, and Foreign Railways.* London: G. Mann, 1845.

Rappaport, Erika Diane. "'The Halls of Temptation': Gender, Politics and the Construction of the Department Store in Late Victorian London." *Journal of British Studies* 35 (1996): 58–83.

———. "'A Husband and His Wife's Dresses': Consumer Credit and the Debtor Family in England, 1864–1914." In *The Sex of Things: Gender and Consumption in Historical Perspective.* Ed. Victoria De Grazia and Ellen Furlough. Berkeley: University of California Press, 1996.

———. *Shopping for Pleasure: Women in the Making of London's West End.* Princeton, N.J.: Princeton University Press, 2000.

Raynes, Harold E. *A History of British Insurance.* London: Pitman, 1950.

Reed, John R. "A Friend to Mammon: Speculation in Victorian Literature." *Victorian Studies* 27 (1984): 179–202.

Reed, M. C. *Investment in Railways in Britain, 1820–1844: A Study in the Development of the Capital Market.* Oxford: Oxford University Press, 1975.

*Report from the Select Committee of the House of Lords on Life Assurance Companies.* London: His Majesty's Stationery Office, 1906.

"Report on the Law of Partnership." Appendix to the first report on the "Select Committee on Joint-Stock Companies." *Parliamentary Papers* 7 (1837).

"Return showing . . . the aggregate gross liabilities of the state . . . at the close of each financial year from 1835–6 to 1890–1 . . ." *Parliamentary Papers* 1890–1891 48, pp. 328–31.

Review of *The Senior Partner. Saturday Review* 53 (25 March 1882): 375.

Revill, George. "Liberalism and Paternalism: Politics and Corporate Culture in 'Railway Derby,' 1865–75." *Social History* 24.2 (1999): 196–214.

Rhind, Henry. *Proposals and Rates of the Glasgow Insurance Company.* Glasgow: Scottish Guardian, 1839.

Richards, Paul. "R. A. Slaney, the Industrial Town and Early Victorian Social Policy." *Social History* 4.1 (1979): 85–101.

Richards, R. D. "The Lottery in the History of English Government Finance." *Economic History* 3 (1934): 57–76.

Richards, Thomas. *The Commodity Culture of Victorian England: Advertising and Spectacle, 1851–1914.* Stanford, Calif.: Stanford University Press, 1990.

Richardson, R. J. "Exposure of the Banking and Funding System." *The English Chartist Circular: The Temperance Record for England and Wales* 1.23 (1841): 90–91.

Riddell, Charlotte. *George Geith of Fen Court.* 1864. London: Frederick Warne and Co., n.d.

Rippy, J. Fred. "Early British Investments in the Latin American Republics." *Inter-American Economic Affairs* 6.1 (Summer 1952): 40–51.

Robb, George. "Race Motherhood: Moral Eugenics vs Progressive Eugenics, 1880–1920." In *Maternal Instincts: Visions of Motherhood and Sexuality in Britain, 1875–1925.* Ed. Claudia Nelson and Ann Sumner Holmes. New York: St. Martin's, 1997. 58–74.

———. *White-Collar Crime in Modern England: Financial Fraud and Business Morality, 1845–1929.* Cambridge: Cambridge University Press, 1992.

Robson, A. P. *On Higher than Commercial Grounds: The Factory Controversy, 1830–1852.* London: Garland, 1982.

Rock Life Assurance Company. *Centenary 1806–1906.* London: privately published, 1906.

Rodger, A. K. "The Race for Records." *Transactions of the Insurance and Actuarial Society of Glasgow* 5 (1900): 21–43.

Rodger, Richard. *The Transformation of Edinburgh: Land, Property and Trust in the Nineteenth Century.* Cambridge: Cambridge University Press, 2001.

Romero, Simon. "Bolivia Reaches for a Slice of the Coast That Got Away." *New York Times* (23 Sept. 2006).

Rose, Jonathan. "Was Capitalism Good for Victorian Literature?" *Victorian Studies* 46.3 (Autumn 2004): 489–502.

Rose, Mary B. "Diversification and Investment by the Greg Family, 1800–1914." *Business History* 21.1 (1979): 79–96.

Rose, Nikolas. *Powers of Freedom: Reframing Political Thought.* Cambridge: Cambridge University Press, 1999.

Rotundo, E. Anthony. *American Manhood: Transformations in Masculinity from the Revolution to the Modern Era.* New York: Basic Books, 1993.

Rowntree, B. Seebohm, ed. *Betting and Gambling: A National Evil.* London: MacMillan, 1905.

Royal Commission on Mercantile Law: first report, *Parliamentary Papers* 1791 (1854): 27; second report, 1977 (1854–present): 18.

Rubinstein, W. D. "New Men of Wealth and the Purchase of Land in Nineteenth-Century Britain." *Past and Present* 92 (1981): 125–47.

Russell, Norman. *The Novelist and Mammon: Literary Responses to the World of Commerce in the Nineteenth Century.* Oxford: Oxford University Press, 1986.

Rutterford, Janette, and Josephine Maltby. Editors' Introduction. "Women and Investment." Special issue of *Accounting, Business and Financial History* 16.2 (2006): 133–42.

———. "'Frank Must Marry for Money': Men, Women and Property in the Novels of Anthony Trollope." *Accounting Historians Journal* 33.2 (2006): 169–99.

———. "'She Possessed Her Own Fortune': Women Investors from the Late Nineteenth Century to the Early Twentieth Century." *Business History* 48.2 (2006): 220–53.

———. "'The Widow, the Clergyman and the Reckless'—Women Investors before 1914." *Feminist Economics* 12.1/2 (2006): 111–38.

Ryan, Roger. "The Early Expansion of the Norwich Union Life Insurance Society, 1808–37." *Business History* 28 (1985): 166–96.

———. "A History of the Norwich Union Fire and Life Insurance Societies from 1797 to 1914." Diss., University of East Anglia, Norwich, UK, 1983.

Said, Edward. *Beginnings: Intention and Method.* New York: Basic Books, 1975.

———. *Culture and Imperialism.* New York: Vintage, 1994.

Saint-Clair, William. *Popular View of Life Assurance.* London: Jones and Causton, 1840.

Sater, William F. *Chile and the War of the Pacific.* Lincoln: University of Nebraska Press, 1986.

*Saturday Review of Politics, Literature, Science and Art.* 166 vols. London: 1855–1938.

Saville, J. "The Christian Socialist of 1848." In *Democracy and the Labour Movement.* Ed. J. Saville. London: Lawrence and Wishart, 1954. 135–58.

———. "Sleeping Partnerships and Limited Liability, 1850–1856." *Economic History Review* 8 (1955): 418–33.

Schmitt, Cannon, Nancy Henry, and Anjali Arondekar. "Introduction: Victorian Investments." *Victorian Studies* 45.1 (2002): 7–16.

Schott, John. *Mind over Money.* Boston: Little, 1998.

Schwarz, Daniel R. "Conrad's Quarrel with Politics in *Nostromo*." *College English* 59.5 (Sept. 1997): 548–68.

Scotter, C. J. *Lost in a Bucket Shop: A Story of Stock Exchange Speculation*. London: Field and Tuer, Leadenhall Press; Simpkin, Marshall; Hamilton Adams, n.d. [1890].

Scottish Provident Institution. *Report of the Proceedings of the Fourth Annual Meeting of Contributors*. Edinburgh: privately printed, 1842.

Scratchley, Arthur. *Observations on Life Assurance Societies, and Savings Banks*. London: J. W. Parker, 1851.

Searle, G. R. *Morality and the Market in Victorian Britain*. Oxford: Clarendon, 1998.

Seymour-Smith, Martin. "Introduction." *Nostromo: A Tale of the Seaboard*, by Joseph Conrad. 1904. Reprint, Harmondsworth, UK: Penguin, 1983. 7–24.

Shachtman, Tom. *The Day America Crashed*. New York: Putnam, 1979.

Shammus, Carole. "Re-assessing the Married Women's Property Acts." *Journal of Women's History* 6 (Spring 1994): 9–30.

Shand, A. Innes. "Speculative Investments." *Blackwood's Edinburgh Magazine* 120 (Sept. 1876): 293–316.

Shannon, H. A. "The Coming of General Limited Liability." In *Essays in Economic History*, vol. 1. Ed. E. M. Carus Wilson. London: Arnold, 1954. 358–79.

———. "The First Five Thousand Limited Companies and Their Duration." *Economic History* 2.7 (1932): 396–424.

Sherry, Norman. *Conrad's Western World*. Cambridge: Cambridge University Press, 1971.

Shiller, Robert. *Irrational Exuberance*. Princeton, N.J.: Princeton University Press, 2000.

Shrimpton, Nicholas. "'Even These Metallic Problems Have Their Melodramatic Side': Money in Victorian Literature." In *Victorian Literature and Finance*. Ed. Francis O'Gorman. Oxford: Oxford University Press, 2007. 17–38.

Sidgwick, Henry. "What Is Money?" *Fortnightly Review* 31 (1 April 1879): 563–75.

Sigsworth, E. M. *Black Dyke Mills: A History*. Liverpool: Liverpool University Press, 1958.

Simon, Daphne. "Master and Servant." In *Democracy and the Labour Movement*. Ed. J. Saville. London: Lawrence and Wishart, 1954.

Simpson, A. W. Brian. "General Editor's Preface." In *Private Property and Abuse of Rights in Victorian England: The Story of Edward Pickles and the Bradford Water Supply*. By M. Taggart. Oxford: Oxford University Press, 2002.

———. *Leading Cases in the Common Law*. Oxford: Oxford University Press, 1995.

Sinclair, Catherine. *Sir Edward Graham: or, Railway Speculators*. 3 vols. London: Longman, 1849.

Sinha, Mrinalini. *Specters of Mother India: The Global Restructuring of an Empire*. Durham, N.C.: Duke University Press, 2006.

Siskin, Clifford. *The Historicity of Romantic Discourse*. Oxford: Oxford University Press, 1988.

Slack, Charles. *Hetty: The Genius and Madness of America's First Female Tycoon*. New York: Harper Collins, 2004.

Slakey, Roger L. "Melmotte's Death: A Prism of Meaning in *The Way We Live Now*." *ELH* 34.2 (June 1967): 248–59.

Smiles, Samuel. *The Life of George Stephenson*. London: John Murray, 1858.

Smith, Andrew, ed. "Literature and Money." Special issue of *Victorian Review* 31:2 (2005).

Smith, Robert Freeman. "Latin America, the United States and the European Powers,

1830–1930." In *The Cambridge History of Latin America*. Ed. Leslie Bethell. 11 vols. Cambridge: Cambridge University Press, 1984–1994. 4: 83–119.

Smith, S. A. "Talking Toads and Chinless Ghosts: The Politics of 'Superstitious' Rumors in the People's Republic of China, 1961–1965." *American Historical Review* 3.2 (April 2006): 405–26.

*Society Herald: A Weekly Record of Social, Political, Theatrical, Literary, and Financial Events*. London.

Somers, Margaret R. "Narrativity, Narrative Identity, and Social Action: Rethinking English Working-Class Formation." *Social Science History* 16.4 (1992): 591–629.

Somerset, Sophia Vernon. *A Good Investment; or, For Love or Money*. London: Griffith, Farran, Okeden and Welsh, 1891.

Spangler, George M. "Suicide and Social Criticism: Durkheim, Dreiser, Wharton, and London." *American Quarterly* 31.4 (Autumn 1979): 496–516.

Sparkes, Boyden, and Samuel Taylor Moore. *Hetty Green: A Woman Who Loved Money*. New York: Doubleday, 1930.

*Sporting Life*. London.

*Sporting Opinion*. London.

*Sporting Times [The Pink 'Un]*. London.

Sprague, Thomas Bond. *A Treatis [sic] on Life Assurance Accounts*. London: C. and E. Layton, 1874.

Srebrnik, Patricia Thomas. "Mrs. Riddell and the Reviewers: A Case Study in Victorian Popular Fiction." *Women's Studies* 23 (1994): 69–84.

Standard Life Assurance Company. *Proceedings at a General Meeting . . . for the Purpose of Receiving the Report by the Directors upon the Investigation of the Company's Affairs . . . and Division of Profits*. Edinburgh: privately printed, 1840.

Star Life Assurance Society, Board Minutes. ST 1/5/1, Zurich Financial Service Group Archives, Cheltenham, UK.

Stebbings, Chantal. *The Private Trustee in Victorian England*. Cambridge: Cambridge University Press, 2002.

"Stockbroking and the Stock Exchange." *Fraser's Magazine* 14, New Series (July 1876): 84–103.

*Stock Exchange Answers*. London.

Stone, Irving. "British Direct and Portfolio Investment in Latin America before 1914." *Journal of Economic History* 37.3 (Sept. 1977): 690–722.

Sturrock, John. *The Principles and Practice of Life Assurance*. Dundee, Scotland: W. Middleton, 1846.

Stutfield, G. Herbert. *The Law Relating to Betting, Time-Bargains and Gaming*. 2nd ed. London: Waterlow, 1886.

"Suicide in Cornhill." *Times* (4 March 1868): 10.

Supple, Barry. *The Royal Exchange Assurance: A History of British Insurance 1720–1970*. Cambridge: Cambridge University Press, 1970.

*Supplement to the Journal of the Society of Arts*. London.

Sutherland, John. "Introduction." In *The Way We Live Now*, by Anthony Trollope. 1875. Oxford: Oxford University Press, 1982. vii–xxviii.

Swiney, Frances. *The Cosmic Procession*. London: Ernest Bell, 1906.

Swingle, L. J. *Romanticism and Anthony Trollope: A Study in the Continuities of Nineteenth-Century Literary Thought*. Ann Arbor: University of Michigan Press, 1990.

Szockyj, Elizabeth, and James G. Fox. *Corporate Victimization of Women*. Boston: Northeastern University Press, 1996.

Taggart, M. *Private Property and Abuse of Rights in Victorian England: The Story of Edward Pickles and the Bradford Water Supply.* Oxford: Oxford University Press, 2002.

Talib, I. S. "Conrad's *Nostromo* and the Reader's Understanding of Anachronic Narratives." *Journal of Narrative Technique* 20.1 (Winter 1990): 1–21.

Taylor, James. "Commercial Fraud and Public Men in Victorian Britain." *Historical Research* 78 (2005): 230–52.

———. *Creating Capital: Joint-Stock Enterprise in British Politics and Culture, 1800–1870.* Woodbridge, UK: Boydell Press, 2006.

Taylor, Miles. *The Decline of British Radicalism, 1847–1860.* Oxford: Oxford University Press, 1995.

Thompson, F. M. L. *Gentrification and the Enterprise Culture: Britain, 1780–1980.* Oxford: Oxford University Press, 2001.

———. "Life after Death: How Successful Nineteenth-Century Businessmen Disposed of Their Fortunes." *Economic History Review,* Series 2, 43.1 (1990): 40–61.

Thorpe, C. H. *How to Invest and How to Speculate.* London: Grant Richards, 1901.

Thrift, Nigel. "Performing Cultures in the New Economy." *Annals of the Association of American Geographers* 90.4 (2000): 674–92.

*Times.* London.

Todhunter, Ralph. "On the Requirements of the Life Assurance Companies Act, 1870." *Journal of the Institute of Actuaries* 35 (1899): 1–41.

Train, John. *The New Money Masters: Winning Investment Strategies of Soros, Lynch, Steinhardt, Rogers, Neff, Wanger, Michaelis, Carret.* New York: Harper, 1989.

*Transactions of the National Association for the Promotion of Social Science,* 1860.

"Trappers of Women." *Ladies Home Journal* (Jan. 1920): 43.

Trebilcock, Clive. *Phoenix Assurance and the Development of British Insurance.* 2 vols. Cambridge: Cambridge University Press, 1985–1998.

Trollope, Anthony. *An Autobiography.* 1883. Ed. Michael Sadleir and Frederick Page. Oxford: Oxford University Press, 1992.

———. *Can You Forgive Her?* 1865. Ed. Andrew Swarbrick. Oxford: Oxford University Press, 1991.

———. *The Last Chronicle of Barset.* 1867. Ed. Sophie Gilmartin. London: Penguin, 2002.

———. *The Prime Minister.* 1876. Ed. David Skilton. Harmondsworth, UK: Penguin, 1994.

———. *The Prime Minister.* 1876. Ed. Jenny Uglow. Oxford: Oxford University Press, 2001.

———. *The Three Clerks.* 1858. London: Richard Bentley and Son, 1884.

———. *The Way We Live Now.* 1875. Ed. Frank Kermode. Harmondsworth, UK: Penguin, 1994.

———. *The Way We Live Now.* 1875. Ed. John Sutherland. Oxford: Oxford University Press, 1982.

Turnbull, Annmarie. "Learning Her Womanly Works: The Elementary School Curriculum, 1870–1914." In *Lessons for Life: The Schooling of Girls and Women, 1850–1950.* Ed. Felicity Hunt. Oxford: Basil Blackwell, 1987. 83–100.

Tuttle, Florence. *The Awakening of Woman.* New York: Abington Press, 1915.

Tyson, R. E. "The Sun Mill Company: A Study in Democratic Investment, 1858–1959." Unpublished MA thesis, University of Manchester, 1962.

University Life Assurance Society, Board Minutes. Guildhall Ms. 24,933.

Ursa Minor [pseud.]. *On the Science and Practice of Stock Exchange Speculation*. London: W. W. Gibbings, 1891.

Valenze, Deborah. *The Social Life of Money in the English Past*. Cambridge: Cambridge University Press, 2006.

Vernon, James. *Politics and the People: A Study in English Political Culture, 1815–1867*. Cambridge: Cambridge University Press, 1993.

Vernon, John. *Money and Fiction: Literary Realism in the Nineteenth and Early Twentieth Centuries*. Ithaca, N.Y.: Cornell University Press, 1984.

Vicinus, Martha. *Independent Women*. Chicago: University of Chicago Press, 1985.

Von Arnim, Elizabeth. *The Enchanted April*. New York: Pocket Books, 1992.

Walford, C. *The Insurance Cyclopaedia*. 6 vols. London: Layton, 1871–1880.

Walker, Stephen P. *The Society of Accountants in Edinburgh 1854–1914: A Study of Recruitment to a New Profession*. New York: Garland, 1988.

"A Warning! Insurance Frauds." *Eye-Opener* (29 June 1912): 2.

Watt, Ian. *Conrad in the Nineteenth Century*. Berkeley: University of California Press, 1979.

Watts, Cedric. "*Nostromo* and *Wild Scenes* Again." *Review of English Studies*, New Series, 48.190 (May 1997): 211–17.

———. *A Preface to Conrad*. London: Longman, 1982.

Watts, Reverend J. Stockwell. *The Greatest Crime of the Nineteenth Century and What the Churches Say to It*. London: Liberator Building Fund, 1893.

Weiss, Barbara. *The Hell of the English: Bankruptcy and the Victorian Novel*. Lewisburg, Penn.: Bucknell University Press, 1986.

Wells, H. G. *Tono-Bungay*. 1909. New York: Signet, 1960.

Weskett, John. *A Complete Digest of the Theory, Laws, and Practice of Insurance*. London: Frys, Couchman, and Collier, 1781.

Westbrook, Wayne W. *Wall Street in the American Novel*. New York: New York University Press, 1980.

Wharton, Edith. *The Custom of the Country*. 1913. Ed. R. W. B. Lewis. New York: Library of America, 1985.

———. *The Letters of Edith Wharton*. Ed. R. W. B. Lewis and Nancy Lewis. New York: Simon and Schuster, 1988.

———. *The Writing of Fiction*. New York: Charles Scribner's Sons, 1925.

Whiting, Robert. *The Labour Party and Taxation: Party Identity and Political Purpose in Twentieth-Century Britain*. Cambridge: Cambridge University Press, 2000.

Whitlock, Tammy C. *Crime, Gender and Consumer Culture in Nineteenth-Century England*. Aldershot, UK: Ashgate, 2005.

Wiener, Martin J. *English Culture and the Decline of the Industrial Spirit, 1850–1980*. Cambridge: Cambridge University Press, 1981.

———. "Market Culture, Reckless Passion and the Victorian Reconstruction of Punishment." In *The Culture of the Market: Historical Essays*. Ed. T. Haskell and R. Teichgraeber. Cambridge: Cambridge University Press, 1993. 136–60.

Wilde, Oscar. *The Importance of Being Earnest and Other Plays*. London: Penguin, 1986.

Wills, W. S., and Charles Dickens. "Two Chapters on Bank Note Forgeries, Chapter II." *Household Words* 1 (1850): 615–20.

Wilson, Edmund. *The Shores of Light: A Literary Chronicle of the Twenties and Thirties*. New York: Farrar, Straus and Young, 1952.

Wilson, Henry. *Hints to Railroad Speculators: Together with the Influence Railroads Will Have upon Society, in Promoting Agriculture, Commerce, and Manufactures.* London: Henry Wilson, 1845.

"A Woman and Her Money." *Spectator* (24 Sept. 1892): 413–14.

"A Woman's Adventure in Investments." *World's Work* (Dec. 1913): 144.

"The Woman's Bank of Boston." *Bankers' Magazine* (1880): 351–52.

Woodmansee, Martha, and Mark Osteen, eds. *The New Economic Criticism: Studies at the Intersection of Literature and Economics.* New York: Routledge, 1999.

———. "Taking Account of the New Economic Criticism: An Historical Introduction." In *The New Economic Criticism: Studies at the Intersection of Literature and Economics.* Ed. Martha Woodmansee and Mark Osteen. New York: Routledge, 1999. 3–50.

Yaeger, Mary A. *Women in Business.* 3 vols. Cheltenham, UK: Edward Elgar, 1999.

Zelizer, Viviana A. Rotman. *Morals and Markets: The Development of Life Insurance in the United States.* New Brunswick, N.J.: Transaction, 1983.

Zimmerman, David A. *Panic! Markets, Crises, and Crowds in American Fiction.* Chapel Hill: University of North Carolina Press, 2006.

Žižek, Slavoj. *The Ticklish Subject: The Absent Centre of Political Ontology.* London: Verso, 1999.

# Contributors

**Timothy Alborn** is Associate Professor of History at Lehman College and the City University of New York Graduate Center. He has published *Conceiving Companies: Joint-Stock Politics in Victorian England* (1998) and articles on British business and culture in the *Journal of Modern History, Business History Review, Victorian Studies, Journal of Victorian Culture,* and *Journal of Interdisciplinary History.*

**Ian Baucom,** Professor of English at Duke University and Chair of the Duke English Department, is author of *Out of Place: Englishness, Empire and the Locations of Identity* (1999) and *Specters of the Atlantic: Finance Capital, Slavery, and the Philosophy of History* (2005) and co-editor of *Shades of Black: Assembling Black Arts in 1980s Britain* (2005).

**Martin Daunton** is Professor of Economic History in the University of Cambridge and Master of Trinity Hall. Among his many works are two volumes on the politics of taxation in Britain since 1799. Most recently he has edited a collection titled *Wealth and Welfare: An Economic and Social History of Britain, 1851–1951* (2007). He is currently working on an economic history of the world since 1945.

**Nancy Henry** is Professor of English at the University of Tennessee. She is author of *George Eliot and the British Empire* (2002) and *The Cambridge Introduction to George Eliot* (2008). A co-editor of the *Victorian Studies* special issue on "Victorian Investments" (2002), she is working on a book about Victorian women and finance.

**David C. Itzkowitz,** Professor of History at Macalester College, is author of *Peculiar Privilege: A Social History of English Foxhunting, 1753–1885* (1977). He has also published articles on the creation of identity among nineteenth-century English Jews.

**Audrey Jaffe,** Professor of English at the University of Toronto, is author of *Scenes of Sympathy: Identity and Representation in Victorian Fiction* (2000) and *Vanishing Points: Dickens, Narrative, and the Subject of Omniscience* (1991).

**Donna Loftus** is Lecturer in History at the Open University. Her publications include "The Self in Society: Middle-Class Men and Autobiography," in David Amigoni, ed., *Life Writing and Victorian Culture* (2006).

**Mary Poovey** is Samuel Rudin University Professor in the Humanities and Professor of English at New York University. Her books include *A History of the Modern Fact* (1998) and *Genres of the Credit Economy: Mediating Value in Eighteenth- and Nineteenth-Century Britain* (2008).

**George Robb** is Professor of History at William Paterson University. He is author of *White-Collar Crime in Modern England* (1992) and *British Culture and the First World War* (2002).

**Cannon Schmitt,** Associate Professor of English at the University of Toronto, is author of *Alien Nation: Nineteenth-Century Gothic Fictions and English Nationality* (1997) and *Darwin and the Memory of the Human: Evolution, Savages, and South America* (forthcoming).

# Index

*Italicized page numbers indicate illustrations.*

Cain, P. J., 5

*Can You Forgive Her* (Trollope), 164, 167

capitalism: and Christianity, 45; Conrad on, 184, 194; critiques of, 2, 162, 205; "gentlemanly," 5; and labor, 79–97; and postmodernism, 33–34; speculation as, 157n2

Caruth, Cathy, 25

"case" concept, 31–32

Chadwick, Edwin, 42

*Challenge of Affluence, The* (Offer), 215

Chamberlain, Joseph, 206

*Chance* (Conrad), 138–39

Chandler, James, 31–32

Chartists/Chartism, 44, 83

Christian Socialists, 83–88, 92

City, the: depicted in fiction, 164–67, 178; journalism in, 41–42; suicide in, 170

*City Argus,* the, 107

City of Glasgow Bank collapse, 127

Claflin, Tennessee, 134–36, *135*

Clerical, Medical & General (insurance company), 67

Clews, Henry, 133–34

CNBC cable channel, 143–45

Coaks, Isaac, 70

Cobden, Richard, 83

Collingwood, Luke, 15–16, 28, 30, 31

"Commerce" board game, 131, *132*

commercial information, publication of, 41, 43

Commercial Life (insurance company), 65–66

*Commodity Culture of Victorian England, The* (Richards), 70–71

commodity spectacle, semiotics of, 70–71

Companies Act/Law: of 1837, 81; of 1856, 95–97, 98, 106; of 1862, 45, 98, 106; of 1907, 208

*Complete Digest of the Theory, Laws, and Practice of Insurance, A* (Weskett), 29–30

compound interest, 59

Conference of Capital and Labor, 91–95

Conrad, Joseph: on culture of investment, 184, 188–89, 204; fiction of, 138–39, 185; and imperialism, 6–7, 188–89, 199nn5,8; and Latin American history, 186–89; "material interests" in, 184, 191–92; modernism in, 192–96; realism in, 184–85; and Trollope, 201n19

"consuls," securities, 106

"contango" fee, 106–107

*Conversations in Political Economy* (Marcet), 125

Cooper, Walter, 87–88

*Cosmic Procession, The* (Swiney), 138

Cotton, William, 89

*Country Banker, The* (Rae), 47

"cover system," 113–14

Credit Foncier and Mobilier of England, 44

Crosty, Alice, 128

*Culture and Anarchy* (Arnold), 162

"Culture and Finance Capital" (Jameson), 33–35

culture of investment: aspects of, 2; Conrad on, 184, 188–89; contemporary, 182–84, 197–98; and finance capital, 10–12; gender in, 120–40; information role in, 50; the novel in, 51–57; as shaping everyday life, 4; spread through increase in shares available, 39–40; as structure of feeling, 51–52

*Custom of the Country, The* (Wharton), 165, 176–78

Dance, Caroline, 127

Daunton, Martin, 12

Davis, Lance E., 4–5, 122

"delayed decoding," Watt on, 192, 199–200n12

Derrida, Jacques: 3, 21; on supplement, 48–51, 56–57; on value, 51–52, 54

Deuchar, J. J. W., 70

Dickens, Charles: 12; fiction of, 52, 79, 159n12, 161–65, 176, 207; and journalism, 44–45, 122

Dickinson, Anna, 138

"Disappearance of Lady Frances Carfax, The" (Doyle), 132–33

discourse, economic, 82

*Doll's House, A* (Ibsen), 138–40

dot-com bubble, 1

*Double-Entry Elucidated* (Forster), 48

Doyle, Arthur Conan, 132–33

drama, financial themes in, 128–30, 180n7

Duncan, W. W., 101–102

Eagle (insurance company), 63, 65

East India Company, 2, 5, 39, 122, 209–10

Economic (insurance company), 64, 76n6

*Economist,* the, 42, 44–45, 101, 121, 161, 205

*Edinburgh Review,* the, 41

Egerton, George, 138

"Eldorado Exploring Expedition" (Conrad), 185

Eliot, George, 9, 10, 52–56, 165

employer/employee relations, 91–95, 217–18

Employers' Liability Act, 218

*Enchanted April, The* (Arnim), 137

English State Lottery, 98

Equal Rights Party, 135–36

Equiano, Ouladah, 15

Equitable, the (American, insurance company), 66

Equitable Society, 60–66, 76n4

127–28; woman investor as victim in, 9, 128–40

"Shock Wave from Shanghai, A" (Barboza), 182–84
Shrimpton, Nicolas, 197
Sidgwick, Henry, 45
*signum rememorativum, demonstrativum, prognostikon* (historical sign), 16, 17–18, 22, 32
*Sir William's Speculations, or, the Seamier Side of Finance*, 45
Slack, Ann and Emma, 127
Slaney, Robert A., 83, 85–89, 92, 94
slave trade, 5–6, 15–32, 217
Smiles, Samuel, 129, 205, 215
Smith, Mr. (suicide), 163, 164, 167
Smith, Sidney, 92
Social Science Association, 96
Somerset, Sophia Vernon, 130
South Sea Bubble of 1720, 131
speculation: definition of, 106–108, 151, 158–59n10; vs. investment, 11–12, 45–46, 98–119, 150–57, 158n7, 191, 203–207, 212; in literature, 128–40, 150–57, 159n12, 164–65, 191; regulation of, 61, 99–105, 116–17; and women, 121, 128–32
speculator as villain figure, 12, 126–30, 150–57, 164–65, 191, 216
Spencer, Herbert, 205, 209
*Sporting Life*, 109–10
*Sporting Times*, the, 113
Stanton, Elizabeth Cady, 137–38
"Stockbroking and the Stock Exchange" (Anonymous), 46
Strahan, Paul, and Bates Bank failure, 130
strikes, 91, 94
structure of feeling, 51–57
Sturrock, John, 64
Stutfield, G. Herbert, 103–105
"Suicide in Life and Literature" (Lewes), 169
suicide in response to financial loss: and English law, 167–69; as myth, 161–62, 179nn1,2; as trope in fiction, 12, 156–57, 161–79
Sun (insurance company), 64
supplement, the, 48–51, 56–57
Swiney, Frances, 138

tariffs, 209–10
Taylor, James, 218–19
Tennyson, Alfred, 162–63
Ten Hours Act of 1847, 83–84
Thompson (Thomas) and Company, 108, *109*
*Three Clerks, The* (Trollope), 127–28
time bargain, 102–103, 118–19n2
tontine offices, 65–66

Torok, Maria, 25
trade associations, 92–95
transformation, 12
trauma-theory, 25
Trebilcock, Clive, 67
Trepsack, Mary, 139–40
Trollope, Anthony: approaches to, 9–12; and Conrad, 201n19; and Eliot, 165; feeling and value in, 147–48, 150–51; financial plots in, 145–58, 162–76; and Greenspan, 145; fiction of, 52, 79, 106, 127–28, 196–97; physical vs. spiritual fate in, 167–69; speculation vs. investment in, 150–57, 204, 206, 212; suicide in, 162–76; and Wharton, 176–79
"Truth-Event," 19–26
Tufnell, Henry, 92
Tuttle, Florence, 138

value: Derrida on, 51–52, 54; feeling and, 147–48, 150–51; loss as determining, 6, 25, 27–32, 35–36nn5,6,8; money as, 30, 197; of reputation, 196; specters of, 34; theory of, 29–32
Vanderbilt, Cornelius, 134
*Victorian Studies*, 2
visual representations of investing, *135*, 143–45, *144*, 150–51

wage/price standards, 93–95
wagering contracts, 100, 102–105, 117, 118n1
Wall Street: in fiction, 176–77; women in, 130, 134–36
War of the Pacific, 187, 198n3
Watt, Ian, 192
*Way We Live Now, The* (Trollope), 52, 79, 106, 164–69, 171–72, 196–97
*Weekly*, the, 128
Weskett, John, 29–30
West Middlesex Fire and Life Insurance Co., 207
West of England Bank failure, 131
*Westminster Review*, the, 84–85
Wharton, Edith, 12, 165, 176–79
*Where Your Treasure Is* (Harraden), 137
*Whirlpool, The* (Gissing), 138–39, 164–65, 168–69, 174–76
Wilde, Oscar, 138–39
Wilson, Edmund, 162
Wilson, James, 42
Woman's Bank of Boston, 134
"Woman's Romance in Wall Street, A," 130
women investors: as authors, 128–32; "begging letters" by, 129; brokers catering to, 123–24, 134–36; as financial professionals, 134–37; as irrational, 215; in key sectors, 122–23; as

"passive," 126, 139; property rights of, 7–8, 121–23, 125, 140nn6,7, 215; tropes of in fiction and journalism, 128–40; unmarried, 7–8; as victims of fraud, 8–9, 126–33, 216
Women's Rights Convention, 137–38
Wood, Mrs. Henry, 9, 131
Woodhull, Claflin and Company, 134–36
Woodhull, Victoria, 128, 134–37, *135*
Woodmansee, Martha, 4
working class: as investors, 11, 85–90; limited liability and, 7, 84–97, 217–18
Working Tailors Association, 87–88
Workmen's Compensation Act of 1897, 218

writing, financial: accounting as genre of, 47–48, 56; conventions common to journalism and fiction, 40; and culture of investment, 39, 43, 54–55, 83; historical vs. literary paradigms in, 55–57; modes of as "supplement," 48–51, 56–57; origin of, 39–40; women in, 120–40

York, Newcastle and Berwick railway, 43

Žižek, Slavoj, 19–22, 31
*Zong* slave ship insurance case, 5–6, 15–16, 22–32, 217

Printed and bound by CPI Group (UK) Ltd, Croydon, CR0 4YY

13/04/2025

14656538-0004